Dein Englischbuch enthält folgende Teile:

Introduction	Hier lernst du die jungen Leute von Band 3 kennen.
Units	die fünf Kapitel des Buches
Getting ready for a test	Hier kannst du dich gezielt auf einen Test vorbereiten.
EXTRA: Text File	viele interessante Texte zum Lesen (passend zu den Units)
Skills File (SF)	Beschreibung wichtiger Lern- und Arbeitstechniken
Grammar File (GF)	Zusammenfassung der Grammatik jeder Unit
Vocabulary	Wörterverzeichnis zum Lernen der neuen Wörter jeder Unit
Dictionary	alphabetische Wörterverzeichnisse zum Nachschlagen

Die Units bestehen aus diesen Teilen:

Lead-in	Einstieg in das neue Thema
A-Section	neuer Lernstoff mit vielen Aktivitäten und Background File
Practice	Übungen
Text	eine spannende oder lustige Geschichte
How am I doing?	Hier kannst du dein Wissen und Können überprüfen.

In den Units findest du diese Überschriften und Symbole:

Looking at language	Hier sammelst du Beispiele und entdeckst Regeln.
STUDY SKILLS	Einführung in Lern- und Arbeitstechniken
Dossier	Schöne und wichtige Arbeiten kannst du in einer Mappe sammeln.
All about …	Hier übst du Wortschatz zum Thema der Unit.
WRITING COURSE	Schreibkurs in fünf Kapiteln mit Hilfen zum Schreiben von Texten
EVERYDAY ENGLISH	Übungen zum Bewältigen wichtiger Alltagssituationen
MEDIATION	Hier vermittelst du zwischen zwei Sprachen.
LISTENING	Aufgaben zu Hörtexten auf der CD
Now you	Hier sprichst und schreibst du über dich selbst.
PRONUNCIATION	Ausspracheübungen
REVISION	Übungen zur Wiederholung
WORDS	Übungen zu Wortfamilien, Wortfeldern und Wortverbindungen
Extra	Zusätzliche Aktivitäten und Übungen
👥 👥👥	Partnerarbeit / Gruppenarbeit
🎧 🎧	nur auf CD / auf CD und im Schülerbuch
▷	Textaufgaben
○ ●	leichtere Übungen / schwierigere Übungen
//○ //●	parallele Übungen auf zwei Niveaus
more help	Hier findest du zusätzliche Hilfen für das Lösen einer Aufgabe.

Inhalt

S.	Unit	Inhalte	Sprachliche Mittel: • grammatische Strukturen • Wortfelder	Sonstiges
6	**Introduction** Music for youth	Asif, Katrina, Latisha und Robert lernen sich auf dem *National Festival of Music for Youth* in Birmingham kennen und freunden sich an.		
12	**Unit 1** My London	  Robert besucht Asif in London und erkundet mit seinem neuen Freund die Stadt. • London sights • The London Underground • Multicultural London • A virtual reality game: The Great Fire of London	• REVISION simple past; present perfect • simple past – present perfect: Gegenüberstellung • sights • transport • asking the way • buying tickets • food • at the restaurant	**STUDY SKILLS** Listening **WRITING COURSE (1)** Writing better sentences – a postcard **BACKGROUND FILE** Kids' day out in London **EVERYDAY ENGLISH** LISTENING Travel announcements SPEAKING Asking for and giving information
30	**Unit 2** Island girl	 Einblicke in Katrinas Leben auf den Orkney Islands vor der Küste Schottlands • Electronic media, TV documentary • Peergroup-Verhalten und *bullying*	• REVISION *will*-future • conditional sentences (type 1 / type 2) • electronic media • town and country • film and TV • friendly/unfriendly (Word building)	**STUDY SKILLS** German-English dictionary **WRITING COURSE (2)** Using paragraphs – an e-mail **BACKGROUND FILE** Scotland, traditional and modern **EVERYDAY ENGLISH** MEDIATION Using a mobile SPEAKING Telephone messages
48	**Extra** Getting ready for a test 1 (Revision and Practice Test)			
52	**Unit 3** Sport and more	  Latisha ist eine begeisterte Sportlerin und zeigt Phillip aus Chemnitz ihre Heimatstadt Manchester. • Sport and other free-time activities • An exchange student from Germany • A very special sports star	• REVISION word order (S–V–O) • REVISION conditional sentences • relative clauses (*who/that*) • contact clauses • sports and hobbies • sports equipment • at home • things in a room • chat language	**STUDY SKILLS** Paraphrasing **WRITING COURSE (3)** Collecting and organizing ideas – a report **BACKGROUND FILE** Manchester – a great city for sport **EVERYDAY ENGLISH** SPEAKING Talking to people at meals MEDIATION Where I'm from

Inhalt

S.	Unit	Inhalte	Sprachliche Mittel: • grammatische Strukturen • Wortfelder	Sonstiges
68	**Unit 4** **Growing up in Canada**	Robert tritt als DJ in seinem *community centre* in Toronto auf und hat eine gefährliche Begegnung mit einem Bären. • Youth culture • Bear hunting: for and against • Bear attacks and a fishing trip	• REVISION relative clauses • modals and their substitutes • present progressive with future meaning • reflexive pronouns • *each other / themselves* • growing up • adults and teenagers • weekend activities • numbers • agreeing and disagreeing	**STUDY SKILLS** Brainstorming **WRITING COURSE (4)** The steps of writing – telling a story **BACKGROUND FILE** Canada **EVERYDAY ENGLISH** SPEAKING Classroom discussions MEDIATION At the cabin
84	**Extra** Getting ready for a test 2 (Revision and Practice Test)			
88	**Unit 5** **A teen magazine**	Asif, Robert, Latisha und Katrina schreiben Beiträge für ein *teen magazine*. Die Schüler verfassen in Projektarbeit Beiträge für ihr eigenes Magazin.	• REVISION present progressive with future meaning • numbers and spelling • kinds of music and musical instruments • project work	**STUDY SKILLS** Skimming **WRITING COURSE (5)** Correcting your text – a short biography

101 Partner B

106 Differentiation

114 EXTRA Text File _____ Zusätzliche optionale Lesetexte zur Vertiefung und Binnendifferenzierung

134 Skills File _____ Zusammenstellung von Lern- und Arbeitstechniken – Wiederholung aus Band 2 und neue Skills aus Band 3

148 Grammar File _____ Übersicht über grammatische Themen
157 Grammatical terms (Grammatische Fachbegriffe)
158 Lösungen der Grammar-File-Aufgaben

159 Vocabulary _____ Das chronologische Wörterverzeichnis enthält alle Wörter und Wendungen, die die Schüler/innen produktiv beherrschen sollten.

181 Dictionary _____ Alphabetische Liste aller Wörter und Wendungen, die im Schülerbuch
(English – German) vorkommen, also auch solche, die nicht zum Lernwortschatz gehören.

205 Dictionary _____ Das deutsch-englische Wörterverzeichnis enthält den Lernwortschatz des
(German – English) ersten bis dritten Bandes.

226 List of names
228 Countries and continents
229 English sounds / The English alphabet
230 Irregular verbs
232 Lösungen für *How am I doing?*
234 Quellenverzeichnis
236 Classroom English

Introduction

10,000 young people from all over the UK – Six days of brilliant music and dance – Play, sing, dance and listen to all kinds of music

National Festival of Music for Youth

Birmingham 10–15 July

1 The festival

a) Look at the poster. What kinds of music can you play and listen to at the festival?

b) What else can you do at the festival? The words in the box can help you.

c) **Extra** The young people come from all over the UK. Look at the map. What do you know about the different parts of the UK?

- listen to classical music/folk music/jazz/…
- go to a reggae/pop/rock/RnB/… concert
- learn to DJ/rap/do hip hop dancing/…
- take part in/go to breakdance/… workshops
- play the guitar/steel drum/…
- sing in a choir/rock band/…

▶ SF Learning words (p. 135)

A day at the festival

1 The people

a) Start a profile for Asif, Katrina, Latisha and Robert.

```
Name: ...
From: ...
Music: ...
At the festival because: ...
```

b) Look through the book. Where can you find the four young people from the photo story? Add information about them to your files.

2 The music 🎧

Listen to four recordings from the festival. Which recording goes with which of the four young people? Why? You can use the phrases in the box.

I think the first/second recording goes with ...
because   she plays ...
           he likes ...

3 Now you

a) Look at these questions. Make notes.
– What kinds of music do you like?
– What are your favourite bands or singers?
– When and where do you listen to music?
– Do you sing? When? Where?
– Do you play an instrument? Which one?

drums • electric guitar • flute • guitar • keyboard • piano • recorder • saxophone • trumpet • violin

b) 👥 Now stand (or sit) in a double circle. Ask three different partners the questions from a).

c) Extra Take notes. Report to the class on one of your partners.

▶ SF Learning words (p. 135) • WB 1–3 (pp. 1–3) •
WB Revision (pp. 4–7)

Unit 1

My London

| To: | Katrina, Latisha, Robert |
| Subject: | Meet on Messenger and visit London |

Hi everybody!
Fantastic festival! It was great to meet you all. Let's all meet again on Messenger this Saturday at 6 pm, OK? But before that why don't you visit my website at www.asifspage.co.uk. You'll find five good reasons to visit me here in the capital. You're all welcome!

Asif

PS Robert, it's great that you and your parents are coming. CU soon!

1 The London Eye

This is the famous big wheel on the River Thames. They say you get great views of London from the Eye – it's 135 metres high! But I haven't been on it yet. Visit me and we can go on it together! In this photo you can see the London Eye on the left and the Houses of Parliament and Big Ben on the right. Click here for my sound file.

2 Funland, London Trocadero

It's at Piccadilly Circus, right in the city centre. I've only been here three times and I can't wait to go again. They have hundreds of video and virtual reality games. Come and play with me! Click here for my sound file.

3 Brick Lane Market

This market is near where I live in Tower Hamlets. Lots of young people come on Sunday mornings and look for trendy second-hand clothes. You can also get great Indian and Bangladeshi food there. Click here for my sound file.

My favourite places in London

4 The Tower of London

All the tourists go to the Tower. It's near where I live too. My favourite part is 'Traitors' Gate'. If somebody went into the Tower through that gate, they often lost their head!
Click here for my sound file.

5 Hyde Park

Hyde Park is one of the royal parks – it's quite near Buckingham Palace, where the Queen lives. In the summer it's a great place for open-air concerts.
Click here for my sound file.

1 Asif's sound files

STUDY SKILLS — Listening

a) Before you listen: What do you think you will hear?
b) Sometimes you only need to understand the main ideas.
c) If you have to answer questions, listen for that information only.

a) What do you think will be in Asif's sound files?

b) Listen. Which sound file goes with which photo? What clues help you?

c) Read the questions. Listen again and answer.
1 What is the man in the market selling?
2 What band is playing in the park?
3 What's the video game called? Who wins?
4 How old is the oldest part of the Tower?
5 What time was it when Asif recorded Big Ben?

2 A day out in London

a) **Think:** Choose two things from Asif's website for a day out in London.

b) **Pair:** Compare your lists. Say why you chose your two things. Make one list of two things for both of you.

+ It's fun/cool/fantastic/cheap/…
You can only do/see/… this in London.
I like video games/interesting food/…

– But it's probably very expensive.
I think … is boring/…
You can do that everywhere.

c) **Share:** Discuss your list with another pair. Agree on a list for the group.

▶ SF Listening (p. 139) • P 1 (p. 20) • WB 1 (p. 8)

1 A-Section

All about ... the London Underground

1 At Queensway underground station 🎧

Robert — We have to meet Asif at the London Eye. That's near Waterloo Tube station.
Mr Smith — OK, let's get the tickets. There's the ticket office.
Mrs Smith — Hi. We are visiting London today. Do we need single or return tickets? Or can we buy one-day tickets?
Clerk — Rush hour is over, so you can get one-day Travelcards. You can use them on the buses too.
Mr Smith — What about our son? He's 14.
Clerk — There's a child Travelcard too.
Mrs Smith — Great. Three Travelcards please, two adults and one child. And one of those Tube maps too, please.
Clerk — Sure.

Mr Smith — Now we have to find Waterloo and the best way to get there.
Robert — That's easy, Dad. There's Waterloo. So we take the red line ...
Mrs Smith — That's the Central line.
Robert — Right. We take the Central line eastbound to Bond Street.
Mrs Smith — And then we change to the Jubilee line. We take that southbound to Waterloo.
Mr Smith — Now where's the right platform?

▶ What kind of tickets are there? What is good about Travelcards?
Find Queensway and Waterloo on the map. Follow the Smiths' route. Can you find another route?

London sights	Tube stations
Brick Lane	Aldgate East
Trocadero	Piccadilly Circus
St Paul's Cathedral	St Paul's
Buckingham Palace	Victoria
Tower Bridge	Tower Hill
Houses of Parliament	Westminster

2 👥 Excuse me please, how do I get to ...?

a) Partner A: You're at **Victoria**. – Ask your partner how you can get to the first three sights on the list.

b) Partner B: You're at **King's Cross**. – Ask how you can get to the last three sights on the list.

Take the ... line (westbound/ northbound/...) to ... • Change at ... • Then take the ... line to ...

▶ P 2–3 (pp. 20–21) • WB 2–4 (pp. 9–10)

3 On the London Eye

a) Look at the photos. Then listen to the CD and answer the questions:
– Who is on the London Eye?
– In what order do they take the photos?

b) Listen again. What do you learn about each of the buildings? Take notes.

A 'The Gherkin'

St Paul's Cathedral C

B Buckingham Palace

Hi, from the London Eye! D

4 A postcard home

London Tower Bridge

Dear Grandma

We arrived in London yesterday morning. In the afternoon we went to the Tower and saw Tower Bridge.
Did you know that a London bus once had to jump across the bridge when it started to open with the bus still on it?!
This morning we went on the London Eye – very cool! I'm going to see more of London with a friend this afternoon.
See you soon!   Love, Robert

Extra Write a postcard for Robert from the Eye. Say who was with you. Write about what you saw. Did you like it?

▶ GF 1a: Simple past (p. 149) • P 4–6 (pp. 21–22) • WB 5–8 (pp. 10–12) • **Text File 2** (p. 117)

16   1   A-Section

5   In Brick Lane 🎧

After the Eye, Robert wanted to see where Asif lived. Tower Hamlets was a surprise to Robert.

'There are more Asians than British people here,' he said.

'Actually,' Asif said, 'most people here are British. Like me.'

'Of course. Sorry.'

'Don't worry about it,' Asif said. 'That's my mosque, by the way.'

'It doesn't look like a mosque,' Robert said.

'A mosque doesn't have to be a special building,' Asif explained. 'Anyway, are you hungry, Robert? You can get great Bangladeshi food here in Brick Lane.'

'Cool,' said Robert. 'I've never tried Bangladeshi food. Is it like … curry and stuff?'

'Yeah, it's like Indian food. It can be very spicy, or it can be quite mild.'

'Great,' said Robert. 'You can help me to choose.'

▷ *True or false?*   1 *Asif isn't British.*
2 *Bangladeshi food is like Indian food.*

▶ GF 1b: Present perfect (p. 149) • P 7–10 (pp. 23–24) • WB 9–11 (pp. 13–14)

6   Extra   Time for lunch

Scan the menu and suggest what Robert and Asif can eat.

Robert	I'd like a mild or medium spicy dish.	Asif	I'd like something spicy or very spicy.
	He can try … or …		*Maybe he'd like the …, … or the …*
Robert	I can't eat nuts.	Asif	I'd like a salad.
	He can't have the …		*He can have a …*
Robert	Maybe something with vegetables?	Asif	I think I'll have lamb.

Lunch menu   (from 12 to 2.30 pm)

TIKKA DISHES
We marinate meat in a yogurt sauce, fry it with spices and herbs, then serve it dry with onion and a salad. Spicy.

Chicken Tikka	£3.75
Lamb Tikka	£3.95

BIRYANI DISHES (mild)
Basmati rice with spices, nuts and sultanas

Chicken Biryani	£4.25
Lamb Biryani	£4.25
Prawn Biryani	£4.75
Vegetable Biryani	£3.95

DANSAK DISHES
We cook lentils in a medium spicy sauce, for a sweet and sour taste.

Chicken Dansak	£4.50
Lamb Dansak	£4.50
Prawn Dansak	£4.50
Vegetable Dansak	£4.25

JALFREZI DISHES
We cook meat with fresh green chillies and onion. Very spicy.

Chicken Jalfrezi	£4.50
Lamb Jalfrezi	£4.75
Prawn Jalfrezi	£5.00

▷ *What would you choose?*   ▶ SF Scanning (p. 140)

7 Have you ever tried ...? 🎧

Asif   So, how's your food?
Robert   It's good.
Asif   Yeah, this is a good restaurant. I've been here lots of times.
Robert   Have you ever tried Japanese food? It's my favourite.
Asif   Yes, I have. I tried it at school last year. We had an 'International Day'.
Robert   Yeah, we have those too.
Asif   And have you ever eaten anything really strange?
Robert   I ate crocodile last summer.
Asif   Crocodile? Yuck.

8 Now you

a) *Have students in your group tried interesting things?*

Have you ever tried ... ?

curry • Chinese/Greek/... food • bacon and eggs • English tea • spaghetti ice cream • ...

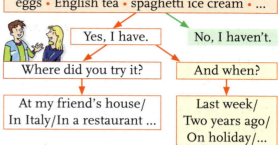

Yes, I have.   No, I haven't.

Where did you try it?   And when?

At my friend's house/ In Italy/In a restaurant ...   Last week/ Two years ago/ On holiday/...

b) *Report to the class:* Max has tried Chinese food. He tried it in a restaurant yesterday.

▶ GF 1c: Present perfect/Simple past (p. 149) • P 11–14 (pp. 24–25) • WB 12–17 (pp. 14–16)

9 Extra Lost! 🎧

Asif   Robert, I think we're lost.
Robert   But you've been to this Trocadero place before.
Asif   Yes, but I didn't take that bus.
Robert   Let's ask that man.
Asif   OK. – Excuse me. Can you tell us the way to Piccadilly Circus?
Man   Yes, of course. Go down this street till you come to a big street. That's the ... fourth one on your right. Turn right, then go straight on. Piccadilly Circus will be on the left.
Asif   Thank you very much.
Man   You're welcome.

▷ Where are the boys – at point 1, 2, 3 or 4?

10 Extra ROLE PLAY Telling the way

a) *Partner A:* Look at the map above. Tell your partner the way to one of the places like this:

Start at ... • Cross ... • Turn right/left into ... • It's on the ... • Go straight on/over/past the ...

b) *Partner B:* Follow the directions. Tell your partner if you don't understand. Where are you?

Can you say that again? • I'm sorry, I didn't get that.

c) *Swap roles.*

Extra | **Background File** | **LONDON** 🎧

Kids' day out in London ... on a budget

London is huge. It's almost twice as big as Berlin. It's also an expensive place. Our tips can help you to see lots of London sights – and save lots of money! ▶ SF Understanding new words (p. 134)

Step 1 Go to a ticket office and buy a Travelcard. You can use it all day on the buses and the Tube. Just check that you buy it for the right zones. Oh, and don't start before 9.30 in the morning. You can only use your Travelcard after the rush hour!

7.5 million people live in London (Berlin: 3.4 million) and another million come into the city to work every morning – so the rush hour is pretty busy.

Step 2 You want to go to one of London's famous musicals, but you're on a budget? No problem! Go to the half-price ticket place at Leicester Square and get your tickets for tonight.

From there it's only five minutes' walk to Trafalgar Square and Nelson's Column. That's a great place for people-watching!

Step 3 What about some shopping? Remember, London is the capital of cool! What the young people are wearing in London today, you'll find in your shops tomorrow.

How can you shop on a budget? Well, don't go to an expensive shop like Harrods. Try the markets at Portobello Road, Camden Lock or Brick Lane. You'll find young designers with interesting new ideas. And, of course, lots of great second-hand clothes!

Step 4 Hungry? The Londoners' favourite lunch is a sandwich. The English invented the sandwich and it comes in every shape and size. If the weather's good, go and sit in one of the parks – sometimes there's even free lunchtime music.

A-Section **1** 19

Step 5 Now it's time for a bit of culture. Don't worry, it won't hurt! Try the Natural History Museum or the British Museum – both are FREE! You can see dinosaurs at one and mummies at the other. And the museum shops are great for interesting souvenirs or gifts.

Step 6 Do your feet need a break? How about a trip on the DLR (Docklands Light Railway)? It goes past the new buildings in the Docklands area.
London is the richest city in Europe and one of the world's most important money centres. Watch the skyscrapers from your window on the DLR. (You can use your Travelcard for this trip.)

Step 7 You're probably hungry again. You need something before the musical. Try a noodle bar – they're cheap and good.
And then, on your way to the theatre, maybe you can spend your last two pounds on the magazine 'The Big Issue'. Homeless people sell it on the street. Every night, in summer and winter, about 200 people – some of them young runaways – sleep on the streets. Buy the magazine and help the homeless.

1 A day in London

a) Make groups (A, B, …). Each group member gets a number (A1, A2, …/B1, B2, …).

b) Each group chooses a different sight or activity in London. Each member of the group collects information about this sight or activity (pp. 12–19, guide books, internet, tourist brochures etc). Discuss everything in your group. Make notes.

c) Make new groups with members of the other groups (A1, B1, C1, …/A2, B2, C2, …). Tell your new group members about your sight and listen to their information.

d) Make a poster of your plan for a day in London.

▶ SF Marking up a text (p. 142) • WB 18 (p. 17)

20 1 Practice

1 WORDS City sights

a) *Find the city words.*
1 Take a b___ t___ on the River Thames and see lots of sights.
2 A m_____ is a building with old, interesting things in it.
3 A p___ is a green place where people can walk, sit or play games.
4 From the top of the London Eye you get a great v___ of London.
5 Every Sunday there's a great m_____ in Brick Lane.
6 A t____ is a high building, or part of a building.
7 The Queen lives in a p_____.

b) Extra Make a city sights mind map. Use group words like *buildings*, *activities* and *other city words*. Put the words from a) into it. Add more if you can.

c) Extra Complete the text. Use your own ideas. Maybe your mind map can help you.

> ■ **Tourists!** Do you need some information for your day out in our city?
> Go to the … It's in the city centre next to the … If it's sunny, you can visit …
> Don't worry if it's rainy. You can go on a bus … You'll see lots of things
> from the bus, like … and …
> At lunchtime, you'll probably need a snack. No problem. There are lots of
> … and … in the city centre. In the afternoon you can … Have a great day!

2 WORDS A transport wheel

a) *Choose words and phrases from the box and put them in a copy of the wheel. You can use some words more than once. The words with* + *are new. Only look them up if you have to. Add more words (e.g. eastbound, bike, …).*

> +airport • bridge • bus • +bus stop •
> car • driver • +ferry • +gate •
> harbour • helicopter • line • +lorry •
> northbound • plane • platform •
> road • river • sea • ship • station •
> +taxi • ticket • train • +tram •
> Travelcard • Tube • Tube map •
> tunnel • underground • …

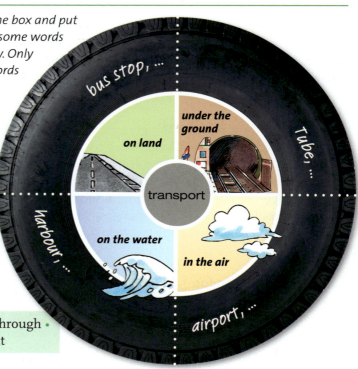

b) Write these verbs and prepositions in your exercise book. Match words from a) to them.

> arrive at • ask for • drive over • drive through •
> get off • get on • go by • wait at

– arrive at the airport, the bus stop, …
– ask for …

c) Extra What verbs can you use with the other words in a)? Check in the dictionary.

Practice **1** 21

3 MEDIATION The ticket machine

Vanessa Beck is visiting London with her parents. They have to buy tickets from a machine before they get on the bus. Help Vanessa.

Herr Beck Also, ein Einzelfahrschein gilt nur für eine Fahrt. Vanessa, gibt es eine Tageskarte? Und gilt sie für alle Busse?
Vanessa Also hier steht …
Frau Beck Gilt die Tageskarte noch heute Abend wenn wir zum Musical wollen?
Vanessa Das Ticket gilt …
Frau Beck Wie viel kostet die Tageskarte für dich?
Vanessa Ich bin 13, also …
Herr Beck Lass uns die Tickets kaufen. Wie viel kostet das insgesamt?
Vanessa …

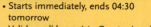

4 REVISION A visit to the London Eye (Simple past) ▶ D p. 106

Put the verbs in brackets in the simple past.

Asif and Robert *had* (have) a really great time yesterday. In the morning the weather … (be) great. Robert and his parents … (take) the Tube to Waterloo. When they … (arrive) at the London Eye, they *didn't see* (see) Asif. But then Asif … (call) Robert on his mobile and they … (find) him quickly. Luckily there … (be) too many tourists there that day, so they … (wait) very long. Soon they … (be) up on the big wheel. The view … (be) fantastic. They … (see) Asif's house, but they … (see) lots of famous London sights. After the ride, Asif and Robert … (stay) with Robert's parents. They … (go) to Asif's part of London and then to the Trocadero.

5 REVISION Yesterday … (Simple past)

a) *Copy the card on a piece of paper. Complete the sentences for yourself.*

Yesterday	Last weekend
I …	I …
I didn't …	I didn't …
In my summer holidays	**Last year**
I …	I …
I didn't …	I didn't …

b) *Make a double circle. Tell your partner about yourself. Then listen to your partner. Take notes about him/her. Here is an example:*

Elsa
Yesterday   Last weekend
rode bike, didn't read   went skating, didn't …
summer holidays   Last year
went > Spain,   moved > new flat
didn't stay at home   didn't …

c) *Talk to two more partners. Is anything the same? What was interesting?*

6 WRITING A postcard (Writing better sentences)

a) *If you use **adjectives**, **time phrases** and **linking words**, you can make your sentences more interesting. Find as many examples as you can in these postcards. Put them in a chart like this.*

adjectives	time phrases	linking words
great, good, …	yesterday, usually, …	and, but, …

Say which postcard you think is more interesting and why.

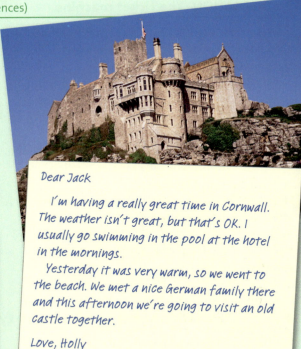

Dear Jack

I'm in Cornwall. It's great. The weather is good. I went to the beach yesterday. I went swimming in the pool this morning. I'm going to visit a castle with friends this afternoon.

Love, Holly

Dear Jack

I'm having a really great time in Cornwall. The weather isn't great, but that's OK. I usually go swimming in the pool at the hotel in the mornings.
 Yesterday it was very warm, so we went to the beach. We met a nice German family there and this afternoon we're going to visit an old castle together.

Love, Holly

b) *Make the sentences more interesting. Add the words from the brackets.*
1 I'm having fun here. (really, lots of)
   I'm really having lots of fun here.
2 We've got a pool. (fantastic)
3 I go there. (usually, in the mornings)
4 We have lunch in restaurants. (different, every day)
5 My parents take me to churches and museums. (in the afternoons, lots of)
6 I don't like the churches, but the museums are interesting. (very much, often)
7 We went to a show. (yesterday, really great)

c) *Use the words in brackets to link the sentences. Make changes if necessary.*
1 We arrived late. There was a problem with our car. (because)
2 The hotel isn't very good. The other guests are really nice. (but)
3 We couldn't go swimming. The hotel pool was closed yesterday. (so)
4 There was a party in the next room. I couldn't sleep last night. (because)
5 We get back home on Sunday. I'm going to send an angry letter to the hotel. (when)

d) more help ▶ D p. 106
Now write a postcard from an imaginary holiday.
– Start with a greeting.
– Say where you are.
– Say what's special about the place.
– Say what you usually do there.
– Say what you did yesterday.
– Say what you are going to do.
– Finish with a closing phrase and your name.
You can put your postcard in your DOSSIER.

I'm writing to you from …
Every day I go to …
Yesterday afternoon we visited …
This evening I'm going to …

Practice **1** 23

7 PRONUNCIATION now [aʊ] – no [əʊ]

a) Listen to the poem. Then read it out loud.

> A mouse wrote a hippo a note.
> 'Let's go to the disco and have a cola!'
> The disco was closed so then they chose
> to go home and sit down on the sofa.

b) Say the words on the right. Which is the odd one out? Listen and check.

1	shout	snow	phone
2	nose	down	photo
3	brown	slow	clown
4	show	grow	town
5	hope	home	house
6	about	cold	cloud
7	pound	mole	throat
8	sofa	sound	soap

8 Extra REVISION A week in London (Present perfect)

Janina and Klara are in London. Look at their list of things to do.

a) Say what Janina and Klara have already done and what they haven't done yet.
1 Janina and Klara have already visited the Tower of London.
2 Janina hasn't written a … yet.
3 Klara …

b) Write the sentences into your exercise book.

```
Things to do in London
J + K    visit the Tower of London ✓
J        write a postcard
K        buy a trendy T-shirt ✓
J        see a musical
J + K    play video games at the Trocadero
J + K    travel on the underground ✓
K        take photos of Buckingham Palace ✓
J        eat Indian food
J + K    have a picnic in Hyde Park
```

9 REVISION The Feely family (Present perfect)

Partner B: Look at p. 101.   Partner A: Ask questions about pictures 1–4.
Picture 1: *A:* Why is Mrs Feely angry?   *B:* …

1 Mrs Feely – angry

2 Mo and Jo Feely – happy

3 Grandpa Feely – sad

4 Mr Feely – tired

Now answer your partner's questions about pictures 5–8.
Picture 5: *B:* …   *A:* She's scared because she's seen a …

5 she – see big dog

6 she – write a nice story

7 he – eat too many sweets

8 they – not close door

10 WORDS Food

a) ⚪ *Which shop sells different things from the box? Which things can't you find in any of the shops? Where can you find them?*

bacon · ⁺beef · biscuits · bread · ⁺butter · cakes · carrots · cheese · cherries · chicken · eggs · ⁺lamb · ⁺lemons · lettuce · meat · ⁺mushrooms · ⁺onions · ⁺peas · ⁺pork · potatoes · rolls · sausages · ⁺steaks · tomatoes · ⁺turkey · ⁺vegetable

b) GAME Extra 👥 *Choose words from the box and find photos or draw pictures. Glue each one on a card. Write each word on a different card. You can use your cards to play a food memory game.*

11 //⚪ What have they done? When did they do it? (Present perfect/Simple past) ▶ D p. 107

Choose the correct verb from the brackets. Say what the people have done and when they did it.

1. Liz (visited/has visited) *has visited* London. She (went/has been) *went* there last summer.
2. Eddie (didn't eat/hasn't eaten) crocodile, but he (ate/has eaten) kangaroo. He (tried/has tried) it when he was in Australia.
3. Charlie (was/has been) on the London Eye. He (went/has been) on it two weeks ago.
4. Diana (didn't write/hasn't written) a postcard to her parents, but she (wrote/has written) postcards to all her friends. She (wrote/has written) them last night.
5. Sarah and Joe (didn't go/haven't been) to Harrods, but they (went/have been) to Brick Lane Market. They (went/have been) there last Sunday.
6. Andy (saw/has seen) a musical in Hyde Park. It (was/has been) two months ago.

12 Extra I've tried that – I tried it last week (Present perfect/Simple past)

a) *Choose six statements from charts A and B and write six sentence pairs.*
Example: I have visited a castle. I visited one last year. / I have been to Turkey. I went there in the holidays.

Chart A

	(try)	Italian/Indian/... food.
	(eat)	curry/bacon and eggs/...
	(play)	a computer game/...
I have	(visit)	a castle/a museum/...
	(have)	a picnic in a park/forest
	(be)	to a zoo/the theatre/...
	(be)	to Britain/Italy/...

Chart B

	(try)	it	
	(eat)	it/them	in the holidays.
	(play)	one	when I was little.
I	(visit)	one	last ...
	(have)	it	in 2007.
	(be)	to one	... ago.
	(go)	there	

b) ⚫ 👥 *Tell different partners what you have done and when and where you did it.*

Practice **1** 25

13 LISTENING Travel announcements

a) ⊙ Look at the pictures. Write down the numbers 1–5. Listen to five announcements and match a picture to each number. The sounds can help you.

b) Listen again and answer these questions. Remember: you needn't understand every word.
1 Which platform do you need if you want the Bristol train?
2 Where must you change if you want to get to Waterloo?
3 What must you keep with you at all times when you're at the airport?
4 Where must Benjamin Müller go now?
5 Which gate do you need if you want to fly to Berlin?

A

B

C

14 SPEAKING Asking for and giving information

1

2

3

a) What questions might people in these pictures ask? Write them down.

How much is	change to the underground?	it from here to Tower Hill?
How long	it for adults?	do we have to wait for the next train?
Can we	get a group ticket?	a ticket to Richmond?	break our journey?
	does the ride take?	does it take from here to the Tower of London?

b) Listen to the dialogues. Which questions do you hear in dialogue 1, 2 and 3? Write the numbers 1, 2 or 3 behind your questions. Then listen again and check

c) more help ▶ D p. 107
Imagine you're in London. With your partner prepare a dialogue like the one in the example. If you need help, listen again to the dialogues in b). Practise your dialogue and act it out in class.

A: Can I help you?
B: How much ...
A: Three pounds.
B: ...

A: ...
B: Thank you.
A: You're welcome.

EVERYDAY ENGLISH

Only a game 🎧

> Do you play video games? Which one do you find the most exciting? Or the most realistic?

When they arrived at the Trocadero, Asif and Robert went to Funland.
'Wow!' Robert said.
'They've got over 250 video games,' Asif said. 'The virtual reality games are the best.'
'I've never played one,' Robert said. 'How do they work?'
'Well,' Asif explained, 'you wear a helmet. Then you can see places all around you. It's like you're really there.'
'Sounds cool,' Robert said. 'Let's try one.'
The two boys looked round. There were so many games! Then Asif saw something in a quiet corner.
'Robert, over here! Look at this.'
There were two VR helmets and a sign in big black letters. Robert read it: 'Danger! Experimental game. Play at your own risk.'
'This is a joke, right?' Robert said.
'Of course it's a joke,' Asif laughed.
'But maybe it is dangerous,' said Robert.
But Asif was already putting on one of the helmets. Robert didn't like it, but he put the other helmet on.
'There's a menu,' Robert said. 'Can you see it too?'
'Yes, I can,' Asif answered. 'We can choose a virtual world.'
'They're all in London. The first one is Roman London. What do you think?' said Robert.
'Everybody in togas. I don't think so,' said Asif. 'The next one is Guy Fawkes. He tried to blow up the Houses of Parliament. And then there's The Great Fire of London.'

> **Tip**
> If you don't know a word and you really need to know it, look it up in an English-German dictionary.

▶ SF English–German dictionary (p. 136)

'That sounds good,' said Robert. 'What do you know about it?'
'It was a huge fire,' said Asif. 'It started in a bakery in Pudding Lane, and it destroyed almost all of London. Do you want to try it?'
'OK,' said Robert. 'But how do we start it?'
'Push the button,' Asif told him.
'Hey, I can see my hand in the game!' Robert said excitedly.
'That's virtual reality,' Asif explained.
A few moments later, London in the year 1666 was all around them.

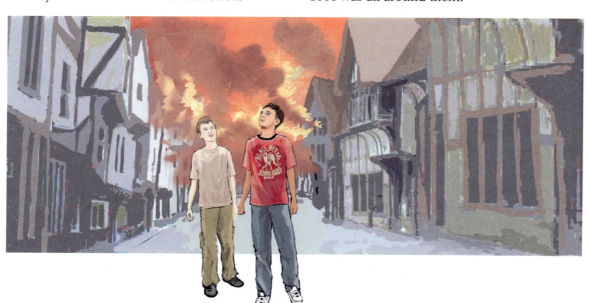

'Wow!' said Robert. 'This is amazing.'

The two boys were in a dark street. The houses were so close that they almost touched. Robert looked up. Between the houses he could see the sky. It was red.

'Look, Asif! The fire!' said Robert. 'Can you smell the smoke? It's so real.'

'Yeah,' said Asif. 'And look at all the people. They look real too. This is great.'

There were lots of people in the street. They had all kinds of things in their arms: bags, boxes, chairs, babies, musical instruments ... Everybody looked scared.

'Come on,' said Robert. 'Let's find the fire.'

'Careful where you walk!' said Asif. 'It's very dirty and smelly here.'

'Oh no!' Robert looked at his shoe. 'Yuck! I've got wet feet now.'

'Look!' shouted Asif. 'There's something in that water. It's moving.'

Robert jumped. Then he shouted, 'Rats! Lots of them. This is getting too realistic for me!'

People stopped and looked at them. They didn't look friendly.

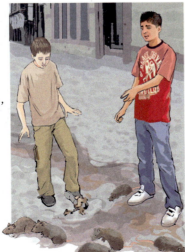

'Who are you? You look and talk funny,' said one woman to Robert.

'There are two of them,' said a man. 'They're not from here.'

'What are you doing here?' asked the woman.

The boys didn't know what to say.

'Er ... We came to see the fire,' said Robert.

'The fire?' said another man.

'Maybe they started the fire!' said the first woman! 'Stop them. Quick!'

Asif shouted to Robert, 'Come on. Let's get out of here. Run!'

They were very near the Tower of London now and they had a good view of the city.

'Oh my God,' said Robert. 'Look, Asif.'

It was terrible. There were fires everywhere and people were screaming.

'You know what?' Robert said. 'This game isn't much fun.'

'Yeah,' Asif answered. 'Let's take the helmets off and try a different game.'

Both boys took off their helmets. But nothing happened.

'We're still here! What's happening?' Asif was scared.

'I don't know! This was your idea,' Robert shouted. 'Do something!'

'I know,' Asif said. 'We can just pull the plug. Without electricity, the game will stop.'

'But where is the plug?' said Robert.

'There must be a plug somewhere,' Asif said. 'Try the walls of the Tower!'

'The walls of the Tower?'

'Just look!' said Asif. He was getting angry. 'It's only a game, Robert.'

Suddenly there was a flash.
'What was that flash?' Robert asked.
'I didn't see anything,' said Asif. 'Just find the plug. And be quick!'
The boys felt the walls. They were hot.
'It's funny,' Asif said. 'I can really feel these walls.'
'So?' asked Robert.
'The thing is, you can see and hear virtual reality. But you can't feel it.'
'And we can feel things,' said Robert. 'So that means …'
'Yeah,' said Asif. 'I think we're really here.'
Just then somebody shouted.
'Stop those two boys. They aren't from here. Maybe they're French. They started the fire.'
People stopped. They looked at the boys.

'We didn't start the fire,' shouted Asif. 'We haven't done anything!'
'They started the fire! Stop them!' another voice shouted.
'What are we going to do, Asif?' cried Robert. 'I'm scared.'
'Run!' said Asif.

Working with the text

1   What happens in the story?
Put the sentences in the right order.
1 They find a game in a quiet corner and want to play it.
2 The Londoners think that the boys started the fire.
3 The game gets too realistic.
4 Robert pushes the button for the virtual world of the Great Fire of London.
5 The boys can't stop the game because they can't find the plug.
6 Robert is scared because he thinks the people will hurt them.
7 Robert and Asif go to Funland because they want to play a virtual reality game.

2   How Robert felt   more help   ▶ D p. 107
Find one point in the story when Robert felt:
a) excited   *b)* nervous   *c)* surprised   *d)* scared
I think Robert felt excited when … (l. 43).

3   The ending
a) What do you think happens to Asif and Robert?

b) Now listen and find out what really happens to them.

4   Only a game?
How do Robert and Asif feel about the game in the end? Will they play an experimental game again? What would you do?

5   Video games – your opinion
a) What makes a video game a good game? *Think of reasons:* realistic pictures, good sounds, exciting story, …

b) What can be bad about video games? The ideas below can help you.
– You sit in front of the computer all the time.
– You hurt or even kill people in the games. That's not funny!
– The games are scary.
– You don't talk to people.
– You don't know what's real.
– …

c) Are video games dangerous in your opinion? Why?

> very dangerous • quite dangerous • not dangerous

▶ WB 19 (p. 18) • **Checkpoint 1** WB (p. 19)

How am I doing?

▶ SF Multiple choice (p. 139)

a) Find or choose the correct answers.

London
1. London is on the River …
2. Another word for the London Underground is the …
3. This bridge opens for ships: …
4. The Trocadero is near a famous square in the centre of London. It's called …
5. The Queen's home in London is …

Words
6. Which word doesn't fit?
   A ticket   B bus   C boat
   D underground
7. Excuse me, how can I … to Victoria Station?
   A come   B find   C get   D move
8. Does this train go to Leicester Square, or do I have to …?
   A change   B leave   C get on   D take
9. Which word is the group word?
   A potato   B vegetable   C carrot
   D lettuce
10. Which word doesn't fit?
    A turkey   B pork   C onion   D beef

Writing
11. It's been rainy, … we've spent most of the holidays inside.
    A because   B so   C when
12. Where can you add 'after' to this sentence?
    … A I spoke to the teacher, … B I tried to work … C harder.
13. Where can you add 'usually' to this sentence:
    I don't A … like food from B … other countries, but I C … liked the food at the Bangladeshi café.
14. Which is not the right way to end a postcard?
    A Love, Lisa   B See you soon!
    C Dear Dora

Grammar
15. The boys … to the Trocadero when Robert … in London last week.
    A go, be   B went, was   C are going, is
16. Robert … lots of photos when he was in London.
    A is taking   B has taken   C took
17. Asif … to France.
    A has been   B was   C is living
18. Have you ever tried Indian food?
    A Yes, I did.   B No, I didn't.
    C Yes, I have.
19. I'm sorry, Mrs Franks, but I … my homework.
    A have done   B haven't done   C did

Everyday English
20. … does the journey take?
    A When   B Can   C How much
    D How long
21. What … do I need for the train to Bath?
    A gate   B platform   C station
    D bus stop

b) Check your answers on p. 232 and add up your points – one point for each correct answer.

c) If you had 17 or more points, well done! If you had 16 points or fewer, it's a good idea to do some more work before you go on to the next unit. Where did you make mistakes? The chart will tell you what you can do to improve your English.

No.	Areas	Find out more	Exercises
1– 5	London facts	Unit 1 (pp. 12–19, P 5 (p. 21)	WB 1–2, 16 (pp. 8–9, 16)
6– 8	Word field: transport	Unit 1 (p. 14)	P 2, 4 (pp. 20, 21), WB 2–4 (pp. 9–10)
9–10	Word field: food	Unit 1 (p. 17), P 11 (p. 24)	WB 11 (p. 14)
11–14	Writing better sentences	P 7 (p. 22)	WB 8 (p. 12)
15–16	Simple past (Revision)	GF 1a (p. 149)	P 5–6 (p. 21), WB 5–6 (pp. 10–11)
17–19	Present perfect/Simple past	GF 1b (p. 149)	P 9–10, 12–13 (pp. 23–24), WB 12–15 (pp. 14–15)
20–21	Everyday English	P 13–14 (p. 25)	WB 17 (p. 16)

Unit 2
Island girl

1 Views of Hoy

a) Look for Hoy, Mainland and Flotta on the map above. Find the Orkney Islands on the map on the inside cover of this book.

b) Match the captions to the photos.

A From Hoy you can see the sea cages of the salmon farms.

B There are lots of cows and sheep on Hoy.

C From the cliffs you can see the Old Man of Hoy. It's a huge rock – 137 metres high.

D On the way to Hoy you can see the oil tanks at Flotta's oil terminal.

E The only way to get to Hoy is by boat.

F The salmon farmer's job is hard work.

2 A journey to Hoy

a) Look at the photos for a minute. Close your eyes and try to remember as much as you can about them.
Then listen – keep your eyes closed – and go on an imaginary journey to the island of Hoy.

b) Did you enjoy the journey? What did you see, hear, smell and feel?

▶ P 1–2 (p. 38) • WB 1–3 (pp. 20–21)

1 To school by ferry 🎧

Katrina McFadden lives with her family on Hoy. Every Monday morning her mum drives her from their home in the north of the island to Lyness, in the south. And every Monday Katrina is late.

'Katrina, love! Come on! We must leave now or we'll be late for the ferry!'

'OK, Mum. Just a minute!'

The journey to Lyness takes about half an hour. Sometimes Katrina doesn't talk much in the car.

'You're very quiet, love. Are you unhappy?'

'I'm OK, Mum. I just don't like Mondays.'

'Oh well, it'll be Friday soon enough. By the way, I won't be able to pick you up on Friday. But Dad will be there. Have a good week, love.'

Katrina takes the ferry from Lyness to Houton, on Mainland. In Houton she gets the school bus to school in Kirkwall. That journey only takes about half an hour.

▷ What time does Katrina have to leave her house on Monday mornings?
What time does she arrive at school?

Hoy – Winter Timetable
Arrivals and departures, 25 Sept until 5 May

Lyness	dep	0650	1405	1640
Flotta	dep	0710	1425	—
Houton	arr	0745	1500	1715
Houton	dep	0800	1520	1730
Flotta	dep	0845	—	—
Lyness	arr	0910	1605	1810

2 Now you

a) How do you get to school? Do you do anything on the way? How long does your journey take? Make notes.

> I usually leave the house at …
> I walk to the …, then …
> I go by bus/tram/train/…
> I ride my bike to the station, and then I take …
> My mum/dad/… drives me.
> I/We pick up my friend at …
> I sometimes stop at a little shop to buy…/…
> I arrive at school at …
> The journey/It takes … minutes.

b) 👥 Tell three or more partners about your journey to school.

c) Extra Which of your partners has the longest journey? Tell the class about his/her journey. Who has the longest journey in your class?

3 An interview for TV 🎧

a) There's going to be a TV documentary about Katrina's school. A film researcher from STV has come to interview students. Look at the questions.
1 How old was Katrina when she left the school on Hoy?
2 Katrina lives far from Kirkwall. Where does she live from Mondays to Fridays?
3 What do we learn about Katrina's dad?
4 What instrument does Katrina play and who does she play with?
5 Katrina uses a local word for a 'dance'. You spell it like this: ceilidh. How do you say it?

Listen and take notes. Then listen again to check.

b) Extra What can Katrina see from her bedroom window? Would you like that view? Why? Why not?

▶ GF 2a: will-future (p. 150) • P 3–4 (pp. 38–39) • WB 4–5 (p. 22)

A-Section **2**   33

All about ... electronic media

4 Keeping in touch 🎧

If you live in a lonely place like the Orkney Islands you need modern media! Katrina's great-grandmother can remember when the boat brought the post to the island once a week. And her grandad remembers when the first people on the island got a telephone.

Today it's different. Katrina can't imagine life without her computer or her mobile.

She goes on the internet all the time and chats with her friends or she visits their websites, and she keeps in touch with her family with text messages and phone calls when she's away at school.

> True or false? Electronic media are not important for people on Hoy.

5 Now you

a) What media do you use? What do you use them for? How often do you use them? Fill in a copy of the chart for yourself (✓).

MEDIA	often	sometimes	never
Mobile phone			
– make phone calls	✓✓✓		
– send text messages to family and mates	✓	✓	✓
– take photos or make videos			
– listen to music		✓	✓
– download personal logos and ringtones			
Computer			
– do homework			
– play games			
– surf the internet			
– watch DVDs			
– download, make or mix music			
– chat or send instant messages			
– talk over the internet			
– visit your friends' websites			

b) 👥👥 Interview two partners. Tick their answers in your chart in a different colour (✓ ✓). Answer your partners' questions.
Do you make phone calls on a mobile phone?
Do you do homework on a computer?
Yes, I do. / No, I don't.
How often do you …?

c) **Extra** 👥👥 Work in a group. Write two or three interesting things about yourself or a partner on a piece of paper and put it in a box. Take a piece of paper from the box and try to guess who the person is.

"I MET SOMEONE WONDERFUL IN A CHAT ROOM... AND THEN I FOUND OUT SHE'S A CAT!"

© 2000 Randy Glasbergen.
www.glasbergen.com

This girl never mixes music on her computer. She sends lots of texts. She has got a brilliant ringtone. Who is she?

▶ P 5–8 (pp. 39–41) • WB 6–9 (pp. 23–25) •
Text File 3 (pp. 118–119)

6 Trendy types 🎧

Linda   So, did the interview go well?
Fiona   Aye, it did.
Alison   If they choose you, you'll be a star.
Linda   Aye ... in a year or two you'll be able to buy us tea every afternoon ...
Fiona   ... and *you'll* be able to ask for my autograph.
Linda   Dream on!
Alison   Oh don't start, you two! Let's go into town after school. I'd like to do some shopping.
Linda   Aye. I want to go to that wee shop in Albert Street. If I don't get there soon, they won't have those new bags any more.
Alison   Which new bags?
Fiona   You know, the bags from that magazine. I'll show you ... here, look! They're really trendy.
Linda   Not like Fishface with her awful old rucksack – so uncool.
Fiona   Well, what do you expect? She comes from Hoy! 'Trendy' isn't even a word on Hoy. I mean, look at her hair. That awful ponytail!
Linda   Oh oh, here comes Fishface.

▶ Who is Fishface?
Do the girls like her? What things do they say?

▶ GF 2b: will-future (p. 150) • GF 3a: Conditional sentences (1) (p. 151) • P 9 (p. 42) • WB 10 (p. 25)

7 Extra POEM Billy doesn't like school really 🎧

Billy doesn't like school really.
It's not because he can't do the work
but because some of the other kids
don't seem to like him that much.

They call him names
and make jokes about his mum.

Everyone laughs ... except Billy.
Everyone laughs ... except Billy.

Paul Cookson

a) Read the poem. What links it to **6**?
In the poem, the other kids ... In 6, the girls ...

b) Do you think Katrina is like Billy? How?
In the poem Billy feels .../doesn't like ...
Katrina probably ...

c) 👥 Why do the girls bully Katrina? Can you think of other reasons why kids bully other kids? Collect ideas with a partner.
Because they are/aren't/...

   cool • different • popular • small • tall • ...

Because of their clothes/...

A-Section **2** 35

8 A Friday night chat 🎧

Katrina was tired and upset when she got back home on Friday evening. She went to her room and turned on the computer.

Katrina I'm so glad I found you online, Tish.
Latisha Me too. How was your week?
Katrina Oh, don't ask!
Latisha Why, what's wrong?
Katrina The Beauties were horrible. They called me names again.
Latisha Hey, don't let them upset you.
Katrina If people called you Fishface, you would be upset too.
Latisha They're just stupid bullies, Katrina. If girls called me names, I wouldn't listen.
Katrina If I looked like you, I wouldn't listen!
Latisha Katrina, you look great. Hey, you are great. Are the Beauties interesting? No! Did the school send them to the music festival in Birmingham? No! If I was you, I'd forget them.
Katrina I'd forget them if they didn't call me names all the time.
Latisha Just don't listen to them. You can do it!

▸ What is Latisha's advice to Katrina?

▶ GF 3b: Conditional sentences (2) (p. 151) • P 10–12 (p. 42) • WB 11–15 (pp. 26–28)

Looking at language

The girls talk about what Latisha *would* do in Katrina's situation (Was sie machen *würde*).
a) Write down the sentences with *if* in **8**.

If-clause	Main clause
If people *called* you Fishface,	you *would be* upset too.
If girls …	

b) Underline the verbs in the two clauses. What verb form is in the *if*-clause? What verb form is in the *main* clause?

c) What's the short form of **would**?

9 Feelings

a) Think of a word to describe the Beauties. Did you think of **gemein**? But what's that in English? Use a German–English dictionary to find out.

> **gemein** *boshaft* mean; *Witz* nasty;
>   *gewöhnlich* common

STUDY SKILLS | German-English dictionary

The dictionary entry gives three translations for **gemein**. Choose the right German word. Then you'll get the correct English translation.

▶ SF German-English dictionary (p. 137) • P 13 (p. 43) • WB 16 (p. 28)

b) Imagine you are chatting online with Katrina. What advice can you give her? There are some ideas in the box. Use a German-English dictionary if you need help.

> (nicht) beachten • um Rat fragen • aus dem Weg gehen • sich an einen Lehrer wenden

10 Extra SONG
If I had a million dollars 🎧

Listen to the song. The singer would buy a few things if he had a million dollars.
How many things can you find in the song?
What would you do if you had a million dollars?

Extra | Background File | SCOTLAND 🎧

Traditional ...

Only 5 million people live in Scotland. (England is almost twice as big and has got 50 million people.) Oh, and by the way, don't call the Scots English! They don't like it.

Tartans

Scottish people often wear their tartans. But they don't buy a tartan dress or trousers just because they like them. They wear the tartan of their family, or 'clan', and the patterns often go back hundreds of years. The pictures show tartans for the MacDonald and MacKay clans.

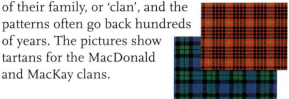

The kilt

For a special day or a traditional festival, the men often get out their kilts. The kilt is like a skirt. The material is a wool tartan – sometimes eight metres of it! What do they wear under their kilts? Don't ask – they'll tell you nothing ...

Highland Games

Every summer, towns and villages in the Highlands and all over Scotland have 'Highland Games'. There are competitions for ceilidh bands and dancers, bagpipers and all kinds of Scottish sports, like 'tossing the caber'.

Music

It isn't just bagpipes. The Scots always enjoy a song – in English or in Gaelic, the traditional language of parts of Scotland. There's a famous one about Scotland's Bonnie Prince Charlie. Maybe you know it!

Food and drink

No special day in Scotland would feel quite right without haggis (a sort of large sausage) or shortbread (not a bread, but a biscuit).

▶ P 14 (p. 43)

... AND MODERN!

From Orkney to Gretna Green, Scotland is a modern country. It's got exciting cities, big oil fields and a lot of high-tech companies.

Technology
Lots of high-tech companies have opened in Scotland. Scientists there were the first in the world to clone a sheep. Now they're doing exciting things with lasers.

Oil
In the 1970s the big oil companies found oil in the North Sea. Now there's lots of money in Aberdeen and other towns near the oil rigs.

Festival time
Every summer, Edinburgh, the capital of Scotland, invites the world to enjoy the Edinburgh International Festival, with music, theatre and dance.

There's lots to do at other times of the year too. Around 31 December for example, you can enjoy four days of concerts and fireworks.

1 Great Scots

a) Work in a group of 4. Each group chooses a person from the box. Find out when and where that person lived or lives and why they are famous. (Use an encyclopedia or the internet.)

b) Make a poster about your person. Think about how you can present it.
– Our poster is about ...
– He/She was born in ... (and died in ...)
– The picture shows ...
– He/She is famous for many things. First, ...
– That's the end of our presentation. Have you got any questions?

> Alexander Graham Bell •
> 'Bonnie Prince Charlie' • Sean Connery •
> Arthur Conan Doyle • Alexander Fleming •
> Mary, Queen of Scots • Ewan McGregor •
> James Watt

c) Put the posters on the wall of your classroom. Give your group members numbers from 1–4. All students with the same number go to one poster. Those who worked on the poster should talk about it. The group moves on and listens to the next presentation.

▶ SF Giving a presentation (p. 138) • WB 17 (p. 29) • **Text File 4** (p. 120)

38 2 Practice

1 WORDS Town and country

In the country

In a town or a city

a) 🔊 Which words go with **country**? Which go with **town**? Which go with both? Can you add more words?

⁺bay • beautiful • ⁺busy • ⁺canal • ⁺car park • cathedral • church • clean • cliffs • ⁺coast • cows • department store • dirty • farmhouse • field • forest • hill • ⁺hilly • hotel • lake • mountain • noisy • park • post office • pub • quiet • river • station • supermarket • theatre • town centre • valley

b) Finish these sentences. Use words from the box.
1 In most towns and cities you can find …
2 Cities are often …
3 In the country there are …
4 People like to walk in/along …

c) Extra Look at the photos again. Where would you like to live? Why?

2 PRONUNCIATION Stress in words with three or more syllables 🎧

a) Write the words from the box in a copy of the chart. Make a blue tick (✓) for each word: Do you think the stress is on the first, second or third syllable?

	1st	2nd	3rd
accident	✓		
alphabet			

accident • alphabet • beautiful • cathedral • cinema • disappear • expensive • helicopter • hospital • information • instrument • parliament • policeman • pullover • telephone • terminal

b) Listen. Where do you hear the stress? Make a red tick (✓) in your chart. Were your ideas in a) correct?

3 🔊 WORDS friendly/unfriendly (Word building)

a) Copy the chart and complete it.

friendly	unfriendly
happy	unhappy
clear	…
cool	
healthy	
fair	
safe	
tidy	

b) Put in an adjective from a).
1 You aren't smiling. Are you … ?
2 Don't eat so much fast food. It's really …
3 Ben can never find anything. He's such an … boy.
4 Jill never says 'hello' when you meet her. She's a really … person.
5 My sister can go out, but I have to stay at home. It's so …
6 Don't go over that bridge. A boat hit it and now it's …

4 REVISION I think Katrina will ... (will-future)

a) How well do you know Katrina? Look at the pictures and write down what you think Katrina will and won't do this weekend. Write like this: *On Friday evening I think Katrina will ... She won't ...*

1 On Friday evening Katrina ...

go to a disco

go shopping

2 On Saturday morning she ...

sleep until 11.30

get up at 8.00

3 On Saturday afternoon Katrina ...

play games

read a book

4 On Saturday evening she ...

go to a ceilidh

chat with her friends

5 On Sunday morning she ...

help Mum

help Dad

6 On Sunday evening she ...

play her fiddle

watch TV

b) **Extra** Read Katrina's diary about the weekend. Did you guess right?

Friday: Dad picked me up at the ferry.
In the evening I met my friends at the disco.

Saturday: Weather terrible. Slept late.
In the afternoon Jamie wanted to play a game. –
OK, just one, I said.
No ceilidh on Saturday. But luckily Latisha
was online and we chatted.

Sunday: Great weather.
Got up early and went out in the boat with Dad.
Mum and Dad went out in the evening, and I
played the fiddle.

5 WORDS Electronic media

a) Complete the text with the words below.

> chat • computer • download (2×) • logo •
> plays • ringtone • send • surf • text messages

Katrina has got her own ... in her room at home. She uses it to ... with friends and to ... the internet. It's cheaper for her to ... instant messages to her friends than to send ... on her mobile.

Katrina loves music, so she often spends her pocket money to ... her favourite songs. She hasn't got an MP3 player, but her mobile ... MP3s. Her ... on her mobile is a picture of a fiddle, and of course her ... is fiddle music. But it isn't a ... – it's her on her own fiddle!

b) Choose five words from a) and make your own sentences.

6 WRITING An e-mail to a friend (Using paragraphs)

a) Look at the e-mail and read the notes.

> At the beginning say what your text is about.

> Start a new paragraph for each new idea.

> Finish with a general or personal statement.

Hi Michael
I promised to send you a mail about our trip to the Orkney Islands – well here it is at last!

We had a great time. :-) We were lucky with the weather – lots of sun and not much rain – so we saw a lot. (I'm sending you some photos.)
…
Mail me soon with your news.
Love, Jenny

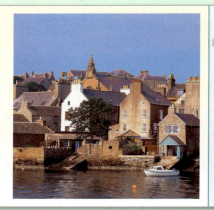

b) Add two paragraphs to Jenny's e-mail in a). Use the following information.

We started on Mainland – yes, the biggest island is really called Mainland. There's lots to see there. The towns of Stromness and Kirkwall are nice, but very quiet! On the third day we took a ferry from Kirkwall to the island of Hoy. There we did the famous walk to see the Old Man of Hoy. The big rock doesn't really look like an old man, but it is quite cool.

c) Rewrite this e-mail. Use paragraphs.

Dear Katie Guess what I did last Thursday – I went to Edinburgh with my gran! We had a very busy day. We arrived at Edinburgh station at 9.30 in the morning. Then we went sightseeing. The best thing was the tour of Edinburgh Castle (photo). In the afternoon we did some shopping on the Royal Mile. Gran bought lots of CDs and I bought a Scottish hat for my dad. We got home very late. I was really tired, but it was a brilliant day! Must stop now. Say hi to your parents. Talk soon! Tom

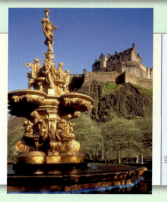

d) [more help] ▶ D p.108
Now write an e-mail to one of your friends about a real or an imaginary day out. Where did you go? Who was with you? What was the weather like? What did you do? What was it like?
You can put the e-mail in your DOSSIER.

Remember:

Start with an interesting opening sentence.	– Guess what happened to me today! – Did I tell you that …?
Start a new paragraph for each new idea.	– After that … – At lunchtime … – Before we …, we …
Finish with something general or personal.	– I hope I'll see you soon. – Must stop now. Please write back soon.

7 MEDIATION Using a mobile

a) *Lucy Parker is staying with Pia Wolf's family in Germany. Read the dialogue and find the English words for the German words in the box.*

> ver-/entriegeln • Knopf drücken • Geheimzahl

b) *Then complete the dialogue.*

Frau Wolf	Sag Lucy, ich kann sie gern abholen. Sie soll einfach anrufen.
Pia	Lucy, Mum says she'll pick you up if you …
Lucy	That's really nice. But I haven't got a mobile with me.
Pia	Ach so. Also, Mama, …
Frau Wolf	Lucy kann mein altes Handy nehmen.
Pia	Well, Mum says you …
Lucy	Thanks. How do I turn it on?
Pia	Wo muss sie es anschalten?
Frau Wolf	Das ist da oben.
Pia	…
Lucy	And how do I lock it and unlock it?
Frau Wolf	'Lock' and 'unlock'? Meint sie 'verriegeln' und 'entriegeln'? Das macht man mit diesen beiden Knöpfen.
Pia	You press …
Lucy	These buttons? Oh yes, I see. If I turn it off and then turn it on again, I'll need the PIN code.
Pia	Ach ja, …
Frau Wolf	Natürlich, 9667.

8 SPEAKING Telephone messages 🎧

a) *Pia is staying with Lucy Parker's family in Britain. Listen to Pia's first phone call and look at the message below. Find the two mistakes and write the correct message.*

From:	Mr McNammara
For:	Mr Parker
Message:	Please ring back 07890-449635

b) *Copy the phrases from Pia's first phone call and fill in the gaps. Then listen again and check.*

- Hello, John McNamara _____.
- Can I _____ Mr Parker, please?
- I'm sorry Mr Parker _____.
- _____ is Pia Wolf _____.
- Can _____ a message?
- Can you ask Mr Parker to _____?

c) Extra *Listen to Pia's second phone call. Write down the message.*

d) 👥 *Look at this message. Prepare a dialogue and practise it.*

From:	Mr Brown from computer shop
For:	Mrs Parker
Message:	Her computer has arrived. Please ring back - 246 788

A: Melde dich.
B: Begrüße A und sag wer du bist. Frag nach dem gewünschten Gesprächspartner.
A: Bedaure, dass er/sie nicht zu Hause ist. Und sag wer du bist.
B: Frag, ob du eine Nachricht hinterlassen kannst.
A: Sag "ja".
B: Diktiere, was A wiedergeben soll.
A: Mach Notizen und sag, wenn du fertig bist.
B: Bedanke und verabschiede dich.
A: Verabschiede dich.

42 **2** Practice

9 REVISION If it's sunny, ... (Conditional sentences type 1)

a) ⊙ *Complete the sentences. Write a positive and a negative statement. Use the ideas on the right.*
1 If it's sunny next Saturday, *I'll go on a bike trip.*
  If it's sunny next Saturday, *I won't practise the fiddle.*
2 If I'm online next weekend, ...
3 If I'm at home alone on Saturday, ...
4 If I'm in town next weekend, ...
5 If I don't see my friends on Sunday, ...
6 If it's warm on Sunday, ...

go dancing/swimming/...

visit ...   watch ...   send text messages

chat with my friends   tidy my room   play ...

go for a walk   have a party for ...

b) **Extra** 👥👥👥 *Make appointments with three students for 10, 11 and 12 o'clock. When your teacher says a time, go to your appointment. Tell your partner what you will and won't do and listen to his/her plans.*

10 //⊙ Fiona's dreams (Conditional sentences type 2) ▸ D p. 108

Fiona often dreams about what it would be like if she lived in London. Match the sentences.
1 If I lived in London,   I would probably see the Queen.
2 If my parents visited me,   I would have a fantastic life.
3 If I waited outside Buckingham Palace,   I would take them on the London Eye.
4 If a film-maker saw me in a school play,   I would be so much happier.
5 If I didn't live in a small town,   I would probably become a film star.

11 //⊙ If I became a film star (Conditional sentences type 2) ▸ D p. 109

a) *Choose the correct forms of the verbs.*
1 If I became a film star, (I'd meet/I met) famous people.
2 If my friends (came/would come) to see me, I'd show them all the film studios.
3 If they (wanted/would want) to see my films, I'd give them free tickets.
4 My photo would be in the newspaper if I (met/would meet) the Queen.

5 I'd be so excited if I (was/would be) in a film.
6 If I (didn't want/wouldn't want) a role, I wouldn't take it.
7 If I didn't like an actor, I (wouldn't work/didn't work) with him.

b) 👥 *What would you do if you were a star? Write three sentences. Compare them.*
If I was a film star / pop star / ..., ...

12 What if ...? (Conditional sentences type 2)

a) *Think: Complete the following sentences.*
1 If I lived on an island, *I'd chat on the internet every night.*
2 If my parents had a million euros, *I'd / we'd ...*
3 If I was 21 years old, ...
4 I would be fitter if ...
5 My English teacher would be really angry if ...
6 People would be happier if ...

love it/hate it/have a boat.
buy a house in .../travel around the world.
drive a car/get married.
do more sport/eat better food.
forget my homework/talk in class.
...

b) 👥 *Pair: Read out your sentences. Then choose your three favourites together.*

c) 👥👥👥 *Share: Present them in class.*

Practice **2** 43

13 STUDY SKILLS Using a German-English dictionary

a) ⃝ *Find the correct English words for the underlined German words in the following sentences.*
1 Katrina hat Latisha um Rat gebeten.
   Katrina asked Latisha _____ .
2 Latisha hatte Mitleid mit Katrina.
   Latisha felt _____ Katrina.
3 Katrina war sehr dankbar für Latishas Hilfe.
   Katrina was very _____ Latisha's help.

b) *Find the correct English translations for these German phrases. Use a dictionary.*
1 im Internet
2 ein Glas Marmelade
3 am Himmel   4 eine Brille
5 Geh ihm aus dem Weg! 6 Er kämmte sich die Haare.

> **Tip**
> What do the short forms mean here?
> Look at p. 159 if you're not sure!
>
> **Rat** advice; *Ratschlag* piece of advice; *Versammlung* council; *jn.* um Rat fragen ask sb. for advice
>
> **Mitleid** pity (*mit* for); ... haben mit feel sorry for
>
> **dankbar** grateful (*jm.* to sb.; *für* for); *lohnend* rewarding

14 Extra 👥 Loch Ness and Edinburgh

Partner B: Look at p. 102.
a) *Partner A: A student has written this text about Loch Ness. There are six mistakes in it. Read it through quietly. Then read it out loud to your partner. He/She will correct the mistakes.*

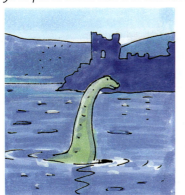

Loch Ness
Loch Ness is one of the most famous places in Wales. It is in the North of Scotland. The word loch is Scottish and means water. Loch Ness is 73 kilometres long. It is the deepest lake in Britain. The water is so dark at the bottom that people can't see when they go down into the lake.
   Some people think that there is a big monster in the lake. They have given it a name: Bessie. Every year hundreds of tourists come to Loch Ness to try and see her. There are even photos of her.
   If you want to find out more about Nessie, you don't have to go to Scotland: there are lots of websites where you can see photos from helicopters over the lake.

b) *Read the box below. Then listen to your partner's text about Edinburgh. When you hear a mistake, say* ***Stop!*** *Correct the sentence with facts from the box.*

> **Facts about Edinburgh**
> 1 Edinburgh is on the east coast of Scotland.
> 2 Edinburgh is the second largest Scottish city.
> 3 More than 13 million tourists come to visit Edinburgh every year.
> 4 Visitors come to see famous places such as Edinburgh Castle, the Royal Mile or Princes Street.
> 5 Alexander Graham Bell had the idea for the first telephone.
> 6 J.K. Rowling wrote her first Harry Potter book in a café in Edinburgh.

Orkney Star 🎧

> *Before you read Orkney Star, look at the pictures. What do you think the story is about?*

Another weekend was over. Katrina looked sadly out of her bedroom window. It was still dark so she couldn't really see the sea. But in her head she could. The sea and the little boat
5 in the bay, ready to go out and check the salmon cages. She liked to go with her dad on the boat …

'Katrina!' her mum called. Katrina put her little old teddy into her bag, took her fiddle,
10 turned off the light and went downstairs.

'There you are, love. I've made some porridge and a cup of tea.'

'I'm not hungry, Mum.'

'Och, you must eat something – it's a long
15 time till lunch – and it will be cold on the ferry. Have you got your scarf?'

'Oh, Mum.'

Her mum always drove her to the ferry at Lyness. The ferry left at ten to seven, so they
20 usually left the house by ten past six. They had to drive slowly because sheep often ran across the road. This Monday morning it was rainy and very windy.

'You'll have to
25 go downstairs on the ferry today,' Katrina's mother said.

'I hate it down
30 there,' Katrina said. 'I always like to have one last look at the island, and down there you can't see anything.'

35 Her mum smiled. 'The island will still be here when you come back on Friday, love!'

When Katrina got to school, there was just time to put her bag in the classroom and then she had to run to Assembly.

40 'And now for some announcements,' the head teacher said. 'I have a letter here from Scottish Television. You all know that they want to make one of their "Going to school in Scotland" documentaries here at our school. Well, they've chosen a student from S3 to be
45 "the star".'

Fiona smiled and whispered to Alison, 'Hollywood here I come!'

'… it's … Katrina McFadden. So, good luck to Katrina. And now …'
50 Katrina didn't hear the rest of the announcements. There must be some mistake: Why her? She couldn't believe it.

When she got back to her classroom lots of kids came up to her.
55 'Great, Katrina!' 'Cool, Katrina. It'll be great fun!'

Katrina began to feel very excited.

At break the 'Beauties' came up to her. 'Amazing, Katrina!' Fiona said. 'Were you
60 surprised?'

'Yes, I was,' said Katrina.

'We were too,' said Linda.

'Sshh, Linda,' said Fiona. 'Katrina, we thought you might need some help.'
65 'Help?' Katrina asked, 'Er … with what?'

'With shopping,' said Linda. 'We know some nice wee shops in Kirkwall – we could help you to buy some trendy new clothes …'

'And a new bag!' added Alison.
70 'But I don't need any new clothes, or a new bag,' said Katrina.

'Well what about your hair? I've got this friend. She's a really good hairdresser,' said Fiona.
75 'Maybe the film crew would like to film you at the hairdresser's?' added Linda.

'But why should I go to a hairdresser? My mum always cuts my hair,' said Katrina.
80 'But Katrina, we only want to help. Ponytails just aren't trendy,' said Alison.

'That's OK!' said Katrina. 'When the wind blows I like my hair out of my face. It's just fine, thank you.'
85 The 'Beauties' walked away. 'Once a Fishface, always a Fishface!' said Alison.

'Yes, and now we won't be able to get into the film!' added Linda.

It was cold and windy when the film crew came to school. Katrina walked across from the hostel in her wellies and anorak. She didn't know if she was more excited or more scared.

'Why did they choose me?' she thought. 'Film people are very trendy, aren't they? They'll probably think I'm really boring!'

'Ah, here she is!' said the head teacher. 'This is Katrina McFadden. Katrina, this is the director's assistant, Miss Burns.'

'Hi, Katrina. It's really nice to meet you. Call me Sheena.'

Katrina smiled. Sheena was about 23. She wore jeans, big green wellies and a green anorak. And she wore her hair in a ponytail. 'Hello, Sheena,' she said.

'Now, I'm going to take you to meet the director – Bill. He's really nice. We're going to film in the school today and tomorrow and on Hoy on Thursday and Friday. The head teacher has said you don't have to come to school on Friday. So you'll be allowed to stay on Hoy, OK?'

'OK!' smiled Katrina.

'We're going to start with an interview,' Bill explained, 'Just like the interview with the researcher, but this time we'll film it!'

'Come and sit here,' said Sheena. Katrina sat down.

The electrician smiled at her. 'I'm Fred,' he said, as he moved one of the lights to the right.

'And I'm Emma. I'm the sound assistant and I'm going to put this little microphone on your sweatshirt.'

'And I'm Alistair. I'm the real boss here,' laughed the cameraman. 'If you're nice to me, you'll look good in the film, if you aren't nice to me, well ...'

'Don't worry!' said Sheena, 'He's only joking. Is everybody ready?'

Katrina didn't feel ready, but Bill smiled at her and Sheena smiled at her ...

Bill began to ask questions.

'Katrina, you live on Hoy, but you have to come to school on Mainland. Do you like living away from home?'

'No, I don't,' said Katrina. 'The hostel's not bad, but I'd really like to be at home with my family.'

'Tell us about your journey to school on a Monday morning.'

'Well, ...'

The interview was going well, but then the bell for break rang.

'Oh dear,' said Emma, the sound assistant.

'Don't worry,' said Bill, 'Let's go out and film the kids at break.'

So Katrina and the crew joined the rest of the school for break.

Later, when they went outside to film Katrina as she walked up the hill from the hostel, Sheena whispered, 'Who were those girls, the ones with the disco clothes and too much make-up?'

'Oh,' smiled Katrina, 'You mean the 'Beauties'.'

'Beauties? I don't think so!' said Sheena. 'Clones, maybe, but not beauties!'

165 'They call me 'Fishface',' said Katrina.

'That's not very nice.' Sheena looked at Katrina. 'They must be very jealous.'

'Jealous? Of me?' said Katrina.

'Sure.' Sheena smiled. 'You're great! You're a 170 great fiddle player, and you're the star of our documentary. They must be jealous.'

The filming finished on Friday evening at Katrina's home on Hoy. The crew stayed for dinner – her mum made clapshot, a delicious 175 Orkney dish: stew with meat and potatoes and swedes in it.

And then Mr McFadden said, 'Now you must join us at the community hall for a Friday night ceilidh!'

'Don't worry,' said Katrina, 'It's just a dance.' 180

Katrina and her father took their fiddles and they all went to the community hall. Katrina's uncle and cousin were waiting: 'At last! There you are!' And the dancing began.

Working with the text

1 What's the story about?

a) Here are headings for the different parts of the story. Put them in the right order.
1 Let's go to the ceilidh
2 Katrina meets Sheena
3 The film crew
4 In Assembly
5 Monday morning at home
6 Clones, maybe, but not beauties
7 On the way to the ferry
8 Katrina and the 'Beauties'

b) Write one or two sentences about each part.

2 What did they mean?
more help ▶ D p. 109

a) Who made these statements? When?
1 'The island will still be here when you come back on Friday, love!' (l. 35)
2 'Once a Fishface, always a Fishface.' (l. 86)
3 'I'd really like to be at home with my family.' (l. 145)
4 'Clones, maybe, but not beauties.' (l. 164)

b) ⬤ Why did they say it?

3 ⬤ Katrina

a) The film researcher chose Katrina. What do you think were her reasons?

b) Why were the 'Beauties' horrible to Katrina before (p. 34)? Why are they suddenly nice to her in the story? What do you think of them?

c) Katrina doesn't want help from the 'Beauties' (ll. 64–85). Do you agree with her? Why? Why not?

4 Extra 👥 The interview

The director interviews Katrina. Make up the interview. Start like this …
Director ___ Katrina, where are you from?
Katrina ___ I'm from …
Go on.

5 Extra Film people

a) Film people have a lot of different jobs. Find them in the story. Add more if you know more.
director's assistant, electrician, …

b) Say what each has to do during the filming.

▶ Text File 5 (p. 121) • WB 18–19 (p. 30) • **Checkpoint 2** WB (p. 31) • **Selbsteinschätzung 1–2** WB (pp. 34–35)

How am I doing? **2** 47

How am I doing? ▶ *SF Multiple choice (p. 139)*

a) *Find or choose the correct answers.*

Scotland

1 Hoy and Mainland are two of the ... Islands.
2 Edinburgh is the ... of Scotland.
3 Scotland is famous for a kind of fish. People keep them in special farms in the sea: ...
4 Ceilidhs are a kind of party in Scotland where you can ...
5 The Old Man of Hoy is a huge ...

Words

6 Where won't you find many trees?
   A forest   B city park
   C car park   D country
7 Which word doesn't fit?
   A coast   B mountain   C lake   D river
8 It's usually cheaper to send somebody a ... than to make a phone call.
   A logo   B text message
   C download   D chat
9 You don't do it on a computer!
   A surf the internet   B write e-mails
   C cook dinner   D play games
10 ... me when you're back.
   A Write   B Say   C Text   D Go

German–English dictionary

11 You want to translate 'geht' in the sentence, 'Die Spülmaschine geht nicht.' You look up 'gehen' and find these German meanings. Where will you find the translation – under:
   A laufen?   B funktionieren?
   C dauern?   D handeln?

Grammar

12 If my brother ... to the party, I ... at home.
   A will go/will stay   B go/stayed
   C goes/will stay   D would go/stay
13 If kids in my class ... horrible to me, I ... my teacher.
   A were/would tell   B would be/would tell   C would be/tell   D are/would tell
14 If I ... in my best friend's class, I ... happy.
   A would be, was   B was, would be
   C was, be   D am, would be

Everyday English: On the phone

15 This is Emily ...
   A on the phone.   B speaking.
   C speak.   D talking.
16 Can I leave a ...
   A message?   B news?   C note?
   D newspaper?

b) *Check your answers on p. 232 and add up your points – one point for each correct answer.*

c) *If you had 13 or more points, well done! Maybe you can help students with fewer points. If you had 12 points or fewer, it's a good idea to do some more work before you go on to the next unit.*
Where did you make mistakes?
The chart below will tell you what you can do to improve your English.

No.	Areas	Find out more	Exercises
1– 5	Scotland facts	Unit 2 (pp. 30–37)	WB 1, 17 (pp. 20, 29)
6– 7	Word field: town and country	Unit 2 (pp. 30–31)	P 1 (p. 38), WB 2 (p. 21)
8–10	Word field: electronic media	Unit 2 (p. 32)	P 5 (p. 39), WB 6 (p. 23)
11	German-English dictionary	Unit 2, A9 (p. 35), SF (p. 137)	P 13 (p. 43), WB 16 (p. 28)
12	Conditional sentences (1)	GF 3a (p. 151)	P 9 (p. 42), WB 10 (p. 25)
13–14	Conditional sentences (2)	Unit 2, LaL (p. 35)	P 10–11 (p. 42)
		GF 3a (p. 151)	WB 11, 13–15 (pp. 26, 27–28)
15–16	Everyday English	P 7–8 (p. 41)	WB 9 (p. 25)

48 ✓ Getting ready for a test 1 Revision Extra

1 WORDS In the country

Words about the country are important in the practice test on pp. 50–51.

a) Complete the mind map with country words and phrases.

- IN THE COUNTRY
  - what it's like: quiet, ...
  - animals: horse, ...
  - places and things: forest, river, ...
  - what you can do there: ride a horse, go ...

b) 👥 Swap with a partner and compare. Can you add anything?

2 STUDY SKILLS Describing pictures ▶ SF Describing pictures (p. 138)

In the test you will have to describe a picture.

Where are these people/things in the picture?

| 1 farmer | 3 dog | 5 boy | 7 mountains |
| 2 birds | 4 horse | 6 bike | 8 farmhouse |

> at the top • in the background on the left •
> in the foreground • in front of the farmhouse •
> in the middle • next to the carrot field •
> between two trees • behind the horse

1) *farmer – next to the carrot field*
2) *birds – ...*

3 The birds are flying (Present progressive)

You use the **present progressive** to say what's happening in a picture.

   The birds **are flying**.

   Form of **be** + **-ing-form** of the verb

a) Write the **-ing form** of the verbs in the box. Be careful with the spelling.

> arrive • chat • cycle • eat • fly • give • get •
> hide • meet • play • take • win • write

arrive   –   arriving
chat   –   ...

b) Complete the sentences with verbs from the box in a). Use the **present progressive**.

1 I can see some birds. They**'re flying** through the air.
2 That must be the farmer next to the carrot field. He ... to somebody on his mobile.
3 The dog looks happy. It ... with a red ball.
4 The rabbits are happy too. They ... carrots.
5 I think the girl is the farmer's daughter. She ... the horse an apple.
6 That could be her little brother. He ... behind the horse.

Extra **Revision** Getting ready for a test 1 ✔ **49**

4 Katrina's day (Simple past)

When you write a short story or report, do this in the simple past.
Use the simple past forms of the verbs in the following sentences.

1 Yesterday Katrina … (get up) at twenty to six.
   Yesterday Katrina got up at twenty to six.
2 Later she … (have) a hot breakfast.
3 It … (be) windy and rainy when her mum …
   (drive) her to the ferry at Lyness.
4 Two hours later she … (arrive) at school.

5 At Assembly there … (be) announcements.
6 Katrina … (be) very surprised when she …
   (hear) her name.
7 She … (hear) the other announcements.
8 After school she … (call) her parents and …
   (tell) them the news about the TV film.

5 Spelling (Plural of nouns)

Remember that nouns have different plural forms.
Write the plural of the words from the box in
a copy of the chart.

book · bookshelf · box · class · day · family ·
film · hobby · man · mouse · party · pen ·
sheep · thief · watch · wife · woman

-s	-es	-ies	-ves	irregular
books			bookshelves	

6 STUDY SKILLS Writing (Linking sentences)

Time phrases and linking words can make stories and reports clearer and more interesting.
Read this story. Choose the right word or phrase for each gap.

An appointment in Victoria Road

… (Every day in August/One day in August)
when Asif was having breakfast he found a
note from his brother:

Meet me at 73 Victoria Road
at 11.45.
I need your help.
Hassan

Asif looked at his watch. It was 8.55. He had
enough time to do a few other things before he
met Hassan. … (First/Tomorrow) he checked
his e-mails. … (After that/First) he tidied his
room. … (At two o'clock/Then) he got his bag.
It was very hot, … (because/so) he packed two
bottles of water.

73 Victoria Road was a pet shop. 'What can
Hassan want here?' Asif wondered. 'And
where is he?' He drank some water and

waited, but Hassan didn't come. … (Two hours
later/Two hours earlier) Asif picked up his bag
and went home again.

'Where were you?' Hassan asked when Asif
got home.
   'I waited at that pet shop for hours,' Asif
said.
   'But 73 is a music shop,' Hassan answered.
'I had to get a big new drum for the band. And
… (just/so) I needed help.'

… (Suddenly/Because) Asif had an idea.
'There's more than one Victoria Road in
London, isn't there?' he asked.
   'And you went to the wrong one!' Hassan
said.
   Asif smiled, … (and/but) he didn't really
think that it was very funny.
   'Listen,' he said. '… (If/Then) you want my
help again, just give me the correct address.'

▶ WB (pp. 32–33)

50 ✔ Getting ready for a test 1 **Practice test** Extra

1 Reading

Robin Hood and Little John

Everybody knows that Robin Hood was a famous outlaw[1], and that he stole from the rich and gave the money to the poor. And everybody knows about 'Little' John, the big tall outlaw and Robin's number 2 man. But not so many people know the story of how the two men met.

One day Robin was fed up. He wanted something exciting to do, so he went out into the forest alone to see what he could find.

That same day, John Little, a shepherd[2], was unhappy too. The terrible Sheriff of Nottingham had taken away all his land, and so he had no place where he could keep his sheep. He gave all his sheep away and left his little village to look for work in the nearest town. The road took him through Sherwood Forest, where there were many thieves and robbers.

And so it happened that John and Robin found themselves in the same place at the same time: a very narrow[3] bridge over a river. One man wanted to go one way; the other wanted to go the other way. And so they met in the middle.

Robin spoke first. 'Please go back, sir, so that I can cross the bridge. I was here before you.'

John was sure that that wasn't true, and he didn't want to go back. If he went back, he would have to turn round, and then he

wouldn't be able to see the other man. 'What if he's a thief?' John thought. 'Maybe this is a trick, and he's going to steal my money.'

'No, sir,' John answered, 'I believe I was here first. You go back.'

Robin got his bow[4] ready. When John saw this he said, 'You seem like a fair man, sir. As you can see, I haven't got a bow. You don't want to kill a man who hasn't got a chance, do you?'

Robin agreed. 'You're carrying a staff[5], I see. If you wait here, I will quickly make a staff. Then we can have a fair fight[6].'

John waited on the bridge as Robin cut a tree and made a staff for himself. Some minutes later Robin went back on the bridge and the fight began.

It didn't take long till Robin was in the water. John ran down to pull him out of the river.

'You saved me!' said Robin, surprised. 'You are a good man. What's your name, sir?'

'John Little,' answered the big man.

Robin thought that was a very funny name for a man as big as that, and he laughed. 'From now on, I will call you Little John. If you like, Little John, you can join me and my men and wear our green clothes.'

And so it happened that Robin Hood and Little John became best friends and had exciting times in their fight against the Sheriff of Nottingham.

a) *Choose the right answers:*

1 Robin Hood was …
   A a sheep farmer.   B a friend of the poor.
   C Little John's number 2 man.

2 Robin met John Little …
   A in a river.   B on a bridge over a river.
   C under a big tree.

3 When Robin met John, he first wanted to …
   A push him into the water.   B kill him.
   C cross the bridge and move on.

4 John …
   A gave Robin his staff.   B killed Robin.
   C pulled Robin out of the water.

b) *Are these statements right or wrong? Why?*
1 Robin was bored that morning.
   This statement is right / wrong because the story says …
2 Sherwood Forest was a dangerous place.
3 Both John and Robin were fair men.

---

[1] outlaw ['aʊtlɔ:] Geächteter   [2] shepherd ['ʃepəd] *Schafhirte*
[3] narrow ['nærəʊ] *schmal*   [4] bow [bəʊ] Bogen
[5] staff [stɑ:f] *Stock*   [6] fight [faɪt] *Kampf*

Extra   Practice test   Getting ready for a test 1   51

2 Speaking

a) Describe the picture. Say:
– what kind of place you can see
– where the things/people/animals are
– what's happening.

> It's a picture of the country. In the background you see the coast. There's …

b) Say more about the two people in the foreground:
– what kind of people you think they are
– how you think they feel at the moment

Give reasons for your ideas.

> The man looks …

> I think the woman is rich. She's checking her watch. So she's probably in a hurry because …

3 Writing

a) Read the beginning of a story about the man and the woman in the picture above.

★ A meeting on a country road

One hot day in June a young woman was driving along a country road. She was in a hurry because she was late for an appointment. Suddenly she saw lots of sheep on the road, so she had to stop. She jumped out of the car and went over to the shepherd.
'Good afternoon,' he said. 'Nice day, isn't it?'

b) Finish the story in about 80 words. Say if
– the woman argued with the man
– she arrived at her appointment in time
– she ever saw the man again.

Remember

When you finish your story:
- Count the words.
- Check the spelling.
- Check the grammar.
- Did you use linking words?

Unit 3
Sport and more

53

1 A teenager's room

a) Look at the room. Make notes about what you see.

b) 👥 Talk about the room. Is it a boy's room or a girl's room? Why? What is he/she interested in?
I think it's a boy's/girl's room because ...
His/Her favourite colour/... is ...
I can see ..., so I think he/she is interested in ...
I think he/she likes/does ...

2 The profile

a) Look at the profile. Who's footie_girl?

PROFILE	footie_girl
age	13
sex	female
location	Manchester, UK
about me	I like football a lot. My favourite

b) Look at your notes from 1a). Complete footie_girl's profile. Use headings like:
My favourite team/film/things/place/...

3 Now you

a) Write your own profile. You can add a picture and put it in your DOSSIER.

b) Extra Describe your room. Does it show what you are interested in? There are useful phrases in the box. Remember: you can use a German-English dictionary if you don't know a word.

– I share my room with .../I've got my own room.
– I've got a ... in my room, so I can ...
– On the walls/In the corner I have got ...
– There is ... on the floor/desk/...
– My family comes from ..., so I love ...
– My dream is to ... You can see that because ...

▶ P 1 (p. 60) • WB 1–2 (pp. 36–37)

All about ... sport

1 Are you sporty? 🎧

I love football because it's fun to play with my team. Matches are really exciting – as a player or as a supporter. I'm a Manchester United fan and I play for United U14s.

We wear red football shirts so we're easy to spot on the pitch! We usually train once a week. Our last match was a draw – 2 all. I scored both goals! Our coach said: 'Not bad.'

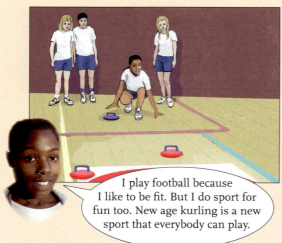

I play football because I like to be fit. But I do sport for fun too. New age kurling is a new sport that everybody can play.

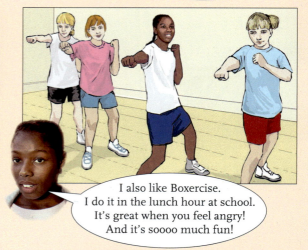

I also like Boxercise. I do it in the lunch hour at school. It's great when you feel angry! And it's soooo much fun!

▶ Why does Latisha do sport? What about you? Are you sporty? Why? Why not?

2 Now you

a) Choose your favourite sport or activity. Make a mind map. If you don't know a word, use a dictionary.

b) 👥 Talk about your mind maps.

3 ACTIVITY

a) On a piece of paper write a short text (4 to 6 sentences) about your sport or activity.

> I love basketball because it's fun to run around a lot after school. I'm an Alba Berlin fan and …

> I'm not sporty, but I do other activities. I like …

b) **Extra** Draw pictures or add photos to your texts.

c) Hang up your work in the classroom. Walk round the classroom. Choose your favourite.

▶ P 2–3 (p. 60–61) • WB 3–4 (pp. 37–38)

A-Section **3** 55

4 A Friday evening chat with friends

scottie	so how's your exchange student?
[banglaboy has entered the room]	
footie_girl	don't know really – he arrived this aft. bad timing – big match on sat
banglaboy	hi room. footie_girl: who r u talking about?
footie_girl	hi banglaboy. the german boy who's staying with us
banglaboy	a holiday friend?
footie_girl	no, it's an exchange that we do at my school every year
scottie	cool
footie_girl	oops, mum is calling me 4 dinner. hafta go! bye all
[footie_girl has left the room]	

> 1 Do you understand chat language? Match.

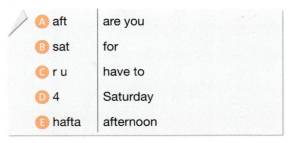

A aft	are you
B sat	for
C r u	have to
D 4	Saturday
E hafta	afternoon

> 2 Why are there no capital letters?

Footie_girl ran downstairs to the dining room.

────────── 🎧 ──────────

Mrs Byrd   There you are, Latisha. The food is getting cold.
Latisha   Sorry, Mum. Hi, Philipp.
Philipp   Hi, Latisha.
Mrs Byrd   Maybe you can do something with Philipp after dinner. Have you finished your homework?
Latisha   Homework? Oh right. No. There's still some Maths that I have to do. Then I have to practise the drums.
Mrs Byrd   Latisha, we have a guest who has come a long way. I'm sure you can find some time for him.
Latisha   Yes, Mum.
Mrs Byrd   Well, Philipp, I've made stewed chicken. It's a dish that my grandma brought with her from Trinidad.
Philipp   That sounds very nice, Mrs Byrd.
Mrs Byrd   Please start, Philipp.
Philipp   Er, OK, … Do you say 'Good appetite' in English?
Mrs Byrd   No, we don't. Is that what you say in German?
Philipp   Yes. So what do you say in English?
Mrs Byrd   I don't know really. Sometimes we say 'Enjoy'. But we usually just start.

> What does Latisha want to do after dinner? What doesn't she want to do?

Looking at language

In **4** Latisha and her mum describe people and things more closely.

a) Complete these sentence parts from **4**:
– the German boy *who*'s staying with us
– an exchange *that* we do at my school every year
– some Maths … I have to do
– a guest … has come a long way
– a dish … my grandma brought

b) What do *who* and *that* refer to?
In the first sentence, *who* refers to 'boy':
– the German boy who is staying with us

In the second sentence, *that* refers to …

▶ GF 4: Relative clauses (p. 152) • P 4–6 (pp. 61–62) • WB 5–7 (pp. 38–39)

5 A Saturday in Manchester 🎧

As Latisha and Philipp got off the bus in the city centre they saw this poster.

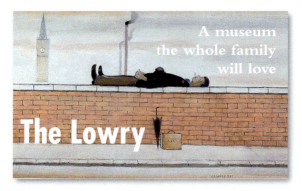

'I really like that picture,' Philipp said. 'But I don't understand the words.'

'Well,' Latisha explained, 'it means the Lowry is a museum that everybody in the family will love.'

'Oh, OK,' Philipp said. 'And what does Lowry mean?'

'Lowry was an artist from Manchester.'

'An artist? You mean he worked in a circus?'

'No!' Latisha laughed. 'An artist is somebody who paints pictures. That's a picture Lowry painted. – OK. Can we go to Old Trafford now?'

'What's Old Trafford?'

'It's the stadium you can see over there. It's the place where Manchester United play.'

'Oh,' Philipp said. 'I'm not really interested in football. Can we go to the museum?'

'OK, let's make a deal. I'll go with you to the Lowry if you go to my match this afternoon.'

'I think that's fair. OK.'

▸ What do Latisha and Philipp agree to do?

▸ GF 5: Contact clauses (p. 153) •
P 7 (p. 62) • WB 8 (p. 40)

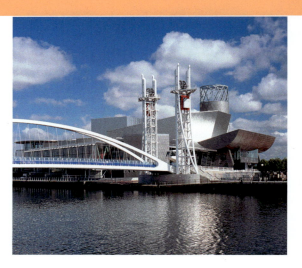

STUDY SKILLS Paraphrasing

How does Latisha explain 'artist' to Philipp? To explain a word, you start with a more general word (somebody, something, ...), then go on with one of these phrases:

It's somebody who ...
an animal that ...
something that you use to ...
a place where ...

6 GAME Paraphrasing

Paraphrase a word from the box.
Can the others in the group guess the word?

anorak • apple • camera • caretaker • choir • classmate • customer • drum • frog • guitar • hairdresser • microphone • pet • rain • roll • shopping centre • tennis

| This is | something/an instrument/... | that ... |
| | somebody/a person/... | who ... |

▸ SF Paraphrasing (p. 144) • P 8–10 (p. 63) •
WB 9–11 (pp. 41–42)

7 The match 🎧

Listen and find out about Latisha's match. Then answer these questions:
1 What's the name of Latisha's team?
2 What's the score two minutes before the end of the match?
3 Who scores the last goal for Manchester?
4 Who's shouting at the end?

8 A match report

Manchester
JUNIOR FOOTBALL NEWS

United U14s beat Dale
Manchester United U14s will play in the cup final after their win against Rochdale in an exciting semi-final in Manchester on Saturday. Although both teams played a good game, Manchester was the stronger team in the end. The score was 1–1 at half-time. Rochdale came back with an early second-half goal by Charlene Gordon. Sandra O'Keefe quickly followed with a goal for Manchester. It looked like a draw till the 59th minute, when Manchester's Latisha Byrd scored the final goal of the match.

Rochdale goalkeeper Sue Waites couldn't stop Byrd's goal

> What was the final score? Copy and complete the chart about the report.

Who played?	Manchester United U14 girls and Rochdale
When was the match?	
Where was the match?	
What was the final score?	
Why did they win?	

▶ P 11 (p. 63)

9 You and sports

a) Make a card like the one on the right for yourself. Write down reasons for your answers.

b) Make a double circle. Talk to three different partners about their answers. Take notes.
A: What's a sport that you don't like?
B: I don't like golf.
A: Why don't you like golf?
B: Because nothing happens. It's really boring.

c) **Extra** Tell the class three interesting things you learned about your classmates.

The sport that I like best:	A sport that I don't like:
hockey – fast, exciting	golf – boring, nothing happens
The sports star who I like best:	A sports star who I don't like:
Podolski – funny, …	…

▶ P 12–14 (p. 64–65) • WB 12–17 (pp. 42–45) • **Text File 6** (p. 122)

58 3 A-Section

Extra | **Background File** | **MANCHESTER – a great city for sport**

1 This week's programme 🎧

a) Write down the numbers 1–4. Listen to the radio programme and match each section of the programme to a number.

b) Listen again and write down one or two facts about each sports venue.

❶ Manchester is probably most famous for its very successful football team, Manchester United.

❷ If it gets too hot, take a dive into the Aquatic Centre.

A-Section **3** 59

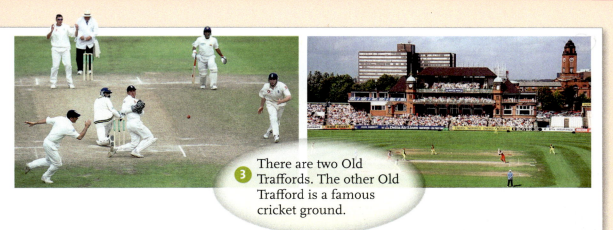

③ There are two Old Traffords. The other Old Trafford is a famous cricket ground.

④ The strangest-looking sports venue in Manchester is surely the Velodrome! They have great cycle races there – for the disabled too.

2 Now you

a) Choose a sport, a sportsperson or a sports venue. Collect information and pictures (internet, magazines, …).

b) Prepare and give a short presentation.
c) You can put your work into your DOSSIER.

▶ SF Giving a presentation (p. 138) • WB 18 (p. 45) •
Text File 7 (p. 123)

1 WORDS Rooms

Partner B: Go to p. 103.
a) *Partner A: Describe the room below to your partner. Use words and phrases from the box.*

> in the foreground/background • next to • on the right/left • in the middle • between • …

b) *When you've finished, compare your partner's picture with this one.*

c) *Draw an empty room. Your partner can help you. Listen to your partner. Put the things into the room. Ask questions if you don't understand.*

"There's a clock on the wall on the left. There's a desk under the clock."

d) **Extra** *Draw another room with lots of things. Describe it to your partner.*

▶ SF Describing pictures (p. 138)

2 WORDS Sports

a) ○ *Look at the pictures 1 to 8. Something is missing from each one. Find the missing things. In picture 1 the skates and pads are missing. In picture 2 …*

rugby ball • ⁺Equipment: • badminton⁺racket • skates and ⁺pads • ⁺saddle • table tennis⁺bat • ⁺swimming trunks/ ⁺swimsuit • ⁺skis • running shoes

b) *Now match a location to each sport:*

> ⁺court • pitch • ⁺half-pipe • pool • ⁺bridle path • ⁺ski slope • sports hall • ⁺running track

c) **Extra** *Write two sentences about each sport: Where do you do it? What do you need?*
1 You go skating in a half-pipe. You need skates, pads and a helmet.
2 If you want to go swimming, you need …

Practice **3** 61

~~Homework~~

3 REVISION Hobbies (Word order in subordinate clauses) ✓

	S V O	S V O
English:	Latisha wears a red shirt	when she plays football.
German:	Latisha trägt ein rotes Hemd,	wenn sie Fußball spielt.
	S V O	S O V

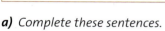

a) Complete these sentences.
1. Latisha likes football because (it / an exciting game / is).
2. She goes to the fan shop when (a new Manchester United poster / wants / she).
3. She would be excited if (one of the players / she / met).
4. Asif doesn't want to go back to the Trocadero after (he / so many problems there / had).
5. Asif would like to play in his brother's band because (their music / likes / he).
6. Robert is happy when (ice hockey matches / he / is watching).
7. Katrina and her dad play at a lot of ceilidhs because (well / the fiddle / they play).[1]
8. Katrina is always happy when (gets / she / a message from Latisha).

b) Extra On a piece of paper, write five sentences about your hobbies and free time activities. Say why you do them.

c) Extra Put your pieces of paper in a box. Take a piece of paper and read it out. Can the group guess who wrote the sentences?

4 What would you like? (Relative clauses) ▶ D p. 109

a) Write sentences.

I'd like	a teacher a friend a brother an aunt	who	doesn't tell our parents when I do something wrong. gives me lots of nice presents when she visits. explains things well and is funny. listens to my problems.
I'd like	a car a computer a room a dog	that	comes and sits with me when I'm lonely. is fun to drive. is really fast and easy to use. is big and has a nice view.

b) Extra What would you like? Make your own sentences.

5 Can you help me? (Relative clauses) ▶ D p. 110 ✓

Make questions. Use **who** or **that**. Then try to answer the questions. Check your answers on p. 180.
1. What's the name of the big wheel … you can see in London?
2. Who's that boy … is visiting the Byrds?
3. What's the name of the instrument … is in Latisha's room?
4. What's the name of the dish … Latisha's grandma brought from Trinidad?
5. What's the name of the team … Latisha supports?
6. What's the name … Latisha uses in the chat room?
7. What's the name of the boy … J. K. Rowling wrote books about?
8. Who's the actor … is in that new action film?

3 Practice

6 Who's that? (Relative clauses) jeder, jede*

Make a sentence about each famous person.

- **Wayne Rooney**
- a footballer
- plays for Manchester United

- **Robbie Williams**
- a singer
- millions of fans love him

1 Wayne Rooney is a footballer who plays ...   2 Robbie Williams is a singer who millions ...

- **Keira Knightley**
- the actor *Schauspielerin
- plays Elizabeth Swann in 'Pirates of the Caribbean'

- **Emma Watson**
- the actor
- you can see her in the Harry Potter films

- **Sir Arthur Conan Doyle**
- the writer
- wrote the Sherlock Holmes stories

- **J. K. Rowling**
- a writer
- lots of people know her

7 The Petersons and their pets (Relative clauses without relative pronouns)

a) Find out the names of the people and pets.
Copy and complete the chart.
1 Pepper is a name you give a black animal.
2 Pepper is the dog Peter and Paul are touching.
3 Pat is the dog Peter is holding.
4 Pat is the dog Paula is touching.
5 Petunia is the dog Pamela is holding.

father	
mother	
boy	
girl	
big black dog	
small brown dog	
small white dog	

b) Extra You can leave out **who** or **that** in two of these sentences. Which two?

1 I'm the pet that isn't in the picture.
2 I'm the pet that the dogs hate.
3 Pamela is the person who feeds me.
4 She's the person who I like best.

8 STUDY SKILLS Paraphrasing

Partner B: Go to p. 103.
a) Partner A: Explain the English words on the right to your partner – but don't use the word. Phrases from the blue box can help you.

> It's somebody/a person who …
> It's something/a vegetable/a … that …
> It's something that you use to …
> It's a thing/an animal that …
> It's a place where …

> coach • cooker • department store • lion • potato • waitress

b) Listen to your partner and guess his/her words – Oh, do you mean a … ?

c) Explain the German words to your partner.

> Fernseher • Hausmeister • Krankenschwester • Tennisschläger • Verkäufer

9 REVISION If Latisha … (Conditional sentences)

Complete these sentences.
1 If Latisha *goes* (goes/will go) to the museum with Philipp, he *will be* (is/will be) happy.
2 Latisha … (is/will be) sad if her team … (won't win/doesn't win) the football match.
3 Latisha … (doesn't play/won't play) well in her match if she … (goes/will go) to bed late.
4 If Latisha's team … (will win/wins) the match, they … (are/will be) in the final.
5 If I … (went/would go) to Manchester, I … (would go/went) to Old Trafford.
6 If I … (had/would have) a ticket, I … (would go/went) to a Manchester United match.

10 PRONUNCIATION (Different stress in English and German words)

a) Copy the German words and the English words. Where is the stress in each word? Underline the stressed syllables.
Appetit • April • brillant • Instrument • Problem • Programm • Pullover • Temperatur
appetite • April • brilliant • instrument • problem • programme • pullover • temperature

b) Listen and check. Were you right?

11 Extra LISTENING Keep fit in your English lesson

a) Match the instructions and the pictures.

… and let your arms hang down.
… and stretch your fingers out.
… and turn your head.
… and bring your knees up, keep your back straight!

1

2

3
4

b) Listen and do the exercises.

12 WRITING A report (Collecting and organizing ideas)

a) When you read a report on a match or another event, you want:
– quick information on what happened
– the important information first, details later

> **Tip**
> A good report usually answers the 5 Ws:
> **Who? What? Where? When? Why?** – and sometimes **How?**

Which of these is the better report? Why?

> Manchester United beat Chelsea 2–1 in a fast and exciting match in London last Saturday. There were no goals until the last minute of the first half, when Manchester's Wayne Rooney scored a beautiful goal past Chelsea goalkeeper Petr Cech.
> Chelsea looked nervous after the

> It was a fine and sunny day last Saturday when Manchester United and Chelsea met for their big match. 'A great day for football,' I thought. 'Not too warm and not too cold.'
> The match started a few minutes after 2 pm because the Chelsea players arrived

b) You are going to write a report on a football match. You need to organize the information.

- Bristol South against Redcliffe
- the first match of the year
- boys' U14 football
- the first half ended 0–0
- slow start
- final score: South 1, Redcliffe 0
- on the pitch
- 19th October
- second half very fast
- South's Tim Hooley best player
- lots of mistakes by Redcliffe

1 You can collect your ideas in a **mind map**:

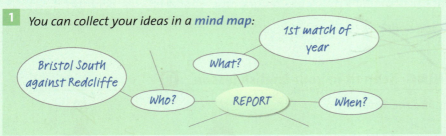

2 Or maybe a **chart** works better for you:

Who?	What?	Where?	When?	Why?	How?
			19th Oct		

Use one of the methods and organize the information.

c) [more help] ▶ D p. 110
Use your ideas from b) to write a short report (two or three paragraphs) on the match between Bristol South and Redcliffe. Use the **simple past**.

d) ● Think of a match you played in, went to or watched on TV. Make notes like the ones in b). Then write your own report.
You can put it in your DOSSIER.

Practice **3** 65

13 SPEAKING Talking to people at meals 🎧

a) ⭘ *The Byrds and their guest are sitting at the dinner table. Listen. Put the phrases below in the right order.*

A Well first we went to the Lowry ...
B Would you like some more rice, Philipp?
C Yes please, Mrs Byrd.
D Well, please start!
E And what about you? What did you do today?
F Mmm, that looks good.
G What did you do today, Philipp?
H Thank you. Enjoy!
I Thank you, Mr Byrd.

> **Remember**
> Here are some 'rules' for sounding friendly when you talk to people:
> – Say 'please' and 'thank you'.
> – Use the other person's name.
> – Don't answer with just one word.
> – Don't just talk about yourself – ask questions too.

b) *A foreign visitor is having dinner at your home. Write a dialogue. Make the visitor sound friendly.*

You ____ I hope you like sausages, Michael.
Visitor ____ I love sausages, thank you.
You ____ Well, please start.
Visitor ____ ...

14 MEDIATION Where I'm from [more help] ▶ D p. 111

Philipp has brought a book about Chemnitz, his home town, as a present for the Byrd family. Imagine you're Philipp. Explain the page.

> **Remember**
> Don't try to translate the texts – just give an idea of what they're about.

Chemnitz und das Erzgebirge

Chemnitz liegt am Rande des Erzgebirges und ist wichtiges Zentrum für die gesamte Region. Die drittgrößte Stadt Sachsens bietet eine aufregende Kombination aus Alt und Neu.

Im Erzgebirge denkt man das ganze Jahr an Weihnachten. Hier werden die herrlichen Holzfiguren geschnitzt, die auf der ganzen Welt beliebt sind. Einige Werkstätten, wie die hier abgebildete in **Seiffen**, kann man das ganze Jahr über besichtigen. Es ist sehr interessant, die Kunsthandwerker bei ihrer Arbeit zu beobachten.

Bergbau. Noch immer baut man im Erzgebirge das Erz ab, von dem es seinen Namen hat. Zinn und Silber werden hier abgebaut.

Erzgebirge — Ore Mountains
Holzfigur — wooden figure
Zinn — tin
Silber — silver
Bergbau — mining

EVERYDAY ENGLISH

Who needs legs?

Partner B: Go to p.104.
Partner A: Work with this text.

Nathan Stephens was born in a village in Wales on 11th April 1988. (The name Nathan means 'happy and brave'.) When he was a baby he learned to walk early. 'He took his first steps when he was only ten months old,' says his mother Helen. 'He just got up and walked.'

As a little boy Nathan loved sport. At school he played football and in his free time he learned to ride. He loved animals. 'When I grow up, Mum,' he said, 'I'm going to work with animals.'

For his ninth birthday Nathan asked his parents for a pair of riding boots and a new riding hat. And he was really excited when he came down to breakfast on 11th April 1997 and there they were.
'Thanks Mum and Dad! They're great!'

After school that day, some cousins and friends came to tea. It was a sunny spring day, so after tea the boys asked if they could go down to the old railway line to play. There were no trains there any more so it was a favourite place for kids to play.

'Just remember to stay away from the new railway line,' called Nathan's mum as they ran outside.

Nathan remembers that afternoon. 'It was my ninth birthday. I went out to play with my friends. Our parents always said to us, "Don't go near the new railway line where the trains are" – but you know, boys often do things they aren't allowed to do! Well, I saw this slow train. "I'll jump onto it and take a ride," I thought. I jumped, but I fell … under the train. It cut off both my legs.'

'A doctor and paramedics were already there when I arrived,' says Nathan's mum. 'I knew that he understood how bad it was because he asked, "Will I have to be in a wheelchair now?" All he said to me as they put him in the ambulance was "Sorry, Mum".'

Working with the text

1 Who is Nathan Stephens?

a) *Read the text. Take notes on these questions:*
– When and where was Nathan born?
– What sports did he do as a little boy?
– Where did he go on his ninth birthday?
– What happened there?

b) *Answer your partner's questions. Then ask him/her what happened next. Take notes.*
– When did Nathan learn to walk again?
– What sports did he do when he was ten?
– When did he win his first athletics medals?
– What are his hopes?

c) *What kind of a boy is Nathan? Why do you think that?*
I think he's brave/hard-working/sporty/… because …

2 Timeline

a) *Copy and complete this timeline with your partner. Scan both texts again if necessary.*

b) **Extra** *What did Nathan do after 2006? Find out with the help of the internet.*

DOSSIER *Timeline for …*

Find out about an interesting person (a sports star, a film star, …). Draw a timeline for him/her.

▶ **Text File 8** *(pp. 124–126)* • WB 19 *(p. 46)* •
Checkpoint 3 *WB (p. 47)*

How am I doing?

a) *Find or choose the correct answers.*

Reading – Facts from the unit

*If you can't remember the answers to these
questions, go back into the unit.*

1 What instrument does Latisha play?
2 What's the name of a Manchester
   museum the whole family will love?
3 What's the name of the football stadium
   where Manchester United plays?
4 What's the name of the young sports star
   who lost his legs when he was nine?

Paraphrasing

5 Which of these is *not* a general word?
   A place   B somebody   C dinner
   D thing
6 Which is the best way to paraphrase
   helmet? It's ...
   A black and hard.   B a thing for skaters.
   C like a hat.   D something skaters wear
   on their heads.

Everyday English

7 Which answer to the question 'Where are
   you from?' is a bit unfriendly?
   A I'm from Germany.   B Berlin.
   C I'm from Berlin, in Germany.
   D I'm from Berlin, the German capital.
8 Which of these is *not* a good idea when
   you talk to English people?
   A Use the people's names often.
   B Say something nice about England.
   C Use complete sentences or short
   answers.
   D Talk about yourself all the time.

Words

9 Another word for 'fan' is ...
   A match   B score   C supporter
   D pitch
10 Which word doesn't fit?
    A racket   B saddle   C bat
    D sports hall
11 Match the sports and the places:
    1 tennis   2 ice hockey   3 football
    4 skiing
    A pitch   B slope   C ice rink   D court
12 What's 'unentschieden' in English?
13 Match the rooms and the things in them:
    1 living room   2 bathroom
    3 bedroom
    A wardrobe   B armchair   C shower
14 Which of these things will you probably
    not find in a kitchen?
    A sink   B fridge   C cooker   D lift

Grammar

15 I've just met a girl ... comes from England.
    A which   B where   C who   D how
16 Put the words in the right order to finish
    the sentence: Manchester is a city ...
    I / to visit / that / want
17 "Frau Marx is the teacher most students at
    our school like best."
    What does the sentence mean?
    A Frau Marx likes the students.
    B Most students like Frau Marx.
    C Frau Marx likes the school.
    D Most students like the school.

b) *Check your answers on p. 232 and add up your points – one point for each correct answer.*

c) *If you had 14 or more points, well done! Maybe you can help students who had fewer points. If you
had 13 points or fewer, it's a good idea to do some more work before you go on to the next unit. Where
did you make mistakes? The chart below will tell you what you can do to improve your English.*

No.	Areas	Find out more	Exercises
1– 4	Facts from the unit	Unit 3 (pp. 52–57, 66)	WB 3, 18–19 (pp. 37, 45–46)
5– 6	Paraphrasing	Unit 3 (p. 56), SF (p. 144)	P 8 (p. 63), WB 9 (p. 41)
7– 8	Talking to people	Unit 3 P 13 (p. 65)	
9–12	Word field: sports	Unit 3 (p. 56)	P 2 (p. 60), WB 3–4 (pp. 37–38)
13–14	Word field: the house	Unit 3 (p. 52)	P 1 (p. 60), WB 1 (p. 36)
15–17	Relative clauses	Unit 3 (p. 55), GF 4 (p. 152)	P 4–7 (pp. 61–62), WB 5–8 (pp. 38–40)

68 Unit 4

Growing up in Canada

A

B

C

D

E

F

1 Growing up in Canada

a) What do young people in Canada do in their free time?
In photo **A** I can see …
Young people in Canada probably …

> go camping • go canoeing • go hunting •
> go into town • go on trips in the USA •
> go shopping • go snowshoeing •
> hang out with friends • have sleepovers •
> play ice hockey …

b) Do you and your friends do the same things as Canadians in their free time?
I/Some of my friends often/sometimes …
I/We don't …
I/We never …

2 Young Canadians talking

a) Listen to the young people. Put the pictures in the right order.

b) True or false? Listen again and check your answers. Correct the false sentences.
1. Toronto is the capital of Canada.
2. Ottawa is the biggest city in Canada.
3. Hockey is a popular sport.
4. The most important languages in Canada are English and German.
5. A lot of Canadians have cabins.
6. Bears like shampoo.
7. You can't shoot bears in Canada.
8. Canada is part of the USA.
9. People come from all over the world to live in Canada.
10. Canadian winters are short.

c) **Extra** List three interesting facts about Canada. Would you like to live in Canada? Why? Why not?

▶ P 1–2 (p. 76) • WB 1 (p. 48)

All about ... adults and teenagers

1 They just don't understand 🎧

Robert: My mom always complains about my music. She doesn't like the lyrics of the rap songs. And I'm not allowed to play loud music. It's not fair.

Emily: I have to go to bed really early on school nights. My friends don't have to go to bed early. They're allowed to watch TV till midnight. It's not fair.

Ashley: I had big problems with my parents last month. The phone bill was huge and they say it's my fault. Now I'm not allowed to use the house phone. But I have to talk to my friends. I think my parents are too strict.

Sam: I wanted to colour my hair, but I wasn't allowed to. All my friends have piercings. I know that I won't be allowed to get one. It's not fair. My parents are so old-fashioned.

Jordan: My parents didn't have much money when they came to Canada. So they want me to work hard and get a good job. Well, I did badly in the last test and now I'm not allowed to go out for a week. I'm grounded. But it's not my fault. Nobody was able to answer the questions.

Jessica: My mom is quite easy-going, but my dad is annoying. He says I spend too much money on clothes. It's not true. I haven't got anything to wear.

▷ 1 What things do these kids argue about with their parents?
2 Do you think their parents are too strict **or** quite strict **or** OK?

▶ P 3 (p. 76) • WB 2 (p. 49)

2 Are you allowed to ...?

a) Write down three things you're allowed to do and three things you aren't allowed to do.

b) 👥 Draw a window like the one on the right. Talk to your partner and fill in the window.

A: I'm allowed to watch TV till midnight. What about you?
B: I'm not allowed to do that. But I'm allowed to sleep till 12 o'clock on Saturdays. What about you?

c) Report to the class.
I'm allowed to watch TV till midnight, but Marcel isn't. He's allowed to ...

	My partner is allowed to ...	My partner isn't allowed to ...
I'm allowed to ...	My partner and I are allowed to ...	I'm allowed to watch TV till midnight, but my partner isn't.
I'm not allowed to ...	I'm not allowed to ..., but my partner is.	My partner and I aren't allowed to ...

▶ GF 6: Modal substitutes (p. 154) • P 4–5 (p. 77) • WB 3–4 (p. 50)

3 Plans for the weekend 🎧

Ashley   Hey, guys! Who's coming to my party on Saturday?
Emily   I'm coming.
Ashley   And you, Jordan? Are you coming?
Jordan   I haven't asked my parents yet, but I'm sure I won't be allowed to go.
Robert   Why not?
Jordan   I'm grounded, remember!
Jessica   Well, I'm allowed to go, but I have to be home by ten o'clock.
Robert   Ten? Your parents are worse than mine. I'm allowed to stay out till 11 if there's no school the next day.
Jordan   So are you going to the party?
Robert   No, we're driving out to our cabin for the weekend.
Jordan   When are you leaving?
Robert   Saturday morning early. I'm doing a gig at the youth centre on Friday.

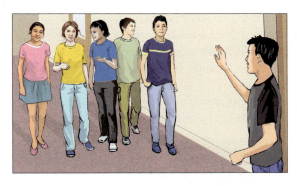

Jordan   Cool.
Jessica   I'm not doing anything on Sunday morning. What about you, Em? Do you want to meet in High Park?
Emily   Sure, why not. Look, here's Sam.
Sam   Hi, guys. Robert, I have to talk to you.

▷ Who's going to the party? Who isn't going? Why not?

4 Plans for your dream weekend

a) Think about a dream weekend. What can you do? Brainstorm your ideas.

> **STUDY SKILLS Brainstorming**
>
> 1 Write down all your ideas as they come into your head. Don't worry if they are good or bad.
> 2 Look at your ideas. Choose the best ones.

▶ SF Brainstorming (p. 145)

b) Choose the best ideas from a) and plan your weekend.

	Saturday	**Sunday**
morning	stay in bed late	meet Tim
afternoon	play football in park	visit Grandma

c) 👥 Compare your diary plans. Who has the most exciting dream weekend?
A: What are you doing on Saturday morning?
B: I'm visiting my cousin. What about you?
A: …

d) Write about your plans for your dream weekend for your DOSSIER.

5 Extra Dragon boats 🎧

a) Listen. What does Sam want from Robert?

b) Read the questions below. Then listen again and answer them.
1 What is a dragon boat?
2 How many people are there in a dragon boat crew?
3 How many people race dragon boats in Toronto?
4 What does Robert's mum think about his hobby?
5 What does Robert decide?

▶ SF Listening (p. 139)

▶ GF 7: Present progressive with future meaning (p. 155) • P 6–7 (p. 77–78) • WB 5–8 (pp. 50–52)

6 A school discussion – Part 1

In 1999 the Canadian province of Ontario stopped the traditional spring bear hunt. People wanted to protect the bears. Now a lot of people want to bring back the spring bear hunt.

Some students at Robert's school are having a discussion in one of their lessons.

Sam   I think we need the bear hunt. There are too many bears and not enough land.

Jessica   That's a good point. And of course we have to protect ourselves.

Emily   Sorry, I don't agree. You can protect yourself from a bear without the hunt!

Robert   That's true. And another point – the bears were here first, not us.

Jessica   Maybe, but there have been lots of bear attacks in the last few years. The bears aren't afraid of us any more.

Sam   Exactly. And did you know – there's this town in the north where people can't go out because there are bears in the streets.

Robert   Sure, but that's not a very good argument. They can only blame themselves! They built their dump too close to the town and in an area where there are lots of bears.

▶ Who's for the bear hunt? Who's against it? Sam is … because he says …

7 A school discussion – Part 2

a) Look at the discussion in **6**. Copy the chart below and write down the phrases the students use to make a point, to agree and to disagree.

make a new point	agree	disagree
I think	That's a good point.	…

b) Continue the dialogue with these arguments. Use phrases from a) to link the arguments.

1 … I don't want to find myself on a bear's menu just because it's hungry.

2 … A bear just wants to feed itself and its babies.

3 … And hunters often kill mother bears and then their young die.

4 … It's better to kill the bears before they kill us!

c) Read your dialogue to the class.

d) **Extra** Which arguments from **6** and **7** do you agree with? Why?

Looking at language

Write words with **-self/-selves** from **6** and **7** in a copy of this chart.

	-self		-selves
I	myself	we	…
you	…	you	yourselves
he she it	himself herself …	they	…

▶ GF 8: Reflexive pronouns (p. 155) • P 8–9 (p. 79) • WB 9–11 (pp. 53–54) ▶ Text File 9 (p. 127)

8 Robert 'DJ Bobby' Smith 🎧

'How do you feel?' the leader of the youth group asked Robert. The hall at the community centre was full for the junior disco.

'A little nervous,' Robert answered.

'It's time,' said the youth leader and went to the microphone.

'Welcome to our holiday weekend disco. We've got three young DJs tonight. All three have taught themselves to DJ. And maybe they'll learn a thing or two from each other tonight.

'Our first DJ is somebody you all know – it's Robert 'DJ Bobby' Smith.'

Robert jumped onto the little stage. 'Hi, everybody. I'd like to start with a mix of all your favourite Canadian pop stars. First, Avril Lavigne with one of her first big hits, …'

▶ GF 9: each other (p. 156) • P 10 (p. 79) • WB 12 (p. 54)

9 SONG Sk8er boi 🎧

Sk8er boi *by Avril Lavigne*

He was a boy, she was a girl
Can I make it any more obvious?
He was a punk, she did ballet
What more can I say?
He wanted her, she'd never tell
secretly she wanted him as well.
But all of her friends stuck up their nose
they had a problem with his baggy clothes.

(Chorus)
*He was a sk8er boi, she said see ya later boy
he wasn't good enough for her,
she had a pretty face but her head was up in space,
she needed to come back down to earth.*

a) What does **sk8er boi** mean? What does the girl in the song think about **sk8er boi**?

b) Listen to the song. What happens five years later? What do you think about the girl and about **sk8er boi**?

10 Extra Now you – talking about songs

a) Prepare a DJ's introduction to your favourite song. First brainstorm your ideas.
– What kind of music is it?
– What do you know about the singer/band?
– What's the song about? Why do you like it?

> This song is rap/hip-hop/pop/… •
> The band/singer is from Canada/… •
> It's a really cool/fantastic/… song. •
> I always think of … when I hear this song. •
> easy to listen to • great lyrics • It's about …

b) Bring your song to class and introduce it. The phrases in the box can help you.

▶ P 11–12 (p. 80) • WB 13–16 (p. 55–56)

4 A-Section

Extra Background File CANADA 🎧

	Canada	Germany
Population	32,834,000	82,310,000
Official language	English and French	German
Head of state	British King or Queen	President

P.E.I. = Prince Edward Island
NB = New Brunswick
1 = Charlottetown
2 = Fredericton

Aboriginals of Canada

Aboriginals like the Inuit and the First Nations (Indians) have lived in Canada for thousands of years. Today only about 4.4 % of the Canadian population are Aboriginals.

The Aboriginals have tried to get their traditional lands back. In 1999 the Inuit got a large part of Northern Canada back. They call it Nunavut – 'Our land' in their language. Today 30,000 people live in Nunavut.

Many First Nations live on reserves all across Canada.

loon

Inuit blanket

walrus

Kahasi and the loon – an Inuit legend 🎧

a) *Before you listen, read the questions.*
1 Where and when did Kahasi live?
2 What did he do every day?
3 Why were the people in the village hungry?
4 What did the other boys do every day?
5 What did the loon say to Kahasi?
6 How did Kahasi find the walruses?
7 What happened then?

Now listen and take notes.

b) 👥 *Check your answers with a partner.*

Canadian settlers

Around the year 1000 the Vikings arrived. They were the first people from Europe in Canada.

In 1497 John Cabot left Bristol, crossed the Atlantic and landed in Newfoundland, now part of North East Canada.

In the 16th century the first French settlers in Canada lived near a mountain that they called *Mont Réal*. Canada became a French colony, New France. But in 1763 France lost Canada to the British.

Today people in the province of Quebec still speak French and *Mont Réal* has become Montréal, Canada's second biggest city.

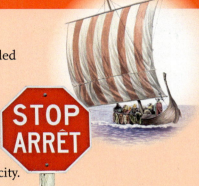

Immigration to Canada

Today Canada is an independent country. About 50% of Canadians still have French or British roots. But 50% have roots in other countries. So now Canada is a really multicultural place.

Canadian sports

Canadian First Nations played the game of **lacrosse** first, hundreds of years ago. Today it's Canada's national summer sport.

The players have to get a small ball into a goal with the crosse – a stick with a net.

Ice hockey is Canada's national winter sport – the Canadians just call it 'hockey'. Toronto's team – the Maple Leafs – is one of the best teams in the country.

1 Interesting facts about Canada

a) What do you find most interesting on these two pages? Why?

It was interesting to read that …
I thought Canada was …
I didn't know Canada was …

b) ● Choose one interesting fact about Germany and write a short text about it. Add pictures. You can put it in your DOSSIER.

▶ WB 17 (p. 57)

4 Practice

1 WORDS Numbers

a) Partner B: Go to p. 105.
Partner A: Read out these numbers to your partner:

17 • 5 • 76 • 104 • 1,516 • 15,243 • 100,000

Then write down the numbers that your partner reads out to you. Swap papers and check.

b) Fill in the gaps in the sentences on the right with words and phrases from the box.

> degrees • million • ⁺per cent (%) •
> ⁺ten-kilometre walk • ⁺sixteen-year-olds •
> ⁺150-kilogram bear • six point seven (6.7) •
> ⁺80 km per hour (kph)

1 More than 30 … people live in Canada.
2 You can't go more than … on most Canadian roads.
3 He was tired when he got home from his …
4 I hope I don't meet a … in the forest!
5 In the summer it can be 40 … in Toronto.
6 … can drive in some places in Canada.
7 French is the first language for … million Canadians. That's about 20 … of all Canadians.

2 REVISION Canada (Relative clauses)

Match the sentence halves and make sentences with **who** or **that**.

1 Canada is a country
2 Snowshoeing is something
3 Avril Lavigne is a singer
4 French is the language
5 French-Canadians are people
6 A snowmobile is something
7 The black bear is one of the many animals

lots of Canadians do in winter.
was born in Canada.
almost 7 million Canadians speak.
live in Canada and speak French.
you can find in the Canadian forests.
lots of Canadians drive in winter.
is near the USA.

Avril Lavigne

snowmobile

3 WORDS Adults and teenagers

a) Find the opposites in the green box.

> cool • easy-going • fair • nervous •
> old-fashioned • ⁺relaxed • strict • trendy •
> uncool • unfair

b) What kind of things do adults say? What do teenagers say? Make two lists.

> It's not fair. • It's too loud. • You never tidy your room. • They don't understand. • They're too strict. • It's not my fault. • They're so annoying. • You're not allowed to have a sleepover. • I'm not allowed to get a piercing. • You have to do more homework. • My parents are OK. • You're grounded.

c) Extra Do you fight with your parents? Write a short text.
I sometimes/never fight with my mum/dad.
He/She always says …
I have to/I'm not allowed to/I'm allowed to …
I think he/she is …
You can put your text in your DOSSIER.

Practice **4**   77

4 Robert wasn't able to … (*be able to* and *be allowed to*)

a) Make sentences about Robert. Use the information in the charts.

be able to	5 years ago	in 5 years
– speak French	–	+
– ride a bike	+	+
– climb through small windows	+	–

be allowed to	5 years ago	in 5 years
– stay out late	–	+
– go to nightclubs	–	+
– go on holiday alone	–	+

Five years ago Robert wasn't able to speak French.
In five years he'll be able to speak French.

Five years ago Robert wasn't allowed to …
In five years …

b) Make sentences about yourself like the sentences in a). Compare them with a partner's.

5 Crazy School 2050 (Modal substitutes) ▶ D p. 112

Look at the picture of Crazy School. Are the sentences true or false? Correct the false sentences.

1 At Crazy School the teachers will have to wear uniforms.
2 The students won't have to wear uniforms.
3 They won't be able to use computers.
4 They'll be allowed to sleep at school.
5 Students won't be allowed to skateboard in school.
6 They won't be allowed to eat in the classrooms.
7 They'll have to turn off their mobile phones in the classroom.
8 Nobody will be able to speak English.

6 Plans for the week (Present progressive with future meaning)

Partner B: Go to p. 105.
a) *Partner A:* Ask your partner about his/her plans. Find out when you're doing the same things.
A: On Monday evening I'm going to basketball training. What about you?
B: I'm going to … On Tuesday evening I'm … What about you?
A: …

	afternoon ☀	evening ☾
MON		go to basketball training
TUE		make cakes for the party
WED	play a basketball match	
THU		help Dad in garden
FRI		visit Grandpa with Mum
SAT	have a picnic	meet mates at youth club

b) Report to the class.
   We're doing the same thing on … and …

c) **Extra** Write about your plans for next week.

4 Practice

7 WRITING Telling a story (The steps of writing)

a) Read the beginning of this story.

It was a warm and sunny Sunday morning. Jessica and Emily were walking through High Park in the centre of Toronto. Suddenly they heard a voice behind them. The two girls saw a boy, about 14 years old. He looked a bit sad.
 'Excuse me,' he said, 'where is this place?'
 'High Park,' Jessica answered.
 They could see that the boy didn't know where High Park was.
 'Are you OK?' asked Emily.
 'Not really,' said the boy. 'Can you help me?'

b) Write the rest of the story. Do this in three steps:

Step 1

Brainstorm ideas
You can …
- write a list
- make a mind map

Thought bubbles: from another country? • from another planet? • ? • from the past? • from the future?

Who is the boy?   from another country
Why is he in Toronto? on holiday
Where are his parents? in their hotel
What is his problem?   can't find hotel
How do Em + Jess help?   …

▶ SF Brainstorming (p. 145)

Step 2

Write | more help | ▶ D p. 112
- Use **adverbs** and **adjectives** to make sentences interesting.
- Use **relative clauses** to make better sentences.
- Use **time phrases** and **linking words** to make things clearer.
 Don't forget:
- Start a new paragraph for each new idea.
- Find a good way to finish your story.
- Give the story a title.

▶ He looked at them *shyly* with his *big, brown* eyes

▶ He gave them the note *that was in his pocket*.
We'll find somebody *who can help you*.

▶ *a bit later* • *after that* • *early in the morning* • *because* • *so* • *although*

▶ Writing course 1: Writing better sentences (p. 22) • Writing course 2: Using paragraphs (p. 40)

Step 3

Check and revise | more help | ▶ D p. 112
- Is your story clear?
- Do you need more details?
- Check the spelling, verb forms, word order …
 Correct your text.

When they at the hotel arrived, | word order |
the boy's parents are outside. | verb form |
They were very hapy to | spelling |
see there son … | spelling |

▶ SF Correcting mistakes (p. 147)

Practice **4** 79

8 Mum and Dad are on strike (Reflexive pronouns) ▶ D p. 113

Complete the sentences with the reflexive pronouns myself, yourself, herself, ourselves, yourselves, themselves.

1 Mr and Mrs Jones are on strike, so <u>the children</u> have to cook for <u>themselves</u>.
2 Mr Jones usually looks after Jill in the afternoon, but today <u>she</u> has to look after …
3 Mrs Jones usually teaches Jack the guitar, but he knows, 'Today <u>I</u>'ll have to teach …'
4 Mr and Mrs Jones usually shop for the children, but today Jack told Jill, 'Mum and Dad are on strike, so <u>we</u> have to shop for …'
5 'Why are you on strike?' the children asked. Their parents said, '<u>You</u> two will have to ask …!'
6 Jill's mum usually puts her to bed, but today she told her, 'Sorry, Jill, but <u>you</u>'ll have to put … to bed tonight.'

9 Lucky Larry's not-so-lucky day (Reflexive pronouns)

Decide if you need a reflexive pronoun or not. You can look at the blue box on p. 177 for help.

Today has been an awful day. My friend and I wanted to meet … after breakfast. But when I went into the bathroom to clean … my teeth, there was no water. 'That's OK,' I said to …, 'I can get water in the kitchen.' But then I remembered … that there was a sign in the street about a water problem. So I got … dressed and went to buy some water. I felt … dirty so I walked quickly back home. But when I put the key in the door, it didn't open … ! 'What can I do?' I asked … Then I remembered … that my bedroom window doesn't close. I was able to pull … up to it, but it was so small that I wasn't able to get in! I was just moving … back when a policeman came. Now I'm here at the police station. And the policeman said, 'Oh well, you can only blame … for that!'

10 Are they looking at themselves or each other? (each other/themselves)

Write sentences about the pictures. Use each other or themselves.

1 *A boy and a girl are looking at themselves.*   2 *Robert and …*

1 look at
2 take photos of
3 think of
4 teach
5 think of
6 look at
7 teach
8 take photos of

11 SPEAKING A classroom discussion

a) Listen to three songs by Canadian musicians. What do you think of each one? Who would like it?

| brilliant • nice • cool • great • fun • easy to listen to • interesting • great lyrics … | boring • old-fashioned • nothing special • strange • not bad • terrible lyrics … |

b) Think of different ways to complete the dialogue. Then listen to the dialogues. Write down the phrases the people use.

A: _____ the first song was boring. My parents like that kind of music.
B: Exactly! I think it's music for older people.
C: _____ it was easy to listen to. I think it was OK.

B: What about the second song? I think that was nice.
C: _____ In my opinion it was nothing special. It's like lots of other songs.
A: _____ I think it was boring.

C: What about the third song? I think that was brilliant. And the lyrics were nice too.
A: _____ People in our class like that kind of music.
B: _____ I thought it was really boring.

c) Work in a group of three. Discuss the songs in the same way. Take turns to start.

d) Report to the class. Which song did your group like best? Did you all like different songs?

12 MEDIATION At the cabin

a) Do you remember how you can paraphrase a word? Use phrases like the ones in the box on the right. Now write explanations for these words:

Hütte • Campingplatz • Lachs • Jäger

It's – an animal/something that …
– a place where …
– a person/somebody who …

STUDY SKILLS Mediation

If you don't know an important English word, try to paraphrase it.

b) Lisa and her mother want to spend a week in a cabin. How can Lisa explain 'Gasflasche' in the situation below?

Frau Kraft   Ich glaube, man braucht hier Gasflaschen zum Kochen. Frag mal, wo wir hier welche kriegen können.
Lisa   Ich probier's. – Excuse me, we're looking for … Sorry, I don't know the word in English … it's …

c) Listen and go on with the rest of the dialogue.

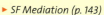

▶ SF Mediation (p. 143)

Two bear attacks

1 Dog helps to kill bear
JULY 22, 2006

A man killed a black bear with a 15-cm hunting knife yesterday. The man said the bear saw him as 'lunch' and attacked him and his dog while he was canoeing in north Ontario.

Tom Tilley, a 55-year-old from Waterloo, Ontario, said his dog Sam warned him, then ran to protect him when the bear came towards them in the woods north of Wawa.

As Sam fought the 90-kg bear, Tilley jumped on it and killed it with his knife.

Doctors say Tilley and his dog will be fine.

2 Woman victim of latest bear attack
SEPTEMBER 12, 2007

A bear killed an Ontario woman and hurt her husband badly at Missinaibi Lake on Saturday. Different groups are again asking parliament to bring back the spring bear hunt. Without the hunt, they say, bears are not afraid of people and see us as 'food'.

The attack happened late on Saturday afternoon.

The victims were camping at the lake, about 80 km north of Chapleau, Ontario. Police gave their names as Sarah Bennett, 31, and Marc Bennett, 30. Mrs Bennett was a doctor.

"The man attacked the bear with a knife, but he couldn't save his wife," policewoman Karen Farand said.

"The bear escaped into the forest."

Working with the text

1 Right or wrong?

Look at the two articles. Correct the wrong statements.
1 Both attacks happened in Toronto.
2 A doctor and his wife died in a bear attack.
3 Tom Tilley and his dog saved each other.
4 Some people think the bears aren't afraid of people any more.
5 The bears died in both attacks.

2 The 5 Ws

Make a chart with the 5 Ws (who, what, when, where, why) for each of the articles.

3 Extra   An interview

Imagine one of you is a reporter, the other is Tom Tilley. The reporter interviews Tom about his canoe trip and the attack.

Reporter	Mr Tilley, where were you yesterday?
Tom Tilley	Well, I was canoeing in north Ontario?
Reporter	Were you alone?
Tom Tilley	No, …

▶ **Text File 10** (pp. 128–129) • **WB 18** (p. 58) • **Checkpoint 4** WB (p. 59) • **Selbsteinschätzung 3–4** WB (pp. 62–63)

4 Text

Extra A fishing trip 🎧

> Look at the pictures. Who are the people in them?
Try and guess the right order of the pictures. Then listen and check.

Working with the text

1 Right or wrong?

Listen again and correct the wrong statements.
1. The Smiths went on a hunting trip.
2. They didn't get any fish.
3. They paddled safely through the rapids.
4. Robert lost his canoe.
5. They had to get past the bear.
6. Robert threw the fish to the bear.
7. They escaped, but the bear followed them.
8. The bear ran away when it saw Robert's knife.

2 A report [more help] ▶ D p. 113

Pick out six or seven key facts about Robert and his dad's fishing trip. Continue this newspaper report. Write about 80–100 words.

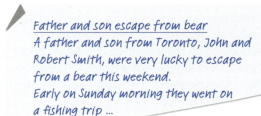

Father and son escape from bear
A father and son from Toronto, John and Robert Smith, were very lucky to escape from a bear this weekend.
Early on Sunday morning they went on a fishing trip …

How am I doing?

a) *Find or choose the correct answers.*

Canada

1 The capital of Canada is ..., and ... is the biggest city.
2 Many Canadians enjoy sports like ..., ... or ...
3 Avril Lavigne is a famous Canadian ...
4 Toronto is in the Canadian ... of Ontario.

Words

5 About 6 million Canadians speak French – that's over 20 ...
   A degrees. B point. C per cent.
   D pounds.
6 I can stay out late. My parents are very ...
   A strict. B easy-going. C nervous.
   D uncool.
7 Why are you so excited? Try to be more ...
   A fair. B relaxed. C nervous.
   D trendy.
8 That's a good ..., but can we talk about it later?
   A bridge B news C point
   D homework
9 My sister made a mistake, but I don't ... her for it.
   A be angry with B should C grumble
   D blame
10 Do you know how you can protect yourself ... bears?
   A from B about C for D over
11 I love that song. The music is good, but what I really like are the ...
   A units. B lyrics. C books.
   D pages.

Writing

12 You can write a story in three steps: ... ideas, ... the text and finally check and ... it.
13 You can write down your ideas from brainstorming in a ... or in a ...
14 Your sentences often sound more interesting if you use ... and ...

Grammar

15 I ... go to the disco because my parents think I'm too young.
   A have to B don't have to
   C am allowed to D am not allowed to
16 I can't swim, but I'm sure I'll ... swim after a few lessons.
   A can B be allowed to C be able to
   D can't
17 If you want to travel, you'll ... work hard and make lots of money.
   A must B have to C had to
   D needn't
18 What are Robert's plans for Friday evening? – He ... a gig at the youth centre.
   A did B can do C is doing D does
19 I thought John was talking to ... but he was actually speaking on his mobile.
20 A better way to say 'Robert took a photo of Sam and Sam took a photo of Robert' is 'Sam and Robert took photos of ...'

b) *Check your answers on p. 232 and add up your points – one point for each correct answer.*

c) *If you had 16 or more points, well done! Maybe you can help students who had fewer points. If you had 15 points or fewer, it's a good idea to do some more work before you go on to the next unit. Where did you make mistakes? The chart below will tell you what you can do to improve your English.*

No.	Areas	Find out more	Exercises
1– 4	Canada facts	Unit 4 (pp. 68–75)	P 2 (p. 76), WB 1, 14, 17 (pp. 48–57)
5–11	Words	Vocabulary Unit 4 (pp. 175–176)	WB 2, 7, 9, 16 (pp. 49, 51, 53)
12–14	Writing	P 7 (p. 78)	WB 8 (p. 52)
15–17	Modal substitutes	GF 6 (p. 154)	P 4–5 (p. 77), WB 3–4 (p. 50)
18	Present progressive with future meaning	GF 7 (p. 155)	P 6 (p. 77), WB 6 (p. 51)
19–20	Reflexive pronouns and verbs	Unit 4 (p. 72), GF 8 (p. 155)	P 8–10 (p. 79), WB 10–12 (pp. 53–54)

84 ✓ Getting ready for a test 2 **Revision** `Extra`

1 👥 STUDY SKILLS Understanding new words ▶ SF Understanding new words (p. 134)

If you read or hear a new word in a test, you can often guess the meaning.

Guess what the green words mean in German.

1 North Rhine-Westphalia and Saxony are two of Germany's 16 states.
2 Beer is a traditional German product. Almost every part of Germany produces beer.
3 It's important to pack glasses and other breakable goods carefully.
4 Greenpeace is an organization that tries to save whales and other animals.
5 Recycling is easy: just take your old glass to the bottle bank.
6 It was a terrible storm. Almost everybody on the ship was seasick.
7 In this factory robots do all the work.

2 SPELLING Same sound, different words

Different words sometimes sound the same. Be careful when you write them.

Fill in the missing words

1 **hour – our** ['auə]
The train was late. I waited for over an ...
Is that ... train on platform 3?
2 **son – sun** [sʌn]
The Browns have a ... and a daughter.
They both wear hats when the ... shines.
3 **their – there** [ðeə]
Who's ... ? – Oh, it's Malte and Hauke.
They've got ... new bikes with them.
4 **know – no** [nəʊ]
Do you ... our new teacher, Mrs Sprengel?
... , I haven't met her yet.
5 **hear – here** [hɪə]
There are lots of birds ... in the forest.
Can you ... the woodpecker?
6 **sea – see** [siː]
We stayed in a caravan near the ...
You could ... the beach from there.
7 **wear – where** [weə]
... is my new dress?
I'd like to ... it to Matt's party.
8 **weak – week** [wiːk]
Last ... the doctor told my grandma she had a ... heart.

3 WRITING The 5 Ws and how ▶ Writing course 3: A report (p. 64)

In a test you could have to write a report. Remember to answer these questions: what, when, where, who and why. Often it's also important to say how something happened.

a) *Write the text on the right with the phrases in the box.*

> the whole family • we went by bus •
> on a Sunday • our visit to the zoo •
> it was my little sister's birthday •
> only three miles from our house

b) *Which question does each phrase answer?*

1) our visit to the zoo = what
2) ...

A great day in the school holidays

The best thing about my school holidays was ... (1). We don't often go there, because it's so expensive. But ...(2), so Dad asked her where she wanted to go, and she chose the zoo. Dad said that ... (3) could go.

I couldn't wait, but at last the day came. We went ... (4) because Dad didn't have to go to work. I wanted to cycle because the zoo is ... (5), but Mum said it was too far, so ... (6).

It was great to see all the animals. We stayed all day and we enjoyed every minute.

Extra **Revision** Getting ready for a test 2 ✔ **85**

4 Ashley's visit to Niagara Falls (Word order)

Remember that English word order is often different from German word order.

Choose the right place in the sentences for the words in brackets.
1 Ashley and her dad went **?** to Niagara Falls **?** . (last June)
 Ashley and her dad went to Niagara Falls last June.
2 Their bus left Toronto at six am, so they had to **?** get up **?** (very early)
3 And they almost didn't get the bus because Ashley **?** her rucksack **?** . (forgot)
4 She hurried back to the house **?** the rucksack **?** . (to get)
5 When they got to Niagara, **?** they **?** the amazing waterfalls. (watched)
6 They had **?** lunch at one of the many restaurants **?** . (at 12.45)
7 Ashley's dad went **?** after lunch **?** . (to Victoria Park)
8 Everything was so interesting that Ashley wanted to stay **?** there **?** . (all weekend)

5 I've always dreamed of ... (Prepositions)

Complete the sentences with the correct prepositions.

1 I have always dreamed ... a trip to Toronto. (from/of) *of*
2 We listened to the weather report ... the radio. (in/on)
3 There wasn't a cloud ... the sky. (in/on)
4 We left early ... the morning and arrived late ... night. (in/on, at/in)
5 There were lots of cars ... the city centre. (in/on)

6 Our friends had warned us ... the traffic. (about/for)
7 It was quicker to walk than to go ... car. (by/with)
8 I was really interested ... the railway museum. (in/on)
9 All the information was ... English. (in/of)
10 I had to translate it ... German. (in/into)

6 If we go to Toronto ... (Conditional sentences types 1 and 2)

a) You're on holiday in Canada. You're planning a day trip to Toronto with a friend. Complete the conditional sentences (type 1).
1 If we go to Toronto, we ... (need) lots of information.
 ... we'll need ...
2 If we leave early, we ... (have) more time in Toronto.
3 We won't be able to explore the city if we ... (have) a good map.
4 If we take sandwiches with us, we ... (can eat) them in a park.
5 If it rains while we're there, we ... (have to do) something inside.
6 If we check on the internet, we ... (know) when the museums open.

b) Your mother thinks it would be better if you went to Ottawa. You don't agree. Complete the conditional sentences (type 2).
1 You: If we went to Ottawa, the journey ... (take) much longer.
 ... would take ...
2 Mother: If you left early enough, you ... (have) lots of time.
3 Mother: And if you ... (stay) at a youth hostel, you could have a second day in Ottawa.
4 You: If we spent the night in Ottawa, the trip ... (be) too expensive.
5 Mother: If you ... (go) to Ottawa, you'd see the parliament building.
6 You: I wouldn't be upset if we ... (see) the Canadian parliament.

▶ WB (pp. 60–61)

Getting ready for a test 2 Practice test Extra

1 Listening

A visit to Green Gables

Michael is a student in Canada and he's working as a tour guide[1] on Prince Edward Island this summer. He's taking a tour group to the farmhouse Green Gables today.

Part 1:
The journey to Green Gables

Listen. Choose the correct answer for each question.

1 Lucy Maud Montgomery …
  A is a singer at a festival.
  B wrote books for children.
  C helped a young girl without parents.

2 Anne of Green Gables …
  A is a girl in a famous children's book.
  B is a Canadian writer.
  C comes from Ottawa.

3 Linda …
  A is a girl who has lost her parents.
  B works as a bus tour guide.
  C knows a lot about Anne of Green Gables.

4 Green Gables is …
  A the house where Linda lives.
  B a place for children without parents.
  C a famous farmhouse.

Part 2:
Lucy Maud Montgomery

a) Read all the questions. Then listen and take notes about the dates and numbers you hear. Choose the correct answer for each question.

1 Lucy Maud Montgomery was born in …
  A 1847.
  B 1874.
  C 1908.

2 You can read Montgomery's books in …
  A more than 50 languages.
  B more than 3 languages.
  C more than 12 languages.

3 Every year Green Gables has …
  A 200,000 visitors.
  B 2,200 visitors.
  C 6,000 visitors.

b) Are these statements right or wrong? Give a reason for your answer.
1 'Montgomery left Prince Edward Island because she hated it.'
2 'Montgomery's books tell people a lot about Canada.'

I think statement 1 is right/ wrong because …

---
[1] tour guide [gaɪd] *Reiseleiter/in*

Extra **Practice test** Getting ready for a test 2 87

2 Reading

Partner B: Go to p. 105. Partner A: Read about St. Jacobs, a village near Toronto, Canada, where Mennonites[1] live. Then answer the questions on the right.

The Mennonite Story
Mennonites are a religious group that came from Europe to America to be free. Since 1800 they have lived on farms around St. Jacobs. What do they believe? Why do many of them use horses, not cars? At the Visitor Centre you can learn about Mennonite history and culture. See the 13-minute DVD presentation, lots of photos and other documents. $3 per person

Visit St. Jacobs
Explore St. Jacobs on foot with our new walking-tour brochure. On sale at the Visitor Centre: $2

The Model Railway
See Waterloo County in miniature. Watch the old trains as they go past farms, a Mennonite Meeting House and the village of St. Jacobs.

1 You can buy a $2 brochure about …
  A how to see St. Jacobs on foot.
  B Mennonite history.
  C railway history in Ontario.

2 Mennonites came to America because …
  A there weren't enough horses in Europe.
  B they wanted to live in the St. Jacobs area.
  C they weren't free in Europe.

3 At the Visitor Centre you can …
  A watch a DVD.
  B go to a market.
  C see model trains.

3 Speaking

Partner A and Partner B: You're planning a day trip to St. Jacobs. Read the instructions below. You can make notes to help you with your dialogue. Then act out the dialogue.

Partner A	Partner B
Say you'd like to go to the Mennonite Story.	Ask what that is.
Answer. Say when and why Mennonites came to America.	Tell your partner about the Mennonites and the Farmers' Market.
Say why you'd like to visit the market.	Describe the Mennonite Farm Tour.
Say you'd like to stay in the village. Tell your partner about the walking-tour brochure.	Ask what your partner wants to see in the village.
Tell your partner about the model railway.	Say it's enough to do two or three things.
Agree. Say what you want to do and why.	Agree or disagree with your partner's ideas.

4 Writing

Yesterday you visited St. Jacobs. Write a report about your visit (80–90) words. Remember the 5 Ws.

[1] Mennonites [ˈmenənaɪts] *Mennoniten*

Unit 5

A teen magazine

⊙ Harbourfront centre

Harbourfront Community Centre · Toronto · Youth Group

The Harbourfront Community Centre Youth Group announces its latest project:

A TEEN MAGAZINE !

What will be in it?

THAT'S UP TO YOU!

So far our magazine has the following sections and editors:

Editor:
Samantha Kowalski

Editor:
Robert Smith

Editor:
Mitsu Nagora

Editor:
Nathalie L'Estane

> Look at the poster. Describe the youth group's latest project.
What's the difference between a magazine and an e-zine?

1 Now you

What teen magazines and e-zines do you know? What are they about? How often do you read them? Which sections (fashion, music, problem pages, ...) do you like best?

WE WANT YOU

Who will produce this magazine?
YOU WILL!

Everybody who's interested can send an article. If it's good, we'll publish it! Send your articles (with photos or drawings) to the editors.

What's next?

If the magazine is a success, we'd like to do an *e-zine* and put it on the centre's website. The e-zine can have more photos – and of course sound files and videos too.

2 The photos

a) Describe the photos. The words below will help you.

> headphones • microphone • monitor • webcam

– In the photo at the top of p. 88, Robert is …

b) **Extra** What do you remember about the people in the photos? Collect ideas in the chart.

name	lives in	hobbies

▶ SF Describing pictures (p. 138)

3 A video chat

a) Read the questions, then listen to the CD.
1 Who asked for the video chat? Why?
2 Who comes later than the others? Why?
3 What kinds of articles does Robert want?
4 Who worries about the time? How much time do they have?

b) Listen again. What ideas for articles do the four have? Take notes.
Katrina: favourite …

c) What do you think is the most interesting idea?

▶ P 1–2 (p. 95) • WB 1–2 (p. 64)

1 The music section

a) What have Robert and his friends written about? Skim the articles A–D on pp. 90–92 and find out.

Robert	– an instrument
Asif	– Manchester music scene
Latisha	– DJing
Katrina	– summer songs
	– life without music
	– a biography

b) Extra Does anything surprise you? What and why?

▶ SF Skimming (p. 141) • P 3 (p. 96) • WB 3–4 (p. 65)

> **STUDY SKILLS Skimming**
>
> Skimming is useful when you want to find the main ideas of a long text quickly.
> – Don't read the text word for word.
> – Look first at the title, the words in bold print, pictures and their captions.

music

Editor: Robert Smith

A Music in my life
by Latisha Byrd

What would a day without music be like? I think it would be very strange.

When I wake up in the morning the first thing I do is turn on my MP3 player. Then I take it with me to the bathroom. And I bring it back with me so that I can listen to music while I get dressed.

When I go down to breakfast Mum has got the radio on – her kind of music, not mine, but that's OK. It's music!

After breakfast I clean my teeth, get my school bag and put on my headphones. Then it's my music all the way to school.

If there was a day without music I would have to wash and get dressed in silence. Breakfast would be very quiet. And the journey to school would be quiet – and really boring.

It would be boring at lunchtime in school without the school radio. After school no steel drums – impossible! In the evening how would I relax without music?
I think a day without music would be terrible!

Music when I wake up!

Music everywhere!

Music is the best!

▶ When does Latisha listen to music? Collect words and phrases she uses to describe her daily routine.
when I wake up, the first thing, in the morning, ...

2 Now you
What's your day like? When do you listen to music? Write a short text about music in your life for your DOSSIER.

B A riddle
by Katrina McFadden

I'm a musical instrument. I was born far, far away in Iran, over two thousand years ago.

From there I travelled all over Europe. You probably know me best as an instrument from one part of Great Britain.

I look very interesting: my body is leather and lots of pipes stick out of me! You blow into one. The other ones let the air out.

How do you play me? Well, you have to be very clever to play me. First you have to blow air into me. I keep it in my body. Then you have to squeeze it out again – very carefully – through the pipes. That's what makes the music.
Can you guess what I am?

C Mika – the story of a singer
by Asif Azad

Mika was born in Beirut, the capital of Lebanon, in 1983.

His dad is American, his mum Lebanese. When he was one, the family moved to Paris. Then, when he was ten, the family moved again – this time to London.

At first Mika was very unhappy. The only thing he really enjoyed was music. And he was very good at it. His mum sent him to a Russian music teacher, who taught him to sing. When he was 12 he sang in an opera at Covent Garden in London.

After that Mika started to write pop songs. When he was twenty-three he released his first single – 'Relax, take it easy' – and it was sold out in two days. Next came his first album, and a track from that – 'Grace Kelly' – went to number one in the UK in one week!
A real success story!

▶ What's the answer to Katrina's riddle?

A recorder B bagpipes C trumpet D flute

Extra Think of a good topic for a riddle or a quiz. It could be an instrument. But it could also be a famous person, somebody you know, a sport, sports equipment, a hobby, a place, …
▶ P 4 (p. 97)

▶ In which country was Mika born? Where does he live now? Make a profile for Mika.

PROFILE
Name: ____
Born: ____
Family: ____
1st single: ____
1st no 1 single: ____

▶ P 5–6 (p. 97–98) • WB 5 (p. 66)

3 **Extra** SONG Relax, take it easy
Listen to the song. Is the singer happy or sad? Why do you think so?

School's out for the summer – my top five countdown

by Robert 'DJ Bobby' Smith

5 'School's out'
by Alice Cooper

School is finishing for the summer soon so this had to be on my list. You always hear it on the radio just before summer vacation – and I think it's great. (Of course if we get an e-zine off the ground, this is where the sound link would be!)

4 'This love'
by Maroon 5

Do you have a crush on somebody? Then this is the song for you. And summer is the time!

3 'The Sound of San Francisco'
by Global Deejays

Summer is the time to travel. This great mix takes you to London, Paris, … and San Francisco. And if you can't go that far, at least you can get up and dance!

2 'Summer in the city'
by The Lovin' Spoonful

Everybody thinks you have to be by a lake or by the sea in the summer, but I don't agree. This is a great song for all of you who are staying in the city this summer.

1 'Come on over'
by Shania Twain

Vacation is a time to hang out with friends – it's what I like best. That's what this song is about. And Shania Twain is a great Canadian singer.

▶ P 7 (p. 99) • WB 6–8 (pp. 67–68) • Text File 11 (pp. 130–133)

4 Now you
Which of the four articles do you like best/like least? Why? Make notes, then talk to your group.

▶ P 8 (p. 99) • Checkpoint 5 WB (p. 69)

– I like …'s article best/least because it's funny/ interesting/…
– My favourite article is Asif's, because …
– Really? I don't like that one.

Extra Project: Our teen mag

In this project you will write an article for a teen magazine (or e-zine). Then put the mag together in your group. You can write about music or other topics that you are interested in (sport, fashion, your hobby, films, ...).

1 Step 1: Choose your topic

a) What would you like to write about? Brainstorm ideas. Make notes – you can use a list or a mind map.
▶ SF Brainstorming (p. 145)

b) 👥 Talk about all your ideas. Agree with your group on who will write what.

> I'd like to write about ...

> We can't have two articles about ... What's your second favourite?

- My top 5 songs / films / sports stars / computer games / ring tones / ...
- A sports / music / ... quiz
- A riddle – which football team is it?
- Something about a pop star, e.g. Madonna?
- A report about the handball final
- What are people wearing this summer
- ~~An interview with a teacher~~
- The lyrics of my favourite song

2 Step 2: Collect information

You have to collect information for your article. Where can you get the information you need?

Tip
- Use English sources if you can.
- If you find too much information, skim. That helps you to decide which texts are useful.
- Make sure the information you use is reliable.

Sources of information	Good for
library, encyclopedia	facts about people, ...
internet	lyrics, ...
magazines	interviews, ...
other people, teachers	surveys, ...

▶ SF English–German dictionary (p. 136) • SF Skimming (p. 141)

3 Step 3: Write and correct your article

a) Write your article and get it ready to show your group.

Tip
- Don't just copy articles. You must write your own text.

▶ Writing course: The steps of writing (p. 78)

b) 👥 Correct each other's work in your group.

▶ Writing course: Correcting your text (p. 98)

Tip

Try a **correcting circle**:
1. Each student in the group watches for one kind of mistake, e.g.
   – spelling
   – 'He, she, it, das "s" muss mit!'
   – ...
2. Give your article to the person on your right. Read the article that your partner has given you. Look only for one kind of mistake. If you find one, correct it. Then look at the next article.
3. When you have your own article back, rewrite it if necessary.

94 5 Extra Project

4 Step 4: Publish your mag

a) Agree how you will publish your mag.

> **Tip**
> If you're doing an e-zine, you can add sound files, videos and links to other interesting web pages.

You can …
… write the articles on paper/on the computer
… make a poster, put it on the classroom wall
… make an e-zine, put it on the school website

b) Decide who will do the different jobs.

> Finish articles – EVERYBODY!!
> Look for pictures – EVERYBODY!!!
> Layout pages on computer – Aisha and Elias
> Design front page – Laura
> Make photocopies – Oleg

c) Put your mag together and publish it. Maybe you want to show it to other classes, parents at parents' evening, …

> **Tip**
> Don't forget to keep a copy of your article for your DOSSIER!

Practice **5** 95

1 WORDS All about music ▶ D p. 113

a) *Read the definitions and find the correct music words from the green box on the right.*
1 a group of people who sing together
2 a round instrument you hit to make music
3 a part of a song that you sing more than once
4 you can download music onto this machine
5 the words of a song
6 you can listen to CDs on this machine
7 a place where people dance to music
8 something you can enjoy in a park

> CD player • choir • chorus • club • drum • lyrics • MP3 player • open-air concert

b) *Make a* MUSIC *network.*
– Use the words from the green box in a).
– If you know more music words you can add them.
– You can use the words from this box too:

> ⁺album • ⁺bagpipes • ⁺career • classical music • microphone • ⁺musician • ⁺opera • ⁺record • recording • (to) release • ⁺single • ⁺tune • ⁺track

c) *Match the phrases in the blue box to one or more nouns in the yellow box. Write six sentences.*
1 *Hassan has to rehearse for a gig next week.*

> buy tickets for • go to • listen to • play • rehearse for • release • sing • whistle

> an album • a club • a disco • a festival • a gig • a musical • a new record • an instrument • an open-air concert • an opera • a rehearsal • a show • a song • a tune • my favourite track

2 LISTENING Numbers and spelling 🎧

a) *Listen to* **part 1** *on the CD. Write down the numbers. Compare with a partner. Listen again and check.*

b) *Listen to* **part 2** *on the CD. Write down the names. Compare with your partner. Listen again and check.*

c) Extra *Choose four names from this book. Write them down. Dictate them to your partner. Check.*

My name is Annabel Tonkins. Please phone me on 01554562317. That's Annabel: A–double N– ...

3 STUDY SKILLS Skimming

a) Imagine the topic of your project is 'Robbie Williams – the career of the famous singer'. Skim the two articles below to decide which article will be more useful.

1 Robbie Williams

Robbie Williams was born on 13 February, 1974, in Newcastle-under-Lyme in North Staffordshire, UK. He began his career with the band Take That, then he left the band in 1995 for a solo career. He has sold more than 50 million albums and 15 million singles around the world.

Family
Williams grew up in Burslem, Stoke-on-Trent, Staffordshire. His parents are Catholic, but he does not see himself as a religious person. He still sees his mother quite often and she has even been on stage with him at some of his concerts.

Williams isn't married, but he has had a few girlfriends, some of them famous.

Charity work
Robbie Williams loves giving, so in June 2000 he started the charity 'Give it sum' because he wanted to give something back to his hometown. 'Give it sum' has given over two million pounds to projects there. He said, 'I'm glad that the little help that I give can do great things.'

With the help of his friend Jonathan Wilkes he also organized a charity football match to collect money for Africa.

2 Robbie Williams

The English singer Robbie Williams (born **Robert Peter Williams** on 13 February, 1974, in Newcastle-under-Lyme, UK) has sold more than 50 million albums and 15 million singles around the world. In the UK he has sold more albums than any other solo singer in history. His success has made him very rich: he has probably got more than £100 million.

Take That (1990–1995)
Williams' early pop career started with the boy band **Take That**. (Of the band's nine UK number 1 singles, seven were with Robbie Williams.) His relationship with the others in the band was difficult. They said he was not interested enough in the work of the group. Williams left Take That in 1995.

Solo success
In 1996 Williams sang his own version of the George Michael song 'Freedom' – it was more successful than Michael's original. His first solo album followed in late 1997. His name appears in the list of the Top 100 best-selling albums in UK history six times.

Although Williams has been very popular all over the world, he hasn't been as successful in **North America**. His best record in the US – 'Angels'– was only number 41 in the charts.

b) Which article would you read to find out about these things? Article 1? Article 2? Both articles?
1 ... why Robbie Williams left Take That
2 ... his family
3 ... how much money he has got
4 ... his solo career
5 ... how many records he has sold
6 ... how he helps other people

Practice **5** 97

4 Extra STUDY SKILLS Research on the internet (Using key words and phrases)

a) To find information on the internet, you will have to use a search engine. Read these tips.

Tips for internet research

- Think carefully: what are you looking for?
- Use a key word or phrase and enter it in your search engine.
- If your results are not good enough or if there are too many websites:
  – add more key words or phrases
  – use different key words.
- To look for a phrase, use quotation marks, e.g. "interview with Shakira".
- Check your spelling.

Remember: The information you find on the internet isn't always reliable!

b) Which key words would you use to answer the following questions? Write them down.
1. When and where was Elvis Presley born?
   "Elvis Presley" born
2. Who sang the 2001 hit 'Can't get you out of my head' and where is he/she from?
3. What was the name of the Beatles' first album?
4. What name did Madonna give her first child?
5. What musical instruments did the Bechstein family make?
6. What group did Phil Collins and Peter Gabriel belong to?

c) Now try your key words from b) in an online search engine. Can you find the answers?

5 Extra STUDY SKILLS Adapting a text

a) Imagine you have found this information on the singer Katie Melua. Use it to write about her life. First find the important facts and mark them up in a copy of the text.

Ketevan 'Katie' Melua is a British singer and musician.

She was born in Kutaisi, Georgia, in 1984 and spent her first years with her grandparents in the capital Tbilisi. Then she moved with her parents and brother to the town of Batumi where her father worked as a heart specialist. During this time the family was so poor that they lived in a flat without running water.

In 1993 the family moved to Belfast, Northern Ireland, where her father took up a position at the Royal Victoria Hospital. When Melua was fourteen the family relocated to Redhill in England. Because she lived in so many different places at an early age, Melua can speak three languages: Georgian, Russian and English.

In November 2003, at the age of just 19, Melua released her first album 'Call off the search'. It reached the top of the United Kingdom album charts and sold 1.2 million copies within five months. Her second album, 'Piece by piece', was released in September 2005 and has gone platinum four times.

Melua is the UK's biggest-selling female artist and Europe's biggest-selling European female artist (2006).

b) Then take notes:
Katie Melua: British singer; born Georgia 1984, ...

c) ⬤ Use your notes and write your own text.
Katie Melua is one of the most successful British singers. She was born in ... She can speak ...

▶ SF Marking up a text (p. 142)

5 Practice

6 WRITING A short biography (Correcting your text)

a) A student has written the beginning of a short biography of Shakira. Be careful: there are lots of mistakes in it! How many can you find?

Shakira

Shakira was born in 1977. She was born in Colombia in South <u>america</u>. She <u>have</u> six brothers and sisters. One <u>off</u> them is her road manager. Shakira begun to rite songs at eight. The songs were in spanish. Soon was she on television, in a show for childs. When she is thirteen she sang some songs for the managers of a big music company. They sayed she could make three albums. That was the main reason why her career realy started. Shakira released her first album 'Magia' ('Magic'). She was 15.
It wasn't a success - the shops only selled about 1,000 copies.

b) ● There are 12 mistakes in the text. Did you find them all? If not, use this checklist:
– Spelling – for example capital letters (<u>america</u>), missing letters (<u>rite</u>), plural forms (<u>childs</u>)
– Grammar – for example verb forms (<u>she have, begun</u>), tenses (<u>when she is thirteen</u>), word order (<u>Soon was she</u>)

> **Tip**
> Make a list of the kinds of mistakes you often make. Use the list as your own personal checklist.

My mistakes		
spelling	verb	word order
– bigger – making (NOT makeing)	go, past = went (NOT goed) she / he / it likes English Every day / On Mondays I play … BUT: Now I'm playing …	Yesterday I went … (NOT went I)

c) **Extra** Write the text about Shakira again. Correct the mistakes and make these changes.
– Start a paragraph for each new idea.
  (Make three paragraphs.)
– Make longer sentences
  (Make one sentence from the first two.
  Make one sentence from the last three – use the <u>linking words</u> 'when' and 'but' here.)
– Write a new, more helpful first sentence.
  (Maybe some readers don't know that Shakira is a singer.)

d) Write a short biography of a star. Write about:
– when and where your star was born
– his/her family
– his/her school days
– how his/her career began
– his/her first CD/film/big match/…
– …
Correct your biography carefully. Write it again.

7 REVISION   What are your plans? (Present progressive with future meaning)

a) Write about the people's plans for the summer.   1 Robert is staying at home. He isn't …

1 Robert – stay at home – this summer.
He – not go – England – this year.
He – work – in uncle's shop.

2 Jill – not go – on holiday.
She – move – London with family.
Jill – start – a new school – September.

3 John – visit – Germany – with family – August. They – fly – Frankfurt. Then – they – go – Berlin.

4 Lena – go – sea – with family.
They – not go – camping. They – stay – nice house – near beach.

b) What are your plans for the summer? Talk to people in your group.

— What are you doing this summer?
— I'm staying at home.
— I'm going to France/Turkey/the North of Germany/…
— I'm visiting my grandparents/aunt/…

8   SPEAKING   Working in a group

a) Asemina (A), Bea (B) and Christopher (C) are talking in English about the material they have collected for their article. Write the dialogue.

A: Zeig den anderen zwei Fotos deines Lieblingsschauspielers.
B: Sag, du findest das zweite Foto besser.
C: Schlag vor, beide Fotos zu nehmen.
A: Stimm zu und sag, ihr müsst auch über die Biografie reden.
B: Das stimmt. Sag, du hast diesen Text im Internet gefunden, aber er ist lang und schwierig.
C: Sag, du möchtest ihn sehen. Stell fest, dass er voller neuer Wörter ist.
A: Schlag vor, den Text zu überfliegen. Dann seht ihr, ob ihr ihn nehmen könnt.
B: Sag, das ist eine gute Idee und schlag vor, dass jeder einen Teil liest.
C: Stimm zu und sag, du möchtest die erste Seite lesen, und dass ihr anfangen solltet.

b) Compare your dialogue with the CD. Then practise the dialogue.

1–5 How am I doing?

How am I doing? – Units 1–5

This page will help you to check what you have learned in the whole of this book, not just in the last unit.

a) *Find or choose the correct answers.*

Facts about Britain

1 The three countries on the main island of the United Kingdom are England, ... and ...
2 The capital of the UK is ... It's on the River ...
3 The quickest way to travel in London is on the ...
4 The Orkney Islands are a group of islands in the north of ...
5 Old Trafford is the name of the football stadium in the northern English city of ...

Words

Add at least three words to each of the word fields. Name the word fields for extra points.

6 ticket, train, ferry, line, ...
7 mobile phone, download, website, ...
8 car park, theatre, traffic, ...
9 training, supporter, draw, stadium, ...
10 gig, DJ, hip-hop, ...
11 forest, river, mountain, bear, ...

Study Skills

12 If you want to find a word in a long text, you can ... the text for the word.
13 If you want to find the main ideas of a long text quickly, you can ... it.
14 If you don't know a word, you can use other words to explain it. You can ... it.
15 If you want to collect lots of ideas, you can ... – alone or in a group.

Writing

16 The main idea of a paragraph is usually in the ...
17 Your writing will be clearer if you use time phrases and ...
18 What are the 5 Ws? What can you use them for?
19 Explain one 'trick' you can use to find mistakes in something you have written.

Grammar

20 If you ... (be) in London now, what ... (want) to do?
21 My class is planning a trip to London. If we ... (go) in May, I ... (not be able to go) with them.
22 *Use a relative clause to make one sentence:* I knew the girl. She was hurt in the accident.
23 *Use a relative clause to make one sentence:* I haven't read the book. The teacher gave us the book.
24 *Correct the mistakes:*
   a) The film was very exciting. It was about two spies who were trying to catch <u>the other</u>.
   b) My sister and I aren't allowed to ride our bikes in the street because my mum is afraid we'll hurt <u>us</u>.
   c) I felt <u>myself</u> ill and stayed at home.
   d) In three years I <u>can speak</u> English better.

b) *Check your answers and the number of points for each correct answer on p. 233. Add up your points.*

c) *If you had 29 or more points, well done! Maybe you can help students who had fewer points. If you had 28 points or fewer, it's a good idea to do some more work before you go on to the next unit. Where did you make mistakes? The chart below will tell you what you can do to improve your English.*

No.	Areas	Find out more	Exercises
1– 5	Britain facts	Units 1–4	–
6–11	Word fields	pp. 6, 11, 14, 20, 33, 38, 54, 60, 95	WB pp. 3, 4, 9, 10, 14, 21, 23, 37, 38, 44, 49, 56, 64, 67
12–15	Study Skills	Skills File, pp. 140, 141, 144, 145	WB pp. 28, 41, 56, 65
16–19	Writing	Writing course, pp. 22, 40, 64, 78, 98	WB pp. 12, 24, 43, 52, 66
20–24	Grammar	GF 6, 8, 9, pp. 154–156	WB pp. 50, 53–54

Unit 1

9 REVISION The Feely family (Present perfect) ▸ Unit 1 (p. 23)

Partner B: answer your partner's questions about pictures 1–4.

Picture 1 A: …
　　　　　　B: Mrs Feely is angry because her kids haven't …

Picture 2 A: …
　　　　　　B: Mo and Jo …

1 kids – not tidy room

2 they – have bath

3 parrot – die

4 he – not sleep enough

Now ask your partner questions about pictures 5–8.

Picture 5 B: Why is Kitty Feely scared?
　　　　　　A: …

5 Kitty Feely – scared

6 Julie Feely - proud

7 Tommy Feely – ill

8 Jill and Jenny Feely – cold

B Partner

Unit 2

14 Extra Loch Ness and Edinburgh ▸ Unit 2 (p. 43)

a) Read the box below. Then listen to your partner's text about Loch Ness. When you hear a mistake, say **Stop!** Correct the sentence with facts from the box.

> **Facts about Loch Ness**
> 1. It is one of the most famous places in Scotland.
> 2. The word loch [lɒx] means lake.
> 3. Loch Ness is 37 kilometres long.
> 4. They have given it a name: Nessie.
> 5. Every year thousands of tourists come to Loch Ness.
> 6. There are lots of websites with webcams from around the lake.

b) A student has written this text about Edinburgh. There are six mistakes in it. Read it through quietly. Then read it out to your partner. He/She will correct the mistakes.

Edinburgh

Edinburgh is on the west coast of Scotland. It is the largest city in Scotland. It's also the capital of Scotland.

Today more than 40 million tourists from all over the world come to visit Edinburgh every year. Visitors come to see the famous old buildings and places such as Buckingham Palace, the Royal Mile or Princes Street.

Edinburgh was also the home of some famous people, like Alexander Graham Bell. He had the idea for the first computer. And only a few people know that J. K. Rowling wrote her first Harry Potter book in her house in Edinburgh.

Partner **B** 103

Unit 3

1 WORDS Rooms ▶ Unit 3 (p. 60)

a) Draw an empty room like this.

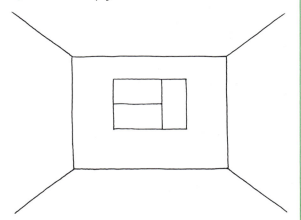

b) Listen to your partner. Put these things into the room. Ask questions if you don't understand.

c) Now describe the room below to your partner. Use words and phrases from the box.

> in the foreground/background • next to •
> on the right/left • in the middle • between •
> ...

There's a fridge at the back on the left. There's a sink under the window next to ...

d) When you've finished, compare your partner's picture with this one.

e) **Extra** Draw another room with lots of things. Describe it to your partner.

8 STUDY SKILLS Paraphrasing ▶ Unit 3 (p. 63)

a) Listen to your partner and guess his/her words.

b) Explain the following English words to your partner – but don't use the word.

> banana • breakfast • crocodile •
> doctor • library • teacher

Phrases from the blue box on the right can help you.
It's a person who ...
– Oh, do you mean a ...?

> It's somebody/a person who ...
> It's something/a fruit/a ... that ...
> It's something that you use to ...
> It's a thing/an animal that ...
> It's a place where ...

c) Now explain these German words to your partner.

> Cousine • Eisdiele • Flaschenöffner •
> Schiedsrichter • Wörterbuch

B Partner

Who needs legs? ▶ Unit 3 (p. 66)

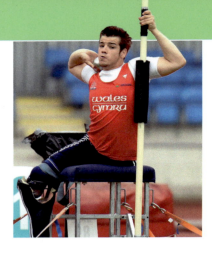

> Birthday boy Nathan was fighting for his life yesterday after a two-hour operation. His mother Helen is by his bed where last night he was very very ill.

That was the report in the Sunday Mirror, a national newspaper, on 13th April 1997.

Three months later Nathan took his second 'first steps', this time with artificial legs. And soon after that he was back at school!

'Yes, Nathan has lost his legs, but he's as mad about sport as he was before,' his mum said a few months later. 'He still goes riding. And he plays football at school, as a goalkeeper. He sits in the goal and stops the ball.'

When he was ten years old Nathan started to play sledge hockey – ice hockey for the disabled. Coaches quickly spotted his talent.

Then when he was 14, Nathan also started to do athletics in the summer. A year later he won gold medals for javelin, discus and shot put at the Junior British Championships.

When Nathan was sixteen, in April 2004, he played for Great Britain at the World Sledge Hockey Championships – he was the youngest player. In 2006 he represented Wales at the Melbourne Commonwealth Games and Great Britain at the Winter Paralympics in Turin.

The BBC asked Nathan Stephens what his hopes were. Nathan's answer: 'I hope I will be able to be in the next Summer and Winter Paralympics. I hope we win more medals than before. If there's a lot about us on TV, people will understand better what we do.'

Working with the text

1 Who is Nathan Stephens?

a) Read the text. Take notes on these questions:
– When did Nathan learn to walk again?
– What sports did he do when he was ten?
– When did he win his first athletics medals?
– What are his hopes?

b) Ask your partner about Nathan's earlier life. Take notes.
– When and where was Nathan born?
– What sports did he do as a little boy?
– Where did he go on his ninth birthday?
– What happened there?
Then answer your partner's questions.

c) What kind of a boy is Nathan? Why do you think that?
I think he's brave/hard-working/sporty/… because …

2 Timeline

a) Copy and complete this timeline with your partner. Scan both texts again if necessary.

Nathan born
1988 1997 1998 2002 2004 2006 After 2006

b) **Extra** What did Nathan do after 2006? Find out with the help of the internet.

DOSSIER Timeline for …

Find out about an interesting person (a sports star, a film star, …). Draw a timeline for him/her.

Partner **B**   105

Unit 4

1 WORDS Numbers ▶ Unit 4 (p. 76)

a) Write down the numbers that your partner reads out to you.
Then read out these numbers to your partner:
Swap papers and check.

15 • 7 • 93 • 303 • 2,684 • 13,155 • 300,000.

6 Plans for the week (Present progressive with future meaning) ▶ Unit 4 (p. 77)

a) Talk to your partner about your plans for the week.
Find out when you're doing the same things. Your partner will start.

A: On Monday evening I'm going to …
What about you?
B: I'm going to football training. On Tuesday evening I'm … What about you?
A: I'm going …

	afternoon ☀	evening ☾
MON		go to football training
TUE		make cakes for party
WED	help sister with homework	
THU		watch DVDs with mates
FRI		go to party at Kevin's house
SAT	paint kitchen with Dad	meet mates at youth club

Getting ready for a test 2 ▶ p. 87

2 Reading

Read about St. Jacobs, a village near Toronto, Canada, where Mennonites[1] live.
Then answer the questions below.

1 The Mennonite Farm Tour …
 A is seven days a week.
 B is on Thursdays and Saturdays.
 C starts at the Maple Syrup[2] Museum.

2 You do the Mennonite Farm Tour at 12.15. How much time will you have at the market after the tour?
 A under 1 hour
 B between 1 and 2 hours
 C over 2 hours

3 You can buy maple syrup …
 A only at the 'Farm Pantry'[3].
 B at the 'Farm Pantry' and the Farmers' Market.
 C on the Mennonite Farm Tour.

❧ The Mennonite Farm Tour
On market days only. The 1 hour 15 min. tour starts and ends at the Farmers' Market. Travel in a horse-drawn trolley, see the farms at work and enjoy the country. ➔ Adults $ 15. Children $ 7.50

❧ St. Jacobs Farmers' Market
Thurs. and Sat. 7 am to 3.30 pm.
Fresh, healthy food. Great atmosphere. Mennonite farmers travel to market by horse and buggy to sell their vegetables, sausages and maple syrup.

❧ The Maple Syrup Museum
Learn how syrup is produced. You can buy maple syrup products at the 'Farm Pantry' near the museum.

[1] Mennonites ['menənaɪts] *Mennoniten*   [2] maple syrup ['meɪpl ˌsɪrəp] *Ahornsirup*   [3] pantry ['pæntri] *Speisekammer*

106 D Differentiation

Unit 1

4 REVISION A visit to the London Eye (Simple past) ▶ Unit 1 (p. 21)

Twelve verbs are missing. Complete the text with the correct form of the verbs in the box.

> arrive • be • be • be • call • go • find •
> see • not see • not stay • take • not wait

Asif and Robert *had* a really great time yesterday. In the morning the weather ... great. Robert and his parents ... the Tube to Waterloo. When they ... at the London Eye, they *didn't see* Asif. But then Asif ... Robert on his mobile and they ... him quickly. Luckily there weren't too many tourists there that day, so they ... very long. Soon they ... up on the big wheel. The view ... fantastic. They ...

Asif's house, but they ... lots of famous London sights. After the ride, Asif and Robert ... with Robert's parents. They ... to Asif's part of London and then to the Trocadero.

6 WRITING A postcard (Writing better sentences) ▶ Unit 1 (p. 22)

Part 1 — WRITING COURSE

d) more help Now write a postcard from an imaginary holiday in London.

– Start with a greeting. — *Dear Laura • Hi Nate*
– Say where you are. — *I'm writing to you from ... • Hello from ...!*
– Say what's special about the place. — *The weather is great – hot and sunny every day. ... • The hotel/... isn't great, but ...*
– Say what you usually do there. — *Every day I go to ... • Usually we ... in the afternoon because ...*
– Say what you did yesterday. — *Yesterday afternoon we visited a castle / a palace/ ... • In the evening we went to a zoo.*
– Say what you are going to do. — *This evening I'm going to go to the cinema. • Tomorrow we're going to visit a market in the town.*
– Finish with a closing phrase. — *Love, ... • Write soon! • See you soon, ...*

11 What have they done? When did they do it? (Present perfect/Simple past) ▶ p. 24

Put in the correct form of the verbs in brackets. Say what the people have done and when they did it.

1 Liz ... (visit) London. She ... (go) there last summer.
2 Eddie ... (eat) crocodile, but he ... (eat) kangaroo. He ... (try) it when he was in Australia.
3 Charlie ... (be) on the London Eye. He ... (go) on it two weeks ago.
4 Diana ... (write) a postcard to her parents, but she ... (write) postcards to all her friends.
   She ... (write) them last night.
5 Sarah and Joe ... (be) to Harrods, but they ... (be) to Brick Lane Market. They ... (go) there last
   Sunday.
6 Andy ... (see) a musical in Hyde Park. It ... (be) two months ago.

1 Liz has visited London. She went there last summer.
2 Eddie ...

14 SPEAKING Asking for and giving information ▶ Unit 1 (p. 25)

c) more help Imagine you're in London. With your partner work out a dialogue. The sentences below can help you. Practise your dialogue and act it out in class.

What can I do for you?	How much is a ticket to ...?	About ... minutes.
How much is a one day ticket for children?	That's ... pounds.	Thank you.	You're welcome.
How long does it take from here to ...?	How long do I have to wait for the next train?

EVERYDAY ENGLISH

Only a game Working with the text ▶ Unit 1 (p. 28)

2 more help How Robert felt

Complete the sentences. Use the words in the yellow box.

1 Robert felt ... when he saw all the games at the Trocadero. (l. 3)
2 He felt   ... when Asif put on the helmet. (l. 23)
3 He felt   ... when he saw his own hand in the game. (l. 43)
4 He felt   ... when the people shouted at them. (l. 139)

scared • excited •
nervous • surprised

D Differentiation

Unit 2

6 WRITING An e-mail to a friend ▶ Unit 2 (p. 40)

d) more help Now write an e- mail to one of your friends about a real or imaginary day out. Maybe these words and phrases will help you.

Remember:

Start with an interesting opening sentence.	Dear Emily I promised to write you a mail about our day trip to … Well, here it is at last.	Hi Will Guess what I did yesterday – I went to …!
Start a new paragraph for each new idea.	I had a great (fantastic / amazing / …) time.	It is a really interesting (cool / funny / …) place.
	I went with … and … They are always good fun.	The weather was good – … (hot and sunny / cold and sunny / only a bit of rain in the morning) – so we were able to do lots of things.
	The best bit of the day was (the tour of the city / lunch / the afternoon/the match / …)	I really enjoyed it because …
	First we … At lunchtime …	Then we … After that …
Finish with something general or personal.	Must stop now. Please write back soon.	Write soon and tell me all your news. Say hi to your parents from me.
	Love Talk soon! CU soon	

10 Fiona's dreams (Conditional sentences type 2) ▶ Unit 2 (p. 42)

Fiona often dreams about what it would be like if she lived in London. Match the sentences.

1 If I lived in London,
2 If my parents visited me,
3 If I waited outside Buckingham Palace,
4 If a film-maker saw me in a school play,
5 If I didn't live in a small town,

we'd try Indian food.
I'd probably see the Queen.
I'd have a fantastic life.
we'd go on the London Eye.
I'd be so much happier.
I'd probably become a film star.
we'd visit the sights.

Differentiation **D**   **109**

11 // ● **If I became a film star** (Conditional sentences type 2)   ▸ Unit 2 (p. 42)

a) *Fill in the correct forms of the verbs in brackets.*
1 If I became a film star, I (meet) famous people.
2 If my friends (come) to see me, I'd show them all the film studios.
3 If they (want) to see my films, I'd give them free tickets.
4 My photo would be in the newspaper if I (meet) the Queen.

5 I'd be so excited if I (be) in a film.
6 If (not want) a role, I (not take) it.
7 If I (not like) an actor, I (not work) with him.

b) 👥 *What would you do if you were a star? Write three sentences. Compare them with a partner's.*

Orkney Star   Working with the text   ▸ Unit 2 (p. 46)

2 [more help] **What did they mean?**

a) *Who made these statements? When?*
1 'The island will still be here when you come back on Friday, love!' (l. 35)
2 'Once a Fishface, always a Fishface.' (l. 86)
3 'I'd really like to be at home with my family.' (l. 144)
4 'Clones, maybe, but not beauties.' (l. 164)

Katrina's mum		when Katrina went downstairs.
Katrina		when the 'Beauties' helped Katrina with her hair.
Alison		when she saw the 'Beauties'.
Sheena	said it	when Katrina didn't want any help.
Fiona		when Bill asked, 'Do you like living away from home?'
Bill		when Katrina got out of the car at the ferry.

Unit 3

4 // ● **What would you like?** (Relative clauses)   ▸ Unit 3 (p. 61)

a) *Write sentences. Use **who** for people and **that** for things and animals.*

	a teacher		comes and sits with me when I'm lonely.
	a car		is fun to drive.
	a computer		doesn't tell our parents when I do something wrong.
I'd like	a friend	who	listens to my problems.
	a brother	that	gives me lots of nice presents when she visits.
	a dog		is really fast and easy to use.
	a room		explains things well and is funny.
	an aunt		is big and has a nice view.

b) **Extra** *What would you like? Make your own sentences.*

D Differentiation

Unit 3

5 Can you help me? (Relative clauses) ▶ Unit 3 (p. 61)

Make the two sentences into one question.
Use **who** or **that**.
Then try to answer the questions. Check your answers on p. 180.

1 What's the name of the big wheel? You can see the big wheel in London.
   What's the name of the big wheel that you can see in London?
2 Who's that boy? The boy is visiting the Byrds.
   Who's the boy who …
3 What's the name of the instrument? The instrument is in Latisha's room.
4 What's the name of the dish? Latisha's grandma brought the dish from Trinidad.
5 What's the name of the team? Latisha supports the team.
6 What's the name? Latisha uses the name in the chat room.
7 What's the name of the boy? J.K. Rowling wrote books about him.
8 Who's the actor? The actor is in that new action film.

12 more help WRITING A report (Collecting and organizing ideas) ▶ Unit 3 (p. 64)

WRITING COURSE Part 3

c) There are 10 mistakes in this report.
Use your notes to find the mistakes and rewrite the report.

> Bristol South U14 girls' rugby team played Redcliffe last Saturday in Manchester.
> It was the second match of the year, so both teams made a fast start. At half-time the score was 1–1.
> After the break both teams played better. But in the end Redcliffe won because Bristol South made lots of mistakes. The final score was Redcliffe 0 Bristol South 1.
> The best player on the pitch was South's John Hooley. He scored the only goal of the match.

Differentiation D

14 [more help] MEDIATION Where I'm from ▶ Unit 3 (p. 65)

Philipp has brought a book about Chemnitz, his hometown, as a present for the Byrd family.
Imagine you're Philipp.
Answer Latisha's questions.

Is Chemnitz an old city? Is it big?

What does 'Erzgebirge' mean?

What's that woman making?

What do they mine?

Are they for children?

This is a book about Chemnitz, my hometown.

Chemnitz und das Erzgebirge

Chemnitz liegt am Rande des Erzgebirges und ist wichtiges Zentrum für die gesamte Region. Die drittgrößte Stadt Sachsens bietet eine aufregende Kombination aus Alt und Neu.

Im Erzgebirge denkt man das ganze Jahr an Weihnachten. Hier werden die herrlichen Holzfiguren geschnitzt, die auf der ganzen Welt beliebt sind. Einige Werkstätten, wie die hier abgebildete in **Seiffen**, kann man das ganze Jahr über besichtigen. Es ist sehr interessant, die Kunsthandwerker bei ihrer Arbeit zu beobachten.

Bergbau. Noch immer baut man im Erzgebirge das Erz ab, von dem es seinen Namen hat. Zinn und Silber werden hier abgebaut.

Erzgebirge — Ore Mountains
Holzfigur — wooden figure
Zinn — tin
Silber — silver
Bergbau — mining

EVERYDAY ENGLISH

D Differentiation

Unit 4

5 Crazy School 2050 (Modal substitutes) ▶ Unit 4 (p. 77)

Look at the picture of Crazy School. Write sentences about the school.

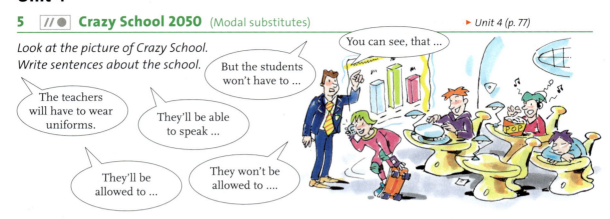

Speech bubbles: "You can see, that …" / "But the students won't have to …" / "The teachers will have to wear uniforms." / "They'll be able to speak …" / "They'll be allowed to …" / "They won't be allowed to …."

7 WRITING Telling a story (The steps of writing) ▶ Unit 4 (p. 78)

Part 4 — WRITING COURSE

Step 2 — more help | Write

a) Make these two paragraphs more interesting. Use the words in the boxes or your own ideas.

Sentence	Word(s)
The boy looked at them.	sadly
'I feel stupid,' he said.	really
'I'm here with my parents.	on holiday
I left our hotel this morning.	early
I wanted to go for a walk.	because
Now I can't find the hotel.'	But/again
The girls wanted to laugh.	at first
It was a funny story.	because / very
They tried to help the boy.	but then
He was worried.	because/clearly/very
He didn't know the name of the hotel or the street.	The problem was that
Then Emily had an idea.	brilliant
'Perhaps you've got something in your pocket. It can help us.'	that

Step 3 — more help | Check and revise

Check this final paragraph.
1. First look at the *blue* verbs. They should all be in the **simple past**. You need to correct five of them.
2. Then check the *spelling* of the words in *green*. You need to correct two of them.
3. Look at the word order in **two sentences**. You need to correct one of them.
4. Read the paragraph again. Perhaps it needs more detail here ***. What could you add here?

The boy *check* his *pockets* quickly. He *find* a ticket for a *swimming pool*.
  'This pool is near the hotel!' he *said*.
  The girls *know* the place because **they sometimes went swimming there.** ***
  When they at the hotel arrived, the boy's parents *are* *outside*. They *were* very *happy* to see *there* son, so they *invited* the girls to a restaurant and they *eat* *delicious* burgers and huge *eiscreams*.

b) Choose a title for the story.

| A day in High Park | Can you help me? | The case of the lost boy |

Differentiation D

8　Mum and Dad are on strike (Reflexive pronouns) ▶ Unit 4 (p. 79)

Complete the sentences with the reflexive pronouns *myself*, *yourself*, *herself*, *ourselves*, *yourselves*, *themselves*.

1. Mr and Mrs Jones are on strike, so the children have to cook for *themselves*.
2. Mr Jones usually looks after Jill in the afternoon, but today she has to look after …
3. Mrs Jones usually teaches Jack the guitar, but he knows, 'Today I'll have to teach … the guitar.'
4. Mr and Mrs Jones usually shop for the children, but today Jack told Jill, 'Mum and Dad are on strike, so we have to shop for …'
5. 'Why are you on strike?' the children asked. Their parents said, 'You two will have to ask …!'
6. Jill's mum usually puts her to bed, but today she told her, 'Sorry, Jill, but you'll have to put … to bed tonight.'

Extra　A fishing trip　Working with the text ▶ Unit 4 (p. 82)

2　more help　A report
Use these ideas to complete the newspaper report.

- The trip – start – well – when Robert – get – big fish
- But then – Mr Smith – see – a bear – so – leave quickly
- When – Mr Smith – lose – canoe – they – in trouble
- They – have to – go past – the bear – Robert – have – great plan
- Mr Smith – throw – Robert's fish – to the bear – and then – he and Robert – escape
- They – think – they – safe – but – the bear – follow – them
- Luckily – bear – run away – when – Mrs Smith – arrive – car

Unit 5

1　WORDS　All about music ▶ Unit 5 (p. 95)

a) Read the definitions and find the music words.
1. goup of people who sing together
2. a round instrument you hit to make music
3. a part of a song that you sing more than once
4. a machine you can download music onto
5. the words of a song
6. you can listen to CDs on this machine
7. a place where people dance to music
8. something you can enjoy in a park

Text File
Inhalt

> **Tip**
> The texts in this **Text File** are extra reading material. The footnotes at the bottom of the pages explain the most important new words. Have fun with the texts!
>
> ▶ *SF Understanding new words (p. 134)*

				Seite	
Intro	TF	1	Pull In Emergency	115	
Unit 1	TF	2	Two Elizabeths	117	
Unit 2	TF	3	Online safety	118	
	TF	4	My blog: Scotch pancakes	120	
	TF	5	The lost girl	121	
Unit 3	TF	6	Football songs	122	
	TF	7	The rules of cricket	123	
	TF	8	Tim, a rock and a rope	124	
Unit 4	TF	9	If you meet a bear …	127	
	TF	10	Poems – the four seasons	128	
Unit 5	TF	11	Fans – a play	130	

TF 1 Pull In Emergency[1] (adapted from 'Children's London', The Times)

Too young to rock? Never! The band Pull In Emergency (13 and 14 years old) tell you how.

Alice Costelloe
13, guitarist in P.I.E.

'I think at 13 it's good to try to go to as many gigs as you can. Some places let you in when you're over 14 – for example the Wireless Festival in Hyde Park (but the tickets are quite expensive). Or there's the Tin Pan Alley Festival in Denmark Street (www.tinpanalleyfestival.co.uk). It's free – and for people of all ages. The Underage Festival[5] in Victoria Park is great because it's for teenagers between 14 and 17 only. We also went to the Love Music Hate Racism Festival in Trafalgar Square.

I buy all my instruments in Denmark Street. They sell guitars for £3000, but if you're in a teenage band you only need a £70 guitar.'

Faith Bale
13, lead singer of the band **Pull In Emergency** from North London

'As most of us are only in Year 8, our friends have a problem: they can't get into our gigs. I went to an under-18s night a few days ago and it was great because everybody there was a teenager.

We haven't got the money for a rehearsal studio, so we practise at our drummer's house. I sit on the washing machine and the others all squash in[2] around it. We're getting a new player soon and I don't know how he is going to fit.

We want to attract people's attention[3] so we try to wear cool clothes *and* sound good.

Old, second-hand clothes are best, but you sometimes have to look at a lot of rubbish in some of the shops. I don't buy whole new outfits: I just add one new thing to an outfit that I already have – this way[4] I save money.'

---

[1] (to) pull in emergency [ɪˈmɜːdʒənsi] *(Notbremse) im Notfall ziehen*   [2] (to) squash in [skwɒʃ] *(sich) hineinquetschen*   [3] (to) attract sb.'s attention [əˈtrækt], [əˈtenʃn] *jn. auf sich aufmerksam machen*   [4] this way *auf diese Weise*   [5] Underage Festival [ˈʌndəreɪdʒ] *Festival für Minderjährige*

Dylan Holmes

13, bass guitarist in P.I.E.

'We have some recording time in a studio with a sound engineer. It's all free because one of our parents knows the owner of the studio.

Young bands have to get help from parents and friends, but even if you can't get a studio, you can still make quite good recordings – on a computer or with a cheap microphone. And if you haven't got enough money for a good guitar, just buy a good effects pedal because it can change your whole sound.'

1 The article
Right or wrong? Correct the wrong statements.
1 P.I.E.'s friends always go to their gigs.
2 P.I.E. practise in a rehearsal studio.
3 P.I.E. aren't interested in their outfits.
4 Alice tries to go to as many concerts as possible.
5 There aren't any concerts for people under 18.
6 P.I.E. play on cheap instruments.
7 Dylan thinks young bands need a recording studio.

2 Young bands
a) Finish this sentence. Can you find more than one ending?
As a young band you have to/you need …

b) What young bands do you know in Germany? Tell your class about them.

3 The song 'Backfoot'
Listen to the song. How do you like it?
– I think the song is …
– The music sounds …

> awful • boring • exciting • great • happy • fantastic • new • nice • sad • …

Backfoot by Pull In Emergency
You say you love me so hold me,
You're running away, why won't you hold me?
Now you seem to[1] say you want me,
Oh running away has never been so easy …
as now.
(…)
You're running off,
You're running off,
Caught on the backfoot[2],
Palm[3] on the handle[4].
(…)

---
[1] (to) seem (to be/do) [siːm] *(zu sein/tun) scheinen*   [2] (to) be caught on the backfoot [kɔːt] *kalt erwischt werden*
[3] palm [pɑːm] *Hand(fläche)*   [4] handle [hændl] *(Tür-)Klinke*

TF 2 Two Elizabeths 🎧

England has had two Queen Elizabeths. Elizabeth I became Queen in 1558, when she was 25 years old. There was always a lot of gossip[1] about her. The big question was: Who will the Queen marry?

Well, she never married anybody, but she had a number of 'favourites'. One of them was Walter Raleigh.

They met, so people say, one rainy evening at Shakespeare's Globe Theatre in London. The Queen wanted to get out of her carriage when she saw a large puddle.

'Why isn't she getting out?' people whispered. Walter Raleigh, a new face at court[2] – young and good-looking – saw why: the puddle. He quickly took off his very expensive new cloak and threw it onto the puddle.

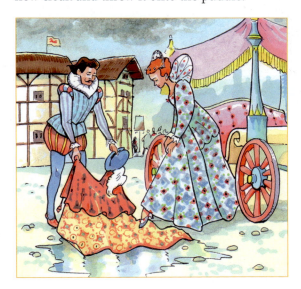

The Queen smiled and allowed Mr Raleigh to help her down. She went into the theatre with dry feet and Raleigh became her new 'favourite'.

Just a few years later the Queen made Walter into 'Sir Walter' and allowed him to start a colony in America.

And what did Sir Walter bring back from America? Gold or jewels? No: a dirty vegetable called 'the potato' and a dry leaf called 'tobacco'.

Which brings us to the second Queen Elizabeth.

She was also very young when she became Queen in 1952 – just 26 years old. But she married and had four children.

One night in 1982, a man called Michael Fagan climbed first into the garden of Buckingham Palace and then into the Palace.

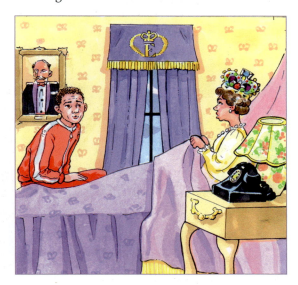

There he went into the Queen's bedroom. And when she woke up in the middle of the night she found a strange[3] man by her bed.

Queen Elizabeth II is famous for being very calm[4]. And that night was an example. She asked the man to sit down and started to talk to him. After a few minutes she asked him, 'Would you like a drink?' He said, 'Yes, please.' So she picked up the phone.

'I'd like two gin and tonics, please. Oh, and my cigarettes,' she said.

The person on the other end of the phone knew that there was something very wrong. Why? Because the Queen has never smoked!

In a few minutes the police were there and took Mr Fagan away.

▶ How does tobacco link the two stories?

---

[1] gossip [ˈɡɒsɪp] *Klatsch*   [2] (at) court [kɔːt] *(am) Hof (der Königin)*   [3] strange [streɪndʒ] *fremd*   [4] calm [kɑːm] *ruhig*

TF 3 Online safety

1 The people

a) Look at the poster: 'm8s' is short for 'mates'. What does 'mates' mean?

b) Who are the two people in the poster? What do you think is going to happen?

c) Why is the person on the stairs wearing a mask?
1. He's playing a trick on his friend.
2. It's Halloween.
3. He wants to hide his face.

2 The message

a) What is the poster saying?
1. Send lots of text messages.
2. Be careful when you meet people online.
3. Be smart: Tell your online mates as much as possible about yourself!

b) Where would you put the poster?
I would put it in schools/libraries/…

3 Keep safe online

Do you know the online safety rules[1]? They are very important! Try this quiz.

Online Safety Quiz

Question 1
When you are online do you use …?
- A: Your real name, age and address?
- B: A nickname[2]?
- C: Your best friend's name?

Question 2
Somebody says: Don't tell your parents about me. What should you do?
- A: Tell your parents quickly.
- B: Don't tell your parents.
- C: Ask why.

Question 3
What information can you get from somebody's real name online?
- A: Only their address.
- B: Only their age.
- C: Their age, address and telephone number.

Question 4
You have met someone online. You want to meet them. What do you do?
- A: Go alone.
- B: Go with a friend.
- C: Go with a parent.

Question 5
How do you stay safe on the internet?
- A: Wear gloves[3].
- B: Don't use the internet.
- C: Be careful and follow safety rules.

The answers are at the bottom of this page. For more on online safety go to … www.EnglishG.de

---

Answers to Online Safety Quiz

Q 1 A NEVER NEVER use your real name. And B NEVER give your address!
C NO, don't do this.
Q 2 A YES, tell your parents QUICKLY! and C NO, tell your parents!
Q 3 A and B NO! You can get more than that!
C You can find out ALL these things about somebody if you know their real name. So NEVER use your real name online.
Q 4 A and B NEVER do this alone or even with a friend.
C YES, DON'T GO if your parents can't come with you!
Q 5 A NO! If you want to stay WARM, wear gloves!
B If you don't want to use the internet, that's OK.
C The internet is cool, BUT you must be careful and follow the rules!

---

[1] rule [ruːl] Regel   [2] nickname ['nɪkneɪm] Spitzname   [3] glove [glʌv] (Finger-)Handschuh

2 Text File

TF 4 My blog[1]   ● Scotch pancakes

Monday November 11

Was a bit bored this weekend and the weather was HORRIBLE!
Luckily some mates came round. We decided to make some Scotch pancakes. They are really easy and VERY GOOD!

1. Put 120 g self-raising flour[2] and 30 g sugar into a bowl.
2. Mix an egg and 150 ml milk in another bowl.
3. Mix the egg and milk mixture into the flour. Now you have to work QUICKLY or your pancakes will be flat[3]!
4. Melt butter in a HOT frying pan. Now put the pancake mixture into the pan with a spoon.
5. When there are lots of bubbles on the pancakes, turn them over.
6. Eat with butter, or butter and jam. If there are some left over[4], you can eat them cold too. BUT we ate them all!

POSTED by Tom at 5.15 pm

COMMENTS

Sugarmonster said ...
Hi Tom! I like your blog! I'm German. I want to make your pancakes. What is self-raising flour??

Tom Scotland said ...
Hi Sugarmonster. You use self-raising flour when you want things to rise (go up). You can use normal flour and baking powder (about a teaspoon). My dictionary says that baking powder is 'Backpulver' in German. Does that sound right?

Sugarmonster said ...
Thanks, Tom! I tried the pancakes. They ARE GOOD! Would you like a German recipe[5]? What about my favourite 'Schokoladenpudding'?

Tom Scotland said ...
Can u do it in English?? My German isn't gr8!

ABOUT ME
TOM Scotland
View my profile

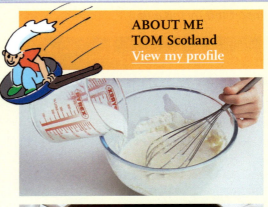

1 What do you need?
If you want to make Scotch pancakes, what do you need? Write a list.

2 Your favourite easy recipe
Write your favourite recipe in English. Choose an easy recipe and explain what to do in a simple way. Use a dictionary if you don't know a word. You can use pictures too.

---

[1] blog [blɒg] *Weblog (Online-Tagebuch)*   [2] flour [ˈflaʊə] *Mehl*   [3] flat [flæt] *flach*   [4] (be) left over [ˌleft ˈəʊvə] *übrig sein*   [5] recipe [ˈresəpi] *Rezept*

TF 5 The lost girl (A folk story from the Orkney Islands) 🎧

A long, long time ago, there was a family on one of the islands in the north of the Orkney Islands. One day the daughter went out to catch some little fish. The father wanted to use them to catch big fish. The girl went out ... but she never came back. Her family looked everywhere, but they couldn't find her.

Years later the father and his two sons went fishing. The weather was fine when they left, but then a thick fog came. They didn't know how to get home. After a time, they came to an island. The three men got off the boat and walked until they came to a big, beautiful house. They knocked on the door, and a good-looking man opened it. He invited them in and said they could stay until the fog was gone.

The three men went inside. They could not believe how beautiful everything was. Then the man introduced[1] them to his wife. It was the lost girl! She welcomed her father and brothers warmly, asked how they were and about her mother and everybody else back home.

As they were talking, the man asked the father if he had any cows to sell. The father answered yes, he had one fine cow, and the man gave him a very good price for the cow. He paid in gold.

Now the father thought that he could find out the name of the island. 'Well,' he said, 'now you'll have to tell me how to get here, or I won't be able to bring the cow to you.'

'Och!' said the man. 'Don't worry about that. I'll come and get the cow.'

Then one of the brothers said, 'Father, the fog is going away.'

'Then we should[2] go,' the father said.

The girl asked, 'Is there anything here that you would like to take home with you?'

'Yes,' her husband said, 'you can take anything[3] in the house. Just say what you would like and take it with you.'

The girl looked at them hopefully. She thought her father would choose her. But he chose a large gold plate.

When they got to the boat, the good-looking man said, 'Just go that way, and you will soon be home.'

The father and his two sons did what he said and took their boat into the fog. As they came out the other side, they found that they were near their own island.

When they got home, the wife was very upset. 'An awful thing has happened,' she said. 'Our cow is dead.'

But the old man smiled. 'Och,' he said, 'that's all right. I got a good price for her.'

Nobody ever saw the island, the man or the girl again.

1 Understanding the story
Right or wrong? Say why.
1 When the father and brothers came to the island, they knew where they were.
2 The girl wanted to go home with her father and brothers.
3 The girl's father loved his daughter more than he loved gold.

---

[1] (to) introduce sb. [ˌɪntrəˈdjuːs] *jn. vorstellen*   [2] Then we should ... [ʃʊd] *Dann sollten wir ...*   [3] you can take anything: *du kannst nehmen, was (immer) du willst*

TF 6 Football songs

You'll never walk alone

When you walk through a storm
Hold your head up high
And don't be afraid of the dark.
At the end of the storm
Is a golden sky
And the sweet, silver song of a lark [1].

Walk on through the wind,
Walk on through the rain,
Though your dreams be tossed and blown [2].
Walk on, walk on with hope in your heart,
And you'll never walk alone,
You'll never walk alone.

by Oscar Hammerstein

We are the champions

We are the champions, my friends
And we'll keep on fighting[3] till the end
We are the champions
We are the champions
No time for losers
'Cause we are the champions
Of the world

by Freddie Mercury

1 The songs
a) Listen to the songs and read the words. Which song do you like better? Why?

> the music is nicer/better ... •
> the singer sound more excited/happier/... •
> the song is about support for others

b) Imagine you are at a match and your team is winning. Which song would you sing? Why?

2 Now you
Which football songs (German or English) do you know? Have you been to a football stadium for a football match/a pop concert/...? How did you like it?

---

[1] lark [lɑːk] *Lerche*   [2] though your dreams be tossed and blown [tɒst] *etwa: auch wenn deine Träume in Gefahr geraten*   [3] (to) keep on fighting ['faɪtɪŋ] *weiterkämpfen*

TF 7 The rules of cricket

Cricket is the second most popular sport (after football) in Britain. People all over the world love cricket too, for example in India, Pakistan, Australia and South Africa.

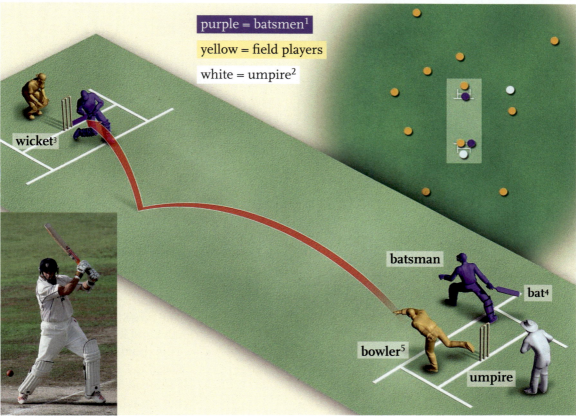

purple = batsmen[1]
yellow = field players
white = umpire[2]

wicket[3]

batsman

bat[4]

bowler[5]

umpire

1 The rules 🎧
Look at the pictures. Then listen and answer the questions about cricket.
1. How long is a match?
2. What equipment[6] do you need?
3. How many people are in a team?
4. What do the players have to do?
   – The bowler has to …
   – The other players have to …
5. How do you score?
   – The … scores one point when …

2 Your favourite sport
a) Answer the questions in 1 for your favourite sport. Use a dictionary if you need to.

b) 👥 Look for somebody who has chosen the same sport. Check your answers. Together give a short presentation about your favourite sport.

---

[1] batsman ['bætsmən] *Schlagmann* [2] umpire ['ʌmpaɪə] *Schiedsrichter* [3] wicket ['wɪkɪt] *Tor* [4] bat [bæt] *Schläger*
[5] bowler ['bəʊlə] *Werfer(in)* [6] equipment [ɪ'kwɪpmənt] *Ausrüstung*

TF 8 Tim, a rock and a rope[1] (adapted from Jacqueline Wilson's novel *Cliffhanger*)

Tim's father has sent him on an adventure[2] holiday for children. There's just one problem. Tim hates sports – all sports. Here's what Tim wrote in one of his postcards:

'OK, Tim. You next.'
'No!'
'Yes,' said Jake, our team leader.
'No,' I said.
'You all have to go sooner or later,' said Jake.
'Later,' I said.
'No. Sooner,' said Jake.
'I can't,' I said.
'Yes you can, Tim,' said Jake and held my hand.
'He's scared,' said Giles.
'We're all scared,' said Jake. 'Especially the first time.' He looked me straight in the eye. 'But you'll see it's easy, Tim. Believe me. Now. Into the harness[4].'
Jake put me into the harness before I could get away. He was telling me things about this rope in this hand, that rope in that hand, but I couldn't listen. All I could hear was this terrible noise inside my head.
'Don't let go of[5] the rope, OK?' said Jake.
The noise in my head got louder and louder.
This couldn't be real. If I closed my eyes maybe it would all be a bad dream and then I'd wake up in bed at home with my teddy bear.
'Tim?' said Jake. 'Open your eyes! Now, your friend Biscuits is waiting for you down there. Come on. Start to walk backwards towards the edge[6].'
I walked backwards one step. Then another. Then I stopped.
'I can't!'
'Yes you can,' said Jake. 'You'll see. Over the edge. Don't worry. You can't fall. You just have to remember, you *don't* let go of the rope.'
I looked at him and started to go back some

> *Do you think Tim is enjoying his holiday? Do you think he wants to go abseiling? Why/ Why not? Look at the pictures. What do you think happens? Now read on.*

[1] rope [rəʊp] *Seil* [2] adventure [ədˈventʃə] *Abenteuer* [3] (to) abseil [ˈæbseɪl] *(sich) abseilen* [4] harness [ˈhɑːnɪs] *(Kletter-)Gurt*
[5] (to) let go of sth. *etwas loslassen* [6] edge [edʒ] *Rand, Kante*

more. Then my feet suddenly lost contact with the ground. I slipped[1] backwards and suddenly ... there I was! I was hanging.

50 'Help!'
I was desperate[2].
I had to hold on to something.
I grabbed at the rock.
I let go of the rope!

55 Suddenly I was sliding[3] backwards, backwards, backwards.
I screamed.
I grabbed the rock. I held on to it. I was crying[4].

60 I heard them up above[5] me. They were shouting. 'He's fallen!'
'He's let go of the rope.'
'I *knew* he would.'
'Of course Tim had to do it wrong!'

65 'He's *stuck*[6].'
'Don't stop, Tim!' Biscuits called from below.
I turned my head and tried to look at him. The whole world started to move
70 this way and that. Biscuits looked like[7] he was millions and millions of miles below[8] me.
'Help!'
'It's OK, Tim. Don't panic,' Jake called
75 down.
'Don't panic, Tim, don't panic!' Kelly shouted. 'He's panicking, isn't he, Jake?'
'Shhh, Kelly. All of you. Go back, eh?' Jake said. 'Now. Tim. Listen.
80 You've let go of the rope.'
'I know!'
'But it's OK. You can't fall. You're safe. Believe me.'
85 'I don't feel safe. I feel sick.[9]'
'Well, you can get down in a few seconds. All you have to do is
90 grab the rope.'

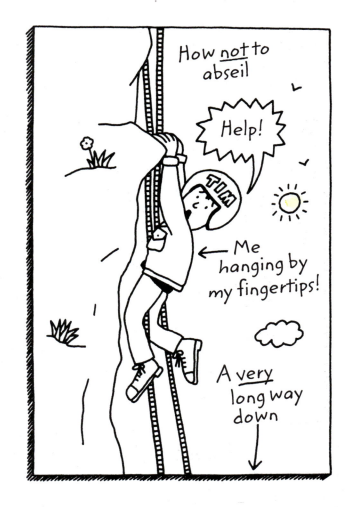

'How???'
'Just let go of the rock and ...'
'I can't!' Was Jake mad? I *couldn't* let go.
'You're safe in your harness,' Jake called.
'You needn't hold on to the rock. 95
You just have to grab the rope. See the rope? Tim! Open your eyes!'
'I can't look down.'
'Look up. At me,' said Jake.
I turned my head up and opened 100
my eyes a little. Jake was leaning right over the edge, not too terribly far away. He gave me a thumbs-up sign.

---

[1] (to) slip [slɪp] *(aus)rutschen* [2] desperate ['dɛspərət] *verzweifelt* [3] (to) slide, slid, slid [slaɪd], [slɪd] *rutschen, gleiten* [4] (to) cry [kraɪ] *weinen*
[5] above [ə'bʌv] *über* [6] (to) be stuck [stʌk] *festsitzen* [7] like *hier: als ob* [8] below [bɪ'ləʊ] *unter* [9] I feel sick. [sɪk] *Mir ist schlecht.*

105 'That's good. Now. It's OK. Have a break if you like. It's not so bad now, is it?'

'Yes!'

'You can hang there all day if you really want,' said Jake.

110 'No!'

'Or you can grab that rope and walk down, one foot at a time, easy-peasy[1]. Mmm?'

I looked up at him.

'Can't you pull me up? Please?' I asked.

115 'We're trying to get you down, Tim, not up!' said Jake. 'You can do it. You're a brave[2] boy, Tim.'

120 He had to be joking!

'So just reach out[3] ...,' Jake said.

I thought about it.

125 My fingers were hurting terribly. I *couldn't* hang there forever. Maybe if I let go and grabbed the rope I could get down. So I let go of the rock, I reached out suddenly, I tried to grab ...

130 I swung round and it was so scary that I closed my eyes and grabbed the rock again.

The others were grumbling. But Jake didn't give up.

'Almost. Try again. Go on.'

135 So I tried again. I reached out. My hand was wet with sweat[4] but I got the rope – I held on

to it – I had it safe!

'Well done!' Jake called. 'There! I knew you could. Just hold on to it this time, eh? Now walk down. One step.' 140

I tried to move my feet. I couldn't feel them inside my boots. I made a little mouse's step downwards.

'Great!' said Jake. 'Now another step.'

My other leg moved. And I moved too. I was 145 going down.

'There we go,' said Jake. 'That's it. You're getting it now.'

'I'm doing it!' I said and I walked down as carefully as I could. 150

'That's right. You're doing it, Tim,' Jake called. 'You're almost halfway down. Doing just great. Go on. Nice and easy. Good boy. Well done.'

'I'm doing it,' I whispered, 'I'm doing it. I'm 155 doing it. It's awful. But I'm doing it.'

I went down quicker and quicker – and then suddenly I was at the bottom and Biscuits hit me on the back and congratulated me.

'You did it, you did it, you did it!' Biscuits 160 sang.

Jake was cheering me from right up at the top of the rock.

'Well done, Tim! It wasn't so bad, was it? Do you want to do it again, eh?' 165

I shook[5] my head so hard that my helmet moved.

'Never ever ever again!'

1 Scary

a) Write Tim's next postcard back to his parents.

b) What's the scariest thing that you've ever done? Make notes (what? where? when? who? how?) and tell the class about it.

POST CARD

Dear Mum and Dad

Mr and Mrs R. Parsons,
10 Rainbow Street,
Didcot,
Oxon

With love from Tim
xxxxxxxx to Mum
x to Dad

---

[1] easy-peasy [ˌiːzi ˈpiːzi] *kinderleicht*   [2] brave [breɪv] *mutig*   [3] (to) reach out [riːtʃ] *die Hand ausstrecken*
[4] wet with sweat [wet], [swet] *schweißnass*   [5] (to) shake, shook, shaken [ʃeɪk], [ʃʊk], [ˈʃeɪkən] *schütteln*

Text File **4** 127

TF 9 If you meet a bear ...

Safety in bear country

If you are in the mountain parks, you are in bear country. **Parks Canada** protects the grizzly and black bears that live here.

Here are our bear safety tips.

AVOID[1] BEARS if you can

Here's how...
- Walk in a group of four or more.
- Make noise. This lets the bears know you are coming and gives them time to move away.
- Watch for fresh bear signs: paw prints, droppings[2], diggings[3].
- Never go near a bear. Stay at least 100 metres away.
- Be extra careful during berry[4] time, from late July to mid-September. Berries are a favourite food of bears.

If you meet a bear ...
- Move away slowly. Never run.
- Stay calm and move carefully. This will help to calm the bear and let it know that you are not dangerous.
- If you are in a group, stay together or join other people who are near you.
- If you have bear spray, get it ready.
- Talk to the bear.
- Leave the area. If this is impossible, wait until the bear moves away. Always leave the bear an escape route[5].

1 What to do in bear country
Right or wrong? Say why.
1 The best way to avoid bears is to be quiet.
2 Stay away from bears as far as you can.
3 If you meet a bear, run as fast as you can.
4 Talk to the bear.
5 In June be extra careful.

---

[1] (to) avoid [əˈvɔɪd] *vermeiden; ausweichen*   [2] droppings (pl) *Kot*   [3] diggings (pl) *Stellen, an denen Bären gegraben haben*
[4] berry [ˈberi] *Beere*   [5] escape route [ɪˈskeɪp ruːt] *Fluchtweg*

128 4 Text File

TF 10 Poems – the four seasons[1]

1 Before you read

a) *Write down the names of the four seasons of the year. Add five words that go with each season.*

b) *Swap and compare with a partner.*

c) *Now read the poems. Which poem goes with which season?*

Who has seen the wind?

Who has seen the wind?
  Neither I nor you[2];
But when the leaves hang trembling[3]
  The wind is passing through.

Who has seen the wind?
  Neither you nor I;
But when the trees bow down[4] their heads
  The wind is passing by.

by Christina Rossetti

August heat

In August when the days are hot,
I like to find a shady spot[5],
And hardly[6] move a single bit

  And sit –

    And sit –

      And sit!

anonymous

---

[1] season ['siːzn] *Jahreszeit* [2] neither I nor you [ˈnaɪðə ... nɔː, ˈniːðə ... nɔː] *weder ich noch du* [3] when the leaves hang trembling [ˈtremblɪŋ] *wenn die Blätter zitternd herabhängen* [4] (to) bow down [ˌbaʊ ˈdaʊn] *senken* [5] a shady spot [ˌʃeɪdi ˈspɒt] *ein schattiger Platz* [6] hardly [ˈhɑːdli] *kaum*

The winter is past

For, lo [1], the winter is past,
The rain is over and gone;
The flowers appear on the earth,
The time of the singing of birds is come,
And the voice of the turtle [2]
   Is heard in our land.

from The Song of Solomon

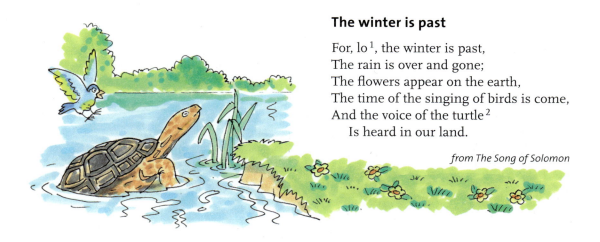

Snow storm

Oh, I am the King of Snowmen,
I've lived here for years and for years.
I've never been slushy [3]
Or melted, or mushy [4],
Or changed to a puddle of tears [5].

Oh, I am the King of Snowmen,
I'm jolly [6] and shiny and fat.
My home, small yet classy,
Has skies blue and glassy
And snowstorms that swirl [7] round my hat.

Oh, I am the King of Snowmen,
I've never been known to complain [8],
But sometimes my world shakes
With TERRIBLE earthquakes –
Take cover! [9] They've started again!

by Clare Bevan

2 Your favourite

a) *Which poem did you like best? Why? Make a few notes.*
I liked … best, because I like the summer/it rhymes/it's funny/easy/…

b) *Make appointments with three partners and compare your notes.*

c) *Learn your favourite poem. Recite it to the class. Say why you like it.*

3 Write your own poem

a) *Write a poem like the one below about one of the seasons. You can use a dictionary.*

  When it's cold and windy outside
   I like it inside:
  No wind, no snow
  Tea and toast and
  English songs on the
  Radio.

b) *Read your poem to the class. You can add a picture and put it in your DOSSIER.*

---

[1] lo [ləʊ] *siehe! seht!* [2] turtle [ˈtɜːtl] *(Wasser-)Schildkröte* [3] slushy [ˈslʌʃi] *matschig* [4] mushy [ˈmʌʃi] *breiig* [5] a puddle of tears [ˈpʌdl], [tɪəz] *eine Tränenpfütze* [6] jolly [ˈdʒɒli] *fröhlich* [7] (to) swirl [swɜːl] *wirbeln* [8] I've never been known to complain [kəmˈpleɪn] *es ist noch nie vorgekommen, dass ich mich beschwert habe* [9] Take cover! [ˈkʌvə] *Geh(t) in Deckung!*

5 Text File

TF 11 FANS – a play   by Ann Cartwright 🎧

1 Before you read
Look at the photo. What are the four teenagers doing? What else can you say about them? What do you think the play could be about?

Now read the play.

Scene:
Four friends are sitting in their form room. The girls are looking at teen magazines. Tim is reading a computer magazine.

Kaz   He's lovely.
5   *Shaz*   He's got lovely hair.
Jaz   Lovely eyes.
Kaz
Shaz ⎱ Ah!
Jaz ⎰
10   *Tim*   Are you talking about me again?
Kaz
Shaz ⎱ No!
Jaz ⎰
Tim   Now you know you are really.
15   *Kaz*
Shaz ⎱ We're not!
Jaz ⎰
Tim   Well, who ARE you on about[1], then?
Shaz   Dermot Devlin!
20   *Jaz*   From the band Celtic Nomads.
Tim   Oh. Him. He's rubbish.
Kaz   He is not!

Tim   He looks like a girl.
Shaz   He does not!   25
Tim   He wears a dress!
Jaz   It's a kaftan, actually. It's ethnic[2].
Tim   You mean hippy.   30
He's stupid. AND he can't sing.
Kaz   I wish he'd walk into the room.[3]
Shaz   I wish he'd walk into the room right   35
now.
Jaz   I wish he'd walk into the room right now – and I'd – and I'd scream.
Kaz
Shaz ⎱ Oo, and *I* would.   40
Tim   What for?
Kaz   Because he's lovely.
Shaz   You just don't understand, Tim. Read your computer magazine.

---

[1] (to) be on about ... *reden von/über ...*   [2] ethnic ['eθnɪk] *exotisch*   [3] I wish he'd walk into the room. [wɪʃ] *etwa: Wenn er (jetzt) hier hereinkäme!*

45	*Jaz*	Yeah. All those hard-drives and mega-nothings.
	Tim	There's more point to this than[1] what you do.
	Jaz	There isn't!
50	*Tim*	There is. At least I can look at these pictures and buy something. You can't look at a picture of Dermot Drill-Head and buy him, can you?
	Kaz	Oo!
55	*Shaz*	Buy Dermot Devlin!
	Jaz	Oo! You've started me off again[2] now!
	Kaz	I'd pay anything[3].
	Tim	But you can't! That's the point. You can't buy him.
60	*Jaz*	We can buy his music.
	Shaz	And videos.
	Kaz	Did you see his latest one?
	Shaz	With him in the boat?
	Jaz	Sailing towards that woman with the flowers in her hair?
65		
	Kaz	And the stars above their heads.
	Shaz	And the breeze flowing softly across the canal.
	Jaz	And he moves that oil-drum out of the way and that big bag of rubbish so that he can get to her.
70		
	Kaz	He's so strong!

	Shaz	He's so romantic.
	Jaz	And singing to her at the same time!
75	*Kaz*	
	Shaz	Wow!
	Jaz	
	Tim	I feel ill.
	Kaz	Oh, shut up.
80	*Shaz*	Have you heard his latest song?
	Jaz	Oh, you mean 'Siren Dream'?
	Shaz	No, no, that was his last one.
	Kaz	Oh, I know the one! 'Tidal Wave Sensation'?
85	*Shaz*	No! That's the CD album. I mean his very latest, 'Flowing From The Heart'.
	Kaz	Oh, yeah! I've heard that one! It's ever so romantic.
90	*Tim*	Got a water fixation[4], hasn't he? Is that because he's a big drip[5]? You do waste your money on that sad singer.
	Jaz	He's not a sad singer! He's THE BUSINESS[6]!
	Tim	It's such a shame[7].
95	*Kaz*	What is?
	Tim	You're just pitiful[8] and totally obsessed[9].
	Shaz	Let's have a look at YOUR magazine, then.
100	*Tim*	Give us that back!

---

[1] there's more point to this than … *das macht mehr Sinn als …*   [2] you've started me off again *etwa: jetzt bringst du mich wieder auf dieses Thema*
[3] anything *hier: alles*   [4] (he's) got a water fixation [fɪkˈseɪʃn] *etwa: der hat wohl einen Wassertick*   [5] a drip [drɪp] *ein Waschlappen, eine Flasche (wörtlich: ein Tropfen)*   [6] the business [ˈbɪznəs] *etwa: er ist DER HIT*   [7] such a shame [ˌsʌtʃˈ_ə ˈʃeɪm] *so ein Jammer, so eine Schande*
[8] pitiful [ˈpɪtɪfl] *jämmerlich*   [9] obsessed [əbˈsest] *besessen*

Kaz — Yeah. Let's see how wonderful it is. Two pounds fifty?! Oh, you do waste your money on this sad computer stuff!

Tim — It's not sad! A madman singer in a dress singing a song about jump-leads to his girlfriend whilst[1] sitting on an oil-drum! Now THAT'S sad!

Jaz — Look at this! Page 14! Wow! New games!

Kaz — 'Deadliest Mortality Blood-Spurt Revenge'[2]? What kind of game's that?

Tim — A really good one.

Shaz — About what?

Tim — Gardening! What do you think?

Jaz — What do you have to do?

Tim — I'm not telling you.

Jaz — Why not?

Tim — 'Cause you'll make fun of me, that's why not.

Kaz — Now why should we make fun of your very serious computer magazine just because you've ripped our beloved Dermot to pieces[3]?

Shaz — We wouldn't do that, would we?

Jaz — Certainly not. We're mature[4].

Kaz — So go on, Tim.

Tim — All right, but you'd better not make fun of it 'cause it's really serious.

Jaz — We won't.

Tim — Well – There's two gangs – The Bloods and the Spurts – and you get to be in one of the gangs and fight the other one.

Kaz —
Shaz — What a load of rubbish!
Jaz —

Tim — I knew it! Shut up!

Kaz — Sounds really boring.

Tim — Boring?! It's brilliant! I've got the whole series.

Shaz — Series? There's more of them?

Tim — Yeah! There's 'Deadliest Mortality Blood-Spurt Revenge: The Beginning' followed by 'Deadliest Mortality Blood-Spurt Revenge: The Battle' followed by 'D.M.B-S.R.: The Hospitalization' followed by –

Jaz — Oh, don't tell me any more!

Kaz — How dreary[5]!

Tim — I'm getting the next one for my birthday! You should see all the stuff I've got. And the posters! And what I really want is a virtual-reality set-up where I can really INTERACT with the gangs!

---

[1] whilst [waɪlst] *während* [2] Deadliest Mortality Blood-Spurt Revenge *Name eines Computerspiels, in dem viel Blut vergossen wird*
[3] (to) rip sth. to pieces [rɪp] *etwas in Stücke reißen* [4] mature [məˈtʃʊə] *reif, vernünftig* [5] dreary [ˈdrɪəri] *öde, langweilig*

	Pause.	
	Kaz	Shame, isn't it?
	Shaz	Yeah. Pitiful.
160	*Kaz*	He's just totally obsessed.
	Tim	Look who's talking![1]
	Kaz	Look out. Teacher's coming.
165	*Shaz*	She'll be in here with her X-Files magazine again.
170	*Jaz*	She's on about that stuff all the time.
	Tim	Was Shakespeare an alien?
175	*Kaz*	Did Wordsworth have a Close Encounter whilst looking at those daffodils?
	Shaz	Now she IS obsessed.
	Kaz	
	Shaz	She's such a fanatic!
	Jaz	
	Tim	

> Say in three or four sentences what the play is about. Were your ideas in **1** right?

2 Right or wrong?

Are the statements right or wrong? Correct the wrong statements.
1. Kaz, Shaz and Jaz are talking about Tim at the beginning of the scene.
2. Tim likes Dermot Devlin.
3. Dermot Devlin is a film star.
4. Kaz, Shaz and Jaz think computer magazines are interesting.
5. Tim thinks the girls are obsessed with Dermot Devlin.
6. Tim likes video games about gardening.
7. The girls don't make fun of Tim.
8. All four make fun of the teacher.

3 Do you agree?

Discuss with a partner.
a) 'It is such a shame (…) You're just pitiful and totally obsessed.' (ll. 94–97)
Do you agree with what Tim says about the three girls? Why (not)?

b) 'Oh, you do waste your money on this sad computer stuff.' (ll. 102–103)
'What a load of rubbish!' (l. 135)
Do you agree with what the three girls say about Tim? Why (not)?

4 Act out the play

Make groups of eight. Four students learn the first half of the play (pp. 130–131), four learn the second half (pp. 132–133). Perform the play for your class.

---

[1] *Look who's talking! Das musst du/müsst ihr gerade sagen!*

Skills File – Inhalt

Seite

STUDY AND LANGUAGE SKILLS

REVISION	Understanding new words	134
REVISION	Learning words	135
	Using an English-German dictionary	136
	Using a German-English dictionary	137
REVISION	Describing pictures	138
REVISION	Giving a presentation	138

LISTENING AND READING SKILLS

REVISION	Listening	139
REVISION	Multiple-choice exercises	139
REVISION	Scanning	140
	Skimming	141
REVISION	Taking notes	142
REVISION	Marking up a text	142

MEDIATION SKILLS

Mediation	143

SPEAKING AND WRITING SKILLS

Paraphrasing		144
Brainstorming		145
WRITING COURSE	Zusammenfassung	146–147

Im **Skills File** findest du Hinweise zu Arbeits- und Lerntechniken. Was du in den Skills-Kästen der Units gelernt hast, wird hier näher erläutert.

Was du bereits aus Band 2 von English G 21 kennst, ist mit **REVISION** gekennzeichnet, z. B.

– **REVISION Understanding new words**, Seite 134
– **REVISION Learning words**, Seite 135.

Viele neue Hinweise helfen dir bei der Arbeit mit Hör- und Lesetexten, beim Sprechen, beim Schreiben von eigenen Texten, bei der Sprachmittlung und beim Lernen von Methoden.

Manchmal gibt es auch Aufgaben dazu.

STUDY AND LANGUAGE SKILLS

SF REVISION   Understanding new words

Immer gleich im Wörterbuch nachschlagen?

Das Nachschlagen unbekannter Wörter im Wörterbuch kostet Zeit und nimmt auf Dauer den Spaß am Lesen. Oft geht es auch ohne Wörterbuch!

Was hilft mir, unbekannte Wörter zu verstehen?

1. Bilder zeigen oft die Dinge, die du im Text nicht verstehst. Schau sie dir deshalb vor dem Lesen genau an.

2. Oft hilft dir der Textzusammenhang, also die Wörter, die vor oder nach dem unbekannten Wort stehen, z. B. *We must hurry. Our train departs in ten minutes.*

3. Viele englische Wörter werden ähnlich wie im Deutschen geschrieben oder klingen ähnlich, z. B. **wonderful**, **electrician**, **president**.

4. Manchmal stecken in neuen Wörtern bekannte Teile, z. B. **arrival**, **a westbound train**, **friendly**, **snowshoes**.

• Alles klar ? Dann überlege, was diese Wörter bedeuten:
  hilly • imaginary • head of state • a winning shot • useful • canal •
  material • realistic • colony • official

Skills File **135**

SF REVISION   Learning words

Worauf solltest du beim Lernen und Wiederholen von Vokabeln achten?

- Führe dein Vokabelverzeichnis, dein Vokabelheft oder deinen Karteikasten aus Klasse 6 weiter.
- Lerne immer 7–10 Vokabeln auf einmal.
- Lerne neue und wiederhole alte Vokabeln regelmäßig – am besten jeden Tag 5–10 Minuten.
- Lerne mit jemandem zusammen. Fragt euch gegenseitig ab oder übt die Wörter mit Lernspielen (z. B. Vokabel-Domino, Schiffe versenken, Quartett, *Vocabulary Action Sheets*).
- Du weißt nach zwei Jahren Englischlernen wahrscheinlich, mit welchen Methoden du am besten Vokabeln lernst: durch Hören und Nachsprechen, durch Bilder, am Computer (z. B. mit deinem *e-Workbook* oder dem *English Coach*) – oder indem du dir eigene Geschichten um die neuen Vokabeln ausdenkst, sie in Texte einbaust oder dich beim Vokabellernen in deinem Zimmer oder der Wohnung bewegst.
- Schreib die neuen Wörter immer auch auf und überprüfe die Schreibweise mithilfe des *Dictionary* oder *Vocabulary*.

Wie kannst du Wörter besser behalten?

Wörter und Wendungen kannst du besser behalten, wenn du sie in Wortgruppen sammelst und ordnest. Dazu gibt es verschiedene Möglichkeiten.

Du kannst …

- **Gegensatzpaare** sammeln, z. B.
  old-fashioned – modern
  spicy – mild
  forget – remember
  sad – happy
  happy – unhappy

old-fashioned   modern   spicy   mild

- Wörter mit **gleicher Bedeutung** sammeln, z. B.
  (to) train – (to) practise; film – movie

- Wörter in **Wortfamilien** sammeln, z. B.
  – shop, shopper, shopping, shopping list, shop assistant
  – (to) ride (a horse/bike), (to) go riding, a bike ride,
  (to) take a ride, riding boots, riding hat

- Wörter in **Wortnetzen** (*networks*)
  sammeln und ordnen.

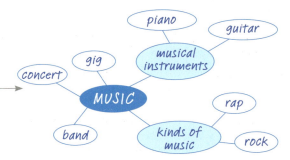

SF Using an English-German dictionary ▶ Unit 1 (p. 26)

Wann brauche ich ein englisch-deutsches Wörterbuch?

Du verstehst einen Text nicht, weil er zu viele Wörter enthält, die dir unbekannt sind? Dann hilft dir ein englisch-deutsches Wörterbuch weiter.
Im Text „Only a game" (S. 26–28) kommen auch Wörter vor, die du nicht kennst und die auch nicht in den EG 21-Wörterverzeichnissen aufgeführt sind, z. B. *experimental*, *at your own risk*, *togas*, *blow up*, *smelly*, *rat*, *God*, *voice*, *cried*. Einige dieser Wörter kannst du sicherlich ableiten oder aus dem Zusammenhang erschließen. Wenn das nicht geht, hilft dir ein englisch-deutsches Wörterbuch.

Play <u>at your own risk</u>.

Then he shouted.
'Rats!'

'They started the fire! Stop them!' another <u>voice</u> shouted.

Wie benutze ich ein englisch-deutsches Wörterbuch?

- Die **Leitwörter** (*running heads*) oben auf der Seite helfen dir, schneller zu finden, was du suchst. Auf der linken Seite steht das erste Stichwort, auf der rechten Seite das letzte Stichwort der Doppelseite.

- **rise** ist das **Stichwort** (*headword*). Stichwörter sind alphabetisch geordnet: **r** vor **s**, **ra** vor **re**, **rhe** vor **rhi** usw.

- Die *kursiv gedruckten* Hinweise helfen dir, die für deinen Text passende Bedeutung zu finden.

- Die **Ziffern 1, 2** usw. zeigen, dass ein Stichwort unterschiedlichen Wortarten angehören kann (z.B. Adjektiv, Nomen, Verb).

- **Beispielsätze** und **Redewendungen** sind dem Stichwort zugeordnet. In den Beispielsätzen und Redewendungen ersetzt eine **Tilde** (~) das Stichwort.

- Die **Lautschrift** gibt Auskunft darüber, wie das Wort ausgesprochen und betont wird (→ *English sounds, p. 229*).

- **Unregelmäßige Verbformen**, **besondere Pluralformen**, die **Steigerungsformen der Adjektive** und ähnliche Hinweise stehen in Klammern.

> **riveting**
> **rink** [rɪŋk] Eisbahn
> **rinse** [rɪns] **1** *Nomen*; *für Haare* Tönung **2** *Verb mit Obj*; *Kleidung*, *Haare* ausspülen; *Geschirr* (ab)spülen
>
> **rise** [raɪz] **1** *Verb ohne Obj* (**rose**, **risen**) *aus Stuhl o. Ä.* aufstehen, sich erheben; *von Sonne* aufgehen; *von Rakete* aufsteigen; *von Preis, Temperatur* ansteigen; *von Wasseroberfläche* (an)steigen **2** *Nomen*; *von Preis, Temperatur* Anstieg; *von Wasseroberfläche* (An)Steigen; *von Sozialismus* Aufstieg; *von Gehalt* Gehaltserhöhung; *give ~ to* verursachen
> **risen** [ˈrɪzn] *Part. Perf.* ☞ **rise**
> **riser** [ˈraɪzə]: *be an early / late ~* ein Frühaufsteher / Langschläfer sein
> **risk** [rɪsk] **1** *Nomen* Risiko; *take a ~* ein Risiko eingehen; *at one's own ~* auf eigene Gefahr **2** *Verb mit Obj* riskieren; *let's ~ it* das Risiko gehen wir ein!
> **risky** [ˈrɪski] (*-ier, -iest*) riskant
> **ritual** [ˈrɪtjʊəl] **1** *Nomen* Ritual **2** *Adj* rituell
> **rival** [ˈraɪvl] **1** *Nomen* Rivale, Rivalin; *von Firma, Mannschaft* Konkurrent(in) **2** *Verb mit Obj* (*-ll-*, *AE -l-*) *Person* rivalisieren mit; *Firma*, *Mannschaft* konkurrieren mit; *I can't ~ that* da kann ich nicht mithalten
> **rivalry** [ˈraɪvlri] (*Pl -ies*) Rivalität; zwi-

- Finde nun heraus, was die folgenden Wörter und Wendungen bedeuten:
  1. *at your own risk*
  2. *'rose'* in *'The rocket rose into the sky.'*
  3. *'rises'* in *'The sun rises in the east.'*
  4. *blow up*
  5. *voice*

- In deinem Wörterbuch werden vermutlich viele Abkürzungen und Symbole verwendet, wie z. B.
  jn.
  Obj
  Pl
  USA
  Finde heraus, was sie bedeuten.

Skills File **137**

SF Using a German-English dictionary ▶ Unit 2 (p. 35)

Wann brauche ich ein deutsch-englisches Wörterbuch?

Stell dir vor, du sollst einen Text über Katrina schreiben. Du findest, dass die Situation im Internat schwer für sie ist. Aber wie drückt man das auf Englisch aus? Was heißt „schwer" in diesem Fall?
Hier hilft dir ein deutsch-englisches Wörterbuch.

Wie benutze ich ein deutsch-englisches Wörterbuch?

Viele Dinge sind dir wahrscheinlich vom **English-German dictionary** dictionary vertraut:

- **Leitwörter** (*running heads*) oben auf den Seiten helfen dir, das gesuchte Wort schneller zu finden.

- Die **Stichwörter** (*headwords*) sind alphabetisch geordnet. **Beispielsätze** und **Redewendungen** sind den Stichwörtern zugeordnet. Die **Tilde** (~) ersetzt das Stichwort.

- Die **kursiv gedruckten** Hinweise helfen dir, die für deinen Text passende Bedeutung zu finden.

- Die **Ziffern 1, 2** usw. zeigen, dass ein Stichwort unterschiedlichen Wortarten angehören kann (z.B. Adjektiv, Nomen, Verb).

- Bei schwierig auszusprechenden Wörtern stehen auch Hinweise zu Aussprache und Betonung.

- Bei kniffligen Wörtern gibt es in vielen Wörterbüchern weitere Hilfen und Hinweise.

Schwester

schwer 1 *Adj*; *gewichtsmäßig* heavy ['hevi] (*auch Musik, Parfüm*); *schwierig* difficult, hard (*auch Arbeit*); *Wein, Zigarre* strong; *Essen* rich; *Krankheit, Fehler, Unfall, Schaden* serious ['sɪərɪəs]; *Strafe* severe; *Gewitter, Kämpfe, Ausschreitungen* heavy, violent; *schwere Zeiten* hard times; **100 Pfund ~ sein** weigh [weɪ] 100 pounds; *es ~ haben* have a hard time; *das ist ~ zu sagen* it's hard to say 2 *Adv*: *~ arbeiten* work hard; *~ beschädigt Haus o.Ä.* severely damaged; *ich bin ~ erkältet* I've got a bad cold; *er ist ~ zu verstehen* it's hard to understand what he's saying; *~ enttäuscht sein* be* bitterly disappointed; *das will ich ~ hoffen* I really hope so; ☞ **schwerfallen, schwertun**

Schwerkraft
☞ **schwer ma**ancholy ['mel..
Schwerpunkt
gen (main) e..
legen put* th..
Schwert sword
schwertun: *sic*..
culty with sth.
Schwerverbrec..
offender
schwerverwun..
schwerwiegen..
['sɪərɪəs]
Schwester sist..
als Anrede

schwer krank

schwer
Das deutsche **schwer** hat drei Hauptbedeutungen:
1) *schwer von Gewicht*: **heavy**;
2) *schwerwiegend, ernst*: **serious, bad**;
3) *schwierig*: **difficult, hard, tough**.

- Welche Entsprechung von **schwer** brauchst du in diesen Sätzen?
  1. Das Leben im Internat ist schwer für Katrina.
  2. Schultaschen sind für jüngere Schüler häufig zu schwer.
  3. Heute Morgen war ein schwerer Unfall auf der Autobahn.
  4. Die Matheaufgabe ist sehr schwer.
  5. Nach einer schweren Krankheit kann er wieder zur Schule gehen.
  6. Letzte Nacht gab es ein schweres Gewitter.

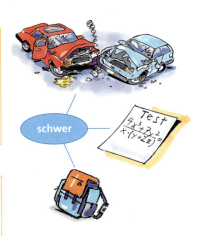

Tipp
Lies immer erst den **gesamten Wörterbucheintrag**, bevor du dich für eine bestimmte Übersetzung entscheidest. Nimm nicht einfach die erste Übersetzung, die dir angeboten wird!

SF REVISION   Describing pictures

Wie kann ich Bilder beschreiben?

Wo?
- Um zu sagen, wo etwas abgebildet ist, benutze:
  at the top/bottom • in the foreground/background •
  in the middle • on the left/right
- Du kannst diese *phrases* auch kombinieren:
  at the bottom on the left • at the top on the right
- Diese Präpositionen sind auch hilfreich:
  behind • between • in front of • next to • under

Wie?
Geh bei der Beschreibung in einer bestimmten Reihenfolge vor, z. B. von links nach rechts, von oben nach unten oder vom Vordergrund zum Hintergrund.

Wie kann ich beschreiben, was die Personen auf dem Bild tun?

Um zu sagen, was die Personen auf dem Bild tun, benutze das **present progressive**.
Robert and Asif are standing inside the London Eye. Robert is taking a photo.

SF REVISION   Giving a presentation

Wie mache ich eine gute Präsentation?

Vorbereitung
- Schreib die wichtigsten Gedanken gut geordnet als Notizen auf, z. B. auf nummerierte Karteikarten oder als Mindmap.
- Bereite ein Poster oder eine Folie vor. Schreib groß und für alle gut lesbar.
- Übe deine Präsentation zu Hause vor einem Spiegel. Sprich laut, deutlich und langsam, mach Pausen.

Durchführung
- Bevor du beginnst, häng das Poster auf bzw. leg deine Folie auf den ausgeschalteten Projektor und sortiere deine Vortragskarten.
- Warte, bis es ruhig ist. Schau die Zuhörer an.
- Erkläre zu Anfang, worüber du sprechen wirst. Lies nicht von deinen Karten ab, sondern sprich frei.

My presentation is about …
First, I'd like to talk about …
Second, …

This picture/photo/… shows …

Schluss
- Sag, dass du fertig bist.
- Frag die Zuhörenden, ob sie Fragen haben. Bedanke dich fürs Zuhören.

That's the end of my presentation. Have you got any questions?

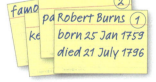

LISTENING AND READING SKILLS

SF REVISION Listening ▶ Unit 1 (p. 13)

Was muss ich beim *listening* beachten?

Vor dem Hören
- Überlege, worum es in dem Hörtext gehen wird. Frag dich, was du schon über das Thema weißt.
- Lies die Aufgabe gut durch, damit du weißt, worauf du achten sollst – auf die Hauptgedanken oder auf bestimmte Informationen wie z. B. einen Namen, eine Uhrzeit, eine Jahreszahl.
- Bereite dich darauf vor, Notizen zu machen. Leg z. B. eine Tabelle oder Liste an.

Beim Hören
- Keine Panik! Du musst nicht alles verstehen. Konzentriere dich auf das Wesentliche. Oft werden wichtige Informationen auch wiederholt.
- Achte auf Geräusche und unterschiedliche Stimmen. Was ein Sprecher/eine Sprecherin besonders betont, das ist wichtig!
- Wenn du gezielt Informationen suchst, denk an die Aufgabe und lass dich nicht von anderen Einzelheiten ablenken.
  Aufgepasst! Die Informationen, die du suchst, kommen vielleicht in einer anderen Reihenfolge vor, als du sie erwartest.
- Manche Signalwörter helfen dir, den Hörtext zu verstehen.
  Aufzählung: **and**, **another**, **too**
  Gegensatz: **although**, **but**
  Grund, Folge: **because**, **so**, **so that**
  Reihenfolge: **before**, **after**, **then**, **next**, **later**, **when**, **at last**, **at the same time**
- Mach nur kurze Notizen, z. B. Anfangsbuchstaben, Symbole oder Stichworte, keine ganzen Sätze.

Nach dem Hören
- Vervollständige deine Notizen sofort.
- Konzentriere dich beim erneuten Hören auf das, was du nicht sicher verstanden hast.

SF REVISION Multiple-choice exercises

Worauf sollte ich bei Multiple-Choice-Aufgaben achten?

- Lies die Frage oder den Satz sehr genau durch.
- Manchmal fällt dir die Lösung sofort ein. Dann findest du die Bestätigung in den Auswahlantworten.
- Lies in jedem Fall alle vorgegebenen Lösungen, bevor du dich entscheidest.
- Sprich die Sätze mit den verschiedenen Lösungsmöglichkeiten leise nach. Oft hört man heraus, was richtig ist.
- Achte darauf, dass du nur **eine** der Antworten ankreuzt.
- Mach erst alle Aufgaben und geh zum Schluss zu den Fragen zurück, bei denen du unsicher bist.

1 Which is a famous London sight?
   A Brandenburg Gate
   B Eiffel Tower
   C Buckingham Palace
   D the Orkney Islands

2 What did Robert and Asif do at the Trocadero?
   A play football
   B eat Indian food
   C visit Asif's family
   D play a new game

SF REVISION Scanning

Lesen, um nach Informationen zu suchen

Du brauchst einen Text nicht genau zu lesen, wenn du nur bestimmte Informationen benötigst. Suche den Text nach Schlüsselwörtern (**key words**) ab und lies nur dort genauer, wo du sie findest.

Manchmal sind in Aufgaben Schlüsselwörter vorgegeben, nach denen du in einem Text suchen sollst. So möchte Asif z. B. in A6 auf S. 16 *something spicy or very spicy*. Auf der Speisekarte findest du dazu solche Speisen unter TIKKA und JALFREZI DISHES, d. h. du brauchst nur dort weiterzusuchen.

Wie gehe ich vor?

Schritt 1: Bevor du auf den Text schaust
Denk an das Schlüsselwort, nach dem du suchst. Es hilft dir, wenn du es aufschreibst.

Schritt 2: Das Schlüsselwort finden
Geh mit deinen Augen sehr schnell durch den Text. Dabei hast du das Schriftbild oder das Bild des Wortes, nach dem du suchst, vor Augen. Das gesuchte Wort wird dir sofort „ins Auge springen".
Du kannst auch mit dem Finger durch den Text gehen: in breiten Schlingen oder Bewegungen wie bei einem „S", „Z" oder „U".
Wenn du das Schlüsselwort gefunden hast, lies nur dort weiter, um Näheres zu erfahren.

Schritt 3: Gegebenenfalls neue Schlüsselwörter finden
Es kann passieren, dass das Schlüsselwort, nach dem du suchst, im Text nicht vorkommt. Dann musst du überlegen, welche anderen Wörter mit der benötigten Information zu tun haben, und nach diesen suchen. Stell dir z. B. vor, du suchst auf einer Speisekarte ein Gericht mit Fleisch. Das Wort *meat* steht aber nirgends. Dann versuch es z. B. mit *lamb*, *chicken* oder *pork*.

> **Tipp**
>
> Wenn du wie bei Aufgabe 6 auf S. 16 nach mehreren Schlüsselwörtern suchen musst, scanne den Text nach jedem Schlüsselwort einzeln.

Skills File 141

SF Skimming ▶ Unit 5 (p. 90)

Lesen, um sich einen Überblick zu verschaffen

Skimming bedeutet, dass du in kurzer Zeit einen Text überfliegst, um dir einen ersten Überblick zu verschaffen, worum es geht. Das ist z. B. sehr nützlich, wenn du herausfinden willst, ob ein Text, den du im Internet oder in einem Buch gefunden hast, die Informationen enthält, nach denen du (z. B. für ein Referat) suchst.

Wie gehe ich vor?

Wichtige Informationen über den Text geben dir

– die **Überschrift**

– **hervorgehobene** Wörter oder Sätze

– die **Bilder** und **Bildunterschriften**

– die **Zwischenüberschriften**

– der **erste Satz** jedes Absatzes

– der **letzte Satz** des Textes

– **Grafiken** und **Statistiken**

– die **Quelle** des Textes

'Hello Glasgow! It's good to be home!'
Franz Ferdinand play fantastic gig in their home town

Review by J. Colthorpe

They have come a long way since they started out playing gigs in Glasgow's local indie clubs back in 2001. Two successful albums and a world tour later, Franz Ferdinand are one of the most popular bands in the world today. But last night they were back playing in their hometown, Glasgow, and this time to a much larger audience than they did six years ago.

Franz Ferdinand get Glasgow dancing

Electric atmosphere
The atmosphere outside the concert hall was electric. The crowd were excited and many fans were already singing their favourite Franz Ferdinand songs. Inside the place was full and noisy; people were pushing through the crowds, hoping to get near the stage. Soon the support band had finished and it was time for Franz Ferdinand to take to the stage.

All the favourite hits
'Hello Glasgow! It's good to be home!' shouted singer Alex Kapranos as he ran onto the stage. The crowd cheered as Alex started with "Jacqueline", the first song off their first album. He was soon joined by Bob Hardy on bass guitar as the song kicked in followed by Paul Thomsen on the drums. All of their popular songs followed to make up a 16-song, 90-minute set. They finished with their classic "Take Me Out" – the perfect song to end an excellent show.

Not only girls
Franz Ferdinand once said that they want to make music that girls can dance to. Well, they have certainly done that; last night everybody was dancing, girls and boys.

New Amsterdam Music Review 18th December 2007

- Überflieg den Artikel, um herauszufinden, worum es darin geht.
- Dann löse die Aufgabe 3 auf Seite 96.

142 Skills File

SF REVISION Taking notes

Worum geht es beim Notizenmachen?

Wenn du beim Lesen oder Zuhören Notizen machst, kannst du dich später besser daran erinnern, wenn du etwas vortragen, nacherzählen oder einen Bericht schreiben sollst.

Wie mache ich Notizen?

In Texten oder Gesprächen gibt es immer wichtige und unwichtige Wörter. Die wichtigen Wörter werden Schlüsselwörter (**key words**) genannt und nur die solltest du notieren. Meist sind das Substantive und Verben, manchmal auch Adjektive oder Zahlen.

> **Tipp**
> - Verwende Ziffern (z. B. „7" statt „seven").
> - Verwende Symbole und Abkürzungen, z. B. ✔ (für Ja) und **+** (für und) oder GB für Great Britain, K. für Katrina.
>   Du kannst auch eigene Symbole erfinden.
> - Verwende **not** oder ✗ statt „doesn't" oder „don't".

Hmm, da hab ich wohl ein paar Symbole zu viel benutzt …

SF REVISION Marking up a text

Wann sollte ich einen Text markieren?

Du hast einen Text mit vielen Fakten vor dir liegen und sollst später über bestimmte Dinge berichten. Dann wird es dir helfen, die für dich wichtigen Informationen im Text zu markieren.

Wie gehe ich am besten vor?

Lies den Text und markiere nur die für dein Thema wichtigen Informationen. Nicht jeder Satz enthält für deine Aufgabe wichtige Wörter und oft reicht es aus, nur ein oder zwei Wörter in einem Satz zu markieren.

– Du kannst wichtige Wörter einkreisen.

– Du kannst sie unterstreichen.

– Du kannst sie mit einem Textmarker hervorheben.

ABER:
Markiere nur auf Fotokopien von Texten oder in deinen eigenen Büchern.

The **British Museum** has one of the largest and most fascinating collections of (mummies) in the world outside of Cairo. The collection of mummies shows the visitor the unusual way the Egyptian people (prepared the dead Pharaoh)s before they

The **British Museum** has one of the largest and most fascinating collections of mummies in the world outside of Cairo. The collection of mummies shows the visitor the unusual way the Egyptian people prepared the dead Pharaohs before they

The **British Museum** has one of the largest and most fascinating collections of mummies in the world outside of Cairo. The collection of mummies shows the visitor the unusual way the Egyptian people prepared the dead Pharaohs before they

MEDIATION SKILLS

SF Mediation 1

REVISION Wann muss ich zwischen zwei Sprachen vermitteln?

Manchmal musst du zwischen zwei Sprachen vermitteln. Das nennt man **mediation**.

1. Du gibst englische Informationen auf Deutsch weiter:
   Du fährst z. B. mit deiner Familie nach Großbritannien und deine Eltern oder Geschwister wollen wissen, was jemand in einem Café gesagt hat oder was an einer Informationstafel steht.

2. Du gibst deutsche Informationen auf Englisch weiter:
   Vielleicht ist bei dir zu Hause eine Austauschschülerin aus England oder Dänemark zu Gast, die kein Deutsch spricht und Hilfe braucht.

3. In schriftlichen Prüfungen musst du manchmal in einem englischen Text gezielt nach Informationen suchen und diese auf Deutsch wiedergeben.

REVISION Worauf muss ich bei *mediation* achten?

– Übersetze nicht alles wörtlich.
– Gib nur das Wesentliche weiter, lass Unwichtiges weg.
– Verwende kurze und einfache Sätze.
– Wenn du ein Wort nicht kennst, umschreibe es oder ersetze es durch ein anderes Wort. ▶ *Mediation 2*

SF Mediation 2   ▶ Unit 4 (p. 80)

Was kann ich tun, wenn ich ein wichtiges Wort nicht kenne?

Vielleicht findest du es manchmal schwer, mündliche Aussagen oder schriftliche Textvorlagen in die andere Sprache zu übertragen, z. B. weil:
– dein Wortschatz nicht ausreicht
– dir bekannte Wörter „im Stress" nicht einfallen
– spezielle Fachbegriffe auftauchen.

Manche Wörter kannst du umschreiben, z. B. mithilfe von Sätzen wie:
It's somebody/a person who …
It's something that you use to …
It's an animal that …
It's a place where …

▶ *Paraphrasing (S. 144)*

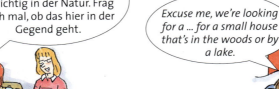

SPEAKING AND WRITING SKILLS

SF Paraphrasing ▶ Unit 3 (p. 56)

Worum geht es beim Paraphrasing?

Paraphrasing bedeutet, etwas mit anderen Worten zu erklären. Man kann vieles umschreiben, z. B. einen Gegenstand, eine Tätigkeit oder eine Person. Paraphrasing ist auch besonders nützlich für **mediation** ▶ Mediation (S. 143)

Wie gehe ich beim Paraphrasing vor?

– Man kann mit einem Wort umschreiben, das dieselbe Bedeutung hat:
  to begin is the same as to start
  Oder man sagt das Gegenteil:
  to win is the opposite of to lose

– Manchmal braucht man mehrere Wörter, z. B. wenn man etwas beschreibt oder erklären will, wie man es verwendet. Dabei benutzt man ein allgemeines Wort (**general word**) und nennt weitere Eigenschaften:
  A half-pipe is a place for skateboarders.

– Oder du beginnst mit **It's like …**:
  It's like a path through the woods or the fields and you can ride on it. (*a bridle path*)

– Du kannst zum Umschreiben auch ein allgemeines Wort nehmen (z. B. **a person**, **something**) und das wird mit einem durch **who**, **that** oder **where** eingeleiteten Satz näher erklärt:
  A coach is a person who trains sports teams.
  A swimsuit is something that girls wear when they go swimming.
  A bakery is a place where people can buy bread and rolls.

---

1. Umschreibe ein Wort aus der linken Spalte mit einem Wort aus der rechten Spalte. Benutze **the same as** oder **the opposite of**.

sad	parents
white	happy
clean	black
brilliant	dirty
mother/father	great

2. Schau dir diese Umschreibungen an. Findest du ein passendes Wort dafür?
  – It's a man or woman who looks funny and works in a circus.
  – It's something you put food on.
  – It's a place where you watch films.
  – It's something that you use to play table tennis.

3. What's wrong here? Correct the sentences.
  – A horse is a place where lots of supporters go to watch a match.
  – A stadium is a meal that you eat in the evening.
  – Dinner is an animal you can ride on.

Skills File **145**

SF Brainstorming ▶ Unit 4 (p. 71)

Wofür ist Brainstorming gut?

Write a text about a great weekend oder *Prepare a presentation on …* – so oder so ähnlich lauten viele Aufgaben, die dir im Unterricht gestellt werden. Immer wenn du selbst etwas schreiben oder präsentieren sollst, ist es nützlich, wenn du im ersten Schritt möglichst viele Ideen zum Thema sammelst. Dabei hilft dir das Brainstorming.

Wie gehe ich beim Brainstorming vor?

Brainstorming erfolgt in zwei Schritten:

Schritt 1:
Schreib alle Ideen so auf, wie sie dir einfallen. Es ist zunächst völlig egal, ob die Ideen gut sind oder nicht. Du kannst die Ideen durcheinander auf einen Zettel schreiben oder schon etwas geordnet, z. B. jede Idee auf eine neue Zeile.

Schritt 2:
Wenn du fertig bist, lies alle deine Ideen durch und wähle die besten aus. Sortiere deine Ideen und fasse sie sinnvoll zusammen.
Beim Sortieren und Zusammenfassen kannst du z. B. die folgenden Techniken anwenden. Sie kommen dir sicher bekannt vor:

no homework
sleep – every morning
watch DVDs
disco/party with friends
swimming pool
no jobs for parents
parents not at home
hang out

Making a mind map
1. Schreib das Thema in die Mitte eines leeren, unlinierten Blattes Papier. Male einen Kreis oder eine Wolke drum herum.
2. Überlege dir, welche Oberbegriffe zu deiner Sammlung von Ideen passen. Verwende unterschiedliche Farben.
3. Ergänze jede Idee, die zu einem Oberbegriff passt, auf einem Nebenast. Nimm dafür nur wichtige Schlüsselwörter. Du kannst auch Symbole verwenden und Bilder ergänzen.

The 5 Ws
Schreib die 5 W-Fragen **Who? What? When? Where? Why?** in eine Tabelle. Die Ideen, die dir zu der jeweiligen Frage kommen, werden darunter geschrieben.

who	what	when	where	why
I + friends	do sports	Friday	at home	no homework
no parents	go to disco	Saturday	at friends'	no jobs to do
	chat		swimming pool	have fun

146 Skills File

WRITING COURSE – ZUSAMMENFASSUNG

The steps of writing

1. Brainstorming – erst Ideen sammeln, dann sortieren (s. S.145).
2. Schreiben. Dabei achte darauf,
   – deine Sätze zu verbinden und auszubauen (*Writing better sentences*)
   – deinen Text gut zu strukturieren (*Using paragraphs*)
   – bei einem Bericht die 5 Ws abzudecken (*Writing a report*).
3. Deinen Text inhaltlich und sprachlich überprüfen (*Correcting your text*).

Writing better sentences ▶ *Unit 1 (p. 22)*

REVISION Linking words

Eine Geschichte klingt interessanter, wenn man die Sätze mit **linking words** miteinander verbindet. Dabei gibt es mehrere Möglichkeiten:
– **Time phrases** wie **at 7 o'clock, every morning, a few minutes later, then, next** ...
– **Konjunktionen** wie **although, and, because, but, so ... that, when, that, while**
– **Relativpronomen** wie **that** und **who**. ▶ *Unit 3 (p.55)*

Adjektive und Adverbien

– Mit Adjektiven kannst du Personen, Orte oder Erlebnisse genauer und interessanter beschreiben. Vergleiche: **The man looked into the room.**
  ▶ **The young man looked into the empty room.**
– Mit Adverbien kannst du beschreiben, **wie** jemand etwas macht:
  The young man looked nervously into the empty room.

Using paragraphs ▶ *Unit 2 (p. 40)*

REVISION Structuring a text

Ein Text ist viel besser zu verstehen, wenn er mehrere Absätze enthält:
– eine Einleitung (**beginning**) – hier schreibst du, worum es geht
– einen Mittelteil (**middle**) – hier schreibst du mehr über dein Thema
– einen Schluss (**end**) – hier bringst du den Text zu einem interessanten Ende.

REVISION Topic sentences

Am Anfang eines Absatzes sind kurze, einleitende Sätze (**topic sentences**) gut, weil sie den Lesern sofort sagen, worum es geht, z. B.
1. Orte: **My trip to ... was fantastic. / ... is famous for ... / ... is a great place.**
2. Personen: **... is great/funny/interesting/clever ...**
3. Aktivitäten: **... is great fun. / Lots of people ... every day.**

Wie kann ich meine Absätze interessant gestalten?

– Beginne mit einem interessanten Einstiegssatz:
  Guess what happened to me today! / Did I tell you that ...?
– Fang für jeden neuen Aspekt einen neuen Absatz an.
– Beende deinen Text mit einer Zusammenfassung oder etwas Persönlichem.

Writing a report – collecting and organizing ideas ▶ Unit 3 (p. 64)

Worauf kommt es bei einem Bericht an?

Wenn du einen Bericht (z. B. über ein Spiel, einen Ausflug) schreibst, beachte:
– Gib dem Leser **eine schnelle Orientierung**, was passiert ist.
– Beginne mit **wichtigen Informationen** und gib erst dann Detailinformationen.
– Ein Bericht gibt immer Antworten auf die **5 Ws**:
   Who? What? When? Where? Why? und manchmal auch How?
– Verwende das **simple past**.

Correcting your text ▶ Unit 5 (p. 98)

Ein Text ist noch nicht „fertig", wenn du ihn zu Ende geschrieben hast. Du solltest ihn immer mehrmals durchlesen:
– einmal, um zu sehen, ob er vollständig und gut verständlich ist
– noch einmal, um ihn auf Fehler zu überprüfen.

REVISION Spelling mistakes

Lies deinen Text langsam, Wort für Wort, Buchstabe für Buchstabe. Wenn du unsicher bist, hilft dir ein Wörterbuch. Beachte folgende Regeln:

tomato [təˈmɑːtəʊ], *pl* tomatoes Tomate II

wife [waɪf], *pl* wives [waɪvz] Ehefrau II

drop (-pp-) [drɒp] fallen lassen I

forget (-tt-) [fəˈget] vergessen I

> **Tipp**
>
> Manche Wörter haben Buchstaben, die man nicht spricht, aber schreibt, z. B. **walk**, **know**.
> Manchmal ändert sich die Schreibweise, wenn ein Wort eine Endung erhält, z. B. take → **taking**, grumble → **grumbled**, happy → **happily**, fly → **flies** (**aber** stay → **stays**), run → **running**, plan → **planned**.

> **Tipp**
>
> – Im **simple present** wird in der 3. Person Singular **-s** angehängt: **she knows**.
> – **Unregelmäßige Verben**: Manche Verben bilden das *simple past* und das Partizip Perfekt (*past participle*) unregelmäßig. Lerne diese Formen. Die Liste steht auf S. 232–233: **go – went – gone; buy – bought – bought**.
> – **Verneinung bei Vollverben**: Im *simple present* mit **don't/doesn't**, im *simple past* mit **didn't**, z. B. **He doesn't speak French, he didn't learn it at school.**
> – **Satzstellung**: Im Englischen gilt immer (auch im Nebensatz):
>   a) subject – verb – object (SVO) … **when I saw my brother.**
>   **als ich meinen Bruder sah.**
>   b) Orts- vor Zeitangabe **I bought a nice book in the city yesterday.**

> **Tipp**
>
> Führe eine Liste der Fehler, die du oft machst und nutze sie beim Schreiben als persönliche Checkliste. Ergänze sie wenn dein Lehrer/deine Lehrerin dich auf weitere Fehler aufmerksam macht. – Ein Beispiel findest du in
> ▶ Unit 5 (p. 98)

148 Grammar File

Grammar File – Inhalt

Seite

Unit 1   **GF 1**   **The present perfect and the simple past in contrast**   **149**
Das *present perfect* und das *simple past* im Vergleich
    a) REVISION **The simple past**   Die einfache Form der Vergangenheit
    b) REVISION **The present perfect**   Das *present perfect*
    c) **Present perfect or simple past?**   *Present perfect* oder *simple past*?

Unit 2   **GF 2**   **The *will*-future for spontaneous decisions**   Das Futur mit *will* für spontane Entschlüsse   **150**
    a) REVISION **The *will*-future**   Das Futur mit *will*
    b) **Spontaneous decisions**   Spontane Entschlüsse
    GF 3   **Conditional sentences**   Bedingungssätze   **151**
    a) REVISION **Conditional sentences (type 1)**   Bedingungssätze (Typ 1)
    b) **Conditional sentences (type 2)**   Bedingungssätze (Typ 2)

Unit 3   **GF 4**   **Relative clauses**   Relativsätze   **152**
    GF 5   **Contact clauses**   Relativsätze ohne Relativpronomen   **153**

Unit 4   **GF 6**   **Modals and their substitutes**   Modale Hilfsverben und ihre Ersatzverben   **154**
    a) „können": *can – (to) be able to*
    b) „dürfen": *can, may – (to) be allowed to*
    c) „müssen": *must – (to) have to*
    GF 7   **The present progressive with future meaning**
    Das *present progressive* mit futurischer Bedeutung   **155**
    GF 8   **Reflexive pronouns**   Reflexivpronomen   **155**
    GF 9   **Reflexive pronoun or *each other*?**   Reflexivpronomen oder *each other*?   **156**

Grammatical terms (Grammatische Fachbegriffe)   **157**

Lösungen der Grammar-File-Aufgaben   **158**

Im **Grammar File** (S. 148–158) wird zusammengefasst, was du in den fünf Units **über die englische Sprache** lernst.

In der **linken Spalte** findest du **Beispielsätze** und **Übersichten**, z.B.

You can protect **yourself** without the hunt. A bear just wants to feed **itself** and its babies.

Reflexive pronouns

Singular
    myself   (ich) mir/mich
    yourself   (du) dir/...

In der **rechten Spalte** stehen **Erklärungen** und nützliche **Hinweise**. Das **rote Ausrufezeichen** (!) macht dich auf besondere Fehlerquellen aufmerksam.

Hinweise wie ▶ Unit 1 (p. 15) • P 4–5 (p. 21) zeigen dir, zu welcher Unit und welcher Seite ein **Grammar-File**-Abschnitt gehört und welche Übungen du dazu im *Practice*-Teil findest.

Die **grammatischen Fachbegriffe** (*grammatical terms*) kannst du auf den Seiten 157–158 nachschlagen.

Am Ende der Abschnitte stehen wieder kleine Aufgaben zur Selbstkontrolle. Schreib die Lösungen in dein Heft. Überprüfe sie dann auf Seite 158.

Unit 1
GF 1 The present perfect and the simple past in contrast
Das *present perfect* und das *simple past* im Vergleich

a) REVISION The simple past

Last weekend Robert **went** to London with his parents.

In the afternoon they **visited** the Tower, and then they **took** the Tube to Waterloo.

Asif **met** them at the London Eye and they all **had** a great time.

▶ Unit 1 (p. 15) • P 4–5 (p. 21)

Die einfache Form der Vergangenheit

Mit dem **simple past** berichtest du über Vergangenes – z. B., wenn du eine Geschichte erzählst.
Das *simple past* drückt aus, dass etwas zu einem **bestimmten Zeitpunkt** oder **in einem bestimmten abgeschlossenen Zeitraum** in der Vergangenheit geschah. (Frage: **Wann?**)
Daher findest du in *simple past*-Sätzen oft **genaue Zeitangaben** wie *last weekend, yesterday, a week ago, in 2005*.

b) REVISION The present perfect

Asif **has** already **visited** the London Trocadero.
… hat schon mal … besucht

He **has always wanted** to go on the London Eye, but he **hasn't done** that **yet**.
… hat schon immer … gehen wollen
… hat … noch nicht getan

He and his friends **have** often **been** to Brick Lane Market.
… sind schon oft … gewesen

▶ Unit 1 (p. 16) • P 8–9 (p. 23)

Das *present perfect*

Mit dem **present perfect** drückst du aus, dass etwas **irgendwann in der Vergangenheit** geschehen ist. Daher findest du oft **Adverbien der unbestimmten Zeit** in *present perfect*-Sätzen, z. B.

already	schon (mal)	always	(schon) immer
just	gerade (eben)	never	(noch) nie
not … yet	noch nicht	often	(schon) oft
ever?	jemals?	yet?	schon?

! Beim *present perfect* ist der genaue Zeitpunkt des Geschehens nicht wichtig oder nicht bekannt.

c) Present perfect or simple past?

1 Have you ever tried Turkish food?
Yes, I have.
2 And when did you try it?
3 We went to a Turkish restaurant last Saturday.

▶ Unit 1 (p. 17) • P 11–12 (p. 24)

Present perfect oder *simple past*?

◀ 1 Asif fragt, ob Robert **überhaupt schon mal** türkisch gegessen hat – also **present perfect**:

Have you *ever* **tried** Turkish food?

◀ 2 Dann möchte er wissen, **wann** das war, und er fragt daher im *simple past*:

And **when did** you **try** it?

◀ 3 Robert antwortet im *simple past*, weil er den **genauen Zeitpunkt** nennt:

We **went** to a Turkish restaurant *last Saturday*.

Present perfect *oder* simple past? *Schreib den vollständigen Dialog in dein Heft.*

A ... you ever (visit) the Tower of London?
B Yes, I ...
A When ... you (go) there?
B We ... (go) in the summer holidays last year.
But I ... (see) Buckingham Palace yet.
A Oh, I ... (visit) that with my aunt und uncle a few months ago.

Unit 2
GF 2 The *will*-future for spontaneous decisions
Das Futur mit *will* für spontane Entschlüsse

---

a) REVISION The *will*-future

Katrina's mum (Vorhersage)	Hurry up, Katrina! We'll be late for the ferry.
Katrina (Vermutung)	No, we won't. I'm ready now. And I think the ferry will be a few minutes late anyway.

▶ Unit 2 (p. 32) • P 4 (p. 39)

Das Futur mit *will*

Mit *will* + Infinitiv kannst du über die Zukunft sprechen. Du verwendest es für Vorhersagen und Vermutungen.

Die Kurzform von *will not* heißt *won't*.

---

b) Spontaneous decisions

Which bags do you mean, Fiona?

The bags from the magazine. I'll **show** you ... here, look.

Die Taschen aus der Zeitschrift.
Ich zeig sie dir ... hier, schau.

▶ Unit 2 (p. 34)

Spontane Entschlüsse

Du verwendest das *will-future* auch, wenn du einen spontanen (nicht geplanten) Entschluss fasst. Oft handelt es sich dabei um Hilfsangebote oder Versprechen.

! Im Deutschen steht bei einem spontanen Entschluss meist die Gegenwart. Im Englischen muss das *will-future* stehen:
I'**ll show** you ...
Ich **zeig** sie dir ...

Wait ... I'll take the boxes.

GF 3 Conditional sentences   Bedingungssätze

a) REVISION Conditional sentences (type 1)

Alison   **If** they **choose** you, you**'ll be** a star.
Wenn sie dich wählen, bist du … /
Wenn sie dich wählen, wirst du … sein.

Linda   **If** I **don't get** to the shop soon,
they **won't have** those trendy new bags
any more.

▶ Unit 2 (p. 34) • P 9 (p. 42)

Bedingungssätze (Typ 1)

Du kennst bereits Bedingungssätze vom Typ 1
(**„Was ist, wenn …"**-Sätze).
Sie sagen aus, was unter bestimmten Bedingungen
geschieht oder nicht geschieht:

if-Satz (Bedingung)	Hauptsatz (Folge)
If they **choose** you,	you**'ll be** a star.
simple present	**will-future**

b) Conditional sentences (type 2)

If a film-maker **chose**
me for one of his films,
I **would be** famous.

Wenn ein Filmemacher mich für
einen seiner Filme auswählen würde,
wäre ich berühmt / würde ich berühmt.

I **wouldn't live** here
if I **was** rich and famous.

Ich würde nicht hier wohnen,
wenn ich reich und berühmt wäre.

▶ Unit 2 (p. 35) • P 10–12 (p. 42)

If I **had** enough money, I **could buy** a new bike.
Wenn ich genug Geld hätte, könnte ich mir ein neues
Rad kaufen.

Bedingungssätze (Typ 2)

Bedingungssätze vom Typ 2 sind
„Was wäre, wenn …"-Sätze.
Sie drücken aus, was unter bestimmten Bedingungen
sein würde, aber doch eher unwahrscheinlich ist (oder
sogar unmöglich):

Es ist unwahrscheinlich, dass Fiona von einem Filmemacher ausgewählt werden wird. Also wird sie wahrscheinlich auch nicht berühmt.

if-Satz (Bedingung)	Hauptsatz (Folge)
If a film-maker **chose** me,	I **would be** famous.
simple past	**would + infinitive**

(Kurzform von *I/you/he/…* would: *I'd / you'd / he'd / …*)

! Im *if*-Satz steht **kein** *would*.
Also nicht:
If a film-maker ~~would choose~~ me, …

Im Hauptsatz kann auch *could* („könnte") stehen.

Vervollständige die Sätze in deinem Heft. Achte auf die richtige Form der Verben.

1 If the other girls … (call) Latisha names, she wouldn't listen.
2 Latisha would forget the girls if she … (be) Katrina.
3 Katrina … (be) much happier if the girls … (call) her Fishface.
4 If the girls … (be) friendly to her, she … (be) upset.
5 If people … (call) you Fishface, you … (be) upset too. Right?
6 What would you do if classmates … (call) you names?

3 Grammar File

Unit 3
GF 4 Relative clauses   Relativsätze

The girl who plays for United U14s is Latisha.
Das Mädchen, das für die U14 von *United* spielt, …
 	
Philipp is **an exchange student** who is staying with Latisha.
… ein Austauschschüler, der bei Latisha wohnt.
 	
Banglaboy is **a boy** who Latisha knows from the festival in Birmingham.
… ein Junge, den Latisha vom Festival … kennt.
 	
There's still **some Maths** that she has to do.
… etwas Mathematik, die sie noch machen muss.
 	
Mrs Byrd has cooked **a dish** that Philipp likes.
… ein Gericht, das Philipp mag.
	Mit Relativsätzen sagst du genauer, wen oder was du meinst.
	
	◂ In Relativsätzen, die **Personen** beschreiben, verwendest du *who*:
	   the man / the woman / people *who* …
	   der Mann, der … / die Frau, die … / Leute, die …
	
	◂ In Relativsätzen, die **Dinge** (und Tiere) beschreiben, verwendest du *that*:
	   the dish / an animal *that* …
	   das Gericht, das … / ein Tier, das …

… **a dish** which Philipp likes **The girl** that plays for United U14s …	Für Dinge (und Tiere) wird auch *which* verwendet. Und manchmal findest du auch *that* für Personen.
The girl **who plays** football … Das Mädchen, **das Fußball spielt** …	❗ Beachte die unterschiedliche Wortstellung in englischen und deutschen Relativsätzen.

▸ Unit 3 (p. 55) • P 4–6 (pp. 61–62)

Wo brauchst du who, *wo brauchst du* that?

1 Philipp is the German boy … is staying with Latisha.
2 Latisha thinks new age kurling is a sport … everybody can do.
3 What's the name of the player … scored two goals in United U14s' last match?
4 Stewed chicken is a dish … comes from Trinidad, isn't it?

Grammar File **3** 153

GF 5 Contact clauses — Relativsätze ohne Relativpronomen

1 An artist is somebody **who** paints pictures.
   ..., **der** Bilder malt.

Das Relativpronomen kann **Subjekt** oder **Objekt** sein.

1 Das Relativpronomen ist **Subjekt des Relativsatzes** (es steht direkt vor dem Verb):

	Subjekt	
An artist is somebody	**who**	paints pictures.
Ein Künstler ist jemand,	**der**	Bilder malt.
The Lowry is a museum	**that**	has something for everybody.
Das Lowry ist ein Museum,	**das**	für jeden etwas hat.

2 Beckham is the only player **who** Philipp knows.
   ..., **den** Philipp kennt.

2 Das Relativpronomen ist **Objekt** des Relativsatzes:

	Objekt	Subjekt	
Beckham is the only player	**who**	Philipp	knows.
Beckham ist der einzige Spieler,	**den**	Philipp	kennt.
Football is a sport	**that**	Latisha	loves.
Fußball ist ein Sport,	**den**	Latisha	liebt.

I don't like football much. David Beckham is the only **player I know**.

Football is a **sport I love**. The **stadium you see** over there is Old Trafford.

◀ Wenn *who* oder *that* **Objekt** des Relativsatzes ist, wird es manchmal **weggelassen** – wie in den Beispielen links.
Relativsätze ohne Relativpronomen nennt man *contact clauses*.

❗ Achtung:
Wenn das **Relativpronomen direkt vor dem Verb** steht, ist es Subjekt – dann darfst du es **nicht** weglassen!

An artist is somebody who paints pictures.
(*not*: An artist is somebody paints pictures.)

The **boy Latisha is chatting with** is Banglaboy.
Der Junge, mit dem Latisha chattet, ist Banglaboy.

The **stadium they are looking at** is Old Trafford.

▶ Unit 3 (p.56) • P 7 (p.62)

❗ Beachte die Stellung der Präposition in Relativsätzen mit Verben wie *talk to, chat with, look at, stay with*. Die Präposition steht an derselben Stelle wie im Hauptsatz:
    Latisha is chatting with Banglaboy.
The boy **Latisha is chatting with** is Banglaboy.

Wo kannst du who *und* that *weglassen? Schreib die Sätze als* contact clauses *in dein Heft.*

1 Philipp is the boy who is staying with the Byrds.
2 Which is the museum that the whole family will love?
3 Football and new age kurling are sports that Latisha likes a lot.
4 David Beckham is a football star who everybody knows.
5 Lowry is an artist who came from Manchester.
6 Let's do something that we both want to do.

Unit 4
GF 6 Modals and their substitutes — Modale Hilfsverben und ihre Ersatzverben

Wenn du sagen willst, dass jemand etwas tun **kann**, **darf** oder **muss**, dann verwendest du *can, may, must* oder ihre **Ersatzverben**:

a) „können": can – (to) be able to

Katrina can play the fiddle.
Robert doesn't play an instrument,
but he's able to DJ.   kann auflegen

Robert was ill last Saturday,
so he wasn't able to DJ.   konnte nicht auflegen

Do you think he'll be able to DJ
at Ashley's party?   wird auflegen können

I could hear music, but I couldn't see anybody.
Ich konnte Musik hören, aber ich konnte niemanden sehen.

„können": can – (to) be able to

- **Gegenwart** (wenn jemand etwas tun **kann**):
  can und *am/is/are able to*

- **Vergangenheit** (wenn jemand etwas tun **konnte**):
  was/were able to

- **Zukunft** (wenn jemand etwas tun **können wird**):
  will be able to

Zu *can* gibt es auch die Vergangenheitsform *could*. Sie steht vor allem in verneinten Sätzen und Fragen und mit Verben der Wahrnehmung (*see, hear, …*).

b) „dürfen": can, may – (to) be allowed to

Can/May I go to Ashley's party, Mum?
Are you allowed to go to Ashley's
party on Saturday?   Darfst du … gehen?

Emily wasn't allowed to go to the
youth centre last month.   durfte nicht gehen

But she'll be allowed to go to Ashley's
party on Saturday.   wird gehen dürfen

„dürfen": can, may – (to) be allowed to

- **Gegenwart** (wenn jemand etwas tun **darf**):
  can, may und *am/is/are allowed to*

- **Vergangenheit** (wenn jemand etwas tun **durfte**):
  was/were allowed to

- **Zukunft** (wenn jemand etwas tun **dürfen wird**):
  will be allowed to

c) „müssen": must – (to) have to

'OK, you can go. But you must be back by ten.'
Emily can go to the party,
but she has to be back by ten.   muss zurück sein

Emily was allowed to go to the party, but
she had to be back by ten.   musste zurück sein

Emily will have to stay at home tomorrow
evening.   wird bleiben müssen

▶ Unit 4 (p. 70) • P 4–5 (p. 77)

„müssen": must – (to) have to

- **Gegenwart** (wenn jemand etwas tun **muss**):
  must und *has/have to*

- **Vergangenheit** (wenn jemand etwas tun **musste**):
  had to

- **Zukunft** (wenn jemand etwas tun **müssen wird**):
  will have to

Vervollständige den Dialog. Es geht um Ashleys Party am kommenden Wochenende.

Emily   My parents are so strict. I'm sure I … (not be allowed to) go to Ashley's party.
Jessica   Well, I'm sure I … (have to) be home by ten again, as always.
Robert   I … (not be able to) go to the party.

Grammar File **4**   155

GF 7 The present progressive with future meaning
Das *present progressive* mit futurischer Bedeutung

I can't come to the phone. **I'm washing** my hair. … Ich wasche mir gerade die Haare.	Das *present progressive* verwendest du, wenn jemand gerade dabei ist, etwas zu tun.
Robert **is doing** a gig on Friday, and he and his parents **are driving** to their cabin on Saturday morning. So Robert **isn't going** to Ashley's party at the weekend. Robert hat am Freitag einen Auftritt, und er und seine Eltern fahren am Samstagmorgen zu ihrer Hütte. Daher wird Robert am Wochenende nicht zu Ashleys Party gehen. ▶ Unit 4 (p. 71) • P 6 (p. 77)	Du kannst mit dem *present progressive* auch über **feste Pläne** und **Verabredungen** sprechen. Dabei muss klar sein, dass es sich um etwas Zukünftiges handelt, z.B. durch eine Zeitangabe wie *on Friday, next week, at the weekend, tomorrow*.

Welche festen Verabredungen hat Robert am Wochenende?

1 On Friday night I … (DJ).
2 On Saturday morning I … (drive) to our cabin with my parents.
3 And on Sunday morning I … (go) fishing with my dad.

GF 8 Reflexive pronouns   Reflexivpronomen

We have to protect **ourselves** from the bears.

You can protect **yourself** without the hunt. **A bear** just wants to feed **itself** and its babies.

Reflexivpronomen (*ourselves, itself, yourself, …*) bezeichnen dieselbe Person oder Sache wie das Subjekt (*we, a bear, you, …*):

Subjekt → **Reflexivpronomen**

We have to protect **ourselves** from the bears.
A bear just wants to feed **itself** and its babies.

Wir müssen uns vor den Bären schützen.
Ein Bär will nur sich und seine Babys ernähren.

Reflexive pronouns

Singular			Plural		
	myself	(ich) mir/mich		ourselves	(wir) uns
	yourself	(du) dir/dich		yourselves	(ihr) euch
	himself	(er) sich		themselves	(sie) sich
	herself	(sie) sich			
	itself	(er/sie/es) sich			

Don't **argue**! **Relax**! Just **imagine** how terrible you would **feel** if you killed a bear!

▶ Unit 4 (p. 72) • P 8–9 (p. 79)

Einige Verben, die im Deutschen mit „sich" gebraucht werden, stehen im Englischen ohne Reflexivpronomen.
Beispiele:
(to) argue	sich streiten
(to) feel	sich fühlen
(to) imagine sth.	sich etwas vorstellen
(to) relax	sich entspannen

(Weitere Beispiele ▶ *Vocabulary*, S. 177)

Schreib die Sätze in dein Heft. In welchen Sätzen brauchst du ein Reflexivpronomen?

1 Do you know how you can protect … from a bear?
2 If you see a bear, don't move … quickly. Walk away slowly.
3 If I saw a bear, I would hide …
4 Bears just want to feed … and their babies.

GF 9 **Reflexive pronoun or *each other*?**   Reflexivpronomen oder *each other*?

Robert and Asif are taking photos of **themselves**.
Robert und Asif machen Fotos von sich (selbst).

Für „**sich**" im Sinne von „**sich selbst**" benutzt du die Pronomen auf **-self/-selves**:
I – myself, he – himself, they – themselves usw.

◀ Robert und Asif machen Fotos von sich selbst – Robert fotografiert sich selbst, und Asif fotografiert sich selbst.

Now they are taking photos of **each other**.
Jetzt fotografieren sie sich gegenseitig. / Jetzt machen sie Fotos voneinander.

▶ Unit 4 (p. 73) • P 10 (p. 79)

Für „**sich**" im Sinne von „**sich gegenseitig**" oder „**einander**" benutzt du **each other**.

◀ Robert und Asif fotografieren sich gegenseitig – Robert fotografiert Asif, und Asif fotografiert Robert.

(Statt *each other* wird auch *one another* verwendet: *Now they are taking photos of one another*.)

Sieh dir die Bilder an. Schreib zu jedem Bild einen kurzen Satz. Brauchst du themselves *oder* each other*?*

1 (laugh at)
They're laughing …

2 (teach – German)
They're teaching …

3 (hurt)
They've hurt …

4 (talk to)
They're …

Grammar File 157

Grammatical terms (Grammatische Fachbegriffe)

adjective ['ædʒɪktɪv]	Adjektiv	*good, red, new, boring, ...*
adverb ['ædvɜːb]	Adverb	*always, badly, here, really, today*
adverb of frequency ['friːkwənsi]	Häufigkeitsadverb	*always, often, never, ...*
adverb of indefinite time [ɪn,defɪnət 'taɪm]	Adverb der unbestimmten Zeit	*already, ever, just, never, ...*
adverb of manner ['mænə]	Adverb der Art und Weise	*badly, happily, quietly, well, ...*
auxiliary [ɔːg'zɪliəri]	Hilfsverb	*be, have, do; will, can, must, ...*
comparison [kəm'pærɪsn]	Steigerung	*old – older – oldest*
conditional sentence [kən,dɪʃənl 'sentəns]	Bedingungssatz	*I'd call him if I knew his number.*
conjunction [kən'dʒʌŋkʃn]	Konjunktion	*and, or, but; because, before, ...*
contact clause ['kɒntækt klɔːz]	Relativsatz ohne Relativpronomen	*She's the girl **I love**.*
future ['fjuːtʃə]	Zukunft, Futur	
going to-**future**	Futur mit *going to*	*I**'m going to watch** TV tonight.*
if-**clause** ['ɪf klɔːz]	*if*-Satz, Nebensatz mit *if*	***If I see Robert**, I'll tell him.*
imperative [ɪm'perətɪv]	Imperativ (Befehlsform)	*Open your books. Don't talk.*
infinitive [ɪn'fɪnətɪv]	Infinitiv (Grundform des Verbs)	*(to) open, (to) see, (to) read, ...*
irregular verb [ɪ,regjələ 'vɜːb]	unregelmäßiges Verb	*(to) go – went – gone*
main clause	Hauptsatz	*I like **Scruffy** because I like dogs.*
modal, modal auxiliary [,məʊdl_ɔːg'zɪliəri]	modales Hilfsverb, Modalverb	*can, could, may, must, ...*
negative statement [,negətɪv 'steɪtmənt]	verneinter Aussagesatz	*I don't like bananas.*
noun [naʊn]	Nomen, Substantiv	*Sophie, girl, brother, time, ...*
object ['ɒbdʒɪkt]	Objekt	*My sister is writing **a letter**.*
object form ['ɒbdʒɪkt fɔːm]	Objektform (der Personalpronomen)	*me, you, him, her, it, us, them*
past [pɑːst]	Vergangenheit	
past participle [,pɑːst 'pɑːtɪsɪpl]	Partizip Perfekt	*cleaned, planned, gone, seen, ...*
past progressive [,pɑːst prə'gresɪv]	Verlaufsform der Vergangenheit	*At 7.30 I **was having** dinner.*
person ['pɜːsn]	Person	
personal pronoun [,pɜːsənl 'prəʊnaʊn]	Personalpronomen (persönliches Fürwort)	*I, you, he, she, it, we, they; me, you, him, her, it, us, them*
plural ['plʊərəl]	Plural, Mehrzahl	
positive statement [,pɒzətɪv 'steɪtmənt]	bejahter Aussagesatz	*I like oranges.*
possessive determiner [pə,zesɪv dɪ'tɜːmɪnə]	Possessivbegleiter (besitzanzeigender Begleiter)	*my, your, his, her, its, our, their*
possessive form [pə,zesɪv fɔːm]	s-Genitiv	*Jo's brother; my sister's room*
possessive pronoun [pə,zesɪv 'prəʊnaʊn]	Possessivpronomen	*mine, yours, his, hers, ours, theirs*
preposition [,prepə'zɪʃn]	Präposition	*after, at, in, next to, under, ...*
present ['preznt]	Gegenwart	
present perfect [,preznt 'pɜːfɪkt]	*present perfect*	*We**'ve made** a cake for you.*
present progressive [,preznt prə'gresɪv]	Verlaufsform der Gegenwart	*The Byrds **are having** lunch.*
pronoun ['prəʊnaʊn]	Pronomen, Fürwort	
pronunciation [prə,nʌnsi'eɪʃn]	Aussprache	
question ['kwestʃən]	Frage(satz)	
question tag ['kwestʃən tæg]	Frageanhängsel	*This place is great, **isn't it**?*
question word ['kwestʃən wɜːd]	Fragewort	*what?, when?, where?, how?, ...*
regular verb [,regjələ 'vɜːb]	regelmäßiges Verb	*(to) help – helped – helped*
reflexive pronoun [rɪ,fleksɪv 'prəʊnaʊn]	Reflexivpronomen	*myself, yourself, themselves, ...*
relative clause [,relətɪv 'klɔːz]	Relativsatz	*There's the girl **who helped me**.*
relative pronoun [,relətɪv 'prəʊnaʊn]	Relativpronomen	*who, that, which*
short answer [,ʃɔːt_'ɑːnsə]	Kurzantwort	*Yes, I am. / No, I don't. / ...*
simple past [,sɪmpl 'pɑːst]	einfache Form der Vergangenheit	*Jo **wrote** two letters yesterday.*
simple present [,sɪmpl 'preznt]	einfache Form der Gegenwart	*I always **go** to school by bike.*

singular ['sɪŋgjələ]	Singular, Einzahl	
spelling ['spelɪŋ]	Schreibweise, Rechtschreibung	
subject ['sʌbdʒɪkt]	Subjekt	*My sister is writing a letter.*
subject form ['sʌbdʒɪkt fɔːm]	Subjektform (der Personalpronomen)	*I, you, he, she, it, we, they*
subordinate clause [sə,bɔːdɪnət 'klɔːz]	Nebensatz	*I like Scruffy **because I like dogs**.*
verb [vɜːb]	Verb	*hear, open, help, go, ...*
will-**future**	Futur mit *will*	*I think it **will be** cold tonight.*
word order ['wɜːd ,ɔːdə]	Wortstellung	
yes/no question	Entscheidungsfrage	*Are you 13? Do you like comics?*

Lösungen der Grammar-File-Aufgaben

p.150
Have you ever **visited** the Tower of London? – Yes, **I have.**
When **did** you **go** there? – We **went** in the summer holidays last year.
But I **haven't seen** Buckingham Palace yet.
Oh, I **visited** that with my aunt and uncle a few months ago.

p.151
1 If the other girls **called** Latisha names, she **wouldn't** listen.
2 Latisha would forget the girls if she **was** Katrina.
3 Katrina **would be** much happier if the girls **didn't call** her 'Fishface'.
4 If the girls **were** friendly to her, she **wouldn't be** upset.
5 If people **called** you 'Fishface', you **would be** upset too. Right?
6 What would you do if classmates **called** you names?

p.152
1 Philipp is the German boy **who** is staying with Latisha.
2 Latisha thinks new age kurling is a sport **that** everybody can do.
3 What's the name of the player **who** scored two goals in United U14s' last match?
4 Stewed chicken is a dish **that** comes from Trinidad, isn't it?

p.153
2 (Which is the museum the whole family will love?)
3 (Football and new age kurling are sports Latisha likes a lot.)
4 (David Beckham is a football star everybody knows.)
6 (Let's do something we both want to do.)

p.154
My parents are so strict. I'm sure I **won't be allowed to** go to Ashley's party.
Well, I'm sure I **will have to** be home by ten again, as always.
I **won't be able to** go to the party.

p.155
1 On Friday night **I'm DJing.**
2 On Saturday morning **I'm driving** to our cabin with my parents.
3 And on Sunday morning **I'm going** fishing with my dad.

p.156/1
1 Do you know how you can protect **yourself** from a bear?
2 If you see a bear, don't move quickly. Walk away slowly.
3 If I saw a bear, I would hide.
4 Bears just want to feed **themselves** and their babies.

p.156/2
1 They're laughing at **each other.**
2 They're teaching **themselves** German.
3 They've hurt **themselves.**
4 They're talking to **each other.**

Vocabulary | 159

Diese Wörterverzeichnisse findest du in deinem Englischbuch:

- Das **Vocabulary** (Vokabelverzeichnis – S. 159–180) enthält alle Wörter und Wendungen, die du lernen musst. Sie stehen in der Reihenfolge, in der sie in den Units vorkommen.
- Das **Dictionary** besteht aus zwei alphabetischen Wörterlisten zum Nachschlagen:
  Englisch – Deutsch: S. 181–204
  Deutsch – Englisch: S. 205–225.

So ist das Vocabulary aufgebaut:

- Hier siehst du, wo die Wörter vorkommen.
  p. 54/A 1 = Seite 54, Abschnitt 1
  p. 60/P 2 = Seite 60, Übung 2

- Die Lautschrift zeigt dir, wie ein Wort ausgesprochen und betont wird.
  (→ Englische Laute: S. 229)

- Eingerückte Wörter lernst du am besten zusammen mit dem vorausgehenden Wort, weil die beiden zusammengehören.

- Diese Kästen solltest du dir besonders gut ansehen.

Tipps zum Wörterlernen findest du im Skills File auf Seite 135.

p.54/A1	(to) **spot** (-tt-) [spɒt]	entdecken	I can't fin
	2 **all**	2 beide (2:2 unentschieden)	
p.60/P2	(to) **score (a goal)** [skɔː], [gəʊl]	ein Tor schießen, einen Treffer erzielen	We won : – Smith
	score [skɔː]	Spielstand; Punktestand	

A football match

What's the score now? – 2–0. *(you say:* **two nil**) ... Wie steht e:
What was the final score? – Chelsea 2, Arsenal 1. ... Wie war der End:
Our last match was a draw, 2–2. *(you say:* **two all**) ... Unser letz

Word field: Sports

EQUIPMENT [ɪˈkwɪpmənt] Ausrüstung ... LO

skis [skiːz]

Abkürzungen:

n	= noun	v	= verb
adj	= adjective	adv	= adverb
prep	= preposition	conj	= conjunction
pl	= plural	no pl	= no plural
p.	= page	pp.	= pages
sb.	= somebody	sth.	= something
jn.	= jemanden	jm.	= jemandem
AE	= American English	BE	= British English
infml	= informal (umgangssprachlich, informell)		

Symbole:

! Hier stehen Hinweise auf Besonderheiten, bei denen man leicht Fehler machen kann.

◄► ist das „Gegenteil"-Zeichen: **slow** ◄► **fast**
(**slow** ist das Gegenteil von **fast**)

~ Die **Tilde** in den Beispielsätzen steht für das neue Wort.
Beispiel: **youth** – In her ~ my grandma was very beautiful.

Introduction

| p.6 | **introduction (to)** [ˌɪntrəˈdʌkʃn] | Einführung (in) | This book is a good ~ **to** a difficult topic. |
| | **youth** [juːθ] | Jugend | the time when you are young
In her ~ my grandma was very beautiful. |
	national [ˈnæʃnəl]	national	**national** ◄► **international**
	festival [ˈfestɪvl]	Fest, Festival, Festspiele	At a ~ you can see lots of bands.
	the United Kingdom (UK) [juːˌnaɪtɪd ˈkɪŋdəm], [juː ˈkeɪ]	das Vereinigte Königreich	**!** **the UK** = Great Britain (England, Scotland, Wales) and Northern Ireland *(Nordirland)*
	from **all over** the UK / the world / England	aus dem gesamten Vereinigten Königreich / aus der ganzen Welt / aus ganz England	Madonna is famous **all over** the world. (= auf der ganzen Welt)

Tipps zum Wörterlernen → S. 135 · Englische Laute → S. 229 · Alphabetische Wörterverzeichnisse → S. 181–204 / S. 205–225

160 Vocabulary **Introduction**

Numbers

Im Englischen steht oft ein **Komma** in Zahlen, die größer als 1 000 sind.	**10,000**	= ten thousand
	10,400	= ten thousand four hundred
❗	**10.4**	= ten **point** four (*deutsch:* 10,4 = zehn **Komma** vier)
	1,100,000	= one million one hundred thousand
❗	**1.1 million**[1]	= one **point** one million (*deutsch:* 1,1 Millionen)

[1] ['mɪljən]

	brilliant ['brɪliənt]	genial, toll	That's ~! You've always got great ideas.
	kind (of) [kaɪnd]	Art	What ~ of music do you like? – Rock music.
			❗ Was für ein Auto ...? = What **kind of** car ...?
	classical ['klæsɪkl]	klassisch	Do you like Mozart? – Oh yes! I love ~ music.
	concert ['kɒnsət]	Konzert	❗ Betonung auf der 1. Silbe: **concert** ['kɒnsət]
	(to) DJ ['diː dʒeɪ]	(Musik/CDs/Platten) auflegen (in der Disko)	noun: **DJ (disc jockey)** – verb: (to) **DJ**
	(to) take part (in) [teɪk 'pɑːt]	teilnehmen (an)	How many people ~ ~ **in** the show?
	workshop ['wɜːkʃɒp]	Workshop, Lehrgang	
	steel drum [ˌstiːl 'drʌm]	Steeldrum	**steel drums**
	steel [stiːl]	Stahl	
	drum [drʌm]	Trommel	❗ (to) **play the drums** (*pl*) = Schlagzeug spielen
p.7	**fiddle** ['fɪdl] (*infml*)	Fiedel, Geige	❗ (to) **play the fiddle** = Geige spielen
	north [nɔːθ]	Norden; nach Norden; nördlich	

north [nɔːθ]	
north-west [ˌnɔːθ'west]	**north-east** [ˌnɔːθ'iːst]
west [west]	**east** [iːst]
south-west [ˌsaʊθ'west]	**south-east** [ˌsaʊθ'iːst]
south [saʊθ]	

p.8	**hostel** ['hɒstl]	Herberge, Wohnheim; Internat	A youth ~ is usually cheaper than a hotel.
	instrument ['ɪnstrəmənt]	Instrument	❗ Betonung auf der ersten Silbe: **instrument** ['ɪnstrəmənt]
	boss [bɒs]	Chef/in, Boss	
	gig [gɪg] (*infml*)	Gig, Auftritt	❗ (to) **do a gig** = einen Auftritt haben, ein Konzert geben
p.9	**mixture** ['mɪkstʃə]	Mischung	
	western ['westən]	westlich, West-	France is one of the biggest countries in ~ Europe.
p.10	**the United States (US)** [juˌnaɪtɪd 'steɪts], [juː_'es]	die Vereinigten Staaten (von Amerika)	
	How about ...?	Wie wär's mit ...?	= What about ...?
	hungry ['hʌŋgri]	hungrig	❗ Ich **habe Hunger**. = I'**m hungry**.
	Nice to meet you.	Nett, dich kennenzulernen.	

Classroom English → S.236 · Personen-, Orts- und Ländernamen → S.226–228 · Unregelmäßige Verben → S.230–231

Vocabulary 1

p.11	half an hour [ˌhɑːf_ən_ˈaʊə]	eine halbe Stunde	❗ Word order: **half an hour** – **eine halbe Stunde**
	half [hɑːf], *pl* **halves** [hɑːvz]	Hälfte	I felt ill and spent ~ of the day in bed.
	(to) **mail** [meɪl]	schicken, senden *(per Post oder E-Mail)*	Julie **~ed** her friends some photos of her birthday party.
	(to) **keep in touch** [ˌkiːp_ɪn ˈtʌtʃ], **kept, kept** [kept]	in Verbindung bleiben, Kontakt halten	It was nice to meet you. – Yes, let's **keep in ~**.
	Wait and see!	Wart's ab!	What's for dinner this evening? – **Wait and ~!**
	recording [rɪˈkɔːdɪŋ]	Aufnahme, Aufzeichnung	
	(to) **go with**	gehören zu, passen zu	The first text **goes ~** the third picture.
	electric [ɪˈlektrɪk]	elektrisch, Elektro-	
	flute [fluːt]	Querflöte	
	recorder [rɪˈkɔːdə]	Blockflöte	
	saxophone [ˈsæksəfəʊn]	Saxophon	
	trumpet [ˈtrʌmpɪt]	Trompete	
	violin [ˌvaɪəˈlɪn]	Violine, Geige	

Unit 1: My London

p.12	**capital** [ˈkæpɪtl]	Hauptstadt	Berlin is the **~** of Germany.
	PS [ˌpiːˈes] (**postscript** [ˈpəʊstskrɪpt])	PS *(Nachschrift unter Briefen)* (Postskript)	
	big wheel [ˌbɪg ˈwiːl]	Riesenrad	
	wheel [wiːl]	Rad	A bike has two **~s**.
	high [haɪ]	hoch	What's the **~est** mountain in the world?
	parliament [ˈpɑːləmənt]	Parlament	❗ Schreibung: **parliament** Betonung auf der 1. Silbe: **par**liament [ˈpɑːləmənt]
	sound file [ˈsaʊnd faɪl]	Tondatei, Soundfile	
	trendy [ˈtrendi]	modisch, schick	
	second-hand [ˌsekənd ˈhænd]	gebraucht; aus zweiter Hand	❗ I bought it **second-hand**. = … **aus** zweiter Hand
p.13	**gate** [geɪt]	Tor	
	royal [ˈrɔɪəl]	königlich	
	queen [kwiːn]	Königin	Elizabeth II is the **Queen** of the UK. (you say: Elizabeth the second)
	open-air [ˌəʊpən_ˈeə]	im Freien; Freilicht-	**~~** concerts/festivals/theatres
	air [eə]	Luft	

Tipps zum Wörterlernen → S.135 · Englische Laute → S.229 · Alphabetische Wörterverzeichnisse → S.181– 204 / S.205–225

162 1 Vocabulary

main [meɪn]	Haupt-	the ~ idea = the most important idea
(to) **listen for** sth.	auf etwas horchen, achten	I'm going to have a bath. Can you **listen ~** the doorbell, please?
(to) **be called** [kɔːld]	heißen, genannt werden	
(to) **record** [rɪˈkɔːd]	(Musik / einen Film) aufnehmen	Let's ~ that film. Then we can watch it later.
day out [ˌdeɪˈaʊt]	Tagesausflug	
everywhere [ˈevriweə]	überall	

Buildings and places in a town

In London:

cathedral [kəˈθiːdrəl]	Kathedrale, Dom	**St Paul's Cathedral** [sənt ˈpɔːlz]
circus [ˈsɜːkəs]	(runder) Platz	**Piccadilly Circus** [ˌpɪkədɪli ˈsɜːkəs]
column [ˈkɒləm]	Säule	**Nelson's Column** [ˌnelsnz ˈkɒləm]
lane [leɪn]	Gasse, Weg	**Brick Lane** [ˌbrɪk ˈleɪn]
lock [lɒk]	Schleuse	**Camden Lock** [ˌkæmdən ˈlɒk]
palace [ˈpæləs]	Palast, Schloss	**Buckingham Palace** [ˌbʌkɪŋəm ˈpæləs]
square [skweə]	Platz	**Leicester Square** ❗ [ˌlestə ˈskweə] **Trafalgar Square** [trəˌfælgə ˈskweə]

p.14/A 1	**the Tube** *(no pl)* [tjuːb] *(BE)*	die Londoner U-Bahn	the underground (in London)
	ticket office [ˈɒfɪs]	Fahrkartenschalter	
	single (ticket) [ˈsɪŋgl]	einfache Fahrkarte *(nur Hinfahrt)*	**single (ticket) ◄► return (ticket)**
	rush hour [ˈrʌʃˌaʊə]	Hauptverkehrszeit	
	Travelcard [ˈtrævlkɑːd]	Tages-/Wochen-/Monats-fahrkarte *(der Londoner Verkehrsbetriebe)*	If you want a one-day ticket in London, buy a ~.
	adult [ˈædʌlt]	Erwachsene(r)	
	way [weɪ]	Art und Weise	A big breakfast is a good ~ to start the day.
	line [laɪn]	(U-Bahn-)Linie	
	central [ˈsentrəl]	Zentral-, Mittel-	❗ Betonung auf der 1. Silbe: <u>**central**</u> [ˈsentrəl]
	eastbound [ˈiːstbaʊnd]	Richtung Osten	**northbound** **westbound** ←→ **eastbound** **southbound**
	(to) **change** [tʃeɪndʒ]	umsteigen	Take the Central line eastbound and ~ to the Bakerloo line at Oxford Circus.
	platform [ˈplætfɔːm]	Bahnsteig, Gleis	The trains to London leave from ~ 3.
p.15/A 4	**once** [wʌns]	einst, früher einmal	**Once** we wrote letters. Now we send e-mails.
	across [əˈkrɒs]	(quer) über	a bridge ~ a river
p.16/A 5	**surprise** [səˈpraɪz]	Überraschung	
	surprised (at sth.**)** [səˈpraɪzd]	überrascht (über/von etwas)	I was ~ **at** the size of their house. It was bigger than I thought.

Classroom English → S.236 · Personen-, Orts- und Ländernamen → S.226–228 · Unregelmäßige Verben → S.230–231

Vocabulary 1

	actually [ˈæktʃuəli]	eigentlich; in Wirklichkeit	**Actually,** I'm not American. I'm from Canada.
	mosque [mɒsk]	Moschee	
	anyway, ... [ˈeniweɪ]	aber egal, ...; wie auch immer, ...; wie dem auch sei, ...	Sorry, I don't agree with you. **Anyway**, let's talk about something different.
	curry [ˈkʌri]	Curry(gericht)	Would you like a **curry** or a pizza?
	spicy [ˈspaɪsi]	würzig, scharf gewürzt	
	mild [maɪld]	mild	! Aussprache: **mild** [maɪld] spicy ◄► mild
p.17/A 7	strange [streɪndʒ]	seltsam, sonderbar; fremd	He looked really ~ in a blouse and skirt. It was a ~ part of town, so I needed a map.
	yuck [jʌk]	igitt	**Yuck!** This soup is really awful.
p.20/P 2	transport [ˈtrænspɔːt]	Beförderung, Transport	

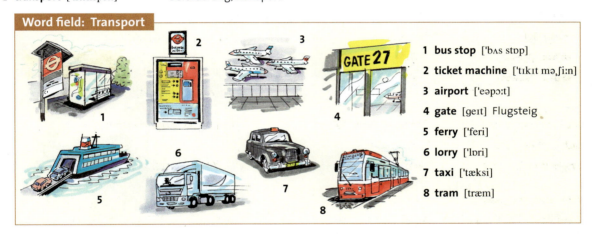

Word field: Transport

1 bus stop [ˈbʌs stɒp]
2 ticket machine [ˈtɪkɪt məˌʃiːn]
3 airport [ˈeəpɔːt]
4 gate [geɪt] Flugsteig
5 ferry [ˈferi]
6 lorry [ˈlɒri]
7 taxi [ˈtæksi]
8 tram [træm]

	ground [graʊnd]	(Erd-)Boden	This railway tunnel is 20 metres under the ~. ! <u>Erd</u>boden = **ground** – <u>Fuß</u>boden = **floor**
p.21/P 3	machine [məˈʃiːn]	Maschine, Gerät *hier:* Automat	
p.22/P 6	course [kɔːs]	Kurs, Lehrgang	My mum does an English ~ on Friday evenings.
p.24/P 10	bakery [ˈbeɪkəri]	Bäckerei	At a ~ you can buy bread and rolls.
	butcher [ˈbʊtʃə]	Fleischer/in, Metzger/in	A ~ sells meat.

at the butcher's/ to the doctor's ...

Wenn der **Ort** gemeint ist, an dem jemand seinen Beruf ausübt – z.B. eine Fleischerei oder eine Arztpraxis – wird oft der **s-Genitiv** benutzt:

Please buy some meat **at the butcher's**.	Kauf bitte etwas Fleisch beim Metzger.
She felt ill and went **to the doctor's**.	Sie fühlte sich krank und ging zum Arzt.
I met Grandpa **at the chemist's** this morning.	Ich habe Opa heute Morgen beim Apotheker getroffen.

	butter [ˈbʌtə]	Butter	
	vegetable [ˈvedʒtəbl]	*(ein)* Gemüse	! **Vegetables <u>are</u>** good for me. = **Gemüse <u>ist</u>** gut ...

Tipps zum Wörterlernen → S.135 · Englische Laute → S.229 · Alphabetische Wörterverzeichnisse → S.181– 204 / S.205–225

1 Vocabulary

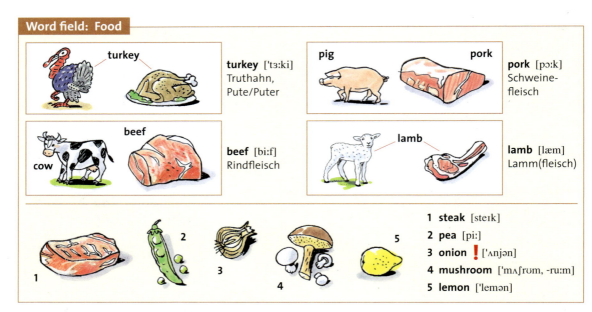

Word field: Food

- **turkey** ['tɜːki] Truthahn, Pute/Puter
- **pork** [pɔːk] Schweinefleisch
- **beef** [biːf] Rindfleisch
- **lamb** [læm] Lamm(fleisch)
- 1 **steak** [steɪk]
- 2 **pea** [piː]
- 3 **onion** ❗ ['ʌnjən]
- 4 **mushroom** ['mʌʃrʊm, -ruːm]
- 5 **lemon** ['lemən]

p.25/P 13	**everyday** (adj) ['evrideɪ]	Alltags-; alltägliche(r, s)	Are you going to wear anything special tonight? – No, just my ~ clothes: jeans and a T-shirt.
	announcement [əˈnaʊnsmənt]	Durchsage, Ansage; Ankündigung, Bekanntgabe	
p.25/P 14	(to) **break a journey** [breɪk], ['dʒɜːni], **broke** [brəʊk], **broken** ['brəʊkən]	eine Reise unterbrechen	
	journey ['dʒɜːni]	Fahrt, Reise	

Only a game

p.26	(to) **work** [wɜːk]	funktionieren	I need your help. My computer doesn't ~.
	helmet ['helmɪt]	Helm	**helmets**

around

herum… / umher…	We walked around till we found a nice café. It's fun to run and jump around in the park after school.	herumlaufen, umherspazieren; herumrennen; herumspringen
in … umher, durch	We walked around the town and looked at the sights. They rode their bikes around the village.	in der Stadt umher, durch die Stadt im Dorf umher, durch das Dorf
um … (herum)	There was water all around them. Let's run around the lake and see who is fastest.	ganz um sie herum um den See (herum)
	❗ (auch zeitlich:) I'll see you around six.	um sechs Uhr herum, gegen sechs

	sign [saɪn]	Schild, Zeichen	The ~ says it's only a mile to the city centre. I'll wait till you give me a ~. Then I'll come in.

Classroom English → S.236 · Personen-, Orts- und Ländernamen → S.226–228 · Unregelmäßige Verben → S.230–231

danger [ˈdeɪndʒə]	Gefahr	

big – large – huge

big / large	**big** und **large** sind oft austauschbar.	a **big/large** family; a **big/large** house
	big ist umgangssprachlicher als **large**, daher solltest du in eher förmlichen Texten besser **large** schreiben.	
	large wird in der Regel nicht verwendet, um Menschen zu beschreiben.	a very **big** man
huge [hjuːdʒ]	**huge** bedeutet „riesig", „sehr groß".	a **huge** suitcase

(to) destroy [dɪˈstrɔɪ]	zerstören	
almost [ˈɔːlməʊst]	fast, beinahe	
button [ˈbʌtn]	Knopf	**buttons**
excited [ɪkˈsaɪtɪd]	begeistert, aufgeregt	❗ He was **excited**. = Er war aufgeregt. It was **exciting**. = Es war aufregend.
moment [ˈməʊmənt]	Moment	I'm almost ready. I'll be with you in a **~**.
p.27 **close (to)** [kləʊs]	nahe (bei, an)	The café isn't far: it's very **~ to** our home. ❗ Aussprache: (to) **close** [kləʊz] schließen **close** (adj) [kləʊs] nahe
smoke [sməʊk]	Rauch	**smoke**
(to) smoke	rauchen	**No smoking!**
wet [wet]	nass	It was a very **~** day – it rained all the time.
realistic [ˌriːəˈlɪstɪk]	realistisch, wirklichkeitsnah	I want to see all the sights in London. – Be **~**. We've only got two days.
friendly [ˈfrendli]	freundlich	
(to) scream [skriːm]	schreien	a German **plug**
plug [plʌg]	Stecker	a British **plug**
electricity [ɪˌlekˈtrɪsəti]	Strom, Elektrizität	noun: **electricity** – adjective: **electric**
p.28 **flash** [flæʃ]	Lichtblitz	
(to) mean [miːn]	bedeuten	I don't understand this word. What does it **~**?
ending [ˈendɪŋ]	Ende, (Ab-)Schluss (einer Geschichte, eines Films usw.)	Not every story can have a happy **~**.
opinion [əˈpɪnjən]	Meinung	❗ In my **opinion** … = Meiner Meinung nach …

Tipps zum Wörterlernen → S.135 · Englische Laute → S.229 · Alphabetische Wörterverzeichnisse → S.181– 204 / S.205–225

How am I doing?

p.29	**How am I doing?**	Wie komme ich voran? *(Wie sind meine Fortschritte?)*	
	area [ˈeərɪə]	Bereich; Gebiet, Gegend	Grammar is my problem ~. I live in an ~ with a lot of restaurants.
	fact [fækt]	Tatsache, Fakt	I've found lots of interesting ~s for my essay on the Music for Youth Festival.

Unit 2: Island girl

p.30	**salmon** [ˈsæmən], *pl* **salmon**	Lachs	❗ stummes „l": **salmon** [ˈsæmən]
	cliff [klɪf]	Klippe, Felsen	
	rock [rɒk]	Fels, Felsen	
	oil [ɔɪl]	Öl	
	farmer [ˈfɑːmə]	Bauer/Bäuerin, Landwirt/in; (Fisch-)Züchter/in	
p.32/A1	(to) **take** [teɪk], **took** [tʊk], **taken** [ˈteɪkən]	dauern, *(Zeit)* brauchen	It ~s about 15 minutes to get home from here. How long does the journey to Lyness ~?
	(to) **be able to** do sth. [ˈeɪbl]	etwas tun können; fähig sein / in der Lage sein, etwas zu tun	Sarah **wasn't ~ to** come to my party last Friday. (= Sarah **couldn't** come …)
	(to) **pick** sb. **up** [ˌpɪk_ˈʌp]	jn. abholen	He's **~ing up** Mr Brown.
	arrival (arr) [əˈraɪvl]	Ankunft	
	departure (dep) [dɪˈpɑːtʃə]	Abfahrt, Abflug; Abreise	**arrival ◄► departure**
	until [ənˈtɪl]	bis	= till
p.32/A3	**from** Monday **to** Friday	von Montag bis Freitag	
	ceilidh [ˈkeɪli]	*Musik- und Tanzveranstaltung, vor allem in Schottland und Irland*	
p.33/A4	**electronic** [ɪˌlekˈtrɒnɪk]	elektronisch	
	media *(pl)* [ˈmiːdɪə]	Medien	It's faster to use ~ like the phone or e-mail than to write letters.
	lonely [ˈləʊnli]	einsam	I felt a bit ~, alone in the big house.
	great-grandmother/-father	Urgroßmutter/-vater	
	post [pəʊst]	Post *(Briefe, Päckchen, …)*	❗ die Post, das Postamt = the **post office**
	once [wʌns]	einmal	
	twice [twaɪs]	zweimal	❗ **once** (1x) – **twice** (2x) – **three times** (3x)
	(once/twice) **a** week	(einmal/zweimal) pro Woche	Our band practises once ~ week.

Classroom English → S.236 · Personen-, Orts- und Ländernamen → S.226–228 · Unregelmäßige Verben → S.230–231

	(to) **imagine** sth. [ɪˈmædʒɪn]	sich etwas vorstellen	
	text message [ˈtekst ˌmesɪdʒ]	SMS	
	message [ˈmesɪdʒ]	Nachricht	
	(to) **text** sb. [tekst]	jm. eine SMS schicken	Have a good trip. And ~ me when you get there.
p.33/A 5	**mate** [meɪt] *(infml)*	Freund/in, Kumpel	a good friend
	personal [ˈpɜːsənl]	persönliche(r, s)	
	ringtone [ˈrɪŋtəʊn]	Klingelton	
	(to) **download** [ˌdaʊnˈləʊd]	runterladen, downloaden	
	(to) **mix** [mɪks]	mischen, mixen	If you ~ blue and yellow, you get green.
	(to) **surf the internet** [sɜːf]	im Internet surfen	
	instant messages *(pl)* [ˌɪnstənt ˈmesɪdʒɪz]	*Nachrichten, die man im Internet austauscht (in Echtzeit)*	
p.34/A 6	**type** [taɪp] *(infml)*	Typ	
	(to) **go well**	gut (ver)laufen, gutgehen	Was the test difficult? – Yes, but it **went ~**.
	(to) **dream (of, about)** [driːm]	träumen (von)	verb: (to) **dream** – noun: **dream**

> ### on („weiter")
>
> | | |
> |---|---|
> | You want to be a rock star? **Dream on**! | ... Träum weiter! |
> | It started to rain, but we **walked on**. | ..., aber wir gingen weiter. |
> | **Read on**. You'll find the information on the next few pages. | Lies weiter. ... |
> | He stopped talking for a moment. Then he **went on**. | ... Dann redete er weiter. |

	not (...) any more	nicht mehr	The Greens do**n't** live here **any more**. They've moved to London.
	rucksack [ˈrʌksæk]	Rucksack	❗ Aussprache: **rucksack** [ˈrʌksæk]
	(to) **expect** [ɪkˈspekt]	erwarten	How many guests are you **~ing** to your party?
	not even	(noch) nicht einmal	I won't tell anybody, **not ~** my best friend.
			❗ • He **even** opened the letter. = Er hat den Brief **sogar** geöffnet! • He **didn't even** open the letter. = Er hat den Brief **nicht einmal** geöffnet!
	ponytail [ˈpəʊniteɪl]	Pferdeschwanz *(Frisur)*	a **ponytail**
p.35/A 8	**upset (about)** [ˌʌpˈset]	aufgebracht, gekränkt, mitgenommen (wegen)	John was ~ because his sister didn't remember his birthday.
	(to) **upset** sb. **(-tt-)** [ʌpˈset]**, upset, upset**	jn. ärgern, kränken, aus der Fassung bringen	It ~**s** me when people are rude to me. The bad news about her father ~ her a lot.
	(to) **turn** sth. **on/off** [tɜːn]	etwas ein-, ausschalten	
	glad [glæd]	froh, dankbar	Tim is a good friend. I'm really ~ that I met him.
	beauty [ˈbjuːti]	Schönheit	adjective: **beautiful** – noun: **beauty**

Tipps zum Wörterlernen → S.135 · Englische Laute → S.229 · Alphabetische Wörterverzeichnisse → S.181– 204 / S.205–225

168 · 2 Vocabulary

(to) **call** sb. **names**	jn. mit Schimpfwörtern hänseln, jm. Schimpfwörter nachrufen	He felt upset because the other kids always **~ed him names** like Carrot-Nose or Rabbit-Ears.
(to) **let** sb. **do** sth. **(-tt-)** [let]**, let, let**	jm. erlauben, etwas zu tun; zulassen, dass jd. etwas tut	My parents never ~ me watch late films. You look hungry. **Let** me make you a sandwich.
I / you / ... **would** ... [wəd, wʊd]	ich würde / du würdest / ...	I don't want to leave my home town. I ~ miss all my friends.
just [dʒʌst]	einfach	I ~ can't find my keys. Do you know where I put them?

---

just

They call you names? **Just** don't listen to them.	... Hör **einfach** nicht hin.
It's **just** a game.	Es ist **nur/bloß** ein Spiel.
They're **just** leaving. / They've **just** left.	Sie gehen **gerade**. / Sie sind **gerade (eben)** gegangen.
Just then the phone rang.	**Genau in dem Moment / Gerade dann** klingelte das Telefon.
You look **just like** your mother.	Du siehst **genau wie** deine Mutter aus.

---

bully ['bʊli]	(Schul-)Tyrann	verb: (to) **bully** – noun: **bully**
p.35/A 9 **feeling** ['fi:lɪŋ]	Gefühl	verb: (to) **feel** – noun: **feeling**
entry ['entri]	Eintrag, Eintragung *(im Wörterbuch/Tagebuch)*	I've got a new dictionary. It has 200,000 **entries**. There's no ~ in Jane's diary for 12th June.
translation [træns'leɪʃn]	Übersetzung	
(to) **translate (from ... into)** [træns'leɪt]	übersetzen (aus ... ins)	We had to ~ the text **from** English **into** German.
correct [kə'rekt]	richtig	

Word field: Town and country

p.38/P 1

hilly ['hɪli] hügelig

bay [beɪ] Bucht

coast [kəʊst] Küste

canal [kə'næl]

car park ['kɑ: pɑ:k]

busy ['bɪzi] belebt, verkehrsreich; hektisch

a **busy** street

---

p.38/P 2 **stress** [stres]	Betonung	
p.40/P 6 **general** ['dʒenrəl]	allgemeine(r,s)	I haven't got all the facts, just ~ information.
statement ['steɪtmənt]	Aussage, Feststellung	I'm afraid I don't agree with that ~.
(to) **be lucky (with)** ['lʌki]	Glück haben (mit)	We **were ~ with** the hotel. It was cheap and clean.

Classroom English → S.236 · Personen-, Orts- und Ländernamen → S.226–228 · Unregelmäßige Verben → S.230–231

	news (no pl) [njuːz]	Neuigkeit(en), Nachricht(en)	**!** Das **sind** gute **Nachrichten**!= That**'s** good **news**! (singular) _Never_: The news ~~are~~ ... or ~~a news.~~
	(to) **guess** [ges]	raten, erraten, schätzen	**Guess** how old I am. – 14? – No, I'm only 13.
p.41/P 7	(to) **lock** [lɒk]	abschließen; sperren	Please ~ the door when you leave the house.
	(to) **unlock** [ˌʌnˈlɒk]	aufschließen; entsperrren	I lost the key, so I couldn't ~ the suitcase.
	(to) **press** [pres]	drücken	
p.42/P 11	**role** [rəʊl]	Rolle	What's your ~ in the play? – I'm the detective.
p.42/P 12	**million** [ˈmɪljən]	Million	**!** one **million** cars (eine Million Autos) – two **million** cars (zwei Million**en** Autos) _But_: **million̲s̲ of** cars (Millionen von Autos)

Orkney Star

p.44	**light** [laɪt]	Licht	
	a **cup of** tea [kʌp]	eine Tasse Tee	**a c☕p of tea**
	scarf [skɑːf], _pl_ **scarves** [skɑːvz]	Schal	
	you	man	How do ~ say 'once more' in German? (= Wie sagt man ...?)
	Assembly [əˈsembli]	Versammlung (morgendliche Schulversammlung, oft mit Andacht)	
	head teacher [ˌhed ˈtiːtʃə]	Schulleiter/in	
	(to) **believe** [bɪˈliːv]	glauben	That can't be true! I don't ~ it.
	(to) **begin (-nn-)** [bɪˈgɪn], **began** [bɪˈgæn], **begun** [bɪˈgʌn]	beginnen, anfangen (mit)	It's time to ~. (= to start) (to) **begin** ◄► (to) **stop**
	you **might** need help [maɪt]	du könntest (vielleicht) Hilfe brauchen	If you wait outside Buckingham Palace, you ~ see the Queen.
	we **could** ... [kəd, kʊd]	wir könnten ...	**!** we **could** = **1.** wir konnten; **2.** wir könnten
	hairdresser [ˈheədresə]	Friseur/in	
	Why **should** I ... ? [ʃəd, ʃʊd]	Warum sollte ich ... ?	Why ~ I go to Jane's party? I really don't like her.
	(to) **cut (-tt-)** [kʌt], **cut, cut**	schneiden	My mum always **cuts** my hair.
	(to) **blow** [bləʊ], **blew** [bluː], **blown** [bləʊn]	wehen, blasen	
p.45	**across** [əˈkrɒs]	hinüber, herüber	Look at that river. How can we get ~?
	anorak [ˈænəræk]	Anorak, Windjacke	
	(to) **be allowed to** do sth. [əˈlaʊd]	etwas tun dürfen	**Are** you ~ **to** use dictionaries in your English tests?

Tipps zum Wörterlernen → S.135 · Englische Laute → S.229 · Alphabetische Wörterverzeichnisse → S.181– 204 / S.205–225

2–3 Vocabulary

„können" und „dürfen"

Du kennst bereits **can** für „können" und für „dürfen":

Ananda **can** play hockey very well.	Ananda kann sehr gut Hockey spielen.
You **can** go to the disco, but be home at 10, please.	Du darfst in die Disko gehen, …

Wenn es um die **Vergangenheit** oder die **Zukunft** geht, verwende

– für **„können"** eine Form von **be able to** und
– für **„dürfen"** eine Form von **be allowed to**.

(to) **be able to**:	The museum was closed on Friday, but we **were able to** go on Saturday.[1]	…, aber wir konnten am Samstag hingehen.
	I **won't be able to** meet you tomorrow.	Ich werde dich morgen nicht treffen können.
(to) **be allowed to**:	**Were** you **allowed to** watch the film last night?	Durftest du den Film gestern Abend sehen?
	When I'm 18 I**'ll be allowed to** drive.	Wenn ich 18 bin, werde ich Auto fahren dürfen.

[1] Es gibt auch eine Vergangenheitsform **could** („konnte"): It was so dark that we **couldn't** really see the sea.

---

microphone ['maɪkrəfəʊn]	Mikrofon	
bell [bel]	Klingel, Glocke	The **bell** rang. = Es klingelte.
p.46 **clone** [kləʊn]	Klon	
jealous (of) ['dʒeləs]	neidisch (auf); eifersüchtig (auf)	You get so much pocket money! I'm really ~. Sarah is ~ **of** her baby brother. She thinks her parents love him more.
dish [dɪʃ]	Gericht (Speise)	What's your favourite ~? – Spaghetti.
stew [stjuː]	Eintopf(gericht)	
community hall [kə'mjuːnəti]	Gemeinschaftshalle, -saal, Gemeindehalle, -saal	

bells

How am I doing?

p.47 (to) **look** sth. **up** [ˌlʊk_'ʌp]	etwas nachschlagen	**Look** ~ the word 'stew' in your dictionary. Can you **look** ~ his new phone number for me?
meaning ['miːnɪŋ]	Bedeutung	verb: (to) **mean** – noun: **meaning**

Unit 3: Sport and more

p.52 **final** ['faɪnl]	Finale, Endspiel	❗ Betonung und Aussprache: **final** ['faɪnl]
final ['faɪnl]	letzte(r, s); End-	The young man saved the girl in the ~ minute of the film.
semi-final [ˌsemi'faɪnl]	Halbfinale	
training session ['seʃn]	Trainingsstunde, -einheit	
p.53 (to) **be interested (in)** ['ɪntrəstɪd]	interessiert sein (an), sich interessieren (für)	❗ I'm **interested** in music. = Ich interessiere mich für Musik. an **interesting** CD = eine interessante CD
profile ['prəʊfaɪl]	Porträt, Steckbrief	

Classroom English → S.236 · Personen-, Orts- und Ländernamen → S.226–228 · Unregelmäßige Verben → S.230–231

Vocabulary 3 · 171

age [eɪdʒ]	Alter	What ~ are you? = How old are you?
sex [seks]	Geschlecht	
female ['fiːmeɪl]	weiblich	
male [meɪl]	männlich	**male** **female**
location [ləʊ'keɪʃn]	Wohn-, Stand-, Einsatzort	
p.54/A1 **sporty** ['spɔːti]	sportlich	
supporter [sə'pɔːtə]	Anhänger/in, Fan	
(to) **support** a team [sə'pɔːt]	eine Mannschaft unterstützen; Fan einer Mannschaft sein	Which football team do you ~? – Manchester United.
(to) **spot** (-tt-) [spɒt]	entdecken	I can't find my key. If you ~ it, please tell me.
pitch [pɪtʃ]	Spielfeld	football/hockey ~
(to) **train** [treɪn]	trainieren	
draw [drɔː]	Unentschieden	I'm a bit upset that we didn't win, but at least it was a ~.
2 all [ˌtuː_'ɔːl]	2 beide (2:2 unentschieden)	
(to) **score (a goal)** [skɔː], [gəʊl]	ein Tor schießen, einen Treffer erzielen	We won 3–2. – Oh, great! Who **scored**? – Smith **scored** all three **goals**.
score [skɔː]	Spielstand; Punktestand	
goal [gəʊl]	Tor (im Sport)	

A football match

What's the score now? – 2–0. (you say: **two nil**)	Wie steht es jetzt? – 2:0.
What was the final score? – Chelsea 2, Arsenal 1.	Wie war der Endstand? – 2:1.
Our last match was a draw, 2–2. (you say: **two all**)	Unser letztes Spiel war ein Unentschieden, 2:2.

coach [kəʊtʃ]	Trainer/in	
p.55/A4 **exchange student** [ɪks'tʃeɪndʒ ˌstjuːdnt]	Austauschschüler/in	
(to) **enter** ['entə]	betreten; eintreten (in)	(to) **enter** a room ◄► (to) **leave** a room
bad timing ['taɪmɪŋ]	schlechtes Timing	
appetite ['æpɪtaɪt]	Appetit	❗ Manchmal sagt man **Enjoy!**, wenn man gemeinsam isst. Aber nie ~~Good appetite!~~
(to) **refer to** (-rr-) [rɪ'fɜː]	sich beziehen auf	This question ~s to line 12 on page 46.
p.56/A5 **whole** [həʊl]	ganze(r, s), gesamte(r, s)	the ~ day = all day
artist ['ɑːtɪst]	Künstler/in	❗ Betonung auf der 1. Silbe: **artist** ['ɑːtɪst] **artist** = Künstler/in (nicht: ~~Artist/in~~)
stadium ['steɪdiəm]	Stadion	

Tipps zum Wörterlernen → S.135 · Englische Laute → S.229 · Alphabetische Wörterverzeichnisse → S.181–204 / S.205–225

172   3   Vocabulary

	(to) **make a deal** [di:l]	ein Abkommen/eine Abmachung treffen	Help me with my Maths, and I'll help you with English. – OK, it's a **deal**! (= Abgemacht!)
	(to) **paraphrase** ['pærəfreɪz]	umschreiben, anders ausdrücken	
p.57/A 8	(to) **beat** [bi:t], **beat**, **beaten** ['bi:tn]	schlagen; besiegen	I **beat** my brother at tennis last Sunday.

cups

	cup [kʌp]	Pokal	
	win [wɪn]	Sieg	verb: (to) **win** – noun: **win**
	against [ə'genst]	gegen	Manchester United won ~ Rochdale.
	although [ɔ:l'ðəʊ]	obwohl	I went to bed early ~ I wasn't really tired.
	in the end	schließlich, zum Schluss	No bus came, so **in the** ~ we walked home. ! **at** the end of the lesson = am Ende / am Schluss der Stunde
	half-time [ˌhɑ:f 'taɪm]	Halbzeit(pause)	the break between the first and the second half of a match ! the first **half** = die erste Halbzeit
	goalkeeper ['ɡəʊlki:pə]	Torwart, Torfrau	goalkeeper

Word field: Sports

p.60/P 2

EQUIPMENT [ɪ'kwɪpmənt] Ausrüstung   **LOCATION** [ləʊ'keɪʃn] Ort

skis [ski:z]     ski slope [sləʊp] Skipiste

table tennis bat [bæt]    sports hall

badminton racket ['rækɪt]    court [kɔ:t] Platz, Court

running shoes    running track [træk] Laufbahn

swimming trunks *(pl)* [trʌŋks] Badehose
swimsuit ['swɪmsu:t] Badeanzug    (swimming) pool

Classroom English → S. 236 · Personen-, Orts- und Ländernamen → S. 226–228 · Unregelmäßige Verben → S. 230–231

Vocabulary 3   173

Word field: Sports

EQUIPMENT		LOCATION	
saddle ['sædl]			bridle path ['braɪdl pɑːθ] Reitweg
helmet, pads [pædz] (Knie-usw.)Schützer			half-pipe ['hɑːfpaɪp]

p.62/P 7	**pepper** ['pepə]	Pfeffer	
	salt [sɔːlt]	Salz	**salt** and **pepper**
p.64/P 12	(to) **organize** ['ɔːgənaɪz]	ordnen, organisieren	
	(to) **end** [end]	enden; beenden	The road ~s here. We'll have to walk now. A hot bath is a good way to ~ the day.
p.65/P 13	**meal** [miːl]	Mahlzeit, Essen	We like to eat a hot ~ in the evenings.
	rice [raɪs]	Reis	
	about yourself [jə'self, jɔː'self]	über dich selbst	

Who needs legs? (Partner A)

p.66	**brave** [breɪv]	tapfer, mutig	! **brave** (English) = *tapfer, mutig* **brav** (German) = *good*
	only ['əʊnli]	erst	I'm not sixteen, I'm ~ fourteen. ! **only** = 1. nur, bloß; 2. erst
	(to) **grow up** [ˌgrəʊ_'ʌp], **grew up** [ˌgruː_'ʌp], **grown up** [ˌgrəʊn_'ʌp]	erwachsen werden; aufwachsen	Dave wants to be a doctor when he ~s up. When my grandparents were ~ing up, they didn't have a television.
	onto ['ɒntə, 'ɒntʊ]	auf (... hinauf)	The cat saw the dog and jumped ~ the table.
	(to) **take a ride** [raɪd]	eine Fahrt machen	
	(to) **cut** sth. **off** (-tt-) [kʌt]	etwas abschneiden, abtrennen	
	ambulance ['æmbjələns]	Krankenwagen	! Betonung und Aussprache: **ambulance** ['æmbjələns]
	athletics [æθ'letɪks]	Leichtathletik	I'm an ~ fan: I love sports like running and jumping.
	medal ['medl]	Medaille	! Betonung auf der 1. Silbe: **medal** ['medl]

Tipps zum Wörterlernen → S.135 · Englische Laute → S.229 · Alphabetische Wörterverzeichnisse → S.181–204 / S.205–225

3–4 Vocabulary

HA: 26.4.16

hope [həʊp]	Hoffnung	noun: **hope** – verb: (to) **hope**
hard-working [ˌhɑːd ˈwɜːkɪŋ]	fleißig, tüchtig	Sam is a ~-~ student.

Who needs legs? (Partner B)

p.104 (to) **fight (for)** [faɪt], **fought** [fɔːt], **fought**	kämpfen (für, um)	Nathan had to ~ **for** his life after his accident.
operation (on) [ˌɒpəˈreɪʃn]	Operation (an)	He had an ~ **on** his knee after he was hurt in the match.
artificial [ˌɑːtɪˈfɪʃl]	künstlich, Kunst-	Are those flowers real or ~? ~ legs = Beinprothesen
(to) **be mad about** sth. [mæd]	verrückt nach/auf etwas sein	He **is mad** ~ chocolate ice cream.

sledge [sledʒ]	Schlitten	a **sledge**
disabled [dɪsˈeɪbld]	(körper)behindert	
talent [ˈtælənt]	Talent, Begabung	❗ Betonung auf der 1. Silbe: **talent** [ˈtælənt]
championship [ˈtʃæmpɪənʃɪp]	Meisterschaft	
(to) **represent** [ˌreprɪˈzent]	repräsentieren, vertreten	There were groups from all over Europe at the festival. A group from Frankfurt ~**ed** Germany.
the Commonwealth [ˈkɒmənwelθ]	*Gemeinschaft der Länder des ehemaligen Britischen Weltreichs*	
Paralympics [ˌpærəˈlɪmpɪks]	Paralympische Spiele *(Olympische Spiele für Sportler/innen mit körperlicher Behinderung)*	

Unit 4: Growing up in Canada

p.69 (to) **go camping** [ˈkæmpɪŋ]	zelten gehen	We **went** ~ last summer.
(to) **camp** [kæmp]	zelten	We ~**ed** near a lake.
(to) **go canoeing** [kəˈnuːɪŋ]	Kanu fahren gehen	
(to) **canoe** [kəˈnuː]	Kanu fahren	
(to) **go hunting** [ˈhʌntɪŋ]	jagen gehen	
(to) **hunt** [hʌnt]	jagen	Do people still ~ lions in Africa?

Verbs and nouns with the same form

(to) **canoe**	paddeln, Kanu fahren	(to) **drive**	*(Auto)* fahren	(to) **link**	verbinden, verknüpfen		
canoe	Kanu, Paddelboot	**drive**	(Auto-)Fahrt	**link**	Verbindung, Verknüpfung		
(to) **colour**	kolorieren, färben bunt an-, ausmalen	(to) **fish**	fischen, angeln	(to) **ski**	Ski fahren		
colour	Farbe	**fish**	Fisch	**ski**	Ski		
(to) **cook**	kochen	(to) **hunt**	jagen	(to) **sleep**	schlafen		
cook	Koch/Köchin	**hunt**	Jagd	**sleep**	Schlaf		

Classroom English → S.236 · Personen-, Orts- und Ländernamen → S.226–228 · Unregelmäßige Verben → S.230–231

(to) **go snowshoeing** ['snəʊʃuːɪŋ]	Schneeschuhwandern gehen	two pairs of **snowshoes**
(to) **have sleepovers** ['sliːpəʊvəz]	Schlafpartys veranstalten	We often **have ~s** at Sally's. She has got a very big room.
(to) **hang out** (with friends) [ˌhæŋ_'aʊt], **hung** [hʌŋ], **hung** (infml)	rumhängen, abhängen (mit Freunden/Freundinnen)	
popular (with) ['pɒpjʊlə]	populär, beliebt (bei)	Ice hockey is a ~ sport in Canada. It's very ~ **with** Canadians.
cabin ['kæbɪn]	Hütte	
(to) **shoot** [ʃuːt], **shot** [ʃɒt], **shot**	schießen, erschießen	
mom [mɒm, AE: mɑːm] (AE)	Mama, Mutti; Mutter	= BE mum
(to) **complain (about** sth.) [kəm'pleɪn]	sich (über etwas) beschweren, beklagen	My mum always **~s about** my loud music.
lyrics (pl) ['lɪrɪks]	Liedtext(e), Songtext(e)	I like this song. What do the ~ mean in German?
bill [bɪl]	Rechnung	Our phone ~ was huge last month. *at a restaurant:* Could we have the ~, please?
It's not my fault. [fɔːlt]	Es ist nicht meine Schuld.	
strict [strɪkt]	streng	Peter's parents are very ~. He isn't allowed to watch TV after 8 o'clock.
(to) **do badly/well (in)**	schlecht/gut abschneiden (in)	Karen **did** very **well/badly in** her English test.
(to) **be grounded** ['graʊndɪd]	Ausgehverbot/Hausarrest haben	I can't hang out with my friends. I**'m ~** for a week because I didn't do my homework.
midnight ['mɪdnaɪt]	Mitternacht	
old-fashioned [ˌəʊld'fæʃnd]	altmodisch	
modern ['mɒdən]	modern	❗ Betonung auf der 1. Silbe: <u>**modern**</u> ['mɒdən]
easy-going [ˌiːzi'gəʊɪŋ]	gelassen, locker	
My dad is annoying. [ə'nɔɪɪŋ]	Mein Vater geht mir auf die Nerven.	Little sisters and brothers can be ~.
(to) **annoy** [ə'nɔɪ]	ärgern, belästigen	Don't ~ the dog. It'll get angry.
guys (pl) [gaɪz] (AE, infml)	Leute	Hey, you ~! Wait for me. I'll come with you.
by ten (o'clock)	bis (spätestens) zehn Uhr	Please be home ~ ten. (= not later than ten)

p.70/A 1

p.71/A 3

German „bis"

until / till („bis")

I can stay up **until / till** eleven o'clock tonight.
We lived in Scotland **until / till** I was 12.

from ... to („von ... bis")

We're open **from** Mondays **to** Saturdays.

by („bis spätestens", „nicht später als")

We need your report **by** Friday (= on or before Friday).
You must be home **by** 5.30 (= at or before 5.30).

Tipps zum Wörterlernen → S.135 · Englische Laute → S.229 · Alphabetische Wörterverzeichnisse → S.181– 204 / S.205–225

4 Vocabulary

p. 71/A 4	(to) **brainstorm** ['breɪnstɔːm]	brainstormen (so viele Ideen wie möglich sammeln)	(to) collect as many ideas as possible
p. 72/A 6	**province** ['prɒvɪns]	Provinz	**!** Betonung auf der 1. Silbe: **prov**ince ['prɒvɪns]
	traditional [trə'dɪʃənl]	traditionell	
	(to) **protect** sb. **(from** sth.) [prə'tekt]	jn. (be)schützen (vor etwas)	Wear a hat – it will ~ you **from** the sun.

Reflexive pronouns (Reflexivpronomen)

I've hurt **myself**.	Ich habe	**mir**	wehgetan / **mich** verletzt.	
You've hurt **yourself**.	Du ...	**dir**	... / **dich** ...	
He's hurt **himself**.	Er ...	**sich**	... / **sich** ...	
She's hurt **herself**.	Sie ...	**sich**	... / **sich** ...	**!** Aussprache/Betonung:
It's hurt **itself**.	Es ...	**sich**	... / **sich** ...	**-self** [-'self]
We've hurt **ourselves**.	Wir ...	**uns**	... / **uns** ...	**-selves** [-'sel<u>vz</u>]
You've hurt **yourselves**.	Ihr ...	**euch**	... / **euch** ...	
They've hurt **themselves**.	Sie ...	**sich**	... / **sich** ...	

---

	attack [ə'tæk]	Angriff	How can I protect my computer from virus ~s?
	(to) **attack**	angreifen	If somebody ~s us, we have to protect ourselves.
	exactly [ɪg'zæktli]	genau	You mean that man is a thief? – **Exactly**.
	argument ['ɑːgjumənt]	Argument, Begründung; Streit	**!** **argument** = **1.** Argument – There are good ~s for and against this idea. **2.** Streit – Mum and dad had an ~ last night. Mum shouted a lot.
	(to) **blame** sb. **(for)** [bleɪm]	jm. die Schuld geben (an); jm. Vorwürfe machen (wegen)	Don't ~ me. It wasn't my fault.
p. 72/A 7	(to) **make a point**	ein Argument vorbringen	He **made** some interesting ~s in the discussion.
	(to) **disagree (with)** [ˌdɪsə'griː]	nicht übereinstimmen (mit); anderer Meinung sein (als)	I thought it was a good point, but the others ~d. (to) **disagree** ◄► (to) **agree**
p. 73/A 8	**leader** ['liːdə]	Leiter/in, (An-)Führer/in	
	each other [iːtʃ_'ʌðə]	einander, sich (gegenseitig)	Paul likes Linda and Linda likes Paul. = Paul and Linda like **each** ~.
	stage [steɪdʒ]	Bühne	At 9 o'clock the band went on ~ and started to play.
	mix [mɪks]	Mix, Mischung	
p. 73/A 9	**chorus** ['kɔːrəs]	Refrain	**!** German „Chor" = English **choir** ['kwaɪə]
p. 76/P 1	**per cent (%)** [pə'sent]	Prozent	Twenty ~ ~ of two hundred is forty.
	per [pɜː, pə]	pro	50 miles ~ hour = 50 miles an hour
	kilometre (km) ['kɪləmiːtə]	Kilometer	1,000 metres = 1 ~
	centimetre (cm) ['sentɪmiːtə]	Zentimeter	100 ~s = 1 **metre**
	kilogram ['kɪləgræm], **kilo** ['kiːləʊ] **(kg)**	Kilogramm, Kilo (kg)	We need two **kilograms/kilos of** oranges for the orange juice.

Classroom English → S. 236 · Personen-, Orts- und Ländernamen → S. 226–228 · Unregelmäßige Verben → S. 230–231

Vocabulary **4**   177

a 150-kilogram bear / a 14-hour flight / ...

a **150-kilogram** bear	ein 150 Kilogramm schwerer Bär	❗ Im Englischen steht das Nomen im Singular:
a **ten-kilometre** walk	eine Zehn-Kilometer-Wanderung	
a **14-hour** flight	ein 14-stündiger Flug, ein 14-Stunden-Flug	a **14-hour** flight
a **24-hour** supermarket	ein Supermarkt, der 24 Stunden geöffnet ist	(*nicht:* a 14-~~hours~~ flight)
a **two-week** holiday	ein zweiwöchiger Urlaub	

	a **sixteen-year-old**	ein/e Sechzehnjährige/r	
	a **sixteen-year-old** girl	ein sechzehnjähriges Mädchen	
p.76/P 3	**relaxed** [rɪˈlækst]	locker, entspannt	
p.77/P 5	**crazy** [ˈkreɪzi]	verrückt	You want to go out in this rain? You must be ~.
p.78/P 7	(to) **revise** [rɪˈvaɪz]	überarbeiten; wiederholen	❗ (to) **revise** 1. überarbeiten – (to) ~ a text, a story, ... 2. wiederholen – (to) ~ vocabulary, grammar, ...
	spelling [ˈspelɪŋ]	(Recht-)Schreibung, Schreibweise	Remember to check your ~ when you revise a text.
p.79/P 8	**strike** [straɪk]	Streik	❗ (to) **be on strike** = streiken, sich im Streik befinden (to) **go on strike** = streiken, in den Streik treten

Reflexiv im Deutschen – nicht reflexiv im Englischen

(to) **calm down**	sich beruhigen		(to) **prepare**	sich vorbereiten
(to) **clean one's teeth**	sich die Zähne putzen		(to) **refer to**	sich beziehen auf
(to) **feel**	sich fühlen; sich anfühlen		(to) **relax**	sich entspannen, sich ausruhen
(to) **get dressed**	sich anziehen		(to) **remember sth.**	sich an etwas erinnern; sich etwas merken
(to) **hide**	sich verstecken			
(to) **imagine sth.**	sich etwas vorstellen		(to) **sit down**	sich hinsetzen
(to) **meet**	sich treffen		(to) **turn**	sich umdrehen
(to) **move**	sich bewegen		(to) **wonder**	sich fragen
(to) **open**	sich öffnen		(to) **worry**	sich Sorgen machen

Two bear attacks

p.81	**knife** [naɪf], *pl* **knives** [naɪvz]	Messer	❗ stummes „k": **knife** [naɪf]

spoon [spuːn]

teaspoon

knife

fork [fɔːk]

while [waɪl]	während	Somebody stole my bike ~ I was in the shop.
(to) **warn** sb. (**about** sth.) [wɔːn]	jn. (vor etwas) warnen	The doctor ~ed him **about** the dangers of smoking.
woods (*pl*) [wʊdz]	Wald, Wälder	Let's go for a walk in the ~.
wood [wʊd]	Holz	a **piece of wood**

Tipps zum Wörterlernen → S.135 · Englische Laute → S.229 · Alphabetische Wörterverzeichnisse → S.181–204 / S.205–225

4–5 Vocabulary

victim ['vɪktɪm]	Opfer	
latest ['leɪtɪst]	neueste(r, s)	The Kooks are great. Have you heard their ~ CD?
(to) **escape (from** sb./sth.) [ɪ'skeɪp]	fliehen (vor jm./aus etwas); entkommen	A lion ~d from its cage at London Zoo last night. The thief ~d in a fast sports car.
p.82 (to) **paddle** ['pædl]	paddeln	
rapids (pl) ['ræpɪdz]	Stromschnellen	

paddle

canoe

rapids

They're **paddling** through the **rapids.**

Unit 5: A teen magazine

p.88 (to) **announce** [ə'naʊns]	ankündigen, bekanntgeben	The form teacher ~d the names of the winners. verb: (to) **announce** – noun: **announcement**
That's up to you.	Das liegt bei dir. / Das kannst/musst du (selbst) entscheiden.	Will I be on the football team? – **That's ~ ~ you**. If you practise hard, you'll have a good chance.
section ['sekʃn]	Abschnitt, Teil, (Themen-)Bereich	❗ Betonung auf der 1. Silbe: <u>**section**</u> ['sekʃn]
editor ['edɪtə]	Redakteur/in	
movie ['muːvi]	Film	= film
p.89 (to) **produce** [prə'djuːs]	produzieren, herstellen	Germany ~s millions of cars every year.
article ['ɑːtɪkl]	(Zeitungs-)Artikel	There was an ~ in the school magazine about the World Cup.
(to) **publish** ['pʌblɪʃ]	veröffentlichen	J. K. Rowling ~ed her first Harry Potter book in 1997.
drawing ['drɔːɪŋ]	Zeichnung	
(to) **draw** [drɔː], **drew** [druː], **drawn** [drɔːn]	zeichnen	verb: (to) **draw** – noun: **drawing**
success [sək'ses]	Erfolg	The party was a big ~. Everybody enjoyed it.
successful [sək'sesfl]	erfolgreich	The band was very ~ in the UK, but not in Canada or the US.
headphones (pl) ['hedfəʊnz]	Kopfhörer	**headphones**
monitor ['mɒnɪtə]	Bildschirm, Monitor	**monitor**
p.90/A1 (to) **skim** a text **(-mm-)** [skɪm]	einen Text überfliegen (um den Inhalt grob zu erfassen)	
biography [baɪ'ɒgrəfi]	Biografie	❗ Betonung auf der 2. Silbe: **b<u>i</u>ography** [baɪ'ɒgrəfi]
useful ['juːsfl]	nützlich	If you don't know a city well, it's ~ to have a street map.
bold print [ˌbəʊld 'prɪnt]	Fettdruck	The names of cities with over a million people are in **bold ~** on this map.
caption ['kæpʃn]	Bildunterschrift	

Classroom English → S.236 · Personen-, Orts- und Ländernamen → S.226–228 · Unregelmäßige Verben → S.230–231

(to) **wake up** [ˌweɪk_ˈʌp], **woke** [wəʊk], **woken** [ˈwəʊkən]	aufwachen	Yesterday I didn't ~ ~ till 8 o'clock and was late for school.
(to) **wake** sb. **(up)**, **woke, woken**	jn. (auf)wecken	This morning my mother **woke** me ~ at 7.
so that	sodass, damit	I'm saving money ~ ~ I can buy a new bike.
silence [ˈsaɪləns]	Stille; Schweigen	There was ~ when the teacher walked into the classroom.

p.91	**riddle** [ˈrɪdl]	Rätsel	
	leather [ˈleðə]	Leder	
	pipe [paɪp]	Pfeife	pipes / a **whistle**
	(to) **stick out of** sth. [stɪk], **stuck, stuck** [stʌk]	aus etwas herausragen, herausstehen	A long pipe **stuck** ~ **of** the old man's mouth.
	(to) **keep** [kiːp], **kept**, **kept** [kept]	(be)halten; aufbewahren	**Keep** your eyes open when you're on the road. You can ~ the book, I don't need it any more. Where do you ~ your drawings? – In my dossier.
	(to) **squeeze** [skwiːz]	drücken; (aus)pressen	She said thank you and ~**d** my arm. For one glass of juice, ~ three or four oranges.
	(to) **be good at** sth.	gut in etwas sein; etwas gut können	(to) **be good at** sth. ◄► (to) **be bad at** sth. She **is good at** Music but **bad at** Maths.
	(to) **release** [rɪˈliːs]	(CD, Film usw.) herausbringen, auf den Markt bringen	
	sold out	ausverkauft; vergriffen	The concert tickets were **sold** ~ in only three days.

p.92	**vacation** [vəˈkeɪʃn, AE: veɪˈkeɪʃn] (AE)	Urlaub, Ferien	= BE holiday
	(to) **get** sth. **off the ground**	etwas auf den Weg bringen; etwas auf die Beine stellen	
	(to) **have a crush on** sb. [krʌʃ]	in jn. verknallt sein	Look, he's smiling at you again. I think he **has a** ~ **on** you.
	that far/good/bad/…	so weit/gut/schlecht/…	I knew you could sing, but I didn't know you were ~ **good**. (= so good)
	least [liːst]	am wenigsten	Which article do you like best, and which do you like ~?

p.95/P 1	**album** [ˈælbəm]	Album	
	bagpipes (pl) [ˈbægpaɪps]	Dudelsack	bagpipes / bag / pipes

Tipps zum Wörterlernen → S.135 · Englische Laute → S.229 · Alphabetische Wörterverzeichnisse → S.181– 204 / S.205–225

career [kə'rɪə]	Karriere	
musician [mju:'zɪʃn]	Musiker/in	
opera ['ɒprə]	Oper	
record ['rekɔ:d]	Schallplatte	❗ • verb: (to) **record** Betonung auf der 2. Silbe: [rɪ'kɔ:d] • noun: **record** Betonung auf der 1. Silbe: ['rekɔ:d]
single ['sɪŋgl]	Single	
tune [tju:n]	Melodie	
track [træk]	Stück, Titel, Track *(auf einer CD)*	Now we'll hear a ~ from their new album.
p.98/P 6 **company** ['kʌmpəni]	Firma, Gesellschaft	
copy ['kɒpi]	Exemplar	I haven't got the book in German, but I've got an English ~.
for example [ˌfər_ɪg'zɑ:mpl]	zum Beispiel	Asif likes lamb, **for ~**.
capital letter [ˌkæpɪtl 'letə]	Großbuchstabe	**CAPITAL LETTERS**
tense [tens]	(grammatische) Zeit, Tempus	

Unit 3 Lösung, p. 61

5 Can you help me? (Relative clauses)

1 London Eye	*3* steel drums	*5* Manchester United	*7* Harry Potter
2 Philipp Franke	*4* stewed chicken	*6* footie_girl	*8* Daniel Craig

Classroom English → S. 236 · Personen-, Orts- und Ländernamen → S. 226–228 · Unregelmäßige Verben → S. 230–231

Dictionary (English – German)   181

Das Dictionary besteht aus zwei alphabetischen Wörterlisten:

Englisch – Deutsch (S. 181–204)
Deutsch – Englisch (S. 205–225).

Das **English – German Dictionary** enthält den Wortschatz der Bände 1 bis 3 von *English G 21*.
Wenn du wissen möchtest, was ein Wort bedeutet, wie man es ausspricht oder wie es genau geschrieben wird,
kannst du hier nachschlagen.

Im **English – German Dictionary** werden folgende **Abkürzungen** und **Symbole** verwendet:

jm. = jemandem	sb. = somebody	*pl* = *plural*	*AE* = *American English*
jn. = jemanden	sth. = something	*no pl* = *no plural*	*infml* = *informal*

° Mit diesem Kringel sind Wörter markiert, die nicht zum Lernwortschatz gehören.

▶ Der Pfeil verweist auf Kästchen im Vocabulary (S. 159–180), in denen du weitere Informationen zu diesem Wort findest.

Die **Fundstellenangaben** zeigen, wo ein Wort zum ersten Mal vorkommt.
Die Ziffern in Klammern bezeichnen Seitenzahlen:

I = Band 1 • II = Band 2 • III = Band 3
III Intro (6)   = Band 3, Introduction, Seite 6
III Intro (6/159)= Band 3, Introduction, Seite 159 (im Vocabulary, zu Seite 6)
III 1 (20)   = Band 3, Unit 1, Seite 20
III 1 (20/163) = Band 3, Unit 1, Seite 163 (im Vocabulary, zu Seite 20)

Tipps zur Arbeit mit dem Dictionary findest du im Skills File auf Seite 136.

A

a [ə]
1. ein, eine I
2. once/twice a week einmal/zweimal pro Woche III 2 (33) • **a bit** ein bisschen, etwas II • **a few** ein paar, einige II • **a lot (of)** eine Menge, viel, viele II • **He likes her a lot.** Er mag sie sehr.
able [ˈeɪbl]: **be able to do sth.** etwas tun können; fähig sein / in der Lage sein, etwas zu tun III 2 (32)
▶ S. 170 „können" und „dürfen"
°**Aboriginal** [ˌæbəˈrɪdʒənl] Ureinwohner/in
about [əˈbaʊt]
1. über I
2. ungefähr II
about yourself [jəˈself, jɔːˈself] über dich (selbst) III 3 (65) • **ask about sth.** nach etwas fragen I
How about ...? Wie wär's mit ...?
III Intro (10) • **This is about Mr Green.** Es geht um Mr Green.
What about ...? 1. Was ist mit ...? / Und ...? I; **2.** Wie wär's mit ...? I
What are you talking about? Wovon redest du? I • **What was the best thing about ...?** Was war das Beste an ...? II
°**above** [əˈbʌv] über, oberhalb (von)
accent [ˈæksənt] Akzent II

accident [ˈæksɪdənt] Unfall II
across [əˈkrɒs]
1. (quer) über III 1 (15)
2. hinüber, herüber III 2 (45)
°**all across Canada** in ganz Kanada
act [ækt] aufführen, spielen I
°**Act out ...** Spiele/Spielt ... vor.
°**action film** [ˈækʃən fɪlm] Actionfilm
activity [ækˈtɪvəti] Aktivität, Tätigkeit I
actor [ˈæktə] Schauspieler/in II
actually [ˈæktʃuəli] eigentlich; in Wirklichkeit III 1 (16)
°**adapt** [əˈdæpt] umstellen, überarbeiten
add (to) [æd] hinzufügen, ergänzen, addieren (zu) I
address [əˈdres] Adresse, Anschrift II
adult [ˈædʌlt] Erwachsene(r) III 1 (14)
°**advice** [ədˈvaɪs] Rat, Ratschläge
afraid [əˈfreɪd]
1. be afraid (of) Angst haben (vor) I
2. I'm afraid leider II
after [ˈɑːftə] nach *(zeitlich)* I
after that danach I
after [ˈɑːftə] nachdem II
afternoon [ˌɑːftəˈnuːn] Nachmittag I • **in the afternoon** nachmittags, am Nachmittag I • **on Friday afternoon** freitagnachmittags, am Freitagnachmittag I

again [əˈgen] wieder; noch einmal I
against [əˈgenst] gegen III 3 (57)
age [eɪdʒ] Alter III 3 (53)
ago [əˈgəʊ]: **a minute ago** vor einer Minute I
agree (on) [əˈgriː] sich einigen (auf) I • **agree with sb./sth.** jm./etwas zustimmen; mit jm./etwas übereinstimmen II
air [eə] Luft III 1 (13/161)
airport [ˈeəpɔːt] Flughafen III 1 (20/163)
album [ˈælbəm] Album III 5 (95)
all [ɔːl] alle; alles I • **2 all** [ˌtuːˈɔːl] 2 beide (2:2 unentschieden) III 3 (54)
°**all across Canada** in ganz Kanada
all day den ganzen Tag (lang) I
all over the world auf der ganzen Welt III Intro (6/159) • **all right** gut, in Ordnung II • **all the time** die ganze Zeit I • °**all the way** den ganzen Weg • **from all over the UK/the world/England** aus dem gesamten Vereinigten Königreich / aus der ganzen Welt / aus ganz England III Intro (6) • **This is all wrong.** Das ist ganz falsch. I
allowed [əˈlaʊd]: **be allowed to do sth.** etwas tun dürfen III 2 (45)
▶ S. 170 „können" und „dürfen"
almost [ˈɔːlməʊst] fast, beinahe III 1 (26)
alone [əˈləʊn] allein I

182 Dictionary (English – German)

along the street [ə'lɒŋ] entlang der Straße / die Straße entlang II
alphabet ['ælfəbet] Alphabet I
°**alphabetical** [ˌælfə'betɪkl] alphabetisch
already [ɔːl'redi] schon, bereits II
also ['ɔːlsəʊ] auch II
although [ɔːl'ðəʊ] obwohl III 3 (57)
always ['ɔːlweɪz] immer I
am [ˌeɪ_'em]: **7 am** 7 Uhr morgens/vormittags I
amazing [ə'meɪzɪŋ] erstaunlich, unglaublich II
ambulance ['æmbjələns] Krankenwagen III 3 (66)
American football [əˌmerɪkən 'fʊtbɔːl] Football I
an [ən] ein, eine I
and [ənd, ænd] und I
angel ['eɪndʒl] Engel II
angry (about sth. / with sb.) ['æŋgri] wütend, böse (über etwas / auf jn.) II
animal ['ænɪml] Tier II
announce [ə'naʊns] ankündigen, bekanntgeben III 5 (88)
announcement [ə'naʊnsmənt] Durchsage, Ansage; Ankündigung, Bekanntgabe III 1 (25)
annoy sb. [ə'nɔɪ] jm. ärgern, belästigen III 4 (70/175)
annoying [ə'nɔɪɪŋ]: **My dad is annoying.** Mein Vater geht mir auf die Nerven. III 4 (70)
anorak ['ænəræk] Anorak, Windjacke III 2 (45)
another [ə'nʌðə] ein(e) andere(r, s); noch ein(e) I • **another 45 p** weitere 45 Pence, noch 45 Pence II
answer ['ɑːnsə] antworten; beantworten I
answer (to) ['ɑːnsə] Antwort (auf) I
any ['eni]: **any ...?** (irgend)welche ...? I • **not (...) any** kein, keine I • **not (...) any more** nicht mehr III 2 (34)
anybody ['enibɒdi] (irgend)jemand II • **not (...) anybody** niemand II
anything ['eniθɪŋ] (irgend)etwas II **not (...) anything** nichts II
anyway ['eniweɪ]
   1. sowieso I
   2. trotzdem II
   3. aber egal, ...; wie auch immer, ...; wie dem auch sei, ... III 1 (16)
anywhere ['eniweə] irgendwo(hin) II • **not (...) anywhere** nirgendwo(hin) II
°**appear** [ə'pɪə] erscheinen, auftauchen
appetite ['æpɪtaɪt] Appetit III 3 (55)
apple ['æpl] Apfel I

appointment [ə'pɔɪntmənt] Termin, Verabredung I
April ['eɪprəl] April I
°**aquatic** [ə'kwætɪk] Wasser-
are [ɑː] bist; sind; seid I • **How are you?** Wie geht es dir/Ihnen/euch? II • **The pencils are 35 p.** Die Bleistifte kosten 35 Pence. I • **You're joking, aren't you?** Du machst Witze, nicht wahr? / Das ist nicht dein Ernst, oder? II
area ['eəriə] Bereich; Gebiet, Gegend III 1 (29)
argue ['ɑːgjuː] sich streiten, sich zanken I
argument ['ɑːgjumənt]
   1. Argument, Begründung III 4 (72)
   2. Streit III 4 (72)
arm [ɑːm] Arm I
armchair ['ɑːmtʃeə] Sessel I
around [ə'raʊnd] um ... (herum); in ... umher, durch III 1 (26/164)
   around six um sechs herum, gegen sechs III 1 (26/164) • **around the lake** um den See (herum) III 1 (26/164) • **around the town** in der Stadt umher, durch die Stadt **jump/run/walk around** herumspringen/-rennen / umherspazieren III 1 (26/164)
   ▶ S.164 around
arrival (arr) [ə'raɪvl] Ankunft III 2 (32)
arrive [ə'raɪv] ankommen, eintreffen II
art [ɑːt] Kunst I
article ['ɑːtɪkl] (Zeitungs-)Artikel III 5 (88)
artificial [ˌɑːtɪ'fɪʃl] künstlich, Kunst- III 3 (104)
artist ['ɑːtɪst] Künstler/in III 3 (56)
as [əz, æz]
   1. als, während II
   2. as old/big as so alt/groß wie II
ask [ɑːsk]
   1. fragen I • **ask about sth.** nach etwas fragen I • **ask questions** Fragen stellen I • **ask sb. the way** jn. nach dem Weg fragen II
   °**2. ask sb. to do sth.** jn. bitten, etwas zu tun
asleep [ə'sliːp]: **be asleep** schlafen I
Assembly [ə'sembli] Versammlung *(morgendliche Schulversammlung, oft mit Andacht)* III 2 (44)
°**assistant** [ə'sɪstənt] Assistent/in
at [ət, æt]: **at 7 Hamilton Street** in der Hamiltonstraße 7 I • **at 8.45** um 8.45 I • **at break** in der Pause *(zwischen Schulstunden)* II • **at home** daheim, zu Hause I • **at last** endlich, schließlich I • **at least** zumindest, wenigstens I

at night nachts, in der Nacht I
at school in der Schule I • **at that table** an dem Tisch (dort) / an den Tisch (dort) I • **at the bottom (of)** unten, am unteren Ende (von) II • **at the butcher's** beim Metzger/Fleischer III 1 (24/163)
at the chemist's beim Apotheker III 1 (24/163) • **at the end (of)** am Ende (von) I • **at the Shaws' house** im Haus der Shaws / bei den Shaws zu Hause I • **at the station** am Bahnhof I • **at the top (of)** oben, am oberen Ende, an der Spitze (von) I • **at the weekend** am Wochenende I • **at work** bei der Arbeit / am Arbeitsplatz I
ate [et, eɪt] *siehe* **eat**
athletics [æθ'letɪks] Leichtathletik III 3 (66)
°**Atlantic** [ət'læntɪk] **the Atlantic** der Atlantische Ozean, Atlantik
attack [ə'tæk] angreifen III 4 (72/176)
attack [ə'tæk] Angriff III 4 (72)
audience ['ɔːdiəns] Publikum; Zuschauer/innen, Zuhörer/innen II
August ['ɔːgəst] August I
aunt [ɑːnt] Tante I • **auntie** ['ɑːnti] Tante II
°**autograph** ['ɔːtəgrɑːf] Autogramm
autumn ['ɔːtəm] Herbst I
away [ə'weɪ] weg, fort I
awful ['ɔːfl] furchtbar, schrecklich II
°**Aye.** [aɪ] Ja. *(besonders in Schottland und Irland gebräuchlich)*

B

baby ['beɪbi] Baby I • **have a baby** ein Baby/Kind bekommen II
°**back** [bæk] Rücken
back (to) [bæk] zurück (nach) I
back door [ˌbæk 'dɔː] Hintertür II
background ['bækgraʊnd] Hintergrund II • **background file** *etwa:* Hintergrundinformation(en) II
bacon ['beɪkən] Schinkenspeck II
bad [bæd] schlecht, schlimm • **bad timing** ['taɪmɪŋ] schlechtes Timing III 3 (55) • **be bad at sth.** in etwas schlecht sein III 5 (91/179)
badly ['bædli]: **do badly (in)** schlecht abschneiden (in) III 4 (70)
badminton ['bædmɪntən] Badminton, Federball I • **badminton racket** ['rækɪt] Badmintonschläger III 3 (60/172)
bag [bæg] Tasche, Beutel, Tüte I
°**baggy** ['bægi] weit (geschnitten)
°**bagpiper** ['bægpaɪpə] Dudelsackpfeifer/in

Dictionary (English – German) 183

bagpipes (pl) ['bægpaɪps] Dudelsack III 5 (95)

bakery ['beɪkəri] Bäckerei III 1 (24)

ball [bɔːl] Ball I

°**ballet** ['bæleɪ] Ballett I

banana [bə'nɑːnə] Banane I

band [bænd] Band, (Musik-)Gruppe I

bank [bæŋk] Bank, Sparkasse I
bank robber ['bæŋk ˌrɒbə] Bankräuber/in I

bar [bɑː] Bar II

baseball ['beɪsbɔːl] Baseball I
baseball cap Baseballmütze II

basket ['bɑːskɪt] Korb I • **a basket of apples** ein Korb Äpfel I

basketball ['bɑːskɪtbɔːl] Basketball I

bath [bɑːθ] Bad, Badewanne II
have a bath baden, ein Bad nehmen II

bathroom ['bɑːθruːm] Badezimmer I

bay [beɪ] Bucht III 2 (38/168)

be [biː], **was/were, been** sein I

beach [biːtʃ] Strand II • **on the beach** am Strand II

bear [beə] Bär II

beat [biːt], **beat, beaten** schlagen; besiegen III 3 (57)

beaten ['biːtn] siehe **beat**

beautiful ['bjuːtɪfl] schön I

beauty ['bjuːti] Schönheit III 2 (35)

became [bɪ'keɪm] siehe **become**

because [bɪ'kɒz] weil I • °**because of** wegen

become [bɪ'kʌm], **became, become** werden II

bed [bed] Bett I • **Bed and Breakfast (B&B)** [ˌbed_ən 'brekfəst] Frühstückspension I • **go to bed** ins Bett gehen II

bedroom ['bedruːm] Schlafzimmer I

beef [biːf] Rindfleisch III 1 (24/163)

been [biːn] siehe **be**

before [bɪ'fɔː] vor (zeitlich) I

before [bɪ'fɔː] bevor II

began [bɪ'gæn] siehe **begin**

begin (-nn-) [bɪ'gɪn], **began, begun** beginnen, anfangen (mit) III 2 (44)

beginning [bɪ'gɪnɪŋ] Beginn, Anfang; Einleitung II

begun [bɪ'gʌn] siehe **begin**

behind [bɪ'haɪnd] hinter II

believe [bɪ'liːv] glauben III 2 (44)

bell [bel] Klingel, Glocke III 2 (45)

°**belong to** [bɪ'lɒŋ] gehören (zu)

°**below** [bɪ'ləʊ] unten

best [best] am besten II • **the best ...** der/die/das beste ...; die besten I • **What was the best thing about ...?** Was war das Beste an ...?

°**best-selling** [ˌbest'selɪŋ] meistgekauft, -verkauft

better ['betə] besser I • **like sth. better** etwas lieber mögen II

between [bɪ'twiːn] zwischen II

big [bɪg] groß I • **big wheel** [ˌbɪg 'wiːl] Riesenrad III 1 (12)
▶ S.165 big – large – huge

bike [baɪk] Fahrrad I • **bike ride** (Rad-)Fahrt I • **ride a bike** Rad fahren I

bill [bɪl] Rechnung III 4 (70)

bin [bɪn] Mülltonne II

biography [baɪ'ɒgrəfi] Biografie III 5 (90)

biology [baɪ'ɒlədʒi] Biologie I

bird [bɜːd] Vogel I

birthday ['bɜːθdeɪ] Geburtstag I
Happy birthday. Herzlichen Glückwunsch zum Geburtstag. I • **My birthday is in May.** Ich habe im Mai Geburtstag. I • **My birthday is on 13th June.** Ich habe am 13. Juni Geburtstag. I • **When's your birthday?** Wann hast du Geburtstag? I

°**biryani** [ˌbɪri'jɑːni] indisches Festtagsgericht, bestehend aus Reis, Fleisch, Gemüse und Jogurt

biscuit ['bɪskɪt] Keks, Plätzchen I

bit: a bit [ə 'bɪt] ein bisschen, etwas II

black [blæk] schwarz I

blame sb. (for) [bleɪm] jm. die Schuld geben (an); jm. Vorwürfe machen (wegen) III 4 (72)

bleep [bliːp] piepsen II

bleep [bliːp] Piepton II

blew [bluː] siehe **blow**

blow [bləʊ], **blew, blown** wehen, blasen III 2 (44)

blown [bləʊn] siehe **blow**

blue [bluː] blau I

board [bɔːd] (Wand-)Tafel I • **on the board** an der/die Tafel I • **notice board** Anschlagtafel, schwarzes Brett I

boat [bəʊt] Boot, Schiff I

body ['bɒdi] Körper I

bold print [ˌbəʊld 'prɪnt] Fettdruck III 5 (90)

book [bʊk] Buch I

boot [buːt] Stiefel I

boring ['bɔːrɪŋ] langweilig I

born [bɔːn]: **be born** geboren sein/werden II

boss [bɒs] Chef/in, Boss III Intro (8)

both [bəʊθ] beide I

bottle ['bɒtl] Flasche I • **a bottle of milk** eine Flasche Milch I

bottom ['bɒtəm] unteres Ende II
at the bottom (of) unten, am unteren Ende (von) II

bought [bɔːt] siehe **buy**

bowl [bəʊl] Schüssel I • **a bowl of cornflakes** eine Schale Cornflakes I

box [bɒks] Kasten, Kästchen, Kiste I • **sandwich box** Brotdose I

°**boxercise** ['bɒksəsaɪz] Sportart, die auf den Fitnessübungen des Boxsports basiert

boy [bɔɪ] Junge I

°**bracket** ['brækɪt] Klammer (in Texten)

brainstorm ['breɪnstɔːm] brainstormen (so viele Ideen wie möglich sammeln) III 4 (71)

brave [breɪv] tapfer, mutig III 3 (66)

bread (no pl) [bred] Brot I

break [breɪk] Pause I • **at break** in der Pause (zwischen Schulstunden) II

break a journey [ˌbreɪk_ə 'dʒɜːni], **broke, broken** eine Reise unterbrechen III 1 (25)

breakfast ['brekfəst] Frühstück I
have breakfast frühstücken I

bridge [brɪdʒ] Brücke I

bridle path ['braɪdl pɑːθ] Reitweg III 3 (60/173)

bright [braɪt] hell, leuchtend II

brilliant ['brɪliənt] genial, toll III Intro (6)

bring [brɪŋ], **brought, brought** (mit-, her)bringen I

British ['brɪtɪʃ] britisch; Brite, Britin II

brochure ['brəʊʃə] Prospekt, Broschüre I

broke [brəʊk] siehe **break**

broken ['brəʊkən] siehe **break**

broken ['brəʊkən] gebrochen; zerbrochen, kaputt II

brother ['brʌðə] Bruder I

brought [brɔːt] siehe **bring**

brown [braʊn] braun I

°**budget** ['bʌdʒɪt]: **be on a budget** mit wenig Geld auskommen müssen

budgie ['bʌdʒi] Wellensittich I

°**buffet** ['bʊfeɪ] Büfett I

build [bɪld], **built, built** bauen II

building ['bɪldɪŋ] Gebäude II

built [bɪlt] siehe **build**

bully ['bʊli] einschüchtern, tyrannisieren II

bully ['bʊli] (Schul-)Tyrann III 2 (35)

bunk (bed) [bʌŋk] Etagenbett, Koje II

bus [bʌs] Bus I • **bus stop** ['bʌs stɒp] Bushaltestelle III 1 (20/163)

184 Dictionary (English – German)

business ['bɪznəs]: **Mind your own business.** Das geht dich nichts an! / Kümmere dich um deine eigenen Angelegenheiten! II

busy ['bɪzi] belebt, verkehrsreich; hektisch III 2 (38/168)

but [bət, bʌt] aber I

butcher ['bʊtʃə] Fleischer/in, Metzger/in III 1 (24) • **at the butcher's** beim Fleischer/Metzger III 1 (24/163)

butter ['bʌtə] Butter III 1 (24)

button ['bʌtn] Knopf III 1 (26)

buy [baɪ], **bought, bought** kaufen I

°**buzz** [bʌz] *hier*: den Summer / die Glocke betätigen

by [baɪ]
 1. von I
 2. an; (nahe) bei II
 3. by car/train/bike/... mit dem Auto/Zug/Rad/... II
 4. bis spätestens; nicht später als **by ten o'clock** bis (spätestens) zehn Uhr III 4 (71)
 5. by the way übrigens II
 ▶ S.175 German „bis"

Bye. [baɪ] Tschüs! I

C

cabin ['kæbɪn] Hütte III 4 (69)

café ['kæfeɪ] *(kleines)* Restaurant, Imbissstube, Café II

cage [keɪdʒ] Käfig I

cake [keɪk] Kuchen, Torte I

calendar ['kælɪndə] Kalender I

call [kɔːl]
 1. rufen; anrufen I
 2. nennen I
 call sb. names jn. mit Schimpfwörtern hänseln, jm. Schimpfwörter nachrufen III 2 (35) • °**call sth. off** etwas absagen, abblasen

call [kɔːl] Anruf, Telefongespräch I

called [kɔːld]: **be called** heißen, genannt werden III 1 (13)

calm down [ˌkɑːm 'daʊn] sich beruhigen II

came [keɪm] *siehe* **come**

camel ['kæml] Kamel II

camera ['kæmərə] Kamera, Fotoapparat I

°**cameraman/-woman** ['kæmrəmən, -wʊmən] Kameramann/-frau

camp [kæmp] zelten III 4 (68/174)

can [kən, kæn]
 1. können I
 2. dürfen I
 Can I help you? Kann ich Ihnen helfen? / Was kann ich für Sie tun? *(im Geschäft)* I
 ▶ S.170 „können" und „dürfen"

canal [kə'næl] Kanal III 2 (38/168)

canoe [kə'nuː] Kanu III 4 (69/174)

canoe [kə'nuː] paddeln, Kanu fahren III 4 (68/174)

canteen [kæn'tiːn] Kantine, Schulmensa II

cap [kæp] Mütze, Kappe II

capital ['kæpɪtl] Hauptstadt III 1 (12)

capital letter [ˌkæpɪtl 'letə] Großbuchstabe III 5 (98)

caption ['kæpʃn] Bildunterschrift III 5 (90)

car [kɑː] Auto I • **car park** Parkplatz III 2 (38/168)

caravan ['kærəvæn] Wohnwagen II

card [kɑːd] (Spiel-, Post-)Karte I

career [kə'rɪə] Karriere III 5 (95)

careful ['keəfl]
 1. vorsichtig II
 2. sorgfältig II

caretaker ['keəteɪkə] Hausmeister/in II

carrot ['kærət] Möhre, Karotte I

cartoon [kɑː'tuːn] Cartoon (Zeichentrickfilm; Bilderwitz) II

case [keɪs] Fall II

castle ['kɑːsl] Burg, Schloss II

cat [kæt] Katze I

catch [kætʃ], **caught, caught** fangen; erwischen II

cathedral [kə'θiːdrəl] Kathedrale, Dom III 1 (14/162)

°**Catholic** ['kæθlɪk] katholisch

caught [kɔːt] *siehe* **catch**

CD [ˌsiː'diː] CD I • **CD player** CD-Spieler I

ceilidh ['keɪli] *Musik- und Tanzveranstaltung, vor allem in Schottland und Irland* III 2 (32)

cent (c) [sent] Cent I • **per cent (%)** [pə'sent] Prozent III 4 (76)

centimetre (cm) ['sentɪmiːtə] Zentimeter III 4 (76/176)

central ['sentrəl] Zentral-, Mittel- III 1 (14)

centre ['sentə] Zentrum, Mitte II **city centre** Stadtzentrum, Innenstadt I • **sports centre** Sportzentrum I

century ['sentʃəri] Jahrhundert II

chair [tʃeə] Stuhl I

champion ['tʃæmpiən] Meister/in, Champion I

championship ['tʃæmpiənʃɪp] Meisterschaft III 3 (104)

change [tʃeɪndʒ] umsteigen III 1 (14)

change [tʃeɪndʒ]
 °**1.** (Ver-)Änderung
 2. Wechselgeld I

°**charity** ['tʃærəti] Wohltätigkeitsorganisation

°**chart** [tʃɑːt] Schaubild, Diagramm, Tabelle, Grafik

charts [tʃɑːts] Charts, Hitliste III 5 (96)

chat (-tt-) [tʃæt] plaudern; chatten II

chat room [tʃæt ruːm] Chatroom III 2 (33)

cheap [tʃiːp] billig I

check [tʃek] (über)prüfen, kontrollieren I

°**checklist** ['tʃeklɪst] Checkliste

checkpoint ['tʃekpɔɪnt] Kontrollpunkt *(hier: zur Selbstüberprüfung)* I

cheer [tʃɪə] jubeln, Beifall klatschen II

cheese [tʃiːz] Käse I

chemist ['kemɪst] Drogerie, Apotheke II • **at the chemist's** beim Apotheker III 1 (24/163)

cherry ['tʃeri] Kirsche II

chicken ['tʃɪkɪn] Huhn; (Brat-)Hähnchen I

child [tʃaɪld], *pl* **children** ['tʃɪldrən] Kind I

chips (pl) [tʃɪps] Pommes frites I

chocolate ['tʃɒklət] Schokolade I

choir ['kwaɪə] Chor I

choose [tʃuːz], **chose, chosen** (sich) aussuchen, (aus)wählen I

chorus ['kɔːrəs] Refrain III 4 (73)

chose [tʃəʊz] *siehe* **choose**

chosen ['tʃəʊzn] *siehe* **choose**

Christmas ['krɪsməs] Weihnachten I

church [tʃɜːtʃ] Kirche I

cinema ['sɪnəmə] Kino I • **go to the cinema** ins Kino gehen II

circus ['sɜːkəs] (runder) Platz III 1 (14/162)

city ['sɪti] (Groß-)Stadt I • **city centre** Stadtzentrum, Innenstadt I

°**clan** [klæn] Clan, Sippe

°**clapshot** ['klæpʃɒt] *schottisches Eintopfgericht*

class [klɑːs] (Schul-)Klasse I **class teacher** Klassenlehrer/in I

classical ['klæsɪkl] klassisch III Intro (6)

classmate ['klɑːsmeɪt] Klassenkamerad/in, Mitschüler/in I

classroom ['klɑːsruːm] Klassenzimmer I

clean [kliːn] sauber II

clean [kliːn] sauber machen, putzen I • **I clean my teeth.** Ich putze mir die Zähne. I

cleaner ['kliːnə] Putzfrau, -mann II

clear [klɪə] klar, deutlich I

°**clerk** [klɑːk] Angestellte(r)

clever ['klevə] schlau, klug I

Dictionary (English – German)   **185**

click on sth. [klɪk] etwas anklicken II

cliff [klɪf] Klippe, Felsen III 2 (30)

climb [klaɪm] klettern; hinaufklettern (auf) I • **Climb a tree.** Klettere auf einen Baum. I

clinic [ˈklɪnɪk] Klinik II

clock [klɒk] (Wand-, Stand-, Turm-) Uhr I

clone [kləʊn] Klon III 2 (46)

close (to) [kləʊs] nahe (bei, an) III 1 (27) • **That was close.** Das war knapp. II

close [kləʊz] schließen, zumachen I

closed [kləʊzd] geschlossen II

°**closing phrase** [ˈkləʊzɪŋ freɪz] Grußformel *(am Briefende)*

clothes *(pl)* [kləʊðz, kləʊz] Kleider, Kleidung(sstücke) II

cloud [klaʊd] Wolke II

cloudy [ˈklaʊdi] bewölkt II

clown [klaʊn] Clown/in II

club [klʌb] Klub; Verein I

°**clue** [klu:] Hinweis, Anhaltspunkt

coach [kəʊtʃ] Trainer/in III 3 (54)

coast [kəʊst] Küste III 2 (38/168)

cola [ˈkəʊlə] Cola I

cold [kəʊld] kalt I • **be cold** frieren I

cold [kəʊld] Erkältung II • **have a cold** erkältet sein, eine Erkältung haben II

collect [kəˈlekt] sammeln I

collector [kəˈlektə] Sammler/in II

°**colony** [ˈkɒləni] Kolonie

colour [ˈkʌlə] kolorieren, färben, bunt an-, ausmalen III 4 (69/174)

colour [ˈkʌlə] Farbe I • **What colour is ...?** Welche Farbe hat ...? I

column [ˈkɒləm] Säule III 1 (14/162)

°**combine** [kəmˈbaɪn] kombinieren, verbinden

come [kʌm], **came, come** kommen I • **come home** nach Hause kommen I • **come in** hereinkommen I • **Come on. 1.** Na los, komm. II; **2.** Ach komm! / Na hör mal! II

comic [ˈkɒmɪk] Comic-Heft I

Commonwealth [ˈkɒmənwelθ]: **the Commonwealth** *Gemeinschaft der Länder des ehemaligen Britischen Weltreichs* III 3 (104)

community hall [kəˈmju:nəti hɔ:l]: Gemeinschaftshalle, -saal, Gemeindehalle, -saal III 2 (46)

company [ˈkʌmpəni] Firma, Gesellschaft III 5 (98)

°**compare** [kəmˈpeə] vergleichen

comparison [kəmˈpærɪsn] Steigerung; Vergleich II

°**competition** [ˌkɒmpəˈtɪʃn] Wettbewerb

complain (about sth.) [kəmˈpleɪn] sich (über etwas) beschweren, beklagen III 4 (70)

°**complete** [kəmˈpli:t] vervollständigen, ergänzen

computer [kəmˈpju:tə] Computer I

concert [ˈkɒnsət] Konzert III Intro (6)

°**context** [ˈkɒntekst]: **from the context** aus dem Zusammenhang, aus dem Kontext

°**continue** [kənˈtɪnju:] fortführen, fortsetzen

cook [kʊk] kochen, zubereiten II

cook [kʊk] Koch/Köchin III 4 (69/174)

cooker [ˈkʊkə] Herd I

cool [ku:l]
1. kühl II
2. cool I

copy [ˈkɒpi] kopieren; abschreiben II

copy [ˈkɒpi]
1. Kopie, Abschrift II
2. Exemplar III 5 (98)

corner [ˈkɔ:nə] Ecke I • **on the corner of Green Street and London Road** Green Street, Ecke London Road II

cornflakes [ˈkɔ:nfleɪks] Cornflakes I

correct [kəˈrekt] berichtigen, korrigieren II

correct [kəˈrekt] richtig III 2 (35)

could [kəd, kʊd]
1. he could ... er konnte ... II
2. he could ... er könnte ... III 2 (44)

count [kaʊnt] zählen II

countdown [ˈkaʊntdaʊn] Countdown III 5 (92)

°**counter** [ˈkaʊntə] Spielstein

country [ˈkʌntri] Land *(auch als Gegensatz zur Stadt)* II • **in the country** auf dem Land II

course [kɔ:s] Kurs, Lehrgang III 1 (22)

course: of course [əv ˈkɔ:s] natürlich, selbstverständlich I

court [kɔ:t] Platz, Court *(für Squash, Badminton, Tennis)* III 3 (60/172)

cousin [ˈkʌzn] Cousin, Cousine I

cover [ˈkʌvə] (CD-)Hülle I

cow [kaʊ] Kuh II

crazy [ˈkreɪzi] verrückt III 4 (77)

°**cricket** [ˈkrɪkɪt] Kricket

crisps *(pl)* [krɪsps] Kartoffelchips I

crocodile [ˈkrɒkədaɪl] Krokodil II

cross [krɒs] überqueren II

cross [krɒs]: **be cross (with)** böse, sauer sein (auf) I

°**crosse** [krɒs] *Sportgerät für Lacrosse*

crush [krʌʃ]: **have a crush on sb.** in jn. verknallt sein III 5 (92)

°**culture** [ˈkʌltʃə] Kultur

cup [kʌp]
1. Tasse • **a cup of tea** eine Tasse Tee III 2 (44)
2. Pokal III 3 (57)

cupboard [ˈkʌbəd] Schrank I

curry [ˈkʌri] Curry(gericht) III 1 (16)

customer [ˈkʌstəmə] Kunde, Kundin II

cut (-tt-) [kʌt], **cut, cut** schneiden III 2 (44) • **cut sth. off** etwas abtrennen, abschneiden III 3 (66)

cycle [ˈsaɪkl] (mit dem) Rad fahren II • **cycle path** Radweg II

D

dad [dæd] Papa, Vati; Vater I

°**daily** [ˈdeɪli] täglich

dance [dɑ:ns] tanzen I

dance [dɑ:ns] Tanz I

dancer [ˈdɑ:nsə] Tänzer/in II

dancing [ˈdɑ:nsɪŋ] Tanzen I **dancing lessons** Tanzstunden, Tanzunterricht I

danger [ˈdeɪndʒə] Gefahr III 1 (26)

dangerous [ˈdeɪndʒərəs] gefährlich II

dark [dɑ:k] dunkel I

date [deɪt] Datum I • °**go on a date** zu einer Verabredung gehen

daughter [ˈdɔ:tə] Tochter I

day [deɪ] Tag I • **one day** eines Tages I • **days of the week** Wochentage I • **day out** Tagesausflug III 1 (13)

dead [ded] tot I

deal [di:l]: **It's a deal.** Abgemacht! III 3 (56/172) • **make a deal** ein Abkommen / eine Abmachung treffen III 3 (56)

dear [dɪə] Schatz, Liebling I • **Oh dear!** Oje! II

dear [dɪə]: **Dear Jay ...** Lieber Jay, ... I

December [dɪˈsembə] Dezember I

°**decide (on)** [dɪˈsaɪd] sich entscheiden (für), beschließen

°**deep** [di:p] tief

deer, *pl* **deer** [dɪə] Reh, Hirsch II

°**definition** [ˌdefɪˈnɪʃn] Definition

degree [dɪˈgri:] Grad II

delicious [dɪˈlɪʃəs] köstlich, lecker II

department store [dɪˈpɑ:tmənt stɔ:] Kaufhaus I

departure (dep) [dɪˈpɑ:tʃə] Abfahrt, Abflug; Abreise III 2 (32)

describe sth. (to sb.) [dɪˈskraɪb] (jm.) etwas beschreiben II

description [dɪˈskrɪpʃn] Beschreibung II

design [dɪˈzaɪn] entwerfen, gestalten II

°**designer** [dɪ'zaɪnə] Designer/in
desk [desk] Schreibtisch I
destroy [dɪ'strɔɪ] zerstören III 1 (26)
detail ['diːteɪl] Detail, Einzelheit II
detective [dɪ'tektɪv] Detektiv/in I
°**dialogue** ['daɪəlɒg] Dialog
diary ['daɪəri] Tagebuch; Termin-kalender I • °**keep a diary** ein Tagebuch führen
dice, *pl* **dice** [daɪs] Würfel II
°**dictate** [dɪk'teɪt] diktieren
dictionary ['dɪkʃənri] Wörterbuch, *(alphabetisches)* Wörterverzeichnis I
did [dɪd] *siehe* **do** • **Did you go ...?** Bist du ... gegangen? / Seid ihr ... gegangen? I • **we didn't sing** ['dɪdnt] wir sangen nicht / wir haben nicht gesungen I
die (of) *(-ing form:* **dying***)* [daɪ] sterben (an) II
°**difference** ['dɪfrəns] Unterschied
different (from) ['dɪfrənt] verschie-den, unterschiedlich; anders (als) I
difficult ['dɪfɪkəlt] schwierig, schwer I
dining room ['daɪnɪŋ ruːm] Ess-zimmer I
dinner ['dɪnə] Abendessen, Abend-brot I • **have dinner** Abendbrot essen I
°**dinosaur** ['daɪnəsɔː] Dinosaurier
°**direction** [dɪ'rekʃən] Richtung
°**director** [də'rektə] Regisseur/in
dirty ['dɜːti] schmutzig II
disabled [dɪs'eɪbld] (körper)be-hindert III 3 (104)
disagree (with) [ˌdɪsə'griː] nicht übereinstimmen (mit); anderer Meinung sein (als) III 4 (72)
disappear [ˌdɪsə'pɪə] verschwinden II
disc jockey (DJ) ['dɪsk dʒɒki, 'diː dʒeɪ] Diskjockey (DJ)
disco ['dɪskəʊ] Disko I
°**discus** ['dɪskəs] Diskuswerfen
°**discuss** [dɪ'skʌs] besprechen; diskutieren (über)
discussion [dɪ'skʌʃn] Diskussion II
dish [dɪʃ] Gericht *(Speise)* III 2 (46)
dishwasher ['dɪʃwɒʃə] Geschirr-spülmaschine I
°**dive** [daɪv] tauchen
°**divide (into)** [dɪ'vaɪd] auf-, einteilen (in)
divorced [dɪ'vɔːst] geschieden I
DJ ['diːdʒeɪ] Diskjockey III Intro (6/160)
DJ ['diːdʒeɪ] (Musik/CDs/Platten) auflegen *(in der Disko)* III Intro (6)
do [duː], **did, done** tun, machen I **Do you like ...?** Magst du ...? I **do a gig** einen Auftritt haben, ein

Konzert geben III Intro (8/160) • **do a good job** gute Arbeit leisten II **do a project** ein Projekt machen, durchführen II • **do an exercise** eine Übung machen II • **do badly/well (in)** schlecht/gut ab-schneiden (in) III 4 (70) • **do sport** Sport treiben I • °**do sth. wrong** etwas ausfressen
doctor ['dɒktə] Doktor; Arzt/Ärztin II • **to the doctor's** zum Arzt III 1 (24/163)
°**documentary** [ˌdɒkju'mentri] Doku-mentarfilm, -beitrag
dog [dɒg] Hund I
°**dollar** ['dɒlə] Dollar
done [dʌn] *siehe* **do**
don't [dəʊnt]: **Don't listen to Dan.** Hör/Hört nicht auf Dan. I • **I don't know.** Ich weiß es nicht. I • **I don't like ...** Ich mag ... nicht. / Ich mag kein(e) ... I
door [dɔː] Tür I
doorbell ['dɔːbel] Türklingel I
dossier ['dɒsieɪ] Mappe, Dossier *(des Sprachenportfolios)* I
double ['dʌbl] zweimal, doppelt, Doppel- I • °**double circle** Dop-pelkreis, „Kugellager" *(als Ge-sprächskreis)*
down [daʊn] hinunter, herunter, nach unten I • **down there** dort unten II • **fall down** hinfallen II
download [ˌdaʊn'ləʊd] runterladen, downloaden III 2 (33)
downstairs [ˌdaʊn'steəz] unten; nach unten I
°**dragon boat** ['drægən] Drachenboot
drama ['drɑːmə] Schauspiel, darstel-lende Kunst I
drank [dræŋk] *siehe* **drink**
draw [drɔː], **drew, drawn** zeichnen III 5 (89/178)
draw [drɔː] Unentschieden III 3 (54) **Our last match was a draw, 2–2.** *(you say: two all)* Unser letztes Spiel war ein Unentschieden, 2:2. III 3 (54/171)
▶ S.171 A football match
drawing ['drɔːɪŋ] Zeichnung III 5 (89)
drawn [drɔːn] *siehe* **draw**
dream (of, about) [driːm] träumen (von) III 2 (34)
dream [driːm] Traum I • **dream house** Traumhaus I
dress [dres] Kleid I
dressed [drest]: **get dressed** sich an-ziehen I
drew [druː] *siehe* **draw**
drink [drɪŋk] Getränk I
drink [drɪŋk], **drank, drunk** trinken I

drive [draɪv], **drove, driven** *(ein Auto/mit dem Auto)* fahren II
drive [draɪv] (Auto-)Fahrt III 4 (69/174)
driven ['drɪvn] *siehe* **drive**
driver ['draɪvə] Fahrer/in II
drop (-pp-) [drɒp] fallen lassen I
drove [drəʊv] *siehe* **drive**
drum [drʌm] Trommel III Intro (6)
drums *(pl)* [drʌmz] Schlagzeug III Intro (6/160) • **play the drums** Schlagzeug spielen III Intro (7/160)
drunk [drʌŋk] *siehe* **drink**
°**dump** [dʌmp] Müllkippe, Schutt-platz
°**during** ['djʊərɪŋ] während
dustbin ['dʌstbɪn] Mülltonne II
DVD [ˌdiː viː' diː] DVD I

E

each [iːtʃ] jeder, jede, jedes (einzel-ne) I • **each other** [iːtʃ_'ʌðə] ein-ander, sich (gegenseitig) III 4 (73)
ear [ɪə] Ohr I
earache ['ɪəreɪk] Ohrenschmerzen II
early ['ɜːli] früh I
earring ['ɪərɪŋ] Ohrring I
°**earth** [ɜːθ] Erde
east [iːst] Osten; nach Osten; öst-lich III Intro (7/160)
eastbound ['iːstbaʊnd] Richtung Osten III 1 (14)
easy ['iːzi] leicht, einfach I
easy-going [ˌiːzi'gəʊɪŋ] gelassen, locker III 4 (70)
eat [iːt], **ate, eaten** essen I
eaten ['iːtn] *siehe* **eat**
editor ['edɪtə] Redakteur/in III 5 (88)
egg [eg] Ei II
electric [ɪ'lektrɪk] elektrisch, Elektro- III Intro (11)
°**electrician** [ɪˌlek'trɪʃn] Elektriker/in
electricity [ɪˌlek'trɪsəti] Strom, Elektrizität III 1 (27)
electronic [ɪˌlek'trɒnɪk] elektronisch III 2 (33)
elephant ['elɪfənt] Elefant I
elevator ['elɪveɪtə] *(AE)* Fahrstuhl, Aufzug II
°**else** [els]: **What else can you do?** Was kannst du sonst noch ma-chen?
e-mail ['iːmeɪl] E-Mail I
empty ['empti] leer I
°**encyclopedia** [ɪnˌsaɪklə'piːdiə] Enzyklopädie, Lexikon
end [end] enden; beenden III 3 (64)
end [end] Ende, Schluss I • **at the end (of)** am Ende (von) I • **in the**

Dictionary (English – German)   187

end schließlich, zum Schluss
III 3 (57)
ending ['endɪŋ] Ende, (Ab-)Schluss
(einer Geschichte, eines Films usw.)
III 1 (28)
enemy ['enəmi] Feind/in II
engineer [ˌendʒɪ'nɪə] Ingenieur/in
II
English ['ɪŋglɪʃ] Englisch; englisch I
enjoy [ɪn'dʒɔɪ] genießen II • **Enjoy yourself.** Viel Spaß / Amüsier dich gut! III 4 (147)
enough [ɪ'nʌf] genug I
enter ['entə] betreten; eintreten (in)
III 3 (55)
entry ['entri] Eintrag, Eintragung
(im Wörterbuch/Tagebuch) III 2 (35)
equipment [ɪ'kwɪpmənt] Ausrüstung III 3 (60/172)
escape (from sb./sth.) [ɪ'skeɪp]
fliehen (vor jm./aus etwas); entkommen III 4 (81)
essay (about, on) ['eseɪ] Aufsatz
(über) I
°**etc.** [et'setərə] usw.
euro (€) ['jʊərəʊ] Euro I
even ['iːvn]
1. sogar I
2. not even (noch) nicht einmal
III 2 (34) • **He didn't even open the letter.** Er hat den Brief nicht einmal geöffnet. III 2 (34/167)
evening ['iːvnɪŋ] Abend I • **in the evening** abends, am Abend I
on Friday evening freitagabends, am Freitagabend I
°**event** [ɪ'vent] Veranstaltung, Ereignis
ever? ['evə] je? / jemals? / schon mal? I
every ['evri] jeder, jede, jedes I
everybody ['evribɒdi] jeder, alle II
everyday *(adj)* ['evrideɪ] Alltags-; alltägliche(r, s) III 1 (25)
°**everyone** ['evriwʌn] jeder, alle
everything ['evriθɪŋ] alles I
everywhere ['evriweə] überall
III 1 (13)
exactly [ɪg'zæktli] genau III 4 (72)
example [ɪg'zɑːmpl] Beispiel
III 5 (98) • **for example** zum Beispiel III 5 (98)
°**except** [ɪk'sept] ausgenommen, bis auf
exchange student [ɪks'tʃeɪndʒ ˌstjuː'dnt] Austauschschüler/in
III 3 (55)
excited [ɪk'saɪtɪd] begeistert, aufgeregt III 1 (26)
exciting [ɪk'saɪtɪŋ] aufregend, spannend I

Excuse me, ... [ɪk'skjuːz miː] Entschuldigung, ... / Entschuldigen Sie, ... I
exercise ['eksəsaɪz] Übung, Aufgabe I • **exercise book** Schulheft, Übungsheft I
expect [ɪk'spekt] erwarten III 2 (34)
expensive [ɪk'spensɪv] teuer I
explain sth. to sb. [ɪk'spleɪn] jm. etwas erklären, erläutern II
explanation [ˌeksplə'neɪʃn] Erklärung II
explore [ɪk'splɔː] erkunden, erforschen I
explorer [ɪk'splɔːrə] Entdecker/in, Forscher/in II
extra ['ekstrə] zusätzlich I
eye [aɪ] Auge I
°**e-zine** ['iːziːn] elektronisches Magazin, elektronische Zeitschrift

F

face [feɪs] Gesicht I
fact [fækt] Tatsache, Fakt III 1 (29)
factory ['fæktri] Fabrik I
fair [feə] fair, gerecht II
fall [fɔːl], **fell, fallen** fallen, stürzen; hinfallen II • **fall down** hinfallen
II • **fall off** herunterfallen (von) II
fallen ['fɔːlən] *siehe* **fall**
°**false** [fɔːls] falsch
family ['fæməli] Familie I • **family tree** (Familien-)Stammbaum I
famous (for) ['feɪməs] berühmt (für, wegen) II
fan [fæn] Fan I
fantastic [fæn'tæstɪk] fantastisch, toll I
far [fɑː] weit (entfernt) II
farm [fɑːm] Bauernhof, Farm II
farmer ['fɑːmə] Bauer/Bäuerin, Landwirt/in; (Fisch-)Züchter/in
III 2 (30)
fashion ['fæʃn] Mode II
fast [fɑːst] schnell II • **fast food**
[ˌfɑːst 'fuːd] Fastfood III 2 (38)
father ['fɑːðə] Vater I
fault [fɔːlt]: **It's not my fault.** Es ist nicht meine Schuld. III 4 (70)
favourite ['feɪvərɪt] Lieblings- I
my favourite colour meine Lieblingsfarbe I
February ['februəri] Februar I
fed [fed] *siehe* **feed** • **be fed up (with sth.)** [ˌfed_'ʌp] die Nase voll haben (von etwas) II
feed [fiːd], **fed, fed** füttern I
feel [fiːl], **felt, felt** sich fühlen; fühlen; sich anfühlen II
feeling ['fiːlɪŋ] Gefühl III 2 (35)

feet [fiːt] *Plural von „foot"*
fell [fel] *siehe* **fall**
felt [felt] *siehe* **feel**
felt tip ['felt tɪp] Filzstift I
female ['fiːmeɪl] weiblich III 3 (53)
ferry ['feri] Fähre III 1 (20/163)
festival ['festɪvl] Fest, Festival, Festspiele III Intro (6)
few [fjuː]: **a few** ein paar, einige II
°**fewer** [fjuːə] weniger
fiddle ['fɪdl] *(infml)* Fiedel, Geige
III Intro (7) • **play the fiddle** Geige spielen III Intro (7/160)
field [fiːld] Feld, Acker, Weide II
in the field auf dem Feld II
fight (for) [faɪt], **fought, fought**
kämpfen (für, um) III 3 (104)
file [faɪl]
°**1.** (Akten-)Ordner, Hefter
2. background file *etwa:* Hintergrundinformation(en) II • **grammar file** *Grammatikanhang* I
skills file *Anhang mit Lern- und Arbeitstechniken* I • **sound file**
Tondatei, Soundfile III 1 (12)
°**fill in** [ˌfɪl_'ɪn]
1. einsetzen
2. ausfüllen
film [fɪlm] Film I • °**film crew**
Filmcrew, Filmteam • °**film researcher** [rɪ'sɜːtʃə] Filmrechercheur/in • **film star** Filmstar I
film studio ['stjuːdɪəʊ] Filmstudio
III 2 (42)
film [fɪlm] filmen III 2 (44)
film-maker ['fɪlm meɪkə] Filmemacher/in III 2 (42)
°**filming** ['fɪlmɪŋ] Dreharbeiten
final ['faɪnl] letzte(r, s); End-
III 3 (52/170) • **final score** Endstand
III 3 (54/171)
▶ S.171 A football match
final ['faɪnl] Finale, Endspiel III 3 (52)
°**finally** ['faɪnəli] zum Schluss, letztlich
find [faɪnd], **found, found** finden I
find out (about) herausfinden
(über) I
finder ['faɪndə] Finder I
fine [faɪn]
1. gut, schön; in Ordnung II
2. *(gesundheitlich)* gut II
I'm/He's fine. Es geht mir/ihm gut. II
finger ['fɪŋgə] Finger I
finish ['fɪnɪʃ] beenden, zu Ende machen; enden I
fire ['faɪə] Feuer, Brand II
fireman/-woman ['faɪəmən, 'faɪə͵wʊmən]
Feuerwehrmann/-frau II
°**fireworks** ['faɪəwɜːks] Feuerwerk

first [fɜːst]
1. erste(r, s) I
2. zuerst, als Erstes I •
be first der/die Erste sein I • **first half** erste Halbzeit III 3 (57/172)

°**First Nations** ['neɪʃnz] *indianische Ureinwohner/innen Kanadas*

fish [fɪʃ] fischen, angeln III 4 (69/174)

fish, *pl* **fish** [fɪʃ] Fisch I

fit (-tt-) [fɪt] passen I

flash [flæʃ] Lichtblitz III 1 (28)

flat [flæt] Wohnung I

flew [fluː] *siehe* **fly**

flight [flaɪt] Flug II • **a 14-hour flight** ein 14-stündiger Flug, ein 14-Stunden-Flug III 4 (76/177)

floor [flɔː] Fußboden I

°**flow chart** ['fləʊ tʃɑːt] Fluss-diagramm

flown [fləʊn] *siehe* **fly**

flute [fluːt] Querflöte III Intro (11)

fly [flaɪ], **flew, flown** fliegen II

fog [fɒg] Nebel II

foggy ['fɒgi] neblig II

folk (music) ['fəʊk ˌmjuːzɪk] Folk (*englische, schottische, irische oder nordamerikanische Volksmusik des 20. Jahrhunderts*) III Intro (6)

follow ['fɒləʊ] folgen; verfolgen I

°**following** ['fɒləʊɪŋ]: **the following ...** die folgenden ...

food [fuːd]
1. Essen; Lebensmittel I
2. Futter I

foot [fʊt], *pl* **feet** [fiːt] Fuß I

football ['fʊtbɔːl] Fußball I • **football boots** Fußballschuhe, -stiefel I

for [fə, fɔː] für I • **for breakfast/lunch/dinner** zum Frühstück/Mittagessen/Abendbrot I • **for example** zum Beispiel III 5 (98)
for lots of reasons aus vielen Gründen I • **for miles** meilenweit II • °**for the festival** wegen des Festivals • **for three days** drei Tage (lang) I • **just for fun** nur zum Spaß I • **What for?** Wofür? II • **What's for homework?** Was haben wir als Hausaufgabe auf? I

foreground ['fɔːgraʊnd] Vorder-grund II

°**foreign** ['fɒrən] ausländisch

forest ['fɒrɪst] Wald II

forget (-tt-) [fə'get], **forgot, forgotten** vergessen I

forgot [fə'gɒt] *siehe* **forget**

forgotten [fə'gɒtn] *siehe* **forget**

fork [fɔːk] Gabel III 4 (81/177)

form [fɔːm]
1. (Schul-)Klasse I • **form teacher** Klassenlehrer/in I
°**2.** Form

°**form** [fɔːm] bilden

fought [fɔːt] *siehe* **fight**

found [faʊnd] *siehe* **find**

fox [fɒks] Fuchs II

free [friː]
1. frei I • **free time** Freizeit, freie Zeit I
2. kostenlos I

°**freedom** ['friːdəm] Freiheit

French [frentʃ] Französisch I

Friday ['fraɪdeɪ, 'fraɪdi] Freitag I

fridge [frɪdʒ] Kühlschrank I

friend [frend] Freund/in I

friendly ['frendli] freundlich III 1 (27)

frog [frɒg] Frosch II

from [frəm, frɒm]
1. aus I
2. von I
from all over the UK/the world/England aus dem gesamten Vereinigten Königreich / aus der ganzen Welt / aus ganz England III Intro (6)
from Monday to Friday von Montag bis Freitag III 2 (32) • **I'm from ...** Ich komme aus ... / Ich bin aus ... I • **Where are you from?** Wo kommst du her? I
▸ S.175 German „bis"

front [frʌnt]: **in front of** vor (*räumlich*) I • **front door** [ˌfrʌnt 'dɔː] Wohnungstür, Haustür I

fruit [fruːt] Obst, Früchte; Frucht I

fruit salad ['fruːt ˌsæləd] Obstsalat I

full [fʊl] voll I

fun [fʌn] Spaß I • **have fun** Spaß haben, sich amüsieren I • **Have fun!** Viel Spaß! I • **just for fun** nur zum Spaß I • **Riding is fun.** Reiten macht Spaß. I

funny ['fʌni] witzig, komisch I

°**fusion** ['fjuːʒn] *aus der Verschmelzung verschiedener Musikrichtungen entstandener Musikstil*

°**future** ['fjuːtʃə] Zukunft

G

°**Gaelic** ['geɪlɪk, 'gælɪk] Gälisch, gälisch

game [geɪm] Spiel I

°**gap** [gæp] Lücke

garage ['gærɑːʒ] Garage II

garden ['gɑːdn] Garten I

gate [geɪt]
1. Tor III 1 (13)
2. Flugsteig III 1 (20/163)

gave [geɪv] *siehe* **give**

general ['dʒenrəl] allgemeine(r,s) III 2 (40)

geography [dʒi'ɒgrəfi] Geografie, Erdkunde I

German ['dʒɜːmən] Deutsch; deutsch; Deutsche(r) I

Germany ['dʒɜːməni] Deutschland I

get (-tt-) [get], **got, got**
1. bekommen, kriegen II
2. holen, besorgen II
3. gelangen, (hin)kommen I
4. get angry/hot/... wütend/heiß/... werden II
5. get off (the train/bus) (aus dem Zug/Bus) aussteigen I • **get on (the train/bus)** (in den Zug/Bus) einsteigen I
6. get up aufstehen I
get dressed sich anziehen I • **get ready (for)** sich fertig machen (für), sich vorbereiten (auf) I • **get sth. off the ground** etwas auf den Weg bringen; etwas auf die Beine stellen III 5 (92) • **get things ready** Dinge fertig machen, vorbereiten I

getting by in English [ˌgetɪŋ 'baɪ] *etwa:* auf Englisch zurechtkommen I

°**gherkin** ['gɜːkɪn] (Essig-)Gurke

ghost [gəʊst] Geist, Gespenst II

°**gift** [gɪft] Geschenk

gig [gɪg] *(infml)* Gig, Auftritt III Intro (8) • **do a gig** einen Auftritt haben, ein Konzert geben III Intro (8/160)

giraffe [dʒə'rɑːf] Giraffe II

girl [gɜːl] Mädchen I

°**girlfriend** ['gɜːlfrend] Freundin I

give [gɪv], **gave, given** geben I

given ['gɪvn] *siehe* **give**

glad [glæd] froh, dankbar III 2 (35)

glass [glɑːs] Glas I • **a glass of water** ein Glas Wasser I

glasses (pl) ['glɑːsɪz] (eine) Brille I

glue [gluː] (auf-, ein)kleben II

glue [gluː] Klebstoff I • **glue stick** ['gluː stɪk] Klebestift I

go [gəʊ], **went, gone** gehen I; fahren II • **go by car/train/bike/...** mit dem Auto/Zug/Rad/... fahren II • **go for a walk** spazieren gehen, einen Spaziergang machen II • **go home** nach Hause gehen I • **go on 1.** weitermachen I, **2.** weiterreden III 2 (34/167) • **Go on.** Mach weiter. / Erzähl weiter. I • °**go on a date** zu einer Verabredung gehen • **go on a trip** einen Ausflug machen • **go on holiday** in Urlaub fahren II • **go riding** reiten gehen I • °**go sightseeing** Sehenswürdigkeiten besichtigen • **go shopping** einkaufen gehen I • **go surfing** wellen-

Dictionary (English – German) 189

reiten gehen, surfen gehen II • **go swimming** schwimmen gehen I **go to bed** ins Bett gehen I • **go to the cinema** ins Kino gehen II • **go together** zusammenpassen, -gehören II • **go well** gut (ver)laufen, gutgehen III 2 (34) • **go with** gehören zu, passen zu III Intro (11) **Let's go.** Auf geht's! I

goal [gəʊl] Tor *(im Sport)* III 3 (54) **score a goal** ein Tor schießen, einen Treffer erzielen III 3 (54)

goalkeeper ['gəʊlkiːpə] Torwart, Torfrau III 3 (57)

golf [gɒlf] Golf III 3 (57)

gone [gɒn] *siehe* **go**

good [gʊd]
1. gut I
2. brav II
Good afternoon. Guten Tag. *(nachmittags)* I • **Good luck (with ...)!** Viel Glück (bei/mit ...)! I • **Good morning.** Guten Morgen. I • **be good at sth.** gut in etwas sein; etwas gut können III 5 (91)

Goodbye. [ˌgʊd'baɪ] Auf Wiedersehen. I • **say goodbye** sich verabschieden I

got [gɒt] *siehe* **get**

got [gɒt]: **I've got ...** Ich habe ... I **I haven't got a chair.** Ich habe keinen Stuhl. I

grammar ['græmə] Grammatik I **grammar file** *Grammatikanhang* I

°**gran** [græn] Oma I

grandad ['grændæd] Opa III 2 (33)

grandchild ['grænt∫aɪld], *pl* **grandchildren** ['-t∫ɪldrən] Enkel/in I

grandfather ['grænfɑːðə] Großvater I

grandma ['grænmɑː] Oma I

grandmother ['grænmʌðə] Großmutter I

grandpa ['grænpɑː] Opa I

grandparents ['grænpeərənts] Großeltern I

granny ['græni] Oma II

great [greɪt] großartig, toll I

great-grandfather [ˌgreɪt 'grænfɑːðə] Urgroßvater III 2 (33)

great-grandmother [ˌgreɪt 'grænmʌðə] Urgroßmutter III 2 (33)

green [griːn] grün I

°**greeting** ['griːtɪŋ] Gruß, Begrüßung I

grew [gruː] *siehe* **grow**

grey [greɪ] grau I

ground [graʊnd] (Erd-)Boden III 1 (20) • **get sth. off the ground** etwas auf den Weg bringen; etwas auf die Beine stellen III 5 (92)

grounded ['graʊndɪd]: **be grounded** Ausgehverbot/Hausarrest haben III 4 (70)

group [gruːp] Gruppe I • **group word** Oberbegriff II

grow [grəʊ], **grew, grown**
1. *(Getreide usw.)* anbauen, anpflanzen II
2. **grow up** [ˌgrəʊ'ʌp] erwachsen werden; aufwachsen III 3 (66)

grown [grəʊn] *siehe* **grow**

grumble ['grʌmbl] murren, nörgeln I

guess [ges] raten, erraten, schätzen III 2 (40)

guest [gest] Gast I

°**guide** [gaɪd] Fremdenführer/in, Reiseleiter/in • °**guide book** Reiseführer

guinea pig ['gɪni pɪg] Meerschweinchen I

guitar [gɪ'tɑː] Gitarre I • **play the guitar** Gitarre spielen I

guys *(pl)* [gaɪz] *(AE, infml)* Leute III 4 (71)

H

had [hæd] *siehe* **have** *und* **have got**

°**haggis** ['hægɪs] *gefüllter Schafsmagen*

hair *(no pl)* [heə] Haar, Haare I

hairdresser ['heədresə] Friseur/in III 2 (44)

half [hɑːf], *pl* **halves** [hɑːvz] Hälfte III Intro (11/161) • **first half** erste Halbzeit III 3 (57/172)

half [hɑːf]: **half an hour** eine halbe Stunde III Intro (11) • **half past 11** halb zwölf (11.30/23.30) I

half-pipe ['hɑːfpaɪp] Halfpipe III 3 (60/173)

°**half-price** [ˌhɑːf 'praɪs] zum halben Preis

half-time [ˌhɑːf 'taɪm] Halbzeit(pause) III 3 (57)

hall [hɔːl] Flur, Diele I

halves [hɑːvz] *Plural von „half"*

hamburger ['hæmbɜːgə] Hamburger I

hamster ['hæmstə] Hamster I

hand [hænd] Hand I

handball ['hændbɔːl] Handball III 5 (93)

hang [hæŋ], **hung, hung: hang out (with friends)** *(infml)* rumhängen, abhängen (mit Freunden/Freundinnen) III 4 (69) • °**hang sth. up** etwas aufhängen

happen (to) ['hæpən] geschehen, passieren (mit) I

happy ['hæpi] glücklich, froh I **Happy birthday.** Herzlichen Glückwunsch zum Geburtstag. I **happy ending** Happyend II

harbour ['hɑːbə] Hafen II

hard [hɑːd] hart; schwer, schwierig II • **work hard** hart arbeiten II

hard-working [ˌhɑːd 'wɜːkɪŋ] fleißig, tüchtig III 3 (66)

hat [hæt] Hut II

hate [heɪt] hassen, gar nicht mögen I

have [həv, hæv], **had, had** haben, besitzen II • **have a baby** ein Baby/Kind bekommen II • **have a bath** baden, ein Bad nehmen II **have a cold** erkältet sein, eine Erkältung haben II • **have a crush on sb.** in jn. verknallt sein III 5 (92) • **have a picnic** ein Picknick machen I • **have a sauna** in die Sauna gehen II • **have a shower** (sich) duschen I • **have a sore throat** Halsschmerzen haben II • **have a temperature** Fieber haben II **have breakfast/dinner** frühstücken / Abendbrot essen I • **have ... for breakfast** ... zum Frühstück essen/trinken I • **have fun** Spaß haben, sich amüsieren I • **have sleepovers** Schlafpartys veranstalten III 4 (69) • **have to do** tun müssen I

have got: I've got ... [aɪv 'gɒt] Ich habe ... I • **I haven't got a chair.** Ich habe keinen Stuhl. I

he [hiː] er I

head [hed] Kopf I • °**head of state** Staatsoberhaupt • **head teacher** Schulleiter/in III 2 (44)

headache ['hedeɪk] Kopfschmerzen II

°**heading** ['hedɪŋ] Überschrift, Titel I

headphones *(pl)* ['hedfəʊnz] Kopfhörer III 5 (89)

healthy ['helθi] gesund II

hear [hɪə], **heard, heard** hören I

heard [hɜːd] *siehe* **hear**

heart [hɑːt] Herz II • °**heart specialist** ['hɑːtˌspe∫əlɪst] Herzspezialist/in

hedgehog ['hedʒhɒg] Igel II

held [held] *siehe* **hold**

helicopter ['helɪkɒptə] Hubschrauber, Helikopter II

Hello. [hə'ləʊ] Hallo. / Guten Tag. I

helmet ['helmɪt] Helm III (26)

help [help] helfen I • **Can I help you?** Kann ich Ihnen helfen? / Was kann ich für Sie tun? *(im Geschäft)* I

help [help] Hilfe I

°**helpful** [ˈhelpfl] hilfsbereit
her [hə, hɜː]
  1. ihr, ihre I
  2. sie; ihr I
here [hɪə]
  1. hier I
  2. hierher I
  Here you are. Bitte sehr. / Hier bitte. I
hers [hɜːz] ihrer, ihre, ihrs II
herself [həˈself, hɜːˈself] sich (selbst) III 4 (72/176)
Hey! [heɪ] Hallo! III Intro (8/160)
Hi! [haɪ] Hallo! I • **Say hi to Dilip for me.** Grüß Dilip von mir. I
hid [hɪd] *siehe* **hide**
hidden [ˈhɪdn] *siehe* **hide**
hide [haɪd], **hid, hidden** sich verstecken; *(etwas)* verstecken I
high [haɪ] hoch III 1 (12) • °**high tech** [ˌhaɪˈtek] Hightech
°**highland** [ˈhaɪlənd] Hochland-
hill [hɪl] Hügel II
hilly [ˈhɪli] hügelig III 2 (38/168)
him [hɪm] ihn; ihm I
himself [hɪmˈself] sich (selbst) III 4 (72/176)
hip hop [ˈhɪp hɒp] Hip Hop III Intro (6)
hippo [ˈhɪpəʊ] Flusspferd II
his [hɪz]
  1. sein, seine I
  2. seiner, seine, seins II
history [ˈhɪstri] Geschichte I
°**natural history** [ˌnætʃrəl ˈhɪstri] Naturkunde
hit (-tt-) [hɪt], **hit, hit** schlagen II
hit [hɪt] Hit III 4 (73)
hobby [ˈhɒbi] Hobby I .
hockey [ˈhɒki] Hockey I • **hockey shoes** Hockeyschuhe I
hold [həʊld], **held, held** halten II • °**hold up** hochhalten
holiday(s) [ˈhɒlədeɪ(z)] Ferien I
  holiday flat Ferienwohnung II
  be on holiday II in Urlaub sein; Ferien haben/machen • **go on holiday** in Urlaub fahren II • **a two-week holiday** ein zweiwöchiger Urlaub III 4 (76/177)
home [həʊm] Heim, Zuhause I
  at home daheim, zu Hause I
  come home nach Hause kommen I • **get home** nach Hause kommen I • **go home** nach Hause gehen I
°**homeless** [ˈhəʊmləs] obdachlos
homework *(no pl)* [ˈhəʊmwɜːk] Hausaufgabe(n) I • **do homework** die Hausaufgabe(n) machen I
  What's for homework? Was haben wir als Hausaufgabe auf? I
Hooray! [huˈreɪ] Hurra! II

hope [həʊp] hoffen II
hope [həʊp] Hoffnung III 3 (66)
horrible [ˈhɒrəbl] scheußlich, grauenhaft II
horse [hɔːs] Pferd I
hospital [ˈhɒspɪtl] Krankenhaus II
hostel [ˈhɒstl] Herberge, Wohnheim III Intro (8)
hot [hɒt] heiß I • **hot chocolate** heiße Schokolade I
hotel [həʊˈtel] Hotel II
hotline [ˈhɒtlaɪn] Hotline II
hour [ˈaʊə] Stunde II • **half an hour** eine halbe Stunde III Intro (11)
  a 14-hour flight ein 14-stündiger Flug, ein 14-Stunden-Flug III 4 (76/177) • **a 24-hour supermarket** ein Supermarkt, der 24 Stunden geöffnet ist III 4 (76/177)
house [haʊs] Haus I • **at the Shaws' house** im Haus der Shaws / bei den Shaws zu Hause I
how [haʊ] wie I • **How about ...?** Wie wär's mit ...? III Intro (10) • **How am I doing?** Wie komme ich voran? *(Wie sind meine Fortschritte?)* III 1 (29) • **How are you?** Wie geht es dir/Ihnen/euch? II • **How do you know ...?** Woher weißt/kennst du ...? I • **how many?** wie viele? I **how much?** wie viel? I • **How much is/are ...?** Was kostet/kosten ...? / Wie viel kostet/kosten ...? I **How old are you?** Wie alt bist du? I • **How was ...?** Wie war ...? I
huge [hjuːdʒ] riesig, sehr groß III 1 (26/165)
▶ S.165 **big – large – huge**
hundred [ˈhʌndrəd] hundert I
hung [hʌŋ] *siehe* **hang**
hungry [ˈhʌŋgri] hungrig III Intro (10)
  I'm hungry. Ich habe Hunger III Intro (10/160)
hunt [hʌnt] jagen III 4 (69/174)
hunt [hʌnt] Jagd III 4 (69/174)
°**hunter** [ˈhʌntə] Jäger
hurry [ˈhʌri] eilen; sich beeilen II **hurry·up** sich beeilen I
hurry [ˈhʌri]: **be in a hurry** in Eile sein, es eilig haben I
hurt [hɜːt], **hurt, hurt** wehtun; verletzen I
hurt [hɜːt] verletzt II
husband [ˈhʌzbənd] Ehemann II
hutch [hʌtʃ] (Kaninchen-)Stall I

I

I [aɪ] ich I • **I'm** [aɪm] ich bin I **I'm from ...** Ich komme aus ... / Ich bin aus ... I • **I'm sorry.** Tut mir

leid. / Entschuldigung. I
ice: ice cream [ˌaɪs ˈkriːm] (Speise-) Eis I • **ice hockey** [ˈaɪs hɒki] Eishockey III 4 (69) • **ice rink** [ˈaɪs rɪŋk] Schlittschuhbahn I
idea [aɪˈdɪə] Idee, Einfall I
if [ɪf]
  1. falls, wenn II
  2. ob II
ill [ɪl] krank II
°**imaginary** [ɪˈmædʒɪnəri] imaginär *(nur in der Vorstellung vorhanden, nicht wirklich)*
imagine sth. [ɪˈmædʒɪn] sich etwas vorstellen III 2 (33)
°**immigration** [ˌɪmɪˈgreɪʃn] Immigration, Einwanderung
important [ɪmˈpɔːtnt] wichtig II
impossible [ɪmˈpɒsəbl] unmöglich II
°**improve** [ɪmˈpruːv] verbessern
in [ɪn] in I • **in ... Street** in der ... straße I • **in English** auf Englisch I • **in front of** vor *(räumlich)* I **in here** hier drinnen I • **in the afternoon** nachmittags, am Nachmittag I • **in the country** auf dem Land I • **in the end** schließlich, zum Schluss III 3 (57) • **in the evening** abends, am Abend I • **in the field** auf dem Feld II • **in the morning** am Morgen, morgens I **in the photo** auf dem Foto I • **in the picture** auf dem Bild I • **in the yard** auf dem Hof II • **in time** rechtzeitig II
°**independent** [ˌɪndɪˈpendənt] unabhängig
infinitive [ɪnˈfɪnətɪv] Infinitiv *(Grundform des Verbs)* I
information (about/on) *(no pl)* [ˌɪnfəˈmeɪʃn] Information(en) (über) II
inside [ˌɪnˈsaɪd]
  1. innen (drin), drinnen I
  2. nach drinnen II
  3. inside the car ins Auto (hinein), ins Innere des Autos II
install [ɪnˈstɔːl] installieren, einrichten II
instant messages *(pl)* [ˌɪnstənt ˈmesɪdʒɪz] *Nachrichten, die man im Internet austauscht (in Echtzeit)* III 2 (33)
instructions *(pl)* [ɪnˈstrʌkʃnz] (Gebrauchs-)Anweisung(en), Anleitung(en) II
instrument [ˈɪnstrəmənt] Instrument III Intro (8)
interested [ˈɪntrəstɪd]: **be interested (in)** interessiert sein (an), sich interessieren (für) III 3 (53)

Dictionary (English – German)   191

interesting ['ɪntrəstɪŋ] interessant I
international [ˌɪntə'næʃnəl] international III Intro (6/159)
internet ['ɪntənet] Internet III 1 (19) • **surf the internet** im Internet surfen III 2 (33)
interview ['ɪntəvjuː] Interview I
interview ['ɪntəvjuː] interviewen, befragen II
into ['ɪntə, 'ɪntʊ] in ... (hinein) I
°**introduce** [ˌɪntrə'djuːs] vorstellen I
introduction (to) [ˌɪntrə'dʌkʃn] Einführung (in) III Intro (6)
°**Inuit** ['ɪnuɪt, 'ɪnjuɪt] Inuit *(eskimoische Volksgruppe in Zentral- und Nordostkanada und Grönland)*
°**invent** [ɪn'vent] erfinden I
invitation (to) [ˌɪnvɪ'teɪʃn] Einladung (zu) I
invite (to) [ɪn'vaɪt] einladen (zu) I
°**irregular** [ɪ'regjələ] unregelmäßig I
is [ɪz] ist I
island ['aɪlənd] Insel II
°**issue** ['ɪʃuː] (Streit-)Frage, Thema, Angelegenheit
it [ɪt] er/sie/es I • **It's £1.** Er/Sie/Es kostet 1 Pfund. I • **It says here: ...** Hier steht: ... / Es heißt hier: ... II
its [ɪts] sein/seine; ihr/ihre I
itself [ɪt'self] sich (selbst) III 4 (72/176)

J

jacket ['dʒækɪt] Jacke, Jackett II
January ['dʒænjuəri] Januar I
°**javelin** ['dʒævlɪn] Speerwerfen
jazz [dʒæz] Jazz III Intro (6)
jealous (of) ['dʒeləs] neidisch (auf); eifersüchtig (auf) III 2 (46)
jeans *(pl)* [dʒiːnz] Jeans I
job [dʒɒb] Aufgabe, Job I
join sb. [dʒɔɪn] sich jm. anschließen; bei jm. mitmachen II
joke [dʒəʊk] Witz I
joke [dʒəʊk] scherzen, Witze machen II
journey ['dʒɜːni] Fahrt, Reise III 1 (25)
judo ['dʒuːdəʊ] Judo I • **do judo** Judo machen I
jug [dʒʌg] Krug I • **a jug of milk** ein Krug Milch I
juice [dʒuːs] Saft I
July [dʒu'laɪ] Juli I
°**jumble** ['dʒʌmbl] gebrauchte Sachen, Trödel
jumble sale ['dʒʌmbl seɪl] Wohltätigkeitsbasar I
jump [dʒʌmp] springen II • **jump around** herumspringen III 1 (26/164)
June [dʒuːn] Juni I

junior ['dʒuːniə] Junioren-, Jugend-I
just [dʒʌst]
1. (einfach) nur, bloß I • **It's just a game.** Es ist nur/bloß ein Spiel. III 2 (35/168)
2. einfach III 2 (35) • **I just can't find my keys.** Ich kann einfach meine Schlüssel nicht finden. III 2 (35/168) • **Just don't listen to them.** Hör einfach nicht hin. III 2 (35/168)
3. gerade (eben), soeben II • **just then** genau in dem Moment / gerade dann III 2 (35/168)
4. **just like your mother** genau wie deine Mutter III 2 (35/168)
▶ S.168 just

K

kangaroo [ˌkæŋgə'ruː] Känguru II
keep [kiːp], **kept, kept** (be)halten; aufbewahren III 5 (91) • °**keep a diary** ein Tagebuch führen °**keep animals** Tiere halten °**keep fit** fit bleiben • **keep in touch** in Verbindung bleiben, Kontakt halten III Intro (11) • **keep sth. warm/cool/open/...** etwas warm/kühl/offen/... halten II • °**keep sth. with you** etwas bei sich haben °**Keep your back straight.** Halte deinen Rücken gerade.
kept [kept] *siehe* **keep**
key [kiː] Schlüssel II • **key ring** Schlüsselring II • **key word** Stichwort, Schlüsselwort I
keyboard ['kiːbɔːd] Keyboard *(elektronisches Tasteninstrument)* III Intro (7)
kid [kɪd] Kind, Jugendliche(r) I
kill [kɪl] töten I
kilogram (kg) ['kɪləgræm], **kilo** ['kiːləʊ] Kilogramm, Kilo (kg) III 4 (76) • **a 150-kilogram bear** ein 150 Kilogramm schwerer Bär III 4 (76/177)
kilometre (km) ['kɪləmiːtə] Kilometer III 4 (76) • **a ten-kilometre walk** eine Zehn-Kilometer-Wanderung III 4 (76/177)
°**kilt** [kɪlt] Kilt, Schottenrock
kind (of) [kaɪnd] Art III Intro (6) **What kind of car ...?** Was für ein Auto ...? III Intro (6/160)
king [kɪŋ] König I
kingdom: the United Kingdom (UK) [juˌnaɪtɪd 'kɪŋdəm, juː'keɪ] das Vereinigte Königreich III Intro (6/159)
kitchen ['kɪtʃɪn] Küche I

kite [kaɪt] Drachen I
kiwi ['kiːwiː] Kiwi II
knee [niː] Knie I
knew [njuː] *siehe* **know**
knife [naɪf], *pl* **knives** [naɪvz] Messer III 4 (81)
know [nəʊ], **knew, known**
1. wissen I
2. kennen I
know about sth. von etwas wissen; über etwas Bescheid wissen II • **How do you know ...?** Woher weißt du ...? / Woher kennst du ...? I • **I don't know.** Ich weiß es nicht. I • **..., you know.** ..., wissen Sie. / ..., weißt du. I • **You know what, Sophie?** Weißt du was, Sophie? I
known [nəʊn] *siehe* **know**

L

°**label** ['leɪbl] beschriften, etikettieren
°**lacrosse** [lə'krɒs] Lacrosse *(Sportart)*
laid [leɪd] *siehe* **lay**
lake [leɪk] (Binnen-)See II
lamb [læm] Lamm(fleisch) III 1 (24/164)
lamp [læmp] Lampe I
land [lænd] landen II
land [lænd] Land, Grund und Boden II
lane [leɪn] Gasse, Weg III 1 (14/162)
language ['læŋgwɪdʒ] Sprache I
large [lɑːdʒ] groß II
▶ S.165 big – large – huge
lasagne [lə'zænjə] Lasagne I
°**laser** ['leɪzə] Laser(gerät)
last [lɑːst] letzte(r, s) I • **the last day** der letzte Tag I • **at last** endlich, schließlich I
late [leɪt] spät; zu spät I • **be late** zu spät sein/kommen I • **Sorry, I'm late.** Entschuldigung, dass ich zu spät bin/komme. I
later ['leɪtə] später I
latest ['leɪtɪst] neueste(r, s) III 4 (81)
laugh [lɑːf] lachen I
laughter ['lɑːftə] Gelächter II
lay the table [leɪ], **laid, laid** den Tisch decken I
°**layout** ['leɪaʊt] Layout, Seitengestaltung
leader ['liːdə] Leiter/in, (An-)Führer/in III 4 (73)
learn [lɜːn] lernen I • **learn sth. about sth.** etwas über etwas erfahren, etwas über etwas herausfinden II
least [liːst] am wenigsten III 5 (92) **at least** zumindest, wenigstens I

leather ['leðə] Leder III 5 (91)
leave [liːv], **left, left**
 1. (weg)gehen; abfahren II
 2. verlassen II
 3. zurücklassen II
left [left] *siehe* **leave**
left [left] linke(r, s) II • **look left** nach links schauen II • **on the left** links, auf der linken Seite II • **turn left** (nach) links abbiegen II
leg [leg] Bein I
°**legend** ['ledʒənd] Legende
leisure centre ['leʒə sentə] Freizeitzentrum, -park II
lemon ['lemən] Zitrone III 1 (24/164)
lemonade [ˌleməˈneɪd] Limonade I
lesson ['lesn] (Unterrichts-)Stunde I • **lessons** *(pl)* ['lesnz] Unterricht I
let [let], **let, let** lassen II • **Let's ...** Lass uns ... / Lasst uns ... I • **Let's go.** Auf geht's! I • **Let's look at the list.** Sehen wir uns die Liste an. / Lasst uns die Liste ansehen. I **let sb. do sth.** jm. erlauben, etwas zu tun; zulassen, dass jd. etwas tut III 2 (35)
letter ['letə]
 1. Buchstabe I • **capital letter** [ˌkæpɪtl 'letə] Großbuchstabe III 5 (98)
 2. **letter (to)** Brief (an) II
lettuce ['letɪs] (Kopf-)Salat II
library ['laɪbrəri] Bibliothek, Bücherei I
life [laɪf], *pl* **lives** [laɪvz] Leben I
lift [lɪft] Fahrstuhl, Aufzug II
light [laɪt] Licht III 2 (44)
like [laɪk] wie I • **What was the weather like?** Wie war das Wetter? II
like [laɪk] mögen, gernhaben I **like sth. better** etwas lieber mögen II • **I like swimming/dancing.** Ich schwimme/tanze gern. I • **I'd like ... (= I would like ...)** Ich hätte gern ... / Ich möchte gern ... I • **I'd like to talk about ... (= I would like to talk about ...)** Ich möchte/würde gern über ... reden I • **Would you like ...?** Möchtest du ...? / Möchten Sie ...? I • **Would you like some?** Möchtest du etwas/ein paar? / Möchten Sie etwas/ein paar? I
line [laɪn]
 1. Zeile II
 °2. Linie
 3. (U-Bahn-)Linie III 1 (14)
link [lɪŋk] verbinden, verknüpfen I
link [lɪŋk] Verbindung, Verknüpfung III 4 (69/174)

linking word ['lɪŋkɪŋ wɜːd] Bindewort II
lion ['laɪən] Löwe II
list [lɪst] Liste I
list [lɪst] auflisten, aufzählen II
listen (to) ['lɪsn] zuhören; sich *etwas* anhören I • **listen for sth.** auf etwas horchen, achten III 1 (13)
listener ['lɪsnə] Zuhörer/in II
little ['lɪtl] klein I
live [lɪv] leben, wohnen I
live music [laɪv] Livemusik II
lives [laɪvz] *Plural von „life"*
living room ['lɪvɪŋ ruːm] Wohnzimmer I
local ['ləʊkl] Orts-, örtlich II
location [ləʊˈkeɪʃn]
 1. (Wohn-)Ort III 3 (53)
 2. (Veranstaltungs-)Ort III 3 (60/172)
lock [lɒk] abschließen; sperren III 2 (41)
lock [lɒk] Schleuse III 1 (14/162)
logo ['ləʊgəʊ] Logo III 2 (33)
lonely ['ləʊnli] einsam III 2 (33)
long [lɒŋ] lang I
look [lʊk]
 1. schauen, gucken I
 2. **look different/great/old** anders/toll/alt aussehen I • **look after sth./sb.** auf etwas/jn. aufpassen; sich um etwas/jn. kümmern II • **look at** ansehen, anschauen I • **look for** suchen II **look left/right** nach links/rechts schauen II • **look round** sich umsehen I • **look sth. up** etwas nachschlagen III 2 (47) • **look up (from)** hochsehen, aufschauen (von) II
°**loon** [luːn] Seetaucher
lorry ['lɒri] Lastkraftwagen III 1 (20/163)
lose [luːz], **lost, lost** verlieren II
lost [lɒst] *siehe* **lose**
lot [lɒt]: **a lot (of)** eine Menge, viel, viele II • **Thanks a lot!** Vielen Dank! I • **He likes her a lot.** Er mag sie sehr. I • **lots more** viel mehr I • **lots of** eine Menge, viele, viel I
loud [laʊd] laut I
love [lʌv] lieben, sehr mögen II
love [lʌv]
 1. Liebe II
 °2. Liebling Liebes **Love ...** Liebe Grüße, ... *(Briefschluss)* I
luck [lʌk]: **Good luck (with ...)!** Viel Glück (bei/mit ...)! I
luckily ['lʌkɪli] zum Glück, glücklicherweise II

lucky ['lʌki]: **be lucky (with)** Glück haben (mit) III 2 (40)
lunch [lʌntʃ] Mittagessen I **lunch break** Mittagspause I
°**lunchtime** ['lʌntʃtaɪm] Mittagszeit
lyrics *(pl)* ['lɪrɪks] Liedtext(e), Songtext(e) III 4 (70)

M

machine [məˈʃiːn] Maschine, Gerät; *hier:* Automat III 1 (21) • **ticket machine** Fahrkartenautomat III 1 (20/163)
mad [mæd] verrückt I • **be mad about sth.** verrückt nach/auf etwas sein III 3 (104)
made [meɪd] *siehe* **make**
°**mag** [mæg] *Abkürzung für* **magazine**
magazine [ˌmægəˈziːn] Zeitschrift, Magazin I
°**magic** ['mædʒɪk] magisch
mail [meɪl] schicken, senden *(per Post oder E-mail)*; mailen III Intro (11) **mail sb.** jn. anmailen II
main [meɪn] Haupt- III 1 (13)
make [meɪk], **made, made** machen; bauen I • **make a deal** ein Abkommen / eine Abmachung treffen III 3 (56) • **make a mess** alles durcheinanderbringen, alles in Unordnung bringen I • °**make notes** sich Notizen machen • **make a point** ein Argument vorbringen III 4 (72) • °**make sth. up** sich etwas ausdenken
make-up ['meɪkʌp] Make-up II
male [meɪl] männlich III 3 (53/171)
man [mæn], *pl* **men** [men] Mann I
manager ['mænədʒə] Manager/in III 5 (98)
many ['meni] viele I • **how many?** wie viele? I
map [mæp] Landkarte, Stadtplan II
March [mɑːtʃ] März I
mark sth. up [ˌmɑːk ˈʌp] etwas markieren, kennzeichnen II
market ['mɑːkɪt] Markt II
marmalade ['mɑːməleɪd] (Orangen-)Marmelade I
married (to) ['mærɪd] verheiratet (mit) I
match [mætʃ] Spiel, Wettkampf I
°**match** [mætʃ]
 1. passen zu
 2. zuordnen
 °**Match the letters and numbers.** Ordne die Buchstaben den Zahlen zu.

Dictionary (English – German)   193

mate [meɪt] *(infml)* Freund/in, Kumpel III 2 (33)
°**material** [məˈtɪərɪəl] Material
maths [mæθs] Mathematik I
matter [ˈmætə]: **What's the matter?** Was ist los? / Was ist denn? II
May [meɪ] Mai I
may [meɪ] dürfen III 4 (154)
maybe [ˈmeɪbi] vielleicht I
me [mi:] mir; mich I • **Me too.** Ich auch. I • **more than me** mehr als ich II • **That's me.** Das bin ich. I **Why me?** Warum ich? I
meal [mi:l] Mahlzeit, Essen III 3 (65)
mean [mi:n], **meant, meant**
1. bedeuten III 1 (28)
2. meinen *(sagen wollen)* II
meaning [ˈmi:nɪŋ] Bedeutung III 2 (47)
meant [ment] *siehe* **mean**
meat [mi:t] Fleisch I
medal [ˈmedl] Medaille III 3 (66)
media *(pl)* [ˈmi:dɪə] Medien III 2 (33)
mediation [ˌmi:dɪˈeɪʃn] Vermittlung, Sprachmittlung, Mediation II
medium [ˈmi:dɪəm] mittel(groß) II
meet [mi:t], **met, met**
1. treffen; kennenlernen I
2. sich treffen II
Nice to meet you. Nett, dich kennenzulernen. III Intro (10)
°**member** [ˈmembə] Mitglied I
men [men] *Plural von „man"*
menu [ˈmenju:] Speisekarte II
mess [mes]: **be a mess** sehr unordentlich sein; fürchterlich aussehen II • **make a mess** alles durcheinanderbringen, alles in Unordnung bringen I
message [ˈmesɪdʒ] Nachricht III 2 (33/167) • **text message** SMS III 2 (33) • **instant messages** [ˌɪnstənt ˈmesɪdʒɪz] *Nachrichten, die man im Internet austauscht (in Echtzeit)* III 2 (33)
met [met] *siehe* **meet**
°**method** [ˈmeθəd] Methode I
metre [ˈmi:tə] Meter II
mice [maɪs] *Plural von „mouse"*
microphone [ˈmaɪkrəfəʊn] Mikrofon III 2 (45)
middle (of) [ˈmɪdl] Mitte I; Mittelteil II
midnight [ˈmɪdnaɪt] Mitternacht III 4 (70)
might [maɪt]: **you might need help** du könntest (vielleicht) Hilfe brauchen III 2 (44)
mild [maɪld] mild III 1 (16)
mile [maɪl] Meile *(= ca. 1,6 km)* II **for miles** meilenweit II
milk [mɪlk] Milch I

million [ˈmɪljən] Million III 2 (42)
mime [maɪm] pantomimisch darstellen, vorspielen II
°**mime** [maɪm] Pantomime
mind map [ˈmaɪnd mæp] Mindmap („Gedankenkarte", „Wissensnetz") I
Mind your own business. [ˌmaɪnd jər‿ˌəʊn ˈbɪznəs] Das geht dich nichts an! / Kümmere dich um deine eigenen Angelegenheiten! II
mine [maɪn] meiner, meine, meins II
mints *(pl)* [mɪnts] Pfefferminzbonbons I
minute [ˈmɪnɪt] Minute I • **Wait a minute.** Warte mal! / Moment mal! II
mirror [ˈmɪrə] Spiegel II
miss [mɪs]
1. vermissen II
2. **Miss a turn.** Einmal aussetzen. II
Miss White [mɪs] Frau White *(unverheiratet)* I
missing [ˈmɪsɪŋ]: **be missing** fehlen II • °**the missing information/words** die fehlenden Informationen/Wörter
mistake [mɪˈsteɪk] Fehler I
mix [mɪks] mischen, mixen III 2 (33) °**mix up** durcheinanderbringen
mix [mɪks] Mix, Mischung III 4 (73)
mixture [ˈmɪkstʃə] Mischung III Intro (9)
°**mobile** [ˈməʊbaɪl] Mobile I
mobile (phone) [ˈməʊbaɪl] Mobiltelefon, Handy I
model [ˈmɒdl] Modell*(-flugzeug, -schiff usw.)* I; (Foto-)Modell II
modern [ˈmɒdən] modern III 4 (70)
mole [məʊl] Maulwurf II
mom [mɒm, *AE:* mɑ:m] *(AE)* Mama, Mutti; Mutter III 4 (70)
moment [ˈməʊmənt] Moment III 1 (26)
Monday [ˈmʌndeɪ, ˈmʌndi] Montag I • **Monday morning** Montagmorgen I
money [ˈmʌni] Geld I
monitor [ˈmɒnɪtə] Bildschirm, Monitor III 5 (89)
monkey [ˈmʌŋki] Affe II
monster [ˈmɒnstə] Ungeheuer, Monster II
month [mʌnθ] Monat I
moon [mu:n] Mond II
more [mɔ:] mehr I • **lots more** viel mehr I • **more than** mehr als II • **more than me** mehr als ich II • **more boring (than)** langweiliger (als) II • **no more music** keine

Musik mehr I • **not (...) any more** nicht mehr III 2 (34)
morning [ˈmɔ:nɪŋ] Morgen, Vormittag I • **in the morning** morgens, am Morgen I • **Monday morning** Montagmorgen I • **on Friday morning** freitagmorgens, am Freitagmorgen I
mosque [mɒsk] Moschee III 1 (16)
most [məʊst] (der/die/das) meiste ...; am meisten II • **most people** die meisten Leute I • **(the) most boring** der/die/das langweiligste ...; am langweiligsten II
mother [ˈmʌðə] Mutter I
mountain [ˈmaʊntən] Berg II
mouse [maʊs], *pl* **mice** [maɪs] Maus I
mouth [maʊθ] Mund I
move [mu:v]
1. bewegen; sich bewegen II **Move back one space.** Geh ein Feld zurück. II • **Move on one space.** Geh ein Feld vor. II
2. **move (to)** umziehen (nach, in) II • **move in** einziehen II • **move out** ausziehen II
movement [ˈmu:vmənt] Bewegung II
movie [ˈmu:vi] Film III 5 (88)
MP3 player [ˌempi:ˈθri: ˌpleɪə] MP3-Spieler I
Mr ... [ˈmɪstə] Herr ... I
Mrs ... [ˈmɪsɪz] Frau ... I
Ms ... [mɪz, məz] Frau ... II
much [mʌtʃ] viel I • **how much?** wie viel? I • **How much is/are ...?** Was kostet/kosten ...? / Wie viel kostet/kosten ...? I • **like/love sth. very much** etwas sehr mögen / sehr lieben II
°**multicultural** [ˌmʌltiˈkʌltʃərəl] multikulturell I
multiple choice [ˌmʌltɪpl ˈtʃɔɪs] Multiple-Choice II
mum [mʌm] Mama, Mutti; Mutter I
°**mummy** [ˈmʌmi] Mumie I
museum [mjuˈzi:əm] Museum I
mushroom [ˈmʌʃrʊm, -ru:m] Pilz III 1 (24/164)
music [ˈmju:zɪk] Musik I
musical [ˈmju:zɪkl] Musical I
musician [mjuˈzɪʃn] Musiker/in III 5 (95)
must [mʌst] müssen I
mustn't do [ˈmʌsnt] nicht tun dürfen II
my [maɪ] mein/e I
myself [maɪˈself] mir/mich (selbst) III 4 (72/176)

N

name [neɪm] Name I • **call sb. names** jn. mit Schimpfwörtern hänseln, jm. Schimpfwörter nachrufen III 2 (35) • **My name is …** Ich heiße … / Mein Name ist … I **What's your name?** Wie heißt du? I

name [neɪm] nennen; benennen II

national ['næʃnəl] national III Intro (6)

°**natural history** [ˌnætʃrəl 'hɪstri] Naturkunde

near [nɪə] in der Nähe von, nahe (bei) I

neat [niːt] gepflegt II • **neat and tidy** schön ordentlich II

°**necessary** ['nesəsəri] notwendig, nötig

need [niːd] brauchen, benötigen I

needn't do ['niːdnt] nicht tun müssen, nicht zu tun brauchen II

neighbour ['neɪbə] Nachbar/in I

nervous ['nɜːvəs] nervös, aufgeregt I

°**net** [net] Netz

°**network** ['netwɜːk] (Wörter-)Netz

never ['nevə] nie, niemals I

new [njuː] neu I • °**new age kurling** [ˌnjuːˈeɪdʒ kɜːlɪŋ] New Age Kurling (abgewandelte Form des Eisstockschießens in Hallen ohne Eisfläche)

news (no pl) [njuːz] Nachrichten, Neuigkeiten III 2 (40) • **That's good news.** Das sind gute Nachrichten. III 2 (40/169)

newspaper ['njuːspeɪpə] Zeitung I

next [nekst]: **be next** der/die Nächste sein I • **the next morning/day** am nächsten Morgen/Tag I • **What have we got next?** Was haben wir als Nächstes? I

next to [nekst] neben II

nice [naɪs] schön, nett I • **Nice to meet you.** Nett, dich/euch/Sie kennenzulernen. III Intro (10)

night [naɪt] Nacht, später Abend I **at night** nachts, in der Nacht I **on Friday night** freitagnachts, Freitagnacht I

nightclub ['naɪtklʌb] Nachtklub III 4 (77)

nil [nɪl] null III 3 (54/171)

no [nəʊ] nein I

no [nəʊ] kein, keine I • **no more music** keine Musik mehr I • **No smoking!** Rauchen verboten! III 1 (27/165) • **No way!** Auf keinen Fall! / Kommt nicht in Frage! II

nobody ['nəʊbədi] niemand II

nod (-dd-) [nɒd] nicken (mit) II

noise [nɔɪz] Geräusch; Lärm I

noisy ['nɔɪzi] laut, lärmend II

°**noodle** ['nuːdl] Nudel

north [nɔːθ] Norden; nach Norden; nördlich III Intro (7)

northbound ['nɔːθbaʊnd] Richtung Norden III 1 (14/162)

north-east [ˌnɔːθ'iːst] Nordosten; nach Nordosten; nordöstlich III Intro (7/160)

°**northern** ['nɔːðən] nördlich

north-west [ˌnɔːθ'west] Nordwesten; nach Nordwesten; nordwestlich III Intro (7/160)

nose [nəʊz] Nase I

not [nɒt] nicht I • **not (…) any** kein, keine I • **not (…) any more** nicht mehr III 2 (34) • **not (…) anybody** niemand II • **not (…) anything** nichts II • **not (…) anywhere** nirgendwo(hin) II • **not even** (noch) nicht einmal III 2 (34) **not (…) yet** noch nicht II

note [nəʊt] Mitteilung, Notiz I °**make notes** sich Notizen machen **take notes** sich Notizen machen I

nothing ['nʌθɪŋ] nichts II

°**notice** ['nəʊtɪs] Notiz, Mitteilung **notice board** Anschlagtafel, schwarzes Brett I

November [nəʊ'vembə] November I

now [naʊ] nun, jetzt I

number ['nʌmbə] Zahl, Ziffer, Nummer I

°**nut** [nʌt] Nuss

O

o [əʊ] null I

°**obvious** ['ɒbvɪəs] offensichtlich

°**och** [ox] ach (besonders in Schottland und Irland gebräuchlich)

o'clock [ə'klɒk]: **eleven o'clock** elf Uhr I

October [ɒk'təʊbə] Oktober I

°**odd** [ɒd]: **What word is the odd one out?** Welches Wort passt nicht dazu / gehört nicht dazu?

of [əv, ɒv] von I • **two kilos of oranges** zwei Kilo Orangen III 4 (76/176)

of course [əv 'kɔːs] natürlich, selbstverständlich I

off [ɒf]: °**call sth. off** etwas absagen, abblasen • **cut sth. off** etwas abtrennen, abschneiden III 3 (66) **fall off** herunterfallen (von) II **get off (the train/bus)** (aus dem Zug/Bus) aussteigen I • **get sth.**

off the ground etwas auf den Weg bringen; etwas auf die Beine stellen III 5 (92) • **take sth. off** etwas ausziehen (Kleidung) II • **take 10 c off** 10 Cent abziehen I • **turn sth. off** etwas ausschalten III 2 (35)

office ['ɒfɪs]: **ticket office** Fahrkartenschalter III 1 (14/162)

°**official** [ə'fɪʃl] offiziell

often ['ɒfn] oft, häufig I

Oh dear! [əʊ 'dɪə] Oje! II

Oh well … [əʊ 'wel] Na ja … / Na gut … I

oil [ɔɪl] Öl III 2 (30) • °**oil rig** ['ɔɪl rɪg] (Öl-)Bohrinsel

OK [əʊ'keɪ] okay, gut, in Ordnung I

old [əʊld] alt I • **a sixteen-year-old** ein/e Sechzehnjährige/r III 4 (76) • **a sixteen-year-old girl** ein sechzehnjähriges Mädchen III 4 (76/177)

old-fashioned [ˌəʊld'fæʃnd] altmodisch III 4 (70)

on [ɒn]
1. auf I
2. be on eingeschaltet sein, an sein (Radio, Licht usw.) I • **turn sth. on** etwas ein-, ausschalten III 2 (35)
3. weiter • **Dream on!** Träum weiter! III 2 (34/167) • **read on** weiterlesen III 2 (34/167) • **walk on** weitergehen III 2 (34/167) • **straight on** geradeaus weiter II • **on 13th June** am 13. Juni I • **on Friday** am Freitag I • **on Friday afternoon** freitagnachmittags, am Freitagnachmittag I • **on Friday evening** freitagabends, am Freitagabend I • **on Friday morning** freitagmorgens, am Freitagmorgen I • **on Friday night** freitagnachts, Freitagnacht I • **on the beach** am Strand II • **on the board** an die Tafel I • **on the corner of Green Street and London Road** Green Street, Ecke London Road II • **on the left** links, auf der linken Seite II • **on the phone** am Telefon I **on the plane** im Flugzeug II • **on the radio** im Radio I • **on the right** rechts, auf der rechten Seite II • **on the train** im Zug I • **on TV** im Fernsehen I • °**be on a budget** mit wenig Geld auskommen müssen • **What page are we on?** Auf welcher Seite sind wir? I • **go on holiday** in Urlaub fahren II
▶ S.167 on („weiter")

once [wʌns]
1. einmal III 2 (33)
2. einst, früher einmal III 1 (15)

Dictionary (English – German)   195

once a week einmal pro Woche
III 2 (33/166)
one [wʌn] eins, ein, eine I • **one
day** eines Tages I • **a new one**
ein neuer / eine neue / ein neues
II • **my old ones** meine alten II
one-day ticket [ˌwʌn deɪ ˈtɪkɪt]
Tages(fahr-)karte III 1 (14/162)
onion [ˈʌnjən] Zwiebel III 1 (24/164)
online [ˌɒnˈlaɪn] online, Online-
III 2 (35)
only [ˈəʊnli]
1. nur, bloß I
2. erst III 3 (66)
3. the only guest der einzige Gast
I
onto [ˈɒntə, ˈɒntʊ] auf (... hinauf)
III 3 (66)
open [ˈəʊpən] öffnen, aufmachen I
open [ˈəʊpən] offen, geöffnet II
open-air [ˌəʊpən ˈeə] im Freien;
Freilicht- III 1 (13)
°**opening sentence** [ˈəʊpnɪŋ]
Anfangssatz
opera [ˈɒprə] Oper III 5 (95)
operation (on) [ˌɒpəˈreɪʃn]
Operation (an) III 3 (104)
opinion [əˈpɪnjən] Meinung III 1 (28)
in my opinion meiner Meinung
nach III 1 (28/165)
opposite [ˈɒpəzɪt] Gegenteil I
or [ɔː] oder I
orange [ˈɒrɪndʒ] orange(farben) I
orange [ˈɒrɪndʒ] Orange, Apfelsine
I • **orange juice** [ˈɒrɪndʒ dʒuːs]
Orangensaft I
°**order** [ˈɔːdə]
1. Reihenfolge • **in the right
order** in der richtigen Reihenfolge • **word order** Wortstellung
2. Befehl
organize [ˈɔːgənaɪz] ordnen,
organisieren III 3 (64)
other [ˈʌðə] andere(r, s) I • **the
others** die anderen I • **the other
way round** anders herum II
Ouch! [aʊtʃ] Autsch! I
our [ˈaʊə] unser, unsere I
ours [ˈaʊəz] unserer, unsere,
unseres II
ourselves [aʊəˈselvz] uns (selbst)
III 4 (72/176)
out heraus, hinaus; draußen II
out of ... aus ... (heraus/hinaus) I
day out Tagesausflug III 1 (13)
outfit [ˈaʊtfɪt] Outfit (Kleidung; Ausrüstung) II
outside [ˌaʊtˈsaɪd]
1. draußen I
2. nach draußen II
3. outside his room vor seinem

Zimmer; außerhalb seines
Zimmers I
over [ˈəʊvə]
1. über, oberhalb von I
2. be over vorbei/zu Ende sein I
over there da drüben, dort drüben
I • **over to ...** hinüber zu/nach ... II
all over the world auf der ganzen
Welt III Intro (6/159) • **from all over
the UK/the world/England** aus
dem gesamten Vereinigten Königreich / aus der ganzen Welt / aus
ganz England III Intro (6)
own [əʊn]: **our own pool** unser
eigenes Schwimmbad II

P

pack [pæk] packen, einpacken II
packet [ˈpækɪt] Päckchen, Packung,
Schachtel I • **a packet of mints**
ein Päckchen/eine Packung Pfefferminzbonbons I
paddle [ˈpædl] paddeln III 4 (82)
paddle [ˈpædl] Paddel III 4 (82/178)
pads (pl) [ˈpædz] (Knie- usw.)
Schützer III 3 (60/173)
page [peɪdʒ] (Buch-, Heft-)Seite I
What page are we on? Auf
welcher Seite sind wir? I
paid [peɪd] siehe pay
paint [peɪnt] (an)malen I
painter [ˈpeɪntə] Maler/in II
pair [peə]: **a pair (of)** ein Paar II
palace [ˈpæləs] Palast, Schloss
III 1 (14/162)
paper [ˈpeɪpə]
1. Papier I
2. Zeitung II
paragraph [ˈpærəgrɑːf] Absatz (in
einem Text) I
Paralympics [ˌpærəˈlɪmpɪks] Paralympische Spiele (Olympische
Spiele für Sportler/innen mit körperlicher Behinderung) III 3 (104)
paramedic [ˌpærəˈmedɪk]
Sanitäter/in II
paraphrase [ˈpærəfreɪz] umschreiben, anders ausdrücken III 3 (56)
parcel [ˈpɑːsl] Paket I
parents [ˈpeərənts] Eltern I
°**parents' night** Elternabend (in
der Schule)
park [pɑːk] Park I
parliament [ˈpɑːləmənt] Parlament
III 1 (12)
parrot [ˈpærət] Papagei I
part [pɑːt] Teil I • **take part (in)**
teilnehmen (an) III Intro (6)
partner [ˈpɑːtnə] Partner/in I
party [ˈpɑːti] Party I

pass [pɑːs] (herüber)reichen, weitergeben I • **pass round** herumgeben I
past [pɑːst] Vergangenheit I
past [pɑːst] vorbei (an), vorüber (an)
II • **half past 11** halb zwölf (11.30/
23.30) I • **quarter past 11** Viertel
nach elf (11.15/23.15) I
path [pɑːθ] Pfad, Weg II • **bridle
path** Reitweg III 3 (60/173)
°**pattern** [ˈpætn] Muster
pay (for) [peɪ], **paid, paid** bezahlen
II
PE [ˌpiːˈiː], **Physical Education**
[ˌfɪzɪkəl edʒuˈkeɪʃn] Turnen, Sportunterricht I
pea [piː] Erbse III 1 (24/164)
pen [pen] Kugelschreiber, Füller I
pence (p) (pl) [pens] Pence (Plural
von „penny")
pencil [ˈpensl] Bleistift I • **pencil
case** [ˈpensl keɪs] Federmäppchen
I • **pencil sharpener** [ˈpensl ˈʃɑːpnə]
Bleistiftanspitzer I
penny [ˈpeni] kleinste britische
Münze I
people [ˈpiːpl] Menschen, Leute I
pepper [ˈpepə] Pfeffer III 3 (62)
per [pɜː, pə] pro III 4 (76/176) • **per
cent (%)** [pə ˈsent] Prozent III 4 (76)
person [ˈpɜːsn] Person II
personal [ˈpɜːsənl] persönliche(r, s)
III 2 (33)
pet [pet] Haustier I • **pet shop**
Tierhandlung I
phone [fəʊn] Telefon I • **on the
phone** am Telefon I • **phone call**
Anruf, Telefongespräch I • **phone
number** Telefonnummer I
phone [fəʊn] telefonieren, anrufen
I
photo [ˈfəʊtəʊ] Foto I • **in the
photo** auf dem Foto I • **take
photos** Fotos machen, fotografieren I
°**photocopy** [ˈfəʊtəʊkɒpi] Fotokopie
°**phrase** [freɪz] Ausdruck, (Rede-)
Wendung
piano [piˈænəʊ] Klavier, Piano I
play the piano Klavier spielen I
pick up [ˌpɪkˈʌp]: **pick sb. up** jn. abholen III 2 (32) • **pick sth. up** etwas
hochheben, aufheben I
picnic [ˈpɪknɪk] Picknick I • **have a
picnic** ein Picknick machen I
picture [ˈpɪktʃə] Bild I • **in the
picture** auf dem Bild I
pie [paɪ] Obstkuchen; Pastete II
piece [piːs]: **a piece of** ein Stück I
a piece of paper ein Stück Papier I
°**piercing** [ˈpɪəsɪŋ] Piercing
pig [pɪg] Schwein III 1 (24/164)

pink [pɪŋk] pink(farben), rosa I
pipe [paɪp] Pfeife III 5 (91)
pirate ['paɪrət] Pirat, Piratin I
pitch [pɪtʃ] Spielfeld III 3 (54)
pizza ['piːtsə] Pizza I
place [pleɪs] Ort, Platz I
°**placemat** ['pleɪsmæt] Set, Platz-deckchen
plan [plæn] Plan I
plan (-nn-) [plæn] planen I
plane [pleɪn] Flugzeug II • **on the plane** im Flugzeug II
planet ['plænɪt] Planet II
plate [pleɪt] Teller I • **a plate of chips** ein Teller Pommes frites I
platform ['plætfɔːm] Bahnsteig, Gleis III 1 (14)
°**platinum** ['plætɪnəm] Platin
play [pleɪ] spielen I • **play football** Fußball spielen I • **play the drums** Schlagzeug spielen III Intro (7/160) **play the fiddle** Geige spielen III Intro (7/160) • **play the guitar** Gitarre spielen I • **play the piano** Klavier spielen I
play [pleɪ] Theaterstück I
player ['pleɪə] Spieler/in I
please [pliːz] bitte (in Fragen und Aufforderungen) I
plug [plʌg] Stecker III 1 (27)
pm [ˌpiːˈem]: **7 pm** 7 Uhr abends / 19 Uhr I
pocket ['pɒkɪt] Tasche (an Klei-dungsstück) II • **pocket money** Taschengeld II
poem ['pəʊɪm] Gedicht I
point [pɔɪnt] Punkt II • **make a point** ein Argument vorbringen III 4 (72) • **10.4 (ten point four)** 10,4 (zehn Komma vier) III Intro (6/151)
▶ S.160 Numbers
point (at/to sth.) [pɔɪnt] zeigen, deuten (auf etwas) II
police (pl) [pəˈliːs] Polizei I **police station** Polizeiwache, Polizeirevier II
policeman [pəˈliːsmən] Polizist II
policewoman [pəˈliːswʊmən] Polizistin II
poltergeist ['pəʊltəgaɪst] Poltergeist I
ponytail ['pəʊniteɪl] Pferdeschwanz (Frisur) III 2 (34)
pool [puːl] (Schwimm-)Becken III 3 (60/172)
poor [pɔː, pʊə] arm I • **poor Sophie** (die) arme Sophie I
pop (music) [pɒp] Pop(musik) III Intro (6/160)
popcorn ['pɒpkɔːn] Popcorn II
popular (with) ['pɒpjʊlə] populär, beliebt (bei) III 4 (69)

°**population** [ˌpɒpjʊˈleɪʃn] Bevölke-rung, Einwohner(zahl)
pork [pɔːk] Schweinefleisch III 1 (24/164)
°**porridge** ['pɒrɪdʒ] Brei
possible ['pɒsəbl] möglich II
post [pəʊst] Post (Briefe, Päck-chen, ...) III 2 (33) • **post office** ['pəʊstˌɒfɪs] Postamt II
postcard ['pəʊstkɑːd] Postkarte II
poster ['pəʊstə] Poster I
potato [pəˈteɪtəʊ], pl **potatoes** Kartoffel I
pound (£) [paʊnd] Pfund (britische Währung) I
practice ['præktɪs] hier: Übungsteil I
practise ['præktɪs] üben; trainieren I
prepare [prɪˈpeə] vorbereiten; sich vorbereiten II • **prepare for** sich vorbereiten auf II
present ['preznt]
1. Gegenwart I
2. Geschenk I
°**present sth. (to sb.)** [prɪˈzent] (jm.) etwas präsentieren, vorstellen
presentation [ˌpreznˈteɪʃn] Präsen-tation, Vorstellung I
presenter [prɪˈzentə] Moderator/in II
°**president** ['prezɪdənt] Präsident/in
press [pres] drücken III 2 (41)
pretty ['prɪti] hübsch I
pretty healthy/good/... ['prɪti] ziemlich gesund/gut/... II
price [praɪs] (Kauf-)Preis I
°**half-price** zum halben Preis
print: bold print [ˌbəʊld ˈprɪnt] Fett-druck III 5 (90)
prize [praɪz] Preis, Gewinn I
probably ['prɒbəbli] wahrscheinlich II
problem ['prɒbləm] Problem II
produce [prəˈdjuːs] produzieren, herstellen III 5 (88)
profile ['prəʊfaɪl] Porträt, Steckbrief III 3 (53)
programme ['prəʊgræm] Programm I
project (about, on) ['prɒdʒekt] Pro-jekt (über, zu) I • **do a project** ein Projekt machen, durchführen II
promise ['prɒmɪs] versprechen II
°**pronounce** [prəˈnaʊns] aussprechen
pronunciation [prəˌnʌnsiˈeɪʃn] Aus-sprache I
proof (no pl) [pruːf] Beweis(e) II
protect sb. (from sth.) [prəˈtekt] jn. (be)schützen (vor) III 4 (72)
proud (of sb./sth.) [praʊd] stolz (auf jn./etwas) II

province ['prɒvɪns] Provinz III 4 (72)
PS [ˌpiːˈes] **(postscript** ['pəʊst-skrɪpt]) PS (Nachschrift unter Briefen) III 1 (12)
pub [pʌb] Kneipe, Lokal II
publish ['pʌblɪʃ] veröffentlichen III 5 (88)
pull [pʊl] ziehen I
pullover ['pʊləʊvə] Pullover II
°**punk** [pʌŋk] Punk / Punker/in
purple ['pɜːpl] violett; lila I
purse [pɜːs] Geldbörse II
push [pʊʃ] drücken, schieben, stoßen I
put (-tt-) [pʊt], put, put legen, stel-len, (etwas wohin) tun I • **put sth. on** etwas anziehen (Kleidung) II °**put sth. on the wall** etwas an die Wand hängen • °**put sth. together** etwas zusammenstellen, zusam-menfügen • °**Put up your hand.** Heb deine Hand. / Hebt eure Hand.
puzzled ['pʌzld] verwirrt II
pyjamas (pl) [pəˈdʒɑːməz] Schlaf-anzug II

Q

quarter ['kwɔːtə]: **quarter past 11** Viertel nach 11 (11.15/23.15) I **quarter to 12** Viertel vor 12 (11.45/23.45) I
queen [kwiːn] Königin III 1 (13)
question ['kwestʃn] Frage I • **ask questions** Fragen stellen I °**question word** Fragewort
quick [kwɪk] schnell I
quiet ['kwaɪət] leise, still, ruhig I
quite bad/quick/good ... [kwaɪt] ziemlich schlimm/schnell/gut/... II
quiz [kwɪz], pl **quizzes** ['kwɪzɪz] Quiz, Ratespiel I
°**quotation mark** [kwəʊˈteɪʃn mɑːk] Anführungszeichen

R

rabbit ['ræbɪt] Kaninchen I
°**race** [reɪs] Rennen
racket ['rækɪt]: **badminton racket** Badmintonschläger III 3 (60/172)
radio ['reɪdiəʊ] Radio I • **on the radio** im Radio I
railway ['reɪlweɪ] Eisenbahn II
rain [reɪn] Regen II
rain [reɪn] regnen II
rainy ['reɪni] regnerisch II
ran [ræn] siehe **run**
rang [ræŋ] siehe **ring**

Dictionary (English – German)   197

rap [ræp] Rap *(rhythmischer Sprech-gesang)* I
rapids *(pl)* ['ræpɪdz] Stromschnellen III 4 (82)
RE [ˌɑːrˈ_ˈiː], **Religious Education** [rɪˌlɪdʒəs_edʒʊˈkeɪʃn] Religion, Religionsunterricht I
°**reach** [riːtʃ] erreichen
read [riːd], **read, read** lesen I
read on weiterlesen III 2 (34/167)
°**read out** vorlesen • °**Read out loud.** Lies laut vor. • °**Read the poem to a partner.** Lies das Gedicht einem Partner / einer Partnerin vor.
read [red] *siehe* **read**
reader ['riːdə] Leser/in II
ready ['redi] bereit, fertig I • **get ready (for)** sich fertig machen (für), sich vorbereiten (auf) I • **get things ready** Dinge fertig machen, vorbereiten I
real [rɪəl] echt, wirklich I
realistic [ˌriːəˈlɪstɪk] realistisch, wirklichkeitsnah III 1 (27)
really ['rɪəli] wirklich I
reason ['riːzn] Grund, Begründung I • **for lots of reasons** aus vielen Gründen I
record [rɪˈkɔːd] *(Musik / einen Film)* aufnehmen III 1 (13)
record ['rekɔːd] Schallplatte III 5 (95)
recorder [rɪˈkɔːdə] Blockflöte III Intro (11)
recording [rɪˈkɔːdɪŋ] Aufnahme, Aufzeichnung III Intro (11)
recycled [ˌriːˈsaɪkld] wiederverwertet, wiederverwendet, recycelt II
recycling [ˌriːˈsaɪklɪŋ] Wiederverwertung, Recycling II
red [red] rot I
refer to (-rr-) [rɪˈfɜː] sich beziehen auf III 3 (55)
reggae ['regeɪ] Reggae III Intro (6)
rehearsal [rɪˈhɜːsl] Probe *(am Theater)* I
rehearse [rɪˈhɜːs] proben *(am Theater)* I
°**relationship** [rɪˈleɪʃnʃɪp] Beziehung, Verhältnis
relax [rɪˈlæks] (sich) entspannen, sich ausruhen II
relaxed [rɪˈlækst] locker, entspannt III 4 (76)
release [rɪˈliːs] *(CD, Film usw.)* herausbringen, auf den Markt bringen III 5 (91)
°**reliable** [rɪˈlaɪəbl] verlässlich, zuverlässig
°**relocate** [ˌriːləʊˈkeɪt] umziehen, übersiedeln

remember sth. [rɪˈmembə]
1. sich an etwas erinnern I
2. sich etwas merken I
°**Remember ...** Denk dran, ...
report (on) [rɪˈpɔːt] Bericht, Reportage (über) I
report (to sb.) [rɪˈpɔːt] (jm.) berichten II
°**reporter** [rɪˈpɔːtə] Reporter,/in Berichterstatter/in I
represent [ˌreprɪˈzent] repräsentieren, vertreten III 3 (104)
rescue helicopter ['reskju: ˌhelɪkɒptə] Rettungshubschrauber II
°**research** [rɪˈsɜːtʃ, 'riːsɜːtʃ] Recherche I
°**researcher** [rɪˈsɜːtʃə, 'riːsɜːtʃə] Rechercheur/in • **film researcher** Filmrechercheur/in
°**reserve** [rɪˈzɜːv] Reservat, Schutzgebiet I
rest [rest] Rest II
restaurant ['restrɒnt] Restaurant II
result [rɪˈzʌlt] Ergebnis, Resultat I
return ticket [rɪˈtɜːn ˌtɪkɪt] Rückfahrkarte II
revise [rɪˈvaɪz]
1. überarbeiten III 4 (78)
2. wiederholen III 4 (78)
revision [rɪˈvɪʒn] Wiederholung *(des Lernstoffs)* I
°**rewrite** [ˌriːˈraɪt], **rewrote, rewritten** umschreiben, neu schreiben I
°**rewritten** [ˌriːˈrɪtn] *siehe* **rewrite**
°**rewrote** [ˌriːˈrəʊt] *siehe* **rewrite**
rhino ['raɪnəʊ] Nashorn II
rice [raɪs] Reis III 3 (65)
rich [rɪtʃ] reich II
ridden ['rɪdn] *siehe* **ride**
riddle ['rɪdl] Rätsel III 5 (91)
ride [raɪd], **rode, ridden** reiten I
go riding reiten gehen I • **ride a bike** Rad fahren I
ride [raɪd]: **(bike) ride** (Rad-)Fahrt II
take a ride eine Fahrt machen III 3 (66)
°**oil rig** (Öl-)Bohrinsel I
right [raɪt] richtig I • **all right** [ɔːl ˈraɪt] gut, in Ordnung II • **be right** Recht haben I • **That's right.** Das ist richtig. / Das stimmt. I • **You need a school bag, right?** Du brauchst eine Schultasche, stimmt's? / nicht wahr? I
right [raɪt] rechte(r, s) II • **look right** nach rechts schauen II • **on the right** rechts, auf der rechten Seite II • **turn right** (nach) rechts abbiegen II
right [raɪt]: **right now** jetzt sofort; jetzt gerade I
ring [rɪŋ] Ring II

ring [rɪŋ], **rang, rung** klingeln, läuten II
ringtone ['rɪŋtəʊn] Klingelton III 2 (33)
river ['rɪvə] Fluss II
RnB [ˌɑːr_ənˈbiː] RnB *(Rhythm and Blues; Form des Blues, in der Rhythmus eine große Rolle spielt; moderner RnB enthält Rap- und Hip Hop-Elemente)* III Intro (6)
road [rəʊd] Straße I • **Park Road** [ˌpɑːk ˈrəʊd] Parkstraße I
rock [rɒk] Fels, Felsen III 2 (30)
rode [rəʊd] *siehe* **ride**
role [rəʊl] Rolle III 2 (42) • **role play** ['rəʊl pleɪ] Rollenspiel I
roll [rəʊl] Brötchen I
Roman ['rəʊmən] römisch; Römer, Römerin II
room [ruːm] Raum, Zimmer I
°**root** [ruːt] Wurzel
round [raʊnd] rund II
round [raʊnd] um ... (herum); in ... umher II • **the other way round** anders herum II
°**route** [ruːt] Weg, Route
°**routine** [ruːˈtiːn] Routine, Tagesablauf
royal ['rɔɪəl] königlich III 1 (13)
rubber ['rʌbə] Radiergummi I
rubbish ['rʌbɪʃ] (Haus-)Müll, Abfall II
rucksack ['rʌksæk] Rucksack III 2 (34)
rude [ruːd] unhöflich, unverschämt II
°**rugby** ['rʌgbi] Rugby I
ruler ['ruːlə] Lineal I
run [rʌn] (Wett-)Lauf II
run (-nn-) [rʌn], **ran, run** laufen, rennen I • **run around** herumrennen III 1 (26/164)
°**runaway** ['rʌnəweɪ] Ausreißer I
rung [rʌŋ] *siehe* **ring**
runner ['rʌnə] Läufer/in II
running shoes ['rʌnɪŋ ˌʃuːz] Laufschuhe III 3 (60/172)
running track ['rʌnɪŋ træk] Laufbahn *(Sport)* III 3 (60/172)
rush hour ['rʌʃ_aʊə] Hauptverkehrszeit III 1 (14)

S

sad [sæd] traurig II
saddle ['sædl] Sattel III 3 (60/173)
safe (from) [seɪf] sicher, in Sicherheit (vor) II
said [sed] *siehe* **say**
sailor ['seɪlə] Seemann, Matrose II
salad ['sæləd] Salat *(als Gericht oder Beilage)* I

Dictionary (English – German)

salmon ['sæmən], *pl* **salmon** Lachs III 2 (30)

salt [sɔ:lt] Salz III 3 (62/173)

same [seɪm]: **the same …** der-/die-/dasselbe …; dieselben … I • **be/look the same** gleich sein/aussehen I

sandwich ['sænwɪtʃ] Sandwich, *(zusammengeklapptes)* belegtes Brot I • **sandwich box** Brotdose I

sang [sæŋ] *siehe* **sing**

sat [sæt] *siehe* **sit**

Saturday ['sætədeɪ, 'sætədi] Samstag, Sonnabend I

sauna ['sɔ:nə] Sauna II • **have a sauna** in die Sauna gehen II

sausage ['sɒsɪdʒ] (Brat-, Bock-)Würstchen, Wurst I

save [seɪv]
1. retten II
2. sparen II

saw [sɔ:] *siehe* **see**

saxophone ['sæksəfəʊn] Saxophon III Intro (11)

say [seɪ], **said, said** sagen I • **It says here: …** Hier steht: … / Es heißt hier: … • **say goodbye** sich verabschieden I • **Say hi to Dilip for me.** Grüß Dilip von mir. I • **say sorry** sich entschuldigen II

scan a text (-nn-) [skæn] einen Text schnell nach bestimmten Wörtern/Informationen absuchen II

scared [skeəd] verängstigt II • **be scared (of)** Angst haben (vor) I

scarf [skɑ:f], *pl* **scarves** [skɑ:vs] Schal III 2 (44)

scary ['skeəri] unheimlich; gruselig I

scene [si:n] Szene I

school [sku:l] Schule I • **at school** in der Schule I • **school bag** Schultasche I • **school subject** Schulfach I

science ['saɪəns] Naturwissenschaft I

°**scientist** ['saɪəntɪst] Wissenschaftler/in

score [skɔ:] Spielstand; Punktestand III 3 (54/171) • **final score** Endstand III 3 (54/171) • **What's the score now? – 2–0.** (you say: two nil) Wie steht es jetzt? *(beim Sport)* – 2:0 III 3 (54/171)
▶ S.171 A football match

score (a goal) [skɔ:], [gəʊl] ein Tor schießen, einen Treffer erzielen III 3 (54)

scream [skri:m] schreien III 1 (27)

sea [si:] Meer, *(die)* See I

°**search engine** ['sɜ:tʃ ˌendʒɪn] Suchmaschine *(im Internet)*

second ['sekənd] zweite(r, s) I

second-hand [ˌsekənd 'hænd] gebraucht; aus zweiter Hand III 1 (12)

°**secretly** ['si:krətli] insgeheim

section ['sekʃn] Abschnitt, Teil, (Themen-)Bereich III 5 (88)

see [si:], **saw, seen**
1. sehen I
2. **see sb.** jn. besuchen, jn. aufsuchen II
See? Siehst du? I • **See you.** Tschüs. / Bis bald. I • **Wait and see!** Wart's ab! III Intro (11)

°**seem (to do)** [si:m] (zu tun) scheinen

seen [si:n] *siehe* **see**

sell [sel], **sold, sold** verkaufen II
be sold out ausverkauft sein; vergriffen sein III 5 (91)

semi-final [ˌsemi'faɪnl] Halbfinale III 3 (52)

send (to) [send], **sent, sent** schicken, senden (an) II

sent [sent] *siehe* **send**

sentence ['sentəns] Satz I

September [sep'tembə] September I

series, *pl* **series** ['sɪəri:z] (Sende-)Reihe, Serie II

°**settler** ['setlə] Siedler/in

setup ['setʌp] Setup II

sex [seks] Geschlecht III 3 (52/53)

shampoo [ʃæm'pu:] Shampoo, Haarwaschmittel III 4 (69)

°**shape** [ʃeɪp] Form, Gestalt

share sth. (with sb.) [ʃeə] sich etwas teilen (mit jm.) I

she [ʃi:] sie I

sheep, *pl* **sheep** [ʃi:p] Schaf II

shelf [ʃelf], *pl* **shelves** [ʃelvz] Regal(brett) I

shine [ʃaɪn], **shone, shone** scheinen *(Sonne)* II

ship [ʃɪp] Schiff I

shirt [ʃɜ:t] Hemd I

shoe [ʃu:] Schuh I

shone [ʃɒn] *siehe* **shine**

shoot [ʃu:t], **shot, shot** schießen, erschießen III 4 (69)

shop [ʃɒp] Laden, Geschäft I
shop assistant ['ʃɒp_əˌsɪstənt] Verkäufer/in I • **shop window** Schaufenster II

shop (-pp-) [ʃɒp] einkaufen (gehen) I

shopping ['ʃɒpɪŋ] (das) Einkaufen I • **go shopping** einkaufen gehen I • **shopping list** Einkaufsliste I

short [ʃɔ:t] kurz I

°**shortbread** ['ʃɔ:tbred] schottischer Butterkeks

shorts *(pl)* [ʃɔ:ts] Shorts, kurze Hose I

shot [ʃɒt] *siehe* **shoot**

°**shot put** ['ʃɒt pʊt] Kugelstoßen I

should [ʃəd, ʃʊd]: **Why should I … ?** Warum sollte ich … ? III 2 (44)

shoulder ['ʃəʊldə] Schulter I

shout [ʃaʊt] schreien, rufen I

show [ʃəʊ] Show, Vorstellung I

show [ʃəʊ], **showed, shown** zeigen I

shower ['ʃaʊə] Dusche I • **have a shower** (sich) duschen I

shown [ʃəʊn] *siehe* **show**

shut up [ˌʃʌt_'ʌp], **shut, shut** den Mund halten II

shy [ʃaɪ] schüchtern, scheu II

side [saɪd] Seite II

sights *(pl)* [saɪts] Sehenswürdigkeiten II

°**sight-seeing** ['saɪtsi:ɪŋ]: **go sightseeing** Sehenswürdigkeiten besichtigen

sign [saɪn] Schild, Zeichen III 1 (26)

silence ['saɪləns] Stille; Schweigen III 5 (90)

silent letter [ˌsaɪlənt 'letə] „stummer" Buchstabe *(nicht gesprochener Buchstabe)* II

silly ['sɪli] albern, dumm I

sing [sɪŋ], **sang, sung** singen I

singer ['sɪŋə] Sänger/in II

single ['sɪŋgl] ledig, alleinstehend I
single (ticket) einfache Fahrkarte *(nur Hinfahrt)* III 1 (14)

single ['sɪŋgl] Single III 5 (95)

sink [sɪŋk] Spüle, Spülbecken I

°**Sir** [sɜ:, sə] Sir *(britischer Adelstitel)*

sister ['sɪstə] Schwester I

sit (-tt-) [sɪt], **sat, sat** sitzen; sich setzen I • **sit down** sich hinsetzen II • **Sit with me.** Setz dich zu mir. / Setzt euch zu mir. I

°**situation** [ˌsɪtʃu'eɪʃn] Situation I

size [saɪz] Größe I

skate [skeɪt] Inliner fahren I

skateboard ['skeɪtbɔ:d] Skateboard I

skater ['skeɪtə] Skateboardfahrer III 3 (67)

skates *(pl)* [skeɪts] Inliner I

sketch [sketʃ] Sketch I

ski [ski:] Ski fahren/laufen III 4 (69/174)

ski [ski:] Ski III 3 (60/172) • **ski slope** ['ski: sləʊp] Skipiste III 3 (60/172)

°**skiing** ['ski:ɪŋ] Skifahren, Skilaufen

skills file ['skɪlz faɪl] Anhang mit Lern- und Arbeitstechniken I

skim a text (-mm-) [skɪm] einen Text überfliegen *(um den Inhalt grob zu erfassen)* III 5 (90)

skirt [skɜ:t] Rock II

sky [skaɪ] Himmel II

Dictionary (English – German)   199

°**skyscraper** ['skaɪskreɪpə] Wolken-
kratzer
slave [sleɪv] Sklave, Sklavin II
sledge [sledʒ] Schlitten III 3 (104)
sleep [sliːp], **slept, slept** schlafen I
sleep [sliːp] Schlaf III 4 (69/174)
sleepover ['sliːpəʊvə] Schlafparty
III 4 (69)
slept [slept] *siehe* **sleep**
slow [sləʊ] langsam II
small [smɔːl] klein I
smart [smɑːt] clever, schlau II
smell [smel] riechen I
smell [smel] Geruch II
smile [smaɪl] lächeln I • **smile at
sb.** jn. anlächeln II
smile [smaɪl] Lächeln II
smoke [sməʊk] rauchen III 1 (27/165)
smoke [sməʊk] Rauch III 1 (27)
smoking: No smoking! [ˌnəʊ
'sməʊkɪŋ] Rauchen verboten.
III 1 (27/165)
snack [snæk] Snack, Imbiss II
snake [sneɪk] Schlange I
snow [snəʊ] Schnee II
snowshoe ['snəʊʃuː] Schneeschuh
III 4 (69/175)
snowshoeing ['snəʊʃuːɪŋ] Schneeschuhwandern III 4 (68)
so [səʊ]
1. also; deshalb, daher I • **So?**
Und? / Na und? II
2. so sweet so süß I
3. so that sodass, damit III 5 (90)
4. Do you really think so? Meinst
du wirklich? / Glaubst du das wirklich? II
soap [səʊp] Seife I
sock [sɒk] Socke, Strumpf I
sofa ['səʊfə] Sofa I
software ['sɒftweə] Software II
sold [səʊld] *siehe* **sell** • **be sold out**
ausverkauft sein; vergriffen sein
III 5 (91)
some [səm, sʌm] einige, ein paar I
some cheese/juice etwas Käse/
Saft I
somebody ['sʌmbədi] jemand I
Find/Ask somebody who ... Finde/
Frage jemanden, der ... II
something ['sʌmθɪŋ] etwas II
sometimes ['sʌmtaɪmz] manchmal
I
somewhere ['sʌmweə] irgend-
wo(hin) II
son [sʌn] Sohn I
song [sɒŋ] Lied, Song I
soon [suːn] bald I
sore [sɔː]: **have a sore throat** Halsschmerzen haben II
sorry ['sɒri]: **(I'm) sorry.** Entschuldigung. / Tut mir leid. I • **Sorry,**

I'm late. Entschuldigung, dass ich
zu spät bin/komme. I • **Sorry?**
Wie bitte? I • **say sorry** sich entschuldigen I
sort [sɔːt] Art, Sorte II
sound [saʊnd] klingen, sich *(gut
usw.)* anhören I
sound [saʊnd] Laut; Klang I
°**sound assistant** ['saʊnd_əˌsɪstənt]
Tonassistent • **sound file** ['saʊnd
faɪl] Tondatei, Soundfile III 1 (12)
soup [suːp] Suppe II
°**source** [sɔːs] (Informations-)Quelle I
south [saʊθ] Süden; nach Süden;
südlich III Intro (7/160)
southbound ['saʊθbaʊnd] Richtung
Süden III 1 (14/162)
south-east [ˌsaʊθ'iːst] Südosten;
nach Südosten; südöstlich
III Intro (7/160)
south-west [ˌsaʊθ'west] Südwesten;
nach Südwesten; südwestlich
III Intro (7/160)
°**souvenir** [ˌsuːvə'nɪə] Souvenir,
Mitbringsel I
space [speɪs]: **Move back one space.**
Geh ein Feld zurück. I • **Move on
one space.** Geh ein Feld vor. II
spaghetti [spə'geti] Spaghetti II
speak (to) [spiːk], **spoke, spoken**
sprechen (mit), reden (mit) II
special ['speʃl]: **a special day** ein
besonderer Tag I
°**speech bubble** ['spiːtʃ bʌbl] Sprech-
blase I
spell [spel] buchstabieren I
spelling ['spelɪŋ] (Recht-)Schrei-
bung, Schreibweise III 4 (78)
spend [spend], **spent, spent: spend
money (on)** Geld ausgeben (für)
II • **spend time (on)** Zeit verbringen (mit) II
spent [spent] *siehe* **spend**
spicy ['spaɪsi] würzig, scharf gewürzt III 1 (16)
spoke [spəʊk] *siehe* **speak**
spoken ['spəʊkən] *siehe* **speak**
spoon [spuːn] Löffel III 4 (81/177)
sport [spɔːt] Sport; Sportart I
do sport Sport treiben I • **sports
centre** Sportzentrum I • **sports
hall** Sporthalle III 3 (60/172)
°**sportsperson** ['spɔːtspɜːsn]
Sportler/in I
sporty ['spɔːti] sportlich III 3 (54)
spot (-tt-) [spɒt] entdecken III 3 (54)
spring [sprɪŋ] Frühling I
spy [spaɪ] Spion/in I
square [skweə] Platz III 1 (14/162)
squeeze [skwiːz] drücken; (aus)
pressen III 5 (91)
squirrel ['skwɪrəl] Eichhörnchen II

stadium ['steɪdiəm] Stadion III 3 (56)
stage [steɪdʒ] Bühne III 4 (73)
stairs *(pl)* [steəz] Treppe; Treppen-
stufen I
stamp [stæmp] Briefmarke I
stand [stænd], **stood, stood** stehen;
sich (hin)stellen II
star [stɑː]
1. Stern II
2. (Film-, Pop-)Star I
start [stɑːt] starten, anfangen, beginnen (mit) I
state [steɪt] Staat III Intro (10)
statement ['steɪtmənt] Aussage,
Feststellung III 2 (40)
station ['steɪʃn] Bahnhof I • **at the
station** am Bahnhof I
statue ['stætʃuː] Statue II
stay [steɪ]
1. bleiben I • **stay out** draußen
bleiben, wegbleiben III 4 (71)
2. wohnen, übernachten II • **stay
with** wohnen bei III 1 (21)
steak [steɪk] Steak III 1 (24/164)
steal [stiːl], **stole, stolen** stehlen II
steel [stiːl] Stahl III Intro (6) • **steel
drum** [ˌstiːl 'drʌm] Steeldrum
III Intro (6)
step [step] Schritt I • **take steps**
Schritte machen/unternehmen
III 3 (66)
stereo ['steriəʊ] Stereoanlage I
stew [stjuː] Eintopf(gericht) III 2 (46)
°**stewed chicken** [stjuːd] geschmor-
tes Hühnchen I
stick out of sth. [stɪk], **stuck, stuck**
aus etwas herausragen, heraus-
stehen III 5 (91)
still [stɪl] (immer) noch I
stole [stəʊl] *siehe* **steal**
stolen ['stəʊlən] *siehe* **steal**
stomach ['stʌmək eɪk] Magen II
stomach ache Magenschmerzen,
Bauchweh II
stone [stəʊn] Stein II
stood [stʊd] *siehe* **stand**
stop (-pp-) [stɒp]
1. aufhören I
2. anhalten I
Stop that! Hör auf damit! / Lass
das! I
storm [stɔːm] Sturm; Gewitter II
stormy ['stɔːmi] stürmisch II
story ['stɔːri] Geschichte, Erzählung I
straight on [streɪt_'ɒn] geradeaus
weiter I
strange [streɪndʒ] seltsam, sonderbar; fremd III 1 (17)
strawberry ['strɔːbəri] Erdbeere II
street [striːt] Straße I • **at 7 Hamilton Street** in der Hamiltonstraße 7
I

stress [stres] Betonung III 2 (38)
°**stressed** [strest] betont
°**stretch out** [ˌstretʃ ˈaʊt] dehnen
strict [strɪkt] streng III 4 (70)
strike [straɪk] Streik III 4 (79) • **be on strike** streiken, sich im Streik befinden III 4 (79/177) • **go on strike** streiken, in den Streik treten III 4 (79/177)
strong [strɒŋ] stark II
structure ['strʌktʃə] strukturieren, aufbauen II
stuck [stʌk] siehe **stick**
student ['stjuːdənt] Schüler/in; Student/in I • **exchange student** Austauschschüler/in III 3 (55)
studio ['stjuːdɪəʊ] Studio III 2 (42)
study skills (pl) ['stʌdi skɪlz] Lern- und Arbeitstechniken I
stuff [stʌf] Zeug, Kram II
stupid ['stjuːpɪd] blöd, dämlich II
subject ['sʌbdʒɪkt]
1. Schulfach I
°**2.** Betreff (in einer E-Mail)
subway ['sʌbweɪ]: **the subway** (AE) die U-Bahn II
success [sək'ses] Erfolg III 5 (88)
successful [sək'sesfl] erfolgreich III 5 (88/178)
°**such** [sʌtʃ] so, solch • °**such as** wie (zum Beispiel)
suddenly ['sʌdnli] plötzlich, auf einmal I
sugar ['ʃʊgə] Zucker II
°**suggest** [sə'dʒest] vorschlagen, empfehlen
suitcase ['suːtkeɪs] Koffer II
°**sum** [sʌm] Summe, Betrag
summer ['sʌmə] Sommer I
sun [sʌn] Sonne II
Sunday ['sʌndeɪ, 'sʌndi] Sonntag I
sung [sʌŋ] siehe **sing**
sunglasses (pl) ['sʌnglɑːsɪz] (eine) Sonnenbrille I
sunny ['sʌni] sonnig II
supermarket ['suːpəmɑːkɪt] Supermarkt II
support a team [sə'pɔːt] eine Mannschaft unterstützen; Fan einer Mannschaft sein III 3 (54/171)
supporter [sə'pɔːtə] Anhänger/in, Fan III 3 (54)
sure [ʃʊə, ʃɔː]: **be sure** sicher sein II
surf [sɜːf]: **surf the internet** im Internet surfen III 2 (33)
surfboard ['sɜːfbɔːd] Surfbrett II
surfing ['sɜːfɪŋ]: **go surfing** wellenreiten gehen, surfen gehen II
surprise [sə'praɪz] Überraschung III 1 (16)
surprise sb. [sə'praɪz] jn. überraschen III 5 (90)

surprised (at sth.) [sə'praɪzd] überrascht (über/von etwas) III 1 (16/162)
survey (on) [sɜːveɪ] Umfrage, Untersuchung (über) II
survive [sə'vaɪv] überleben II
swam [swæm] siehe **swim**
°**swap (-pp-)** [swɒp] tauschen
sweatshirt ['swetʃɜːt] Sweatshirt I
sweet [swiːt] süß I
sweetheart ['swiːthɑːt] Liebling, Schatz II
sweets (pl) [swiːts] Süßigkeiten I
swim (-mm-) [swɪm], **swam, swum** schwimmen I • **go swimming** schwimmen gehen I
swimmer ['swɪmə] Schwimmer/in II
swimming ['swɪmɪŋ]: **swimming pool** [puːl] Schwimmbad, Schwimmbecken I • **swimming trunks (pl)** [trʌŋks] Badehose III 3 (60/172)
swimsuit ['swɪmsuːt] Badeanzug III 3 (60/172)
swum [swʌm] siehe **swim**
syllable ['sɪləbl] Silbe I

T

table ['teɪbl] Tisch I
table tennis ['teɪbl tenɪs] Tischtennis I • **table tennis bat** [bæt] Tischtennisschläger III 3 (60/172)
take [teɪk], **took, taken**
1. nehmen I
2. (weg-, hin)bringen I
3. dauern, (Zeit) brauchen III 2 (32)
take a ride [raɪd] eine Spritztour/Fahrt machen III 3 (66) • **take notes** sich Notizen machen I • **take out** herausnehmen I • **take part (in)** teilnehmen (an) III Intro (6) **take photos** Fotos machen, fotografieren I • **take steps** Schritte machen III 3 (66) • **take sth. off** etwas ausziehen (Kleidung) II **take 10 c off** 10 Cent abziehen I °**Take turns.** Wechselt euch ab. **We'll take them.** (beim Einkaufen) Wir nehmen sie. I
taken ['teɪkən] siehe **take**
talent ['tælənt] Talent, Begabung III 3 (104)
talk [tɔːk]: **talk (about)** reden (über), sich unterhalten (über) I **talk (to)** reden (mit), sich unterhalten (mit) I
°**tartan** ['tɑːtn] Schottenstoff (mit Schottenmuster)
taught [tɔːt] siehe **teach**
taxi ['tæksi] Taxi III 1 (20/163)

tea [tiː] Tee; (auch:) leichte Nachmittags- oder Abendmahlzeit I
teach [tiːtʃ], **taught, taught** unterrichten, lehren I
teacher ['tiːtʃə] Lehrer/in I • **head teacher** Schulleiter/in III 2 (44)
team [tiːm] Team, Mannschaft I
teaspoon ['tiːspuːn] Teelöffel III 4 (81/177)
teen [tiːn] Teenager-, Jugend- III 5 (88)
teenager ['tiːneɪdʒə] Teenager, Jugendliche(r) II
°**technology** [tek'nɒlədʒi] Technik, Technologie
teddy ['tedi] Teddybär III 2 (44)
teeth [tiːθ] Plural von „tooth"
telephone ['telɪfəʊn] Telefon I **telephone number** Telefonnummer I • **What's your telephone number?** Was ist deine Telefonnummer? I
television (TV) ['telɪvɪʒn] Fernsehen I
tell (about) [tel], **told, told** erzählen (von), berichten (über) I • **Tell me your names.** Sagt mir eure Namen. I • **tell sb. the way** jm. den Weg beschreiben II
temperature ['temprətʃə] Temperatur II • **have a temperature** Fieber haben II
tennis ['tenɪs] Tennis I
tense [tens] (grammatische) Zeit, Tempus III 5 (98)
term [tɜːm] Trimester II
°**terminal** ['tɜːmɪnl] Terminal
terrible ['terəbl] schrecklich, furchtbar I
test [test] Test, Prüfung II
text sb. [tekst] jm. eine SMS schicken III 2 (33)
text [tekst] Text I • **text message** ['tekst ˌmesɪdʒ] SMS III 2 (33/167) **skim a text** einen Text überfliegen (um den Inhalt grob zu erfassen) III 5 (90)
than [ðæn, ðən] als II • **more than** mehr als II • **more than me** mehr als ich II
thank [θæŋk]: **Thank you.** Danke (schön). I • **Thanks.** Danke. I **Thanks a lot!** Vielen Dank! I **Thanks very much!** Danke sehr! / Vielen Dank! II
that [ðət, ðæt]
1. das (dort) I
2. jene(r, s) I
That's me. Das bin ich. I • **That's right.** Das ist richtig. / Das stimmt. I • **That's up to you.** Das liegt bei dir. / Das kannst/musst du (selbst)

Dictionary (English – German)   201

entscheiden. III 5 (88) • **That was close.** Das war knapp. II

that [ðət, ðæt] dass I • **so that** sodass, damit III 5 (90)

that [ðət, ðæt] der, die, das; die *(Relativpronomen)* III 3 (55)

that far/good/bad/... [ðæt] so weit/gut/schlecht/... III 5 (92)

the [ðə, ði] der, die, das; die I

theatre ['θɪətə] Theater II

their [ðeə] ihr, ihre *(Plural)* I

theirs [ðeəz] ihrer, ihre, ihrs II

them [ðəm, ðem] sie; ihnen I

themselves [ðəm'selvz] sich (selbst) III 4 (72/176)

then [ðen] dann, danach I

there [ðeə]
1. da, dort I
2. dahin, dorthin I
down there dort unten II • **over there** da drüben, dort drüben I • **there are** es sind (vorhanden); es gibt I • **there's** es ist (vorhanden); es gibt I • **there isn't a ...** es ist kein/e ...; es gibt kein/e ... I

thermometer [θə'mɒmɪtə] Thermometer II

these [ðiːz] diese, die (hier) I

they [ðeɪ] sie *(Plural)* I

thief [θiːf], *pl* **thieves** [θiːvz] Dieb/in II

thing [θɪŋ] Ding, Sache I • **What was the best thing about ...?** Was war das Beste an ...? II

think [θɪŋk], **thought, thought** glauben, meinen, denken I
think about 1. nachdenken über II; **2.** denken über, halten von II
think of 1. denken über, halten von II; **2.** denken an; sich ausdenken II

third [θɜːd] dritte(r, s) I

this [ðɪs]
1. dies (hier) I
2. diese(r, s) I
This is Isabel. Hier spricht Isabel. / Hier ist Isabel. *(am Telefon)* II
this morning/afternoon/evening heute Morgen/Nachmittag/Abend I • **this way** hier entlang, in diese Richtung II

those [ðəʊz] die (da), jene (dort) I

thought [θɔːt] *siehe* **think**

thousand ['θaʊznd] tausend I

threw [θruː] *siehe* **throw**

throat [θrəʊt] Hals, Kehle II

through [θruː] durch II

throw [θrəʊ], **threw, thrown** werfen I

thrown [θrəʊn] *siehe* **throw**

Thursday ['θɜːzdeɪ, 'θɜːzdi] Donnerstag I

°**tick** [tɪk] Häkchen

°**tick** [tɪk] ankreuzen, ein Häkchen machen

ticket ['tɪkɪt]
1. Eintrittskarte I
2. Fahrkarte II
ticket machine Fahrkartenautomat III 1 (20/163) • **ticket office** Fahrkartenschalter III 1 (14) • **one-day ticket** Tages(fahr)karte III 1 (14/162) • **return ticket** Rückfahrkarte II • **single (ticket)** einfache Fahrkarte *(nur Hinfahrt)* III 1 (14)

tidy ['taɪdi] aufräumen I

tidy ['taɪdi] ordentlich, aufgeräumt II

tiger ['taɪgə] Tiger II

till [tɪl] bis *(zeitlich)* I
▶ S.175 German „bis"

time [taɪm]
1. Zeit; Uhrzeit I
2. time(s) Mal(e); -mal II
What's the time? Wie spät ist es? I • **in time** rechtzeitig II • **three times** dreimal III 2 (33/166)

°**timeline** ['taɪmlaɪn] Zeitachse, Zeitleiste

timetable ['taɪmteɪbl]
1. Stundenplan I
2. Fahrplan II

timing ['taɪmɪŋ]: **bad timing** schlechtes Timing III 3 (55)

tip [tɪp] Tipp II

tired ['taɪəd] müde I

title ['taɪtl] Titel, Überschrift I

to [tə, tu]
1. zu, nach I • **to Jenny's** zu Jenny I • °**to the front** nach vorn
2. an e-mail to eine E-Mail an I **write to** schreiben an I
3. quarter to 12 Viertel vor 12 (11.45/23.45) I
4. try to help/to play/... versuchen, zu helfen/zu spielen/... I
5. um zu II
6. from Monday to Friday von Montag bis Freitag III 2 (32)
▶ S.175 German „bis"

toast [təʊst] Toast(brot) I

tobacco [tə'bækəʊ] Tabak II

today [tə'deɪ] heute I

toe [təʊ] Zeh I

together [tə'geðə] zusammen I

toilet ['tɔɪlət] Toilette I

told [təʊld] *siehe* **tell**

tomato [tə'mɑːtəʊ], *pl* **tomatoes** Tomate II

tomorrow [tə'mɒrəʊ] morgen I
tomorrow's weather das Wetter von morgen II

°**tongue-twister** ['tʌŋtwɪstə] Zungenbrecher

tonight [tə'naɪt] heute Nacht, heute Abend I • **tonight's programme** das Programm von heute Abend; das heutige Abendprogramm II

too [tuː]: **from Bristol too** auch aus Bristol I • **Me too.** Ich auch. I

too much/big/... [tuː] zu viel/groß/... I

took [tʊk] *siehe* **take**

tooth [tuːθ], *pl* **teeth** [tiːθ] Zahn I

toothache ['tuːθeɪk] Zahnschmerzen II

top [tɒp]
1. Spitze, oberes Ende I • **at the top (of)** oben, am oberen Ende, an der Spitze (von) I
2. Top, Oberteil I

topic ['tɒpɪk] Thema, Themenbereich I • **topic sentence** *Satz, der in das Thema eines Absatzes einführt* II

tornado [tɔː'neɪdəʊ] Tornado, Wirbelsturm II

tortoise ['tɔːtəs] Schildkröte I

°**tossing the caber** [ˌtɒsɪŋ ðə 'keɪbə] Baumstammwerfen

touch [tʌtʃ] berühren, anfassen II **keep in touch** in Verbindung bleiben, Kontakt halten III Intro (11)

tour (of the house) [tʊə] Rundgang, Tour (durch das Haus) I

tourist ['tʊərɪst] Tourist/in II
tourist information Fremdenverkehrsamt II

towards sb./sth. [tə'wɔːdz] auf jn./etwas zu II

tower ['taʊə] Turm I

town [taʊn] (Klein-)Stadt I

track [træk] Stück, Titel, Track *(auf einer CD)* III 5 (95)

traditional [trə'dɪʃənl] traditionell III 4 (72)

traffic ['træfɪk] Verkehr II

train [treɪn] Zug I • **on the train** im Zug I

train [treɪn] trainieren III 3 (54)

trainers *(pl)* ['treɪnəz] Turnschuhe II

training session ['seʃn] Trainingsstunde, -einheit III 3 (52)

°**traitor** ['treɪtə] Verräter/in

tram [træm] Straßenbahn III 1 (20/163)

translate (from ... into) [træns'leɪt] übersetzen (aus ... ins) III 2 (35/168)

translation [træns'leɪʃn] Übersetzung III 2 (35)

transport ['trænspɔːt] Beförderung, Transport III 1 (20)

travel (-ll-) ['trævl] reisen II

Travelcard ['trævlkɑːd] Tages-/Wochen-/Monatsfahrkarte *(der Londoner Verkehrsbetriebe)* III 1 (14)

tree [tri:] Baum I

trendy ['trendi] modisch, schick III 1 (12)

trick [trɪk]
1. (Zauber-)Kunststück, Trick I • **do tricks** (Zauber-)Kunststücke machen I
2. Streich II

trip [trɪp] Reise; Ausflug I • **go on a trip** einen Ausflug machen II

trouble ['trʌbl] Schwierigkeiten, Ärger II • **be in trouble** in Schwierigkeiten sein; Ärger kriegen II

trousers (pl) ['traʊzəz] Hose II

true [tru:] wahr II

trumpet ['trʌmpɪt] Trompete III Intro (11)

try [traɪ]
1. versuchen I
2. probieren, kosten I
try and do sth. / try to do sth. versuchen, etwas zu tun I • **try on** anprobieren (Kleidung) I

T-shirt ['ti:ʃɜ:t] T-Shirt I

tube [tju:b]: **the Tube** (no pl) die Londoner U-Bahn III 1 (14)

Tuesday ['tju:zdeɪ, 'tju:zdi] Dienstag I

tune [tju:n] Melodie III 5 (95)

tunnel ['tʌnl] Tunnel II

turkey ['tɜ:ki] Truthahn, Pute/Puter III 1 (24/164)

turn [tɜ:n]
1. sich umdrehen II • **turn left/ right** (nach) links/rechts abbiegen II • **turn to sb.** sich jm. zuwenden; sich an jn. wenden I
2. **turn sth. on/off** etwas ein-, ausschalten III 2 (35)

turn [tɜ:n]: **It's your turn.** Du bist dran / an der Reihe. I • **Miss a turn.** Einmal aussetzen. II • °**Take turns.** Wechselt euch ab. • **Whose turn is it?** Wer ist dran / an der Reihe? II

TV [ti:'vi:] Fernsehen I • **on TV** im Fernsehen I • **watch TV** fernsehen I

twice [twaɪs] zweimal • **twice a week** zweimal pro Woche III 2 (33/166)

twin [twɪn]: **twin brother** Zwillingsbruder I • **twins** (pl) Zwillinge I

two all [ˌtu:'ɔ:l] 2 beide (2:2 unentschieden) III 3 (54/171)

type [taɪp] (infml) Typ III 2 (34)

U

uncle ['ʌŋkl] Onkel I

unclear [ˌʌn'klɪə] unklar III 2 (38)

uncool [ˌʌn'ku:l] (infml) uncool III 2 (38)

under ['ʌndə] unter I

underground ['ʌndəgraʊnd]: **the underground** die U-Bahn II

°**underline** [ˌʌndə'laɪn] unterstreichen

°**underlined** [ˌʌndə'laɪnd] unterstrichen

understand [ˌʌndə'stænd], **understood, understood** verstehen, begreifen I

understood [ˌʌndə'stʊd] siehe **understand**

unfair [ˌʌn'feə] unfair, ungerecht III 2 (38)

unfriendly [ʌn'frendli] unfreundlich III 2 (38)

unhappy [ʌn'hæpi] unglücklich III 2 (38)

unhealthy [ʌn'helθi] ungesund III 2 (38)

uniform ['ju:nɪfɔ:m] Uniform I

unit ['ju:nɪt] Lektion, Kapitel I

united: **the United Kingdom (UK)** [juˌnaɪtɪd 'kɪŋdəm] ([ˌju: 'keɪ]) das Vereinigte Königreich (Großbritannien und Nordirland) III Intro (6)
the United States (US) [juˌnaɪtɪd 'steɪts] ([ˌju: '_'es]) die Vereinigten Staaten (von Amerika) III Intro (10)

unlock [ˌʌn'lɒk] aufschließen; entsperren III 2 (41)

unsafe [ʌn'seɪf] nicht sicher, gefährlich III 2 (38)

untidy [ʌn'taɪdi] unordentlich III 2 (38)

until [ən'tɪl] bis III 2 (32)
▶ S.175 German „bis"

up [ʌp] hinauf, herauf, nach oben I
up the hill den Hügel hinauf II
That's up to you. Das liegt bei dir. / Das kannst/musst du (selbst) entscheiden. III 5 (88)

upset sb. (-tt-) [ʌp'set], **upset, upset** jn. ärgern, kränken, aus der Fassung bringen III 2 (35/167)

upset (about) [ʌp'set] aufgebracht, gekränkt, mitgenommen (wegen) III 2 (35)

upstairs [ʌp'steəz] oben; nach oben I

us [əs, ʌs] uns I

use [ju:z] benutzen, verwenden I

°**used** [ju:zd] gebraucht

usually ['ju:ʒuəli] meistens, gewöhnlich, normalerweise I

V

vacation [və'keɪʃn, AE: veɪ'keɪʃn] (AE) Urlaub, Ferien III 5 (92)

valley ['væli] Tal II

vegetable ['vedʒtəbl] (ein) Gemüse III 1 (24)

°**velodrome** ['velədrəʊm] Radrennbahn

°**venue** ['venju:] Austragungsort

°**version** ['vɜ:ʃn] Variante, Version

very ['veri] sehr I • **like/love sth. very much** etwas sehr mögen/ sehr lieben II • **Thanks very much!** Danke sehr! / Vielen Dank! II

victim ['vɪktɪm] Opfer III 4 (81)

video ['vɪdiəʊ] Video III 1 (13)

view [vju:] Aussicht, Blick II

°**Viking** ['vaɪkɪŋ] Wikinger/in

village ['vɪlɪdʒ] Dorf I

violin [ˌvaɪə'lɪn] Violine, Geige III Intro (11)

°**virtual reality** [ˌvɜ:tʃuəl ri'æləti] durch Computerprogramme simulierte Realität

visit ['vɪzɪt] besuchen II

visit ['vɪzɪt] Besuch II

visitor ['vɪzɪtə] Besucher/in, Gast I

vocabulary [və'kæbjələri] Vokabelverzeichnis, Wörterverzeichnis I

°**voice** [vɔɪs] Stimme

volleyball ['vɒlibɔ:l] Volleyball I

W

wait (for) [weɪt] warten (auf) I
Wait a minute. Warte mal! / Moment mal! II • **I can't wait to see ...** ich kann es kaum erwarten, ... zu sehen I • **Wait and see!** Wart's ab! III Intro (11)

waiter ['weɪtə] Kellner II

waitress ['weɪtrəs] Kellnerin II

wake up [ˌweɪk_'ʌp], **woke, woken** aufwachen III 5 (90) • **wake sb. (up)** jn. (auf)wecken III 5 (90/179)

walk [wɔ:k] (zu Fuß) gehen I
walk around herumlaufen, umherspazieren III 1 (26/164) • **walk around the town** in der Stadt umhergehen, durch die Stadt gehen III 1 (26/164)

walk [wɔ:k] Spaziergang II • **a ten-kilometre walk** eine Zehn-Kilometer-Wanderung III 4 (76/177)
go for a walk spazieren gehen, einen Spaziergang machen II

wall [wɔ:l] Wand; Mauer II

°**walrus** ['wɔ:lrəs] Walross

Dictionary (English – German)   203

want [wɒnt] (haben) wollen I • **want to do** tun wollen I

wardrobe ['wɔːdrəʊb] Kleiderschrank I

warm [wɔːm] warm II

warn sb. (about sth.) [wɔːn] jn. (vor etwas) warnen III 4 (81)

was [wəz, wɒz]: **(I/he/she/it) was** siehe **be**

wash [wɒʃ] waschen I • **I wash my face.** Ich wasche mir das Gesicht. I

washing machine ['wɒʃɪŋ məˌʃiːn] Waschmaschine I

watch [wɒtʃ] beobachten, sich etwas ansehen; zusehen I • **watch TV** fernsehen I

watch [wɒtʃ] Armbanduhr I

water ['wɔːtə] Wasser I

wave [weɪv] winken II

way [weɪ]
1. Weg II • **ask sb. the way** jn. nach dem Weg fragen II • **on the way (to)** auf dem Weg (zu/nach) II • **tell sb. the way** jm. den Weg beschreiben II • °**all the way** den ganzen Weg
2. Richtung II • **the other way round** anders herum II • **the wrong way** in die falsche Richtung II • **this way** hier entlang, in diese Richtung II • **which way?** in welche Richtung? / wohin? II
3. Art und Weise III 1 (14)
4. by the way übrigens II
5. No way! Auf keinen Fall! / Kommt nicht in Frage! II

we [wiː] wir I

weak [wiːk] schwach II

wear [weə], **wore, worn** tragen, anhaben (Kleidung) I

weather ['weðə] Wetter II

°**weather forecast** ['weðə fɔːˌkɑːst] Wettervorhersage I

webcam ['webkæm] Webcam III 5 (89)

website ['websaɪt] Website II

Wednesday ['wenzdeɪ, 'wenzdi] Mittwoch I

°**wee** [wiː] (infml) klein (besonders in Schottland gebräuchlich)

week [wiːk] Woche I • **days of the week** Wochentage I • **a two-week holiday** ein zweiwöchiger Urlaub III 4 (76/177)

weekend [ˌwiːk'end] Wochenende I • **at the weekend** am Wochenende I

welcome ['welkəm]
1. Welcome (to Bristol). Willkommen (in Bristol). I
2. You're welcome. Gern geschehen. / Nichts zu danken. I

welcome sb. (to) ['welkəm] jn. begrüßen, willkommen heißen (in) I **They welcome you to ...** Sie heißen dich in ... willkommen I

well [wel]
1. gut II
2. (gesundheitlich) gut; gesund, wohlauf II
do well (in) gut abschneiden (in) III 4 (70) • **go well** gut (ver)laufen, gutgehen III 2 (34) • **You did well.** Das hast du gut gemacht. II
Oh well ... Na ja ... / Na gut ... I
Well, ... Nun, ... / Also, ... I

°**wellies (pl)** ['weliz] (infml) Gummistiefel

Welsh [welʃ] walisisch; Walisisch II

went [went] siehe **go**

were [wə, wɜː]: **(we/you/they) were** siehe **be**

west [west] Westen; nach Westen; westlich III Intro (7/160)

westbound ['westbaʊnd] Richtung Westen III 1 (14/162)

western ['westən] westlich, West- III Intro (9)

wet [wet] nass III 1 (27)

what [wɒt]
1. was I
2. welche(r, s) I
What about ...? 1. Was ist mit ...? / Und ...? I; **2.** Wie wär's mit ...? I
What are you talking about? Wovon redest du? I • **What colour is ...?** Welche Farbe hat ...? I
What for? Wofür? II • **What have we got next?** Was haben wir als Nächstes? I • **What kind of car ...?** Was für ein Auto ...? III Intro (6/160)
What page are we on? Auf welcher Seite sind wir? I • **What's for homework?** Was haben wir als Hausaufgabe auf? I • **What's the matter?** Was ist los? / Was ist denn? II • **What's the time?** Wie spät ist es? I • **What's your name?** Wie heißt du? I • **What's your telephone number?** Was ist deine Telefonnummer? I • **What was the weather like?** Wie war das Wetter? II

wheel [wiːl] Rad III 1 (12) • **big wheel** Riesenrad III 1 (12)

wheelchair ['wiːltʃeə] Rollstuhl I

when [wen] wann I • **When's your birthday?** Wann hast du Geburtstag? I

when [wen]
1. wenn I
2. als I

where [weə]
1. wo I

2. wohin I
Where are you from? Wo kommst du her? I

which [wɪtʃ]: **Which picture ...?** Welches Bild ...? I • **which way?** in welche Richtung? / wohin? II

which [wɪtʃ] der, die, das; die (Relativpronomen) III 3 (152)

while [waɪl] während III 4 (81)

whisky ['wɪski] Whisky II

whisper ['wɪspə] flüstern II

whistle ['wɪsl] pfeifen II

whistle ['wɪsl] (Triller-)Pfeife III 5 (91/179)

white [waɪt] weiß I

who [huː]
1. wer I
2. wen/wem II

who [huː] der, die, das; die (Relativpronomen) III 3 (55) • **Find/Ask somebody who ...** Finde/Frage jemanden, der ... II

whole [həʊl] ganze(r, s), gesamte(r, s) III 3 (56)

whose? [huːz] wessen? II • **Whose are these?** Wem gehören diese? II **Whose turn is it?** Wer ist dran / an der Reihe? II

why [waɪ] warum I • **Why me?** Warum ich? I • **Why should I ... ?** Warum sollte ich ... ? III 2 (44)

wife [waɪf], pl **wives** [waɪvz] Ehefrau II

wild [waɪld] wild II

will [wɪl]: **you'll be cold (= you will be cold)** du wirst frieren; ihr werdet frieren II • **you won't be cold** [wəʊnt] **(= you will not be cold)** du wirst nicht frieren; ihr werdet nicht frieren II

win (-nn-) [wɪn], **won, won** gewinnen I

win [wɪn] Sieg III 3 (57)

wind [wɪnd] Wind I

window ['wɪndəʊ] Fenster I

windy ['wɪndi] windig I

winner ['wɪnə] Gewinner/in, Sieger/in II

winter ['wɪntə] Winter II

with [wɪð]
1. mit I
2. bei I
go with gehören zu, passen zu III Intro (11) • **Sit with me.** Setz dich zu mir. / Setzt euch zu mir. I

°**within** [wɪ'ðɪn] in, innerhalb I

without [wɪ'ðaʊt] ohne I

wives [waɪvz] Plural von „wife"

woke [wəʊk] siehe **wake**

woken ['wəʊkən] siehe **wake**

wolf [wʊlf], pl **wolves** [wʊlvz] Wolf II

woman ['wʊmən], *pl* **women** ['wɪmɪn] Frau I

won [wʌn] *siehe* **win**

wonder ['wʌndə] sich fragen, gern wissen wollen II

won't [wəʊnt]: **you won't be cold (= you will not be cold)** du wirst nicht frieren; ihr werdet nicht frieren II

wood [wʊd] Holz III 4 (81/177)

°**wooden** ['wʊdən] hölzern

woodpecker ['wʊdpekə] Specht II

woods *(pl)* [wʊdz] Wald, Wälder III 4 (81)

°**wool** [wʊl] Wolle

word [wɜːd] Wort I • **word building** Wortbildung II

°**word order** Wortstellung

wore [wɔː] *siehe* **wear**

work [wɜːk]
1. arbeiten I
2. funktionieren III 1 (26)
work hard hart arbeiten II
work on sth. an etwas arbeiten I

work [wɜːk] Arbeit I • **at work** bei der Arbeit / am Arbeitsplatz I

worker ['wɜːkə] Arbeiter/in II

worksheet ['wɜːkʃiːt] Arbeitsblatt I

workshop ['wɜːkʃɒp] Workshop, Lehrgang III Intro (6)

world [wɜːld] Welt I • **all over the world** auf der ganzen Welt III Intro (6/159) • **from all over the world** aus der ganzen Welt III Intro (6)

worn [wɔːn] *siehe* **wear**

worry ['wʌri] Sorge, Kummer II

worry (about) ['wʌri] sich Sorgen machen (wegen, um) I • **Don't worry.** Mach dir keine Sorgen. I

worse [wɜːs] schlechter, schlimmer II

worst [wɜːst]: **(the) worst** am schlechtesten, schlimmsten; der/die/das schlechteste, schlimmste II

would [wəd, wʊd]: **I/you/... would ...** ich würde / du würdest / ... III 2 (35) **I'd like ... (= I would like ...)** Ich hätte gern ... / Ich möchte gern ... I **Would you like ...?** Möchtest du ...? / Möchten Sie ...? I • **Would you like some?** Möchtest du etwas/ein paar? / Möchten Sie etwas/ein paar? I • **I'd like to talk about ... (= I would like to talk about ...)** Ich möchte über ... reden / Ich würde gern über ... reden I

write [raɪt], **wrote, written** schreiben I • **write down** aufschreiben I • **write to** schreiben an I

writer ['raɪtə] Schreiber/in; Schriftsteller/in II

written ['rɪtn] *siehe* **write**

wrong [rɒŋ] falsch, verkehrt I • **be wrong 1.** falsch sein I; **2.** sich irren, Unrecht haben II • °**do sth. wrong** etwas ausfressen • **the wrong way** in die falsche Richtung II

wrote [rəʊt] *siehe* **write**

Y

yard [jɑːd] Hof II • **in the yard** auf dem Hof II

yawn [jɔːn] gähnen II

year [jɪə]
1. Jahr I
2. Jahrgangsstufe I
a sixteen-year-old ein/e Sechzehnjährige/r III 4 (76) • **a sixteen-year-old girl** ein sechzehnjähriges Mädchen III 4 (76/177)

yellow ['jeləʊ] gelb I

yes [jes] ja I

yesterday ['jestədeɪ, 'jestədi] gestern I • **yesterday morning/afternoon/evening** gestern Morgen/Nachmittag/Abend I • **yesterday's homework** die Hausaufgaben von gestern II

yet [jet]: **not (...) yet** noch nicht II **yet?** schon? II

yoga ['jəʊgə] Yoga I

you [juː]
1. du; Sie I
2. ihr I • **you two** ihr zwei I
3. dir; dich; euch I
4. man III 2 (44)

young [jʌŋ] jung I

your [jɔː]
1. dein/e I
2. Ihr I
3. euer/eure I

yours [jɔːz]
1. deiner, deine, deins II
2. Ihrer, Ihre, Ihrs II
3. eurer, eure, eures II

yourself [jɔːˈself] dir/dich (selbst) III 4 (72/176)

yourselves [jɔːˈselvz] euch (selbst) III 4 (72/176)

youth [juːθ] Jugend, Jugend- III Intro (6) • **youth hostel** Jugendherberge III Intro (8/160)

yuck [jʌk] igitt III 1 (17)

Z

zebra ['zebrə] Zebra II

zero ['zɪərəʊ] null I

°**zone** [zəʊn] Zone, Bereich

°**zoo** [zuː] Zoo

Dictionary (German – English)   205

Das **German – English Dictionary** enthält den **Lernwortschatz** der Bände 1 bis 3 von *English G 21*. Es kann dir eine erste Hilfe sein, wenn du vergessen hast, wie etwas auf Englisch heißt.

Wenn du wissen möchtest, wo das englische Wort zum ersten Mal in *English G 21* vorkommt, dann kannst du im **English – German Dictionary** (S. 181–204) nachschlagen.

Im **German – English Dictionary** werden folgende **Abkürzungen** und **Symbole** verwendet:

jm. = jemandem	sb. = somebody	*pl* = plural	BE = British English	infml = informal
jn. = jemanden	sth. = something	*no pl* = no plural	AE = American English	

▶ Der Pfeil verweist auf Kästchen im Vocabulary (S. 159–180), in denen du weitere Informationen findest.

A

abbiegen: (nach) links/rechts abbiegen turn left/right [tɜːn]
Abend evening ['iːvnɪŋ]; *(später Abend)* night [naɪt] • **am Abend, abends** in the evening
Abendbrot, -essen dinner ['dɪnə] **Abendbrot essen** have dinner **zum Abendbrot** for dinner
aber but [bət, bʌt] • **aber egal, ...** *(wie auch immer, ...; wie dem auch sei, ...; na ja, ...)* anyway, ... ['eniweɪ]
abfahren *(wegfahren)* leave [liːv]
Abfahrt *(Abreise)* departure (dep) [dɪ'pɑːtʃə]
Abfall rubbish ['rʌbɪʃ]
Abflug departure (dep) [dɪ'pɑːtʃə]
Abgemacht! It's a deal. [diːl]
abhängen (mit Freunden/Freundinnen) *(rumhängen)* hang out (with friends) [ˌhæŋ_'aʊt]
abholen: jn. abholen pick sb. up [ˌpɪk_'ʌp]
Abkommen: ein Abkommen treffen make a deal [diːl]
Abmachung: eine Abmachung treffen make a deal [diːl]
Abreise departure (dep) [dɪ'pɑːtʃə]
Absatz *(in einem Text)* paragraph ['pærəɡrɑːf]
abschließen lock [lɒk]
Abschluss *(einer Geschichte, eines Films usw.)* ending ['endɪŋ]
abschneiden: etwas abschneiden cut sth. off [ˌkʌt_'ɒf]
Abschnitt section ['sekʃn]
abschreiben *(kopieren)* copy ['kɒpi]
abtrennen: etwas abtrennen *(abschneiden)* cut sth. off [ˌkʌt_'ɒf]
abziehen: 10 Cent abziehen take 10 c off [ˌteɪk_'ɒf]
achten: auf etwas achten *(horchen)* listen for sth. ['lɪsn]
Acker field [fiːld]
addieren (zu) add (to) [æd]
Adresse address [ə'dres]

Affe monkey ['mʌŋki]
Aktivität activity [æk'tɪvəti]
Akzent accent ['æksənt]
albern silly ['sɪli]
Album album ['ælbəm]
alle *(die ganze Gruppe)* all [ɔːl]
allein alone [ə'ləʊn]
alleinstehend single ['sɪŋɡl]
alles everything ['evriθɪŋ]; all [ɔːl]
allgemeine(r, s) general ['dʒenrəl]
alltägliche(r, s), Alltags- everyday ['evrideɪ]
Alphabet alphabet ['ælfəbet]
als 1. *(zeitlich)* when [wen]; *(während)* as [əz, æz]
2. größer/teurer als bigger/more expensive than [ðæn, ðən]
also *(daher, deshalb)* so [səʊ]
 Also, ... Well, ... [wel]
alt old [əʊld]
Alter age [eɪdʒ]
altmodisch old-fashioned [ˌəʊld'fæʃnd]
am 1. am Bahnhof at the station **am oberen Ende (von)** at the top (of) • **am Strand** on the beach **am Telefon** on the phone • **am unteren Ende (von)** at the bottom (of) ['bɒtəm]
2. *(nahe bei)* **am Meer** by the sea
3. *(zeitlich)* **am 13. Juni** on 13th June • **am Morgen/Nachmittag/ Abend** in the morning/afternoon/ evening • **am Ende (von)** at the end (of) • **am Freitag** on Friday **am Freitagmorgen** on Friday morning • **am nächsten Morgen/ Tag** the next morning/day • **am Wochenende** at the weekend
amüsieren: sich amüsieren have fun [hæv 'fʌn] • **Amüsier dich gut!** Enjoy yourself.
an 1. an dem/den Tisch (dort) at that table • **an der Spitze** at the top (of) • **an der/die Tafel** on the board • **an jn. schreiben** write to sb.
2. *(nahe bei)* **an der See** by the sea

3. Was war das Beste an ...? What was the best thing about ...?
4. an sein *(Radio, Licht usw.)* be on
anbauen *(Getreide usw.)* grow [ɡrəʊ]
andere(r, s) other ['ʌðə] • **die anderen** the others
anders (als) different (from) ['dɪfrənt] **anders ausdrücken** *(umschreiben)* paraphrase ['pærəfreɪz] • **anders herum** the other way round
Anfang beginning [bɪ'ɡɪnɪŋ]
anfangen (mit) begin [bɪ'ɡɪn]; start [stɑːt]
anfassen touch [tʌtʃ]
anfühlen: sich gut anfühlen feel good [fiːl]
Anführer/in leader ['liːdə]
angeln fish [fɪʃ]
angreifen attack [ə'tæk]
Angriff attack [ə'tæk]
Angst haben (vor) be afraid (of) [ə'freɪd]; be scared (of) [skeəd]
anhaben *(Kleidung)* wear [weə]
anhalten stop [stɒp]
Anhänger/in *(Fan)* supporter [sə'pɔːtə]
anhören 1. sich etwas anhören listen to sth. ['lɪsn]
2. sich gut anhören sound good [saʊnd]
anklicken: etwas anklicken click on sth. [klɪk]
ankommen arrive [ə'raɪv]
ankündigen announce [ə'naʊns]
Ankündigung announcement [ə'naʊnsmənt]
Ankunft arrival (arr) [ə'raɪvl]
anlächeln: jn. anlächeln smile at sb. [smaɪl]
Anleitung(en) *(Gebrauchsanweisungen)* instructions (pl) [ɪn'strʌkʃnz]
anmailen: jn. anmailen mail sb. [meɪl]
anmalen paint [peɪnt]; *(bunt ausmalen)* colour ['kʌlə]
Anorak anorak ['ænəræk]
anpflanzen *(Getreide usw.)* grow [ɡrəʊ]

anprobieren (Kleidung) try on [ˌtraɪ_'ɒn]

Anruf call; phone call ['fəʊn kɔ:l]

anrufen call [kɔ:l]; phone [fəʊn]

Ansage (Durchsage) announcement [ə'naʊnsmənt]

anschauen look at [lʊk]

Anschlagtafel notice board ['nəʊtɪs bɔ:d]

anschließen: sich jm. anschließen join sb. [dʒɔɪn]

Anschrift address [ə'dres]

ansehen: sich etwas ansehen look at sth. [lʊk]; watch sth. [wɒtʃ]

Antwort (auf) answer (to) ['ɑ:nsə]

antworten answer ['ɑ:nsə]

Anweisung(en) (Gebrauchsanweisungen) instructions (pl) [ɪn'strʌkʃnz]

anziehen: etwas anziehen (Kleidung) put sth. on [ˌpʊt_'ɒn] • **sich anziehen** get dressed [get 'drest]

Apfel apple ['æpl]

Apfelsine orange ['ɒrɪndʒ]

Apotheke chemist ['kemɪst]

Apotheker: beim Apotheker at the chemist's
▶ S.163 at the butcher's / to the doctor's

April April ['eɪprəl]

Appetit appetite ['æpɪtaɪt]

Arbeit work [wɜ:k] • **bei der Arbeit/ am Arbeitsplatz** at work • **gute Arbeit leisten** do a good job

arbeiten (an) work (on) [wɜ:k]

Arbeiter/in worker ['wɜ:kə]

Arbeitsblatt worksheet ['wɜ:kʃi:t]

Arbeits- und Lerntechniken study skills ['stʌdi skɪlz]

Ärger (Schwierigkeiten) trouble ['trʌbl] • **Ärger kriegen** be in trouble

ärgern: jn. ärgern (kränken) upset sb. [ʌp'set]

Argument argument ['ɑ:gjʊmənt] • **ein Argument vorbringen** make a point

Argumentation argument ['ɑ:gjʊmənt]

arm poor [pɔ:, pʊə]

Arm arm [ɑ:m]

Armbanduhr watch [wɒtʃ]

Art 1. (Sorte) sort (of) [sɔ:t]; kind (of) [kaɪnd]
2. Art und Weise way [weɪ]

Artikel article ['ɑ:tɪkl]

Arzt/Ärztin doctor ['dɒktə] • **zum Arzt** to the doctor's
▶ S.163 at the butcher's / to the doctor's

auch: auch aus Bristol from Bristol too [tu:]; also from Bristol ['ɔ:lsəʊ] **Ich auch.** Me too.

auf on [ɒn] • **auf (... hinauf)** onto ['ɒntə, 'ɒntʊ] • **auf dem Bild/Foto** in the picture/photo • **auf dem Feld** in the field • **auf dem Hof** in the yard • **auf dem Land** (im Gegensatz zur Stadt) • in the country; (nicht auf dem Wasser) on land **auf dem Weg (zu/nach)** on the way (to) • **auf der ganzen Welt** all over the world • **auf einmal** suddenly ['sʌdnli] • **auf Englisch** in English • **Auf geht's!** Let's go. • **auf jn./etwas zu** towards sb./sth. [tə'wɔ:dz] • **Auf keinen Fall!** No way! • **Auf welcher Seite sind wir?** What page are we on? • **Auf Wiedersehen.** Goodbye. [ˌgʊd'baɪ]

aufbewahren keep [ki:p]

aufführen (Szene, Dialog) act [ækt]

Aufgabe (im Schulbuch) exercise ['eksəsaɪz]; (Job) job [dʒɒb]

aufgebracht (wegen) upset (about) [ˌʌp'set]

aufgeräumt (ordentlich) tidy ['taɪdi]

aufgeregt (nervös) nervous ['nɜ:vəs]; (begeistert) excited [ɪk'saɪtɪd]

aufheben: etwas aufheben (hochheben) pick sth. up [ˌpɪk_'ʌp]

aufhören stop [stɒp]

auflegen (Musik/CDs/Platten; in der Disko) DJ ['di:dʒeɪ]

auflisten list [lɪst]

aufmachen open ['əʊpən]

Aufnahme (Aufzeichnung) recording [rɪ'kɔ:dɪŋ]

aufnehmen (Musik / einen Film) record [rɪ'kɔ:d]

aufpassen: auf etwas/jn. aufpassen look after sth./sb. [ˌlʊk_'ɑ:ftə]

aufräumen tidy ['taɪdi]

aufregend exciting [ɪk'saɪtɪŋ]

Aufsatz essay ['eseɪ]

aufschauen (von) look up (from) [ˌlʊk_'ʌp]

aufschließen unlock [ˌʌn'lɒk]

aufschreiben write down [ˌraɪt 'daʊn]

aufstehen get up [ˌget_'ʌp]

aufsuchen: jn. aufsuchen see sb. [si:]

Auftritt (Konzert) gig [gɪg] (infml) **einen Auftritt haben** (ein Konzert geben) do a gig

aufwachen wake up [ˌweɪk_'ʌp]

aufwachsen grow up [ˌgrəʊ_'ʌp]

aufwecken: jn. aufwecken wake sb. up [ˌweɪk_'ʌp]

aufzählen (auflisten) list [lɪst]

Aufzeichnung (Aufnahme) recording [rɪ'kɔ:dɪŋ]

Aufzug lift [lɪft] (BE); elevator ['elɪveɪtə] (AE)

Auge eye [aɪ]

August August ['ɔ:gəst]

aus: Ich komme/bin aus ... I'm from ... [frəm, frɒm] • **aus ... (heraus/ hinaus)** out of ... ['aʊt_əv] • **aus der ganzen Welt** from all over the world • **aus dem Zug/Bus aussteigen** get off the train/bus **aus vielen Gründen** for lots of reasons • **aus zweiter Hand** (gebraucht) second-hand [ˌsekənd 'hænd]

ausdenken: sich etwas ausdenken think of sth. [θɪŋk]

ausdrücken: anders ausdrücken (umschreiben) paraphrase ['pærəfreɪz]

Ausflug trip [trɪp] • **einen Ausflug machen** go on a trip

ausgeben: Geld ausgeben (für) spend money (on) [spend]

Ausgehverbot haben be grounded ['graʊndɪd]

ausmalen (bunt anmalen, kolorieren) colour ['kʌlə]

auspressen squeeze [skwi:z]

ausruhen: sich ausruhen relax [rɪ'læks]

Ausrüstung equipment [ɪ'kwɪpmənt]

Aussage statement ['steɪtmənt]

ausschalten turn off [tɜ:n]

aussehen: anders/toll/alt aussehen look different/great/old [lʊk] **fürchterlich aussehen** be a mess [mes]

außerhalb seines Zimmers outside his room [ˌaʊt'saɪd]

aussetzen: Einmal aussetzen. Miss a turn. [tɜ:n]

Aussicht (auf) (Blick) view (of) [vju:]

Aussprache pronunciation [prəˌnʌnsi'eɪʃn]

aussteigen (aus dem Zug/Bus) get off (the train/bus) [ˌget_'ɒf]

aussuchen: (sich) etwas aussuchen choose sth. [tʃu:z]

Austauschschüler/in exchange student [ɪks'tʃeɪndʒ ˌstju:dnt]

ausverkauft sein be sold out [ˌsəʊld_'aʊt]

auswählen choose [tʃu:z]

ausziehen 1. (aus Wohnung) move out [ˌmu:v_'aʊt]
2. etwas ausziehen (Kleidung) take sth. off [ˌteɪk_'ɒf]

Auto car [kɑ:]

Autofahrt drive [draɪv]

Autsch! Ouch! [aʊtʃ]

B

Baby baby ['beɪbi] • **ein Baby bekommen** have a baby

Bäckerei bakery ['beɪkəri]

Badeanzug swimsuit ['swɪmsu:t]

Dictionary (German – English) 207

Badehose swimming trunks *(pl)* [trʌnks]

baden *(ein Bad nehmen)* have a bath [bɑ:θ]

Badewanne bath [bɑ:θ]

Badezimmer bathroom ['bɑ:θru:m]

Badminton badminton ['bædmɪntən]

Badmintonschläger badminton racket ['rækɪt]

Bahnhof station ['steɪʃn] • **am Bahnhof** at the station

Bahnsteig *(Gleis)* platform ['plætfɔ:m]

bald soon [su:n] • **Bis bald.** See you. ['si: ju:]

Ball ball [bɔ:l]

Banane banana [bə'nɑ:nə]

Band *(Musikgruppe)* band [bænd]

Bank *(Sparkasse)* bank [bæŋk]

Bankräuber/in bank robber ['rɒbə]

Bar bar [bɑ:]

Bär bear [beə]

Baseball baseball ['beɪsbɔ:l]

Baseballmütze baseball cap [kæp]

Basketball basketball ['bɑ:skɪtbɔ:l]

Bauchweh stomach ache ['stʌmək_eɪk]

bauen build [bɪld]

Bauer/Bäuerin farmer ['fɑ:mə]

Bauernhof farm [fɑ:m]

Baum tree [tri:]

beantworten answer ['ɑ:nsə]

Becken *(Schwimmbecken)* pool [pu:l]

bedeuten mean [mi:n]

Bedeutung meaning ['mi:nɪŋ]

beeilen: sich beeilen hurry ['hʌri]; hurry up [,hʌri_'ʌp]

beenden finish ['fɪnɪʃ]; end [end]

Beginn beginning [bɪ'gɪnɪŋ]

Beförderung *(Transport)* transport ['trænspɔ:t]

Begabung talent ['tælənt]

begeistert *(aufgeregt)* excited [ɪk'saɪtɪd]

beginnen (mit) begin [bɪ'gɪn]; start [stɑ:t]

begreifen understand [,ʌndə'stænd]

Begründung *(Grund)* reason ['ri:zn]; *(Argument)* argument ['ɑ:gjumənt]

behalten keep [ki:p]

behindert disabled [dɪs'eɪbld]

bei: bei den Shaws zu Hause at the Shaws' house • **bei der Arbeit** at work • **Englisch bei Mr Kingsley** English with Mr Kingsley

beide both [bəʊθ] • **2 beide** *(2:2 unentschieden)* 2 all [,tu:_'ɔ:l]

Beifall klatschen cheer [tʃɪə]

Bein leg [leg] • **etwas auf die Beine stellen** get sth. off the ground

beinahe almost ['ɔ:lməʊst]

Beispiel example [ɪg'zɑ:mpl] • **zum Beispiel** for example

Bekanntgabe announcement [ə'naʊnsmənt]

bekanntgeben announce [ə'naʊns]

beklagen: sich (über etwas) beklagen complain (about sth.) [kəm'pleɪn]

bekommen get [get] • **ein Baby bekommen** have a baby

belästigen: jn. belästigen annoy sb. [ə'nɔɪ]

belebt *(Straße, Ort)* busy ['bɪzi]

beliebt popular ['pɒpjələ]

benennen name [kɔ:l]

benötigen need [ni:d]

benutzen use [ju:z]

beobachten watch [wɒtʃ]

bereit ready ['redi]

Bereich area ['eəriə]; section ['sekʃn]

bereits already [ɔ:l'redi]

Berg mountain ['maʊntən]

Bericht (über) report (on) [rɪ'pɔ:t]

berichten (über) tell (about) [tel] **(jm.) etwas berichten** report sth. (to sb.) [rɪ'pɔ:t]

berichtigen correct [kə'rekt]

beruhigen: sich beruhigen calm down [,kɑ:m 'daʊn]

berühmt famous ['feɪməs]

berühren touch [tʌtʃ]

Bescheid: über etwas Bescheid wissen know about sth. [nəʊ]

beschreiben: (jm.) etwas beschreiben describe sth. (to sb.) [dɪ'skraɪb] **jm. den Weg beschreiben** tell sb. the way

Beschreibung description [dɪ'skrɪpʃn]

beschweren: sich (über etwas) beschweren complain (about sth.) [kəm'pleɪn]

besiegen beat [bi:t]

besitzen have [həv, hæv]

besondere(r, s): ein besonderer Tag a special day ['speʃl]

besorgen *(holen)* get [get]

besser better ['betə]

beste: am besten (the) best [best] **der/die/das beste …; die besten …** the best … • **Was war das Beste an …?** What was the best thing about …?

Besuch visit ['vɪzɪt]

besuchen: jn. besuchen visit sb. ['vɪzɪt]; see sb. [si:]

Besucher/in visitor ['vɪzɪtə]

Betonung stress [stres]

betreten enter ['entə]

Bett bed [bed] • **ins Bett gehen** go to bed

Beutel bag [bæg]

bevor before [bɪ'fɔ:]

bewegen: sich bewegen move [mu:v]

Bewegung movement ['mu:vmənt]

Beweis(e) proof *(no pl)* [pru:f]

bewölkt cloudy ['klaʊdi]

bezahlen: etwas bezahlen pay for sth. [peɪ]

beziehen: sich beziehen auf refer to [rɪ'fɜ:]

Bibliothek library ['laɪbrəri]

Bild picture ['pɪktʃə] • **auf dem Bild** in the picture

Bildschirm monitor ['mɒnɪtə]

Bildunterschrift caption ['kæpʃn]

billig cheap [tʃi:p]

Bindewort linking word ['lɪŋkɪŋ wɜ:d]

Biografie biography [baɪ'ɒgrəfi]

Biologie biology [baɪ'ɒlədʒi]

bis *(zeitlich)* until [ən'tɪl]; till [tɪl] **Bis bald.** See you. ['si: ju:] • **bis (spätestens) zehn Uhr** by ten o'clock • **von Montag bis Freitag** from Mondays to Fridays
► S.175 German „bis"

bisschen: ein bisschen a bit [bɪt]

bitte 1. *(in Fragen und Aufforderungen)* please [pli:z] **2. Bitte sehr. / Hier bitte.** Here you are. **3. Bitte, gern geschehen.** You're welcome. ['welkəm] **4. Wie bitte?** Sorry? ['sɒri]

blasen blow [bləʊ]

blau blue [blu:]

bleiben stay [steɪ] • **draußen bleiben** stay out • **in Verbindung bleiben** keep in touch [,ki:p_ɪn 'tʌtʃ]

Bleistift pencil ['pensl]

Bleistiftanspitzer pencil sharpener ['pensl ʃɑ:pnə]

Blick *(Aussicht)* view [vju:]

Blitz *(Lichtblitz)* flash [flæʃ]

Blockflöte recorder [rɪ'kɔ:də]

blöd stupid ['stju:pɪd]

bloß just [dʒʌst]; only ['əʊnli]

Boden *(Erdboden)* ground [graʊnd]

Boot boat [bəʊt]

böse sein (auf jn.) be cross (with sb.) [krɒs]; be angry (with sb.) ['æŋgri] **böse sein (über etwas)** be angry (about sth.)

Boss boss [bɒs]

Brand fire ['faɪə]

brainstormen *(so viele Ideen wie möglich sammeln)* brainstorm ['breɪnstɔ:m]

brauchen need [ni:d]; *(Zeit brauchen, dauern)* take [teɪk] • **nicht zu tun brauchen** needn't do ['ni:dnt]

braun brown [braʊn]

brav good [gʊd]

Brief (an) letter (to) ['letə]

Briefmarke stamp [stæmp]

Dictionary (German – English)

Brille: (eine) Brille glasses *(pl)* ['glɑːsɪz]
bringen: (mit-, her)bringen bring [brɪŋ] • **(weg-, hin)bringen** take [teɪk] • **alles in Unordnung bringen** make a mess • **etwas auf den Weg bringen** get sth. off the ground
britisch; Brite, Britin British ['brɪtɪʃ]
Broschüre brochure ['brəʊʃə]
Brot bread *(no pl)* [bred]
Brötchen roll [rəʊl]
Brotdose sandwich box ['sænwɪtʃ bɒks]
Brücke bridge [brɪdʒ]
Bruder brother ['brʌðə]
Buch book [bʊk]
Bücherei library ['laɪbrəri]
Buchstabe letter ['letə]
buchstabieren spell [spel]
Bucht bay [beɪ]
Bühne stage [steɪdʒ]
bunt an-, ausmalen colour ['kʌlə]
Burg castle ['kɑːsl]
Bus bus [bʌs]
Bushaltestelle bus stop ['bʌs stɒp]
Butter butter ['bʌtə]

C

Café café ['kæfeɪ]
Cartoon cartoon [kɑːˈtuːn]
CD CD [ˌsiːˈdiː] • **CD-Spieler** CD player [ˌsiːˈdiː ˌpleɪə]
Cent cent (c) [sent]
Charts charts [tʃɑːts]
Chatroom chat room [tʃæt ruːm]
chatten chat [tʃæt]
Chef/in boss [bɒs]
Chor choir ['kwaɪə]
clever clever ['klevə]; smart [smɑːt]
Clown/in clown [klaʊn]
Cola cola ['kəʊlə]
Comic-Heft comic ['kɒmɪk]
Computer computer [kəmˈpjuːtə]
cool cool [kuːl]
Cornflakes cornflakes ['kɔːnfleɪks]
Countdown countdown ['kaʊntdaʊn]
Court *(für Squash, Badminton)* court [kɔːt]
Cousin, Cousine cousin ['kʌzn]
Curry(gericht) curry ['kʌri]

D

da, dahin *(dort, dorthin)* there [ðeə]
  da drüben over there [ˌəʊvə ˈðeə]
daheim at home [ət ˈhəʊm]
daher so [səʊ]
damit *(sodass)* so that
dämlich stupid ['stjuːpɪd]
danach *(zeitl.)* after that [ˌɑːftə ˈðæt]

dankbar thankful ['θæŋkfl]; *(froh)* glad [glæd]
Danke. Thank you. ['θæŋk juː]; Thanks. • **Danke sehr!** Thanks very much! • **Vielen Dank!** Thanks a lot!
dann then [ðen]
darstellende Kunst drama ['drɑːmə]
das 1. *(Artikel)* the [ðə, ði]
  2. *(Relativpronomen)* **das Mädchen, das ...** the girl who ... / the girl that ... • **das Auto, das ...** the car that ... / the car which ...
das (dort) *(Singular)* that [ðət, ðæt]; *(Plural)* those [ðəʊz] • **Das bin ich.** That's me.
dass that [ðət, ðæt]
dasselbe the same [seɪm]
Datum date [deɪt]
dauern *(Zeit brauchen)* take [teɪk]
decken: den Tisch decken lay the table [ˌleɪ ðə ˈteɪbl]
dein(e) ... your ... [jɔː]
deiner, deine, deins yours [jɔːz]
denken think [θɪŋk] • **denken an** think of • **Was denkst du über ...?** What do you think about/of ...?
der 1. *(Artikel)* the [ðə, ði]
  2. *(Relativpronomen)* **der Mann, der ...** the man who ... / the man that ... • **der Laden, der ...** the shop that ... / the shop which ...
derselbe the same [seɪm]
deshalb so [səʊ]
Detail detail ['diːteɪl]
Detektiv/in detective [dɪˈtektɪv]
deuten (auf etwas) *(zeigen)* point (at/to sth.) [pɔɪnt]
deutlich clear [klɪə]
Deutsch; deutsch; Deutsche(r) German ['dʒɜːmən]
Deutschland Germany ['dʒɜːməni]
Dezember December [dɪˈsembə]
dich you [juː] • **dich (selbst)** *(Reflexivpronomen)* yourself [jəˈself, jɔːˈself]
  ▶ S.176 Reflexive pronouns
die 1. *(Artikel)* the [ðə, ði]
  2. *(Relativpronomen)* **die Frau, die ...** the woman who ... / the woman that ... • **die Jacke, die ...** the jacket that ... / the jacket which ...
die (dort) *(Singular)* that [ðət, ðæt]; *(Plural)* those [ðəʊz] • **die (hier)** *(Singular)* this [ðɪs]; *(Plural)* these [ðiːz]
Dieb/in thief [θiːf], *pl* thieves [θiːvz]
Diele hall [hɔːl]
Dienstag Tuesday ['tjuːzdeɪ, 'tjuːzdi] *(siehe auch unter „Freitag")*
dies (hier); diese(r, s) *(Singular)* this [ðɪs]; *(Plural)* these [ðiːz]

dieselbe(n) the same [seɪm]
Ding thing [θɪŋ]
dir you [juː]
Diskjockey DJ ['diːdʒeɪ]
Disko disco ['dɪskəʊ]
Diskussion discussion [dɪˈskʌʃn]
Doktor doctor ['dɒktə]
Dom cathedral [kəˈθiːdrəl]
Donnerstag Thursday ['θɜːzdeɪ, 'θɜːzdi] *(siehe auch unter „Freitag")*
doppelt, Doppel- double ['dʌbl]
Dorf village ['vɪlɪdʒ]
dort, dorthin there [ðeə] • **dort drüben** over there [ˌəʊvə ˈðeə] **dort unten** down there
Dossier dossier ['dɒsieɪ]
downloaden *(runterladen)* download [ˌdaʊnˈləʊd]
Drachen kite [kaɪt]
dran: Ich bin dran. It's my turn. [tɜːn]
draußen outside [ˌaʊtˈsaɪd]; out [aʊt] **nach draußen** outside • **draußen bleiben** stay out
dreimal three times
drinnen inside [ˌɪnˈsaɪd] • **hier drinnen** in here [ˌɪn ˈhɪə] • **nach drinnen** inside
dritte(r, s) third [θɜːd]
Drogerie chemist ['kemɪst]
drüben: da/dort drüben over there [ˌəʊvə ˈðeə]
drücken push [pʊʃ]; *(pressen)* press [pres]; squeeze [skwiːz]
du you [juː]
dumm *(albern)* silly ['sɪli]
dunkel dark [dɑːk]
durch through [θruː]; *(in...umher)* around [əˈraʊnd] • **durch die Stadt** around the town
  ▶ S.164 around
durcheinander: alles durcheinanderbringen make a mess [ˌmeɪk_ə ˈmes]
durchführen: ein Projekt durchführen do a project
Durchsage *(Ansage)* announcement [əˈnaʊnsmənt]
dürfen can [kən, kæn]; may [meɪ]; be allowed to [əˈlaʊd] • **nicht dürfen** mustn't ['mʌsnt]
  ▶ S.170 „können" und „dürfen"
Dusche shower ['ʃaʊə]
duschen; sich duschen have a shower ['ʃaʊə]
DVD DVD [ˌdiːviːˈdiː]

E

echt real [rɪəl]
Ecke corner ['kɔːnə] • **Green Street, Ecke London Road** on the corner of Green Street and London Road

Dictionary (German – English) 209

Ehefrau wife [waɪf], *pl* wives [waɪvz]
Ehemann husband ['hʌzbənd]
Ei egg [eg]
Eichhörnchen squirrel ['skwɪrəl]
eifersüchtig (auf) jealous (of) ['dʒeləs]
eigene(r, s): unser eigenes Schwimmbad our own pool [əʊn]
eigentlich *(in Wirklichkeit)* actually ['æktʃuəli]
Eile: in Eile sein be in a hurry ['hʌri]
eilen *(sich beeilen)* hurry ['hʌri]
eilig: es eilig haben be in a hurry ['hʌri]
ein(e) a, an [ə, ən]; one [wʌn]
ein(e) andere(r, s) ... another ... [ə'nʌðə] • **eine Menge** a lot (of) [lɒt]; lots (of) [lɒts] • **ein neuer / eine neue / ein neues** a new one [wʌn] • **ein paar** some [səm, sʌm] **eines Tages** one day
einander *(sich gegenseitig)* each other [i:tʃ_'ʌðə]
einfach *(nicht schwierig)* easy ['i:zi] **einfach nur** just [dʒʌst] • **einfache Fahrkarte** *(nur Hinfahrt)* single (ticket) ['sɪŋgl]
Einfall *(Idee)* idea [aɪ'dɪə]
Einführung (in) introduction (to) [ˌɪntrə'dʌkʃn]
eingeschaltet sein *(Licht usw.)* be on
einige some [səm, sʌm]; *(einige wenige)* a few [fju:]
einigen: sich einigen (auf) agree (on) [ə'gri:]
einkaufen shop [ʃɒp] • **einkaufen gehen** go shopping; shop
Einkaufen shopping ['ʃɒpɪŋ]
Einkaufsliste shopping list
einladen (zu) invite (to) [ɪn'vaɪt]
Einladung (zu) invitation (to) [ˌɪnvɪ'teɪʃn]
einmal once [wʌns] • **einmal pro Woche** once a week • **auf einmal** suddenly ['sʌdnli] • **Einmal aussetzen.** Miss a turn. [tɜ:n] • **früher einmal** once • **(noch) nicht einmal** not even
einpacken pack [pæk]
eins, ein, eine one ['wʌn]
einsam lonely ['ləʊnli]
Einsatzort location [ləʊ'keɪʃn]
einschalten *(Computer usw.)* turn on [ˌtɜ:n_'ɒn]
einschüchtern bully ['bʊli]
einst *(früher einmal)* once [wʌns]
einsteigen (in den Zug/Bus) get on (the train/bus) [ˌget_'ɒn]
Eintopf(gericht) stew [stju:]
Eintrag *(in Wörterbuch/Tagebuch)* entry ['entri]

Eintragung *(in Tagebuch)* entry ['entri]
eintreffen *(ankommen)* arrive [ə'raɪv]
eintreten (in) enter ['entə]
Eintrittskarte ticket ['tɪkɪt]
Einzelheit detail ['di:teɪl]
einziehen *(in Wohnung)* move in [ˌmu:v_'ɪn]
einzig: der einzige Gast the only guest ['əʊnli]
Eis ice [aɪs]; *(Speiseeis)* ice cream [ˌaɪs 'kri:m]
Eisenbahn railway ['reɪlweɪ]
Eishockey ice hockey ['aɪs hɒki]
Elefant elephant ['elɪfənt]
elektrisch electric [ɪ'lektrɪk]
Elektrizität electricity [ɪˌlek'trɪsəti]
Elektro- electric [ɪ'lektrɪk]
elektronisch electronic [ɪˌlek'trɒnɪk]
Eltern parents ['peərənts]
E-Mail (an) e-mail (to) ['i:meɪl]
End- *(letzte/r/s)* final ['faɪnl]
Ende 1. end [end]; *(einer Geschichte, eines Films usw.)* ending ['endɪŋ] **am Ende (von)** at the end (of) **zu Ende machen** finish ['fɪnɪʃ] • **zu Ende sein** be over ['əʊvə] **2. oberes Ende** *(Spitze)* top [tɒp] **am oberen Ende** at the top **3. unteres Ende** bottom ['bɒtəm] **am unteren Ende** at the bottom ['bɒtəm]
enden finish ['fɪnɪʃ]
endlich at last [ət 'lɑ:st]
Endstand *(beim Sport)* final score [ˌfaɪnl 'skɔ:]
▶ S.171 A football match
Engel angel ['eɪndʒl]
Englisch; englisch English ['ɪŋglɪʃ]
Enkel/in grandchild ['græntʃaɪld], *pl* grandchildren ['græntʃɪldrən]
entdecken spot [spɒt]
Entdecker/in *(Forscher/in)* explorer [ɪk'splɔ:rə]
entkommen escape [ɪ'skeɪp]
entlang der Straße / die Straße entlang along the street [ə'lɒŋ]
entscheiden: Das kannst/musst du (selbst) entscheiden. That's up to you.
entschuldigen: sich entschuldigen say sorry ['sɒri]
Entschuldigung 1. *(Tut mir leid.)* I'm sorry. ['sɒri] • **Entschuldigung, dass ich zu spät bin/komme.** Sorry, I'm late. **2. Entschuldigung, ... / Entschuldigen Sie, ...** *(Darf ich mal stören?)* Excuse me, ... [ɪk'skju:z mi:]
entspannen; sich entspannen relax [rɪ'læks]
entspannt relaxed [rɪ'lækst]

entsperren unlock [ˌʌn'lɒk]
entwerfen design [dɪ'zaɪn]
er 1. *(männliche Person)* he [hi:] **2.** *(Ding, Tier)* it [ɪt]
Erbse pea [pi:]
Erdbeere strawberry ['strɔ:bəri]
Erdboden ground [graʊnd]
Erdkunde geography [dʒi'ɒgrəfi]
erfahren: etwas über etwas erfahren learn sth. about sth. [lɜ:n]
Erfolg success [sək'ses]
erfolgreich successful [sək'sesfl]
erforschen explore [ɪk'splɔ:]
ergänzen add (to) [æd]
Ergebnis result [rɪ'zʌlt]
erinnern: sich erinnern (an) remember [rɪ'membə]
erkältet sein have a cold [kəʊld]
Erkältung cold [kəʊld] • **eine Erkältung haben** have a cold
erklären: jm. etwas erklären explain sth. to sb. [ɪk'spleɪn]
Erklärung explanation [ˌeksplə'neɪʃn]
erkunden explore [ɪk'splɔ:]
erlauben: jm. erlauben, etwas zu tun let sb. do sth. [let]
erläutern: jm. etwas erläutern explain sth. to sb. [ɪk'spleɪn]
erraten guess [ges]
erschießen shoot [ʃu:t]
erst only ['əʊnli]
erstaunlich amazing [ə'meɪzɪŋ]
erste(r, s) first [fɜ:st] • **als Erstes** first • **der erste Tag** the first day **der/die Erste sein** be first
erwachsen werden grow up [ˌgrəʊ_'ʌp]
Erwachsene(r) adult ['ædʌlt]
erwarten expect [ɪk'spekt] • **ich kann es kaum erwarten, ... zu sehen** I can't wait to see ... [weɪt]
erwischen *(fangen)* catch [kætʃ]
erzählen (von) tell (about) [tel]
Erzählung story ['stɔ:ri]
erzielen: einen Treffer erzielen *(ein Tor schießen)* score (a goal) [skɔ:], [gəʊl]
es it [ɪt] • **es gibt** *(es ist vorhanden)* there's; *(es sind vorhanden)* there are
Essen food [fu:d]; *(Mahlzeit)* meal [mi:l]
essen eat [i:t] • **Abendbrot essen** have dinner • **Toast zum Frühstück essen** have toast for breakfast
Esszimmer dining room ['daɪnɪŋ ru:m]
Etagenbett bunk (bed) [bʌŋk]
etwas something ['sʌmθɪŋ]; *(irgendetwas)* anything ['eniθɪŋ]; *(ein bisschen)* a bit [bɪt] • **etwas Käse** some cheese [səm, sʌm]

Dictionary (German – English)

euch you [juː] • **euch (selbst)** yourselves [jəˈselvz, jɔːˈselvz]
▶ S.176 Reflexive pronouns
euer, eure … your … [jɔː]
eurer, eure, eures yours [jɔːz]
Euro euro [ˈjʊərəʊ]
Exemplar copy [ˈkɒpi]

F

Fabrik factory [ˈfæktri]
fähig sein, etwas zu tun be able to do sth. [ˈeɪbl]
Fähre ferry [ˈferi]
fahren go [gəʊ]; *(ein Auto / mit dem Auto)* drive [draɪv] • **in Urlaub fahren** go on holiday • **mit dem Auto/Zug/Rad/… fahren** go by car/train/bike/… • **Inliner/Skateboard fahren** skate [skeɪt] • **Rad fahren** cycle [ˈsaɪkl]; ride a bike [ˌraɪd_ə ˈbaɪk]
Fahrer/in driver [ˈdraɪvə]
Fahrkarte ticket [ˈtɪkɪt] • **einfache Fahrkarte** *(nur Hinfahrt)* single (ticket) [ˈsɪŋgl]
Fahrkartenautomat ticket machine [ˈtɪkɪt məˌʃiːn]
Fahrkartenschalter ticket office [ˈtɪkɪt_ˌɒfɪs]
Fahrplan timetable [ˈtaɪmteɪbl]
Fahrrad bike [baɪk]
Fahrstuhl lift [lɪft] *(BE)*; elevator [ˈelɪveɪtə] *(AE)*
Fahrt journey [ˈdʒɜːni] • **(Auto-)Fahrt** drive [draɪv] • **(Rad-)Fahrt** (bike) ride [raɪd] • **eine Fahrt machen** take a ride [raɪd]
fair fair [feə]
Fakt *(Tatsache)* fact [fækt]
Fall *(Kriminalfall)* case [keɪs]
fallen fall [fɔːl]
fallen lassen drop [drɒp]
falls if [ɪf]
falsch wrong [rɒŋ] • **in die falsche Richtung** the wrong way
Familie family [ˈfæməli]
Fan fan [fæn]; *(Unterstützer/in)* supporter [səˈpɔːtə] • **Fan einer Mannschaft sein** support a team [səˈpɔːt]
fangen catch [kætʃ]
fantastisch fantastic [fænˈtæstɪk]
Farbe colour [ˈkʌlə] • **Welche Farbe hat …?** What colour is …?
färben *(bunt an-, ausmalen)* colour [ˈkʌlə]
Farm farm [fɑːm]
Fassung: jd. aus der Fassung bringen upset sb. [ʌpˈset]
fast almost [ˈɔːlməʊst]

Fastfood fast food [ˌfɑːst ˈfuːd]
Februar February [ˈfebruəri]
Federball badminton [ˈbædmɪntən]
Federmäppchen pencil case [ˈpensl keɪs]
fehlen be missing [ˈmɪsɪŋ]
Fehler mistake [mɪˈsteɪk]
Feind/in enemy [ˈenəmi]
Feld 1. field [fiːld] • **auf dem Feld** in the field
2. *(bei Brettspielen)* **Geh ein Feld vor.** Move on one space. [speɪs] **Geh ein Feld zurück.** Move back one space.
Fels, Felsen rock; *(Klippe)* cliff [klɪf]
Fenster window [ˈwɪndəʊ]
Ferien holidays [ˈhɒlədeɪz] *(BE)*; vacation [vəˈkeɪʃn, *AE:* veɪˈkeɪʃn] *(AE)*
Ferienwohnung holiday flat [ˈhɒlədeɪ flæt]
Fernsehen television [ˈtelɪvɪʒn]; TV [tiˈviː] • **im Fernsehen** on TV
fernsehen watch TV [ˌwɒtʃ tiˈviː]
fertig *(bereit)* ready [ˈredi] • **sich fertig machen (für)** *(sich vorbereiten)* get ready (for) • **Dinge fertig machen (für)** *(vorbereiten)* get things ready (for)
Fest, Festival festival [ˈfestɪvl]
Festspiele festival [ˈfestɪvl]
Fettdruck bold print [ˌbəʊld ˈprɪnt]
Feuer fire [ˈfaɪə]
Feuerwehrfrau firewoman [ˈfaɪəˌwʊmən]
Feuerwehrmann fireman [ˈfaɪəmən]
Fieber haben have a temperature [ˈtemprətʃə]
Fiedel fiddle [ˈfɪdl] *(infml)* • **Fiedel spielen** play the fiddle
Film film [fɪlm]; movie [ˈmuːvi]
Filmemacher film-maker [ˈfɪlmmeɪkə]
filmen film [fɪlm]
Filmstar film star [ˈfɪlm stɑː]
Filmstudio film studio [ˈfɪlm ˌstjuːdiəʊ]
Filzstift felt tip [ˈfelt tɪp]
Finale final [ˈfaɪnl]
finden *(entdecken)* find [faɪnd]
Finder finder [ˈfaɪndə]
Finger finger [ˈfɪŋgə]
Firma company [ˈkʌmpəni]
Fisch fish, *pl* fish [fɪʃ]
fischen fish [fɪʃ]
Fischzüchter/in farmer [ˈfɑːmə]
Flasche bottle [ˈbɒtl] • **eine Flasche Milch** a bottle of milk
Fleisch meat [miːt]
Fleischer butcher [ˈbʊtʃə] • **beim Fleischer** at the butcher's
▶ S.163 at the butcher's / to the doctor's
fleißig hard-working [ˌhɑːdˈwɜːkɪŋ]
fliegen fly [flaɪ]

fliehen (vor jm. / aus etwas) escape (from sb./sth.) [ɪˈskeɪp]
Flug flight [flaɪt] • **ein 14-stündiger Flug, ein 14-Stunden-Flug** a 14-hour flight
Flughafen airport [ˈeəpɔːt]
Flugsteig gate [geɪt]
Flugzeug plane [pleɪn] • **im Flugzeug** on the plane
Flur hall [hɔːl]
Fluss river [ˈrɪvə]
Flusspferd hippo [ˈhɪpəʊ]
flüstern whisper [ˈwɪspə]
folgen follow [ˈfɒləʊ]
Folk folk (music) [ˈfəʊk ˌmjuːzɪk]
Football American football [əˌmerɪkən ˈfʊtbɔːl]
Forscher/in explorer [ɪkˈsplɔːrə]
fort away [əˈweɪ]
Foto photo [ˈfəʊtəʊ] • **auf dem Foto** in the photo • **Fotos machen** take photos
Fotoapparat camera [ˈkæmərə]
fotografieren take photos [teɪk ˈfəʊtəʊz]
Frage question [ˈkwestʃn] • **Fragen stellen** ask questions • **Kommt nicht in Frage!** No way!
fragen ask [ɑːsk] • **nach etwas fragen** ask about sth. • **jn. nach dem Weg fragen** ask sb. the way • **sich fragen** wonder [ˈwʌndə]
Französisch French [frentʃ]
Frau woman [ˈwʊmən], *pl* women [ˈwɪmɪn] • **Frau Brown** Mrs Brown [ˈmɪsɪz]; Ms Brown [mɪz, məz] • **Frau White** *(unverheiratet)* Miss White [mɪs]
frei free [friː] • **freie Zeit** free time **im Freien** *(Freilicht-)* open-air [ˌəʊpən_ˈeə]
Freilicht- open-air [ˌəʊpən_ˈeə]
Freitag Friday [ˈfraɪdeɪ, ˈfraɪdi] **freitagabends, am Freitagabend** on Friday evening • **freitagnachts, Freitagnacht** on Friday night
Freizeit free time [ˌfriː ˈtaɪm]
Freizeitzentrum, -park leisure centre [ˈleʒə sentə]
fremd strange [streɪndʒ]
Fremdenverkehrsamt tourist information [ˈtʊərɪst_ˌɪnfəˌmeɪʃn]
Freund/in friend [frend]; *(Kumpel)* mate [meɪt] *(infml)*
freundlich friendly [ˈfrendli]
frieren be cold [kəʊld]
Friseur/in hairdresser [ˈheədresə] **beim Friseur** at the hairdresser's
▶ S.163 at the butcher's / to the doctor's
froh happy [ˈhæpi]; glad [glæd]
Frosch frog [frɒg]
Frucht, Früchte fruit [fruːt]

Dictionary (German – English)   211

früh early ['ɜːli]
früher *(einst, früher einmal)* once [wʌns]
Frühling spring [sprɪŋ]
Frühstück breakfast ['brekfəst]
  zum Frühstück for breakfast
frühstücken have breakfast
Frühstückspension Bed and Breakfast (B&B) [ˌbed_ən 'brekfəst]
Fuchs fox [fɒks]
fühlen; sich fühlen feel [fiːl]
Führer/in leader ['liːdə]
Füller pen [pen]
funktionieren work [wɜːk]
für for [fə, fɔː] • **Was für ein Auto ...?** What kind of car ...?
furchtbar terrible ['terəbl]; awful ['ɔːfl]
fürchterlich aussehen be a mess [mes]
Fuß foot [fʊt], *pl* feet [fiːt]
Fußball football ['fʊtbɔːl] • **Fußball spielen** play football
Fußballplatz pitch [pɪtʃ]
Fußballschuhe, -stiefel football boots ['fʊtbɔːl buːts]
Fußboden floor [flɔː]
Futter food [fuːd]
füttern feed [fiːd]

G

Gabel fork [fɔːk]
gähnen yawn [jɔːn]
ganze(r, s) whole [həʊl] • **auf der ganzen Welt** all over the world • **aus der ganzen Welt** from all over the world • **den ganzen Tag (lang)** all day • **die ganze Zeit** all the time • **Das ist ganz falsch.** This is all wrong.
Garage garage ['gærɑːʒ]
Garten garden ['gɑːdn]
Gasse lane [leɪn]
Gast guest [gest]; *(Besucher/in)* visitor ['vɪzɪtə]
Gebäude building ['bɪldɪŋ]
geben give [gɪv] • **es gibt** *(es ist vorhanden)* there's; *(es sind vorhanden)* there are • **jm. die Schuld geben (an)** blame sb. (for) [bleɪm]
geboren sein/werden be born [bɔːn]
gebraucht *(aus zweiter Hand)* second-hand [ˌsekənd 'hænd]
gebrochen *(Arm, Bein)* broken ['brəʊkən]
Geburtstag birthday ['bɜːθdeɪ]
  Herzlichen Glückwunsch zum Geburtstag. Happy birthday.
  Ich habe im Mai / am 13. Juni Geburtstag. My birthday is in May /

on 13th June. • **Wann hast du Geburtstag?** When's your birthday?
Gedicht poem ['pəʊɪm]
Gefahr danger ['deɪndʒə]
gefährlich dangerous ['deɪndʒərəs]; *(nicht sicher)* unsafe [ʌn'seɪf]
Gefühl feeling ['fiːlɪŋ]
gegen against [ə'genst] • **gegen sechs** *(um sechs Uhr herum)* around six
  ► S.164 around
gegenseitig: sich gegenseitig each other [iːtʃ_'ʌðə]
Gegenteil opposite ['ɒpəzɪt]
Gegenwart present ['preznt]
gehen 1. go [gəʊ]; *(zu Fuß gehen)* walk [wɔːk]; *(weggehen)* leave [liːv]
  Auf geht's! Let's go. • **einkaufen gehen** go shopping; shop [ʃɒp]
  Geh ein Feld vor. Move on one space. [speɪs] • **Geh ein Feld zurück.** Move back one space. • **in die Sauna gehen** have a sauna • **ins Bett gehen** go to bed • **ins Kino gehen** go to the cinema • **nach Hause gehen** go home • **reiten/schwimmen gehen** go riding/swimming • **spazieren gehen** go for a walk [wɔːk]
  2. Es geht mir/ihm gut. I'm/He's fine. [faɪn]
  3. Es geht um Mr Green. This is about Mr Green.
  4. Das geht dich nichts an! Mind your own business. [ˌmaɪnd jər_ˌəʊn 'bɪznəs]
gehören zu *(passen zu)* go with
Geige violin [ˌvaɪə'lɪn]; fiddle *(infml)* ['fɪdl] • **Geige spielen** play the violin
Geist *(Gespenst)* ghost [gəʊst]
gekränkt (wegen) upset (about) [ˌʌp'set]
Gelächter laughter ['lɑːftə]
gelangen *(hinkommen)* get [get]
gelassen *(locker)* easy-going [ˌiːzi'gəʊɪŋ]
gelb yellow ['jeləʊ]
Geld money ['mʌni] • **Geld ausgeben (für)** spend money (on) [spend]
Geldbörse purse [pɜːs]
Gemeindehalle, -saal community hall [kə'mjuːnəti]
Gemeinschaftshalle, -saal community hall [kə'mjuːnəti]
Gemüse: (ein) Gemüse vegetable ['vedʒtəbl]
genannt werden *(heißen)* be called [kɔːld]
genau exactly [ɪg'zæktli] • **genau in dem Moment** just then • **genau wie du** just like you

genial brilliant ['brɪliənt]
genießen enjoy [ɪn'dʒɔɪ]
genug enough [ɪ'nʌf]
geöffnet open ['əʊpən]
Geografie geography [dʒi'ɒgrəfi]
gepflegt neat [niːt]
gerade at the moment; *(eben, soeben)* just [dʒʌst] • **gerade dann** *(genau in dem Moment)* just then • **jetzt gerade** *(in diesem Moment)* right now [raɪt 'naʊ]
geradeaus weiter straight on [streɪt_'ɒn]
Gerät *(Maschine)* machine [mə'ʃiːn]
Geräusch noise [nɔɪz]
gerecht fair [feə]
Gericht *(Speise)* dish [dɪʃ]
gern: Ich hätte gern ... / Ich möchte gern ... I'd like ... (= I would like ...) • **Ich schwimme/tanze/... gern.** I like swimming/dancing/... • **Ich würde gern über ... reden** I'd like to talk about ... • **Gern geschehen.** You're welcome. ['welkəm]
gernhaben like [laɪk]
Geruch smell
gesamte(r, s) whole [həʊl] • **aus dem gesamten Vereinigten Königreich** from all over the United Kingdom
Geschäft shop [ʃɒp]
geschehen (mit) happen (to) ['hæpən]
Geschenk present ['preznt]
Geschichte 1. story ['stɔːri]
  2. *(vergangene Zeiten)* history ['hɪstri]
geschieden divorced [dɪ'vɔːst]
Geschirrspülmaschine dishwasher ['dɪʃwɒʃə]
Geschlecht sex [seks]
geschlossen closed [kləʊzd]
Gesellschaft *(Firma)* company ['kʌmpəni]
Gesicht face [feɪs]
Gespenst *(Geist)* ghost [gəʊst]
gestalten design [dɪ'zaɪn]
gestern yesterday ['jestədeɪ, 'jestədi]
  gestern Morgen/Nachmittag/Abend yesterday morning/afternoon/evening • **die Hausaufgaben von gestern** yesterday's homework
gesund healthy ['helθi]; well [wel]
Getränk drink [drɪŋk]
Gewinn prize [praɪz]
gewinnen win [wɪn]
Gewinner/in winner ['wɪnə]
Gewitter storm [stɔːm]
gewöhnlich usually ['juːʒuəli]
Giraffe giraffe [dʒə'rɑːf]

212 Dictionary (German – English)

Gitarre guitar [gɪˈtɑː] • **Gitarre spielen** play the guitar

Glas glass [glɑːs] • **ein Glas Wasser** a glass of water

glauben think [θɪŋk]; believe [bɪˈliːv] • **Glaubst du das wirklich?** Do you really think so?

gleich sein/aussehen be/look the same [seɪm]

Gleis *(Bahnsteig)* platform [ˈplætfɔːm]

Glocke bell [bel]

Glück: Glück haben (mit) be lucky (with) [ˈlʌki] • **Viel Glück (bei/mit ...)!** Good luck (with ...)! [gʊd lʌk] • **zum Glück** *(glücklicherweise)* luckily [ˈlʌkɪli]

glücklich happy [ˈhæpi]

glücklicherweise luckily [ˈlʌkɪli]

Golf golf [gɒlf]

Grad degree [dɪˈgriː]

Grammatik grammar [ˈgræmə]

grau grey [greɪ]

grauenhaft horrible [ˈhɒrəbl]

groß big [bɪg]; large [lɑːdʒ]; *(riesig)* huge [hjuːdʒ]
▶ S.165 big – large – huge

Großbuchstabe capital letter [ˌkæpɪtl ˈletə]

großartig great [greɪt]

Größe *(Schuhgröße usw.)* size [saɪz]

Großeltern grandparents [ˈgrænpeərənts]

Großmutter grandmother [ˈgrænmʌðə]

Großstadt city [ˈsɪti]

Großvater grandfather [ˈgrænfɑːðə]

grün green [griːn]

Grund reason [ˈriːzn] • **aus vielen Gründen** for lots of reasons

Gruppe group [gruːp]; *(Musikgruppe)* band [bænd]

gruselig scary [ˈskeəri]

Gruß: Liebe Grüße, ... *(Briefschluss)* Love ... [lʌv]

Grüß Dilip von mir. Say hi to Dilip for me.

gucken look [lʊk]

gut good [gʊd]; *(okay)* OK [əʊˈkeɪ]; *(in Ordnung)* all right [ɔːl ˈraɪt]; *(gesundheitlich gut, wohlauf)* well [wel]; fine [faɪn] • **Es geht mir/ihm gut.** I'm/He's fine. • **gute Arbeit leisten** do a good job • **Guten Morgen.** Good morning. • **Guten Tag.** Hello.; *(nachmittags)* Good afternoon. • **gut abschneiden (in)** do well (in) • **gut in etwas sein / etwas gut können** be good at sth. **gut (ver)laufen** *(gutgehen, klappen)* go well • **Das hast du gut gemacht.** You did well.

gutgehen *(gut (ver)laufen, klappen)* go well

H

Haar, Haare hair *(no pl)* [heə]

Haarwaschmittel shampoo [ʃæmˈpuː]

haben have got [hæv gɒt]; have [həv, hæv] • **Ich habe keinen Stuhl.** I haven't got a chair. • **Ich habe am 13. Juni/im Mai Geburtstag.** My birthday is on 13th June/in May. **Wann hast du Geburtstag?** When's your birthday? • **haben wollen** want [wɒnt] • **Was haben wir als Hausaufgabe auf?** What's for homework?

Hafen harbour [ˈhɑːbə]

Hähnchen chicken [ˈtʃɪkɪn]

halb: eine halbe Stunde half an hour [ˌhɑːf_ən_ˈaʊə] • **halb zwölf** half past 11 [hɑːf]

Halbfinale semi-final [ˌsemiˈfaɪnl]

Halbzeit half • **die erste Halbzeit** the first half • **Halbzeit(pause)** half-time [ˌhɑːf ˈtaɪm]

Halfpipe half-pipe [ˈhɑːfpaɪp]

Hälfte half [hɑːf], *pl* halves [hɑːvs]

Hallo! Hi! [haɪ]; Hello. [həˈləʊ]; Hey! [heɪ]

Hals throat [θrəʊt]

Halsschmerzen haben have a sore throat [sɔː ˈθrəʊt]

halten 1. hold [həʊld]
2. *(aufbewahren)* keep [kiːp] **etwas warm/kühl/offen/... halten** keep sth. warm/cool/open/...
3. *(behalten)* keep • **Kontakt halten** keep in touch [ˌkiːp_ɪn ˈtʌtʃ]
4. Halt den Mund! Shut up. [ˌʃʌt_ˈʌp]
5. Was hältst du von ...? What do you think about/of ...?

Hamburger hamburger [ˈhæmbɜːgə]

Hamster hamster [ˈhæmstə]

Hand hand [hænd] • **aus zweiter Hand** *(gebraucht)* second-hand

Handball handball [ˈhændbɔːl]

Handy mobile (phone) [ˈməʊbaɪl]

hänseln: jn. mit Schimpfwörtern hänseln call sb. names

Happyend happy ending [ˌhæpi_ˈendɪŋ]

hart hard [hɑːd] • **hart arbeiten** work hard

hassen hate [heɪt]

häufig often [ˈɒfn]

Haupt- main [meɪn]

Hauptstadt capital [ˈkæpɪtl]

Hauptverkehrszeit rush hour [ˈrʌʃ_aʊə]

Haus house [haʊs] • **im Haus der Shaws / bei den Shaws zu Hause** at the Shaws' house • **nach Hause gehen** go home [həʊm] • **nach Hause kommen** come home; get home • **zu Hause** at home

Hausarrest haben be grounded [ˈgraʊndɪd]

Hausaufgabe(n) homework *(no pl)* [ˈhəʊmwɜːk] • **die Hausaufgabe(n) machen** do homework • **Was haben wir als Hausaufgabe auf?** What's for homework?

Hausmeister/in caretaker [ˈkeəteɪkə]

Haustier pet [pet]

Haustür front door [ˌfrʌnt ˈdɔː]

Heim home [həʊm]

heiß hot [hɒt]

heißen 1. *(genannt werden)* be called [kɔːld] • **Ich heiße ...** My name is ... • **Wie heißt du?** What's your name?
2. Sie heißen dich in ... willkommen They welcome you to ... [ˈwelkəm]

helfen help [help]

Helikopter helicopter [ˈhelɪkɒptə]

hell *(leuchtend)* bright [braɪt]

Helm helmet [ˈhelmɪt]

Hemd shirt [ʃɜːt]

herauf up [ʌp]

heraus out [aʊt] • **aus ... heraus** out of ... [ˈaʊt_əv]

herausbringen *(Buch, CD, Film usw. auf den Markt bringen)* release [rɪˈliːz]

herausfinden find out [ˌfaɪnd_ˈaʊt] **etwas über etwas herausfinden** learn sth. about sth. [lɜːn]

herausnehmen take out [ˌteɪk_ˈaʊt]

herausragen aus etwas stick out of sth. [stɪk]

herausstehen aus etwas *(herausragen)* stick out of sth. [stɪk]

Herberge hostel [ˈhɒstl]

herbringen bring [brɪŋ]

Herbst autumn [ˈɔːtəm]

Herd cooker [ˈkʊkə]

hereinkommen come in [ˌkʌm_ˈɪn]

Herr Brown Mr Brown [ˈmɪstə]

herstellen produce [prəˈdjuːs]

herum: anders herum the other way round [raʊnd] • **um ... herum** round, around • **um sechs Uhr herum** *(gegen sechs)* • around six
▶ S.164 around

herum-: etwas herumgeben pass sth. round [ˌpɑːs ˈraʊnd] • **herumgehen** walk around [əˈraʊnd]

herumrennen run around

herumspringen jump around
▶ S.164 around

Dictionary (German – English) 213

herunter down [daʊn]
herunterfallen (von) fall off [ˌfɔːl ˈɒf]
Herz heart [hɑːt]
Herzlichen Glückwunsch zum Geburtstag. Happy birthday. [ˌhæpi ˈbɜːθdeɪ]
heute today [təˈdeɪ] • **heute Morgen/Nachmittag/Abend** this morning/afternoon/evening
heute Nacht tonight [təˈnaɪt]
das Programm von heute today's programme
heutig: das heutige Programm today's programme
hier here [hɪə] • **Hier bitte.** (Bitte sehr.) Here you are. • **hier drinnen** in here [ˌɪn ˈhɪə] • **hier entlang** this way [ˈðɪs weɪ] • **Hier spricht Isabel. / Hier ist Isabel.** (am Telefon) This is Isabel. • **Hier steht: ... / Es heißt hier: ...** (im Text) It says here: ...
hierher here [hɪə]
Hilfe help [help]
Himmel sky [skaɪ]
hinauf up [ʌp] • **den Hügel hinauf** up the hill • **auf ... hinauf** onto [ˈɒntə, ˈɒntʊ]
hinaufklettern (auf) climb [klaɪm]
hinaus out [aʊt] • **aus ... hinaus** out of ... [ˈaʊt_əv]
hinein: in ... hinein into ... [ˈɪntə, ˈɪntʊ]
hinfallen fall [fɔːl]; fall down
hinkommen (gelangen) get [get]
hinsetzen: sich hinsetzen sit down
hinstellen: sich hinstellen stand [stænd]
hinter behind [bɪˈhaɪnd]
Hintergrund background [ˈbækɡraʊnd]
Hintertür back door
hinüber zu/nach ... over to ... [ˈəʊvə]
hinunter down [daʊn]
hinzufügen (zu) add (to) [æd]
Hirsch deer, pl deer [dɪə]
Hit hit [hɪt]
Hitliste charts [tʃɑːts]
Hobby hobby [ˈhɒbi], pl hobbies
hoch high [haɪ]
hochheben: etwas hochheben pick sth. up [ˌpɪk_ˈʌp]
hochsehen (von) look up (from) [ˌlʊk_ˈʌp]
Hockey hockey [ˈhɒki]
Hockeyplatz, -feld hockey pitch [ˈhɒki pɪtʃ]
Hockeyschuhe hockey shoes [ˈhɒki ʃuːz]
Hof yard [jɑːd] • **auf dem Hof** in the yard
hoffen hope [həʊp]
Hoffnung hope [həʊp]
holen (besorgen) get [get]

Holz wood [wʊd]
horchen: auf etwas horchen (achten) listen for sth. [ˈlɪsn]
hören hear [hɪə] • **Na hör mal! Come on.** [ˌkʌm_ˈɒn]
Hose trousers (pl) [ˈtraʊzəz]
Hotel hotel [həʊˈtel]
Hotline hotline [ˈhɒtlaɪn]
hübsch pretty [ˈprɪti]
Hubschrauber helicopter [ˈhelɪkɒptə]
Hügel hill [hɪl]
hügelig hilly [ˈhɪli]
Huhn chicken [ˈtʃɪkɪn]
Hülle cover [ˈkʌvə]
Hund dog [dɒɡ]
hundert hundred [ˈhʌndrəd]
Hunger haben be hungry [ˈhʌŋɡri]
hungrig sein be hungry [ˈhʌŋɡri]
Hurra! Hooray! [huˈreɪ]
Hut hat [hæt]
Hütte cabin [ˈkæbɪn]

I

ich I [aɪ] • **Ich auch.** Me too. [ˌmiː ˈtuː] • **Das bin ich.** That's me. **Warum ich?** Why me?
Idee idea [aɪˈdɪə] • **Ideen sammeln** brainstorm [ˈbreɪnstɔːm]
Igel hedgehog [ˈhedʒhɒɡ]
igitt yuck [jʌk]
ihm him; (bei Dingen, Tieren) it
ihn him; (bei Dingen, Tieren) it
ihnen them [ðəm, ðem]
Ihnen (höfliche Anrede) you [juː]
ihr (Plural von „du") you [juː] • **ihr zwei** you two [ˌjuː ˈtuː]
ihr: Hilf ihr. Help her. [hə, hɜː]
ihr(e) (besitzanzeigend) (zu „she") her [hə, hɜː]; (zu „they") their [ðeə]
Ihr(e) (höfliche Anrede) your [jɔː]
ihrer, ihre, ihrs (zu „she") hers [hɜːz]; (zu „they") theirs [ðeəz]
Ihrer, Ihre, Ihrs (höfliche Anrede) yours [jɔːz]
im: im Fernsehen on TV • **im Flugzeug** on the plane • **im Haus der Shaws** at the Shaws' house • **im Mai** in May • **im Radio** on the radio • **im Zug** on the train
Imbiss snack [snæk]
Imbissstube café [ˈkæfeɪ]
immer always [ˈɔːlweɪz] • **immer noch** still [stɪl]
in in • **in ... (hinein)** into ... [ˈɪntə, ˈɪntʊ] • **in den Zug/Bus einsteigen** get on the train/bus • **in der Stadt umher** around the town • **in der ...straße** in ... Street • **in der Hamiltonstraße 7** at 7 Hamilton Street • **in der Nacht** at night

in der Nähe von near • **in der Pause** (zwischen Schulstunden) at break • **in der Schule** at school **in die falsche Richtung** the wrong way • **in die Sauna gehen** have a sauna • **in Eile sein** be in a hurry **ins Bett gehen** go to bed • **ins Kino gehen** go to the cinema • **in Urlaub fahren** go on holiday • **in Verbindung bleiben** keep in touch [ˌkiːp_ɪn ˈtʌtʃ] • **in welche Richtung?** which way? • **in Wirklichkeit** (eigentlich) actually [ˈæktʃuəli]
Information(en) (über) information (about/on) (no pl) [ˌɪnfəˈmeɪʃn]
Ingenieur/in engineer [ˌendʒɪˈnɪə]
Inliner skates [skeɪts] • **Inliner fahren** skate
innen (drin) inside [ˌɪnˈsaɪd]
Innenstadt city centre [ˌsɪti ˈsentə]
Insel island [ˈaɪlənd]
installieren install [ɪnˈstɔːl]
Instrument instrument [ˈɪnstrəmənt]
interessant interesting [ˈɪntrəstɪŋ]
interessieren: sich interessieren (für) be interested (in) [ˈɪntrəstɪd]
interessiert sein (an) be interested (in) [ˈɪntrəstɪd]
international international [ˌɪntəˈnæʃnəl]
Internet internet [ˈɪntənet] • **im Internet surfen** surf the internet [sɜːf]
Interview interview [ˈɪntəvjuː]
interviewen interview [ˈɪntəvjuː]
irgendetwas anything [ˈeniθɪŋ]
irgendjemand anybody [ˈenibɒdi]
irgendwelche any [ˈeni]
irgendwo(hin) somewhere [ˈsʌmweə]; anywhere [ˈeniweə]
irren: sich irren be wrong [rɒŋ]

J

ja yes [jes]
Jacke, Jackett jacket [ˈdʒækɪt]
Jagd hunt [hʌnt]
jagen hunt [hʌnt]
Jahr year [jɪə]
Jahrgangsstufe year [jɪə]
Jahrhundert century [ˈsentʃəri]
...jährig: ein(e) Sechzehnjährige(r) a sixteen-year-old • **ein sechzehnjähriges Mädchen** a sixteen-year-old girl
Januar January [ˈdʒænjuəri]
Jazz jazz [dʒæz]
je? (jemals?) ever? [ˈevə]
Jeans jeans (pl) [dʒiːnz]
jede(r, s) ... (Begleiter) 1. every ... [ˈevri] 2. (jeder einzelne) each ... [iːtʃ]

214 Dictionary (German – English)

jeder *(alle)* everybody ['evribɒdi]
jemals? ever? ['evə]
jemand somebody ['sʌmbədi]; *(irgend-jemand)* anybody ['enibɒdi]
jene(r, s) *(Singular)* that [ðət, ðæt]; *(Plural)* those [ðəʊz]
jetzt now [naʊ] • **jetzt gerade, jetzt sofort** right now
Job job [dʒɒb]
jubeln cheer [tʃɪə]
Judo judo ['dʒuːdəʊ] • **Judo machen** do judo
Jugend youth [juːθ]
Jugend- junior ['dʒuːniə]; *(Teenager-)* teen [tiːn]
Jugendherberge youth hostel ['juːθ ˌhɒstl]
Jugendliche(r) kid [kɪd]; teenager ['tiːneɪdʒə]
Juli July [dʒuˈlaɪ]
jung young [jʌŋ]
Junge boy [bɔɪ]
Juni June [dʒuːn]
Junioren- junior ['dʒuːniə]

K

Käfig cage [keɪdʒ]
Kalender calendar ['kælɪndə]
kalt cold [kəʊld]
Kamel camel ['kæml]
Kamera camera ['kæmərə]
kämpfen (für, um) fight (for) [faɪt]
Kanal canal [kəˈnæl]
Känguru kangaroo [ˌkæŋgəˈruː]
Kaninchen rabbit ['ræbɪt]
Kantine canteen [kænˈtiːn]
Kanu canoe [kəˈnuː] • **Kanu fahren** canoe [kəˈnuː]
Kappe cap [kæp]
kaputt broken ['brəʊkən]
Karotte carrot ['kærət]
Karriere career [kəˈrɪə]
Karte *(Post-, Spielkarte)* card [kɑːd]
Kartoffel potato [pəˈteɪtəʊ], *pl* -toes
Kartoffelchips crisps *(pl)* [krɪsps]
Käse cheese [tʃiːz]
Kästchen, Kasten box [bɒks]
Kathedrale cathedral [kəˈθiːdrəl]
Katze cat [kæt]
kaufen buy [baɪ]
Kaufhaus department store [dɪˈpɑːtmənt stɔː]
Kehle throat [θrəʊt]
kein(e) no; not a; not (...) any • **Ich habe keinen Stuhl.** I haven't got a chair. • **keine Musik mehr** no more music
Keks biscuit ['bɪskɪt]
Kellner waiter ['weɪtə]
Kellnerin waitress ['weɪtrəs]

kennen know [nəʊ]
kennenlernen meet [miːt] • **Nett, dich/euch/Sie kennenzulernen.** Nice to meet you.
kennzeichnen mark up [ˌmɑːkˈʌp]
Keyboard *(elektronisches Tasten-instrument)* keyboard ['kiːbɔːd]
Kilogramm, Kilo (kg) kilogram (kg) ['kiːləgræm], kilo ['kiːləʊ] • **ein 150 Kilogramm schwerer Bär** a 150-kilo-gram bear
Kilometer (km) kilometre (km) ['kɪləmiːtə] • **eine Zehn-Kilometer-Wanderung** a ten-kilometre walk
Kind child [tʃaɪld], *pl* children ['tʃɪldrən]; kid [kɪd] • **ein Kind be-kommen** have a child
Kino cinema ['sɪnəmə] • **ins Kino gehen** go to the cinema
Kirche church [tʃɜːtʃ]
Kirsche cherry ['tʃeri]
Kiste box [bɒks]
Kiwi kiwi ['kiːwiː]
Klang sound [saʊnd]
klar clear [klɪə]
Klasse class [klɑːs]; form [fɔːm]
Klassenkamerad/in classmate ['klɑːsmeɪt]
Klassenlehrer/in class teacher; form teacher
Klassenzimmer classroom ['klɑːsruːm]
klassisch classical ['klæsɪkl]
klatschen: Beifall klatschen cheer [tʃɪə]
Klavier piano [piˈænəʊ] • **Klavier spielen** play the piano
kleben: (auf-, ein)kleben glue [gluː]
Klebestift glue stick ['gluː stɪk]
Klebstoff glue [gluː]
Kleid dress [dres]
Kleider *(Kleidungsstücke)* clothes *(pl)* [kləʊðz, kləʊz]
Kleiderschrank wardrobe ['wɔːdrəʊb]
Kleidung(sstücke) clothes *(pl)* [kləʊðz, kləʊz]
klein little ['lɪtl]; small [smɔːl]
Kleinstadt town [taʊn]
klettern climb [klaɪm] • **Klettere auf einen Baum.** Climb a tree.
Klingel bell [bel]
klingeln ring [rɪŋ]
Klingelton ringtone ['rɪŋtəʊn]
klingen sound [saʊnd]
Klinik clinic ['klɪnɪk]
Klippe cliff [klɪf]
Klon clone [kləʊn]
Klub club [klʌb]
klug clever ['klevə]
knapp: Das war knapp. That was close. [kləʊs]
Kneipe pub [pʌb]

Knie knee [niː]
Knieschützer *(pl)* pads *(pl)* [pædz]
Knopf button ['bʌtn]
Koch cook [kʊk]
kochen cook [kʊk]
Köchin cook [kʊk]
Koffer suitcase ['suːtkeɪs]
Koje *(Etagenbett)* bunk (bed) [bʌŋk]
kolorieren colour ['kʌlə]
komisch funny ['fʌni]
Komma: 10,4 (zehn Komma vier) 10.4 (ten point four)
▶ S.160 Numbers
kommen come [kʌm]; *(hinkommen)* get [get] • **Ich komme aus ...** I'm from ... • **Wo kommst du her?** Where are you from? • **nach Hause kommen** come home; get home • **zu spät kommen** be late **Kommt nicht in Frage!** No way! **Ach komm!** Come on. [ˌkʌmˈɒn] **Na los, komm.** Come on.
König king [kɪŋ]
Königin queen [kwiːn]
königlich royal ['rɔɪəl]
Königreich: das Vereinigte König-reich *(Großbritannien und Nord-irland)* the United Kingdom (UK) [juˌnaɪtɪd 'kɪŋdəm, juːˈkeɪ]
können can [kən, kæn]; be able to ['eɪbl] • **etwas gut/schlecht kön-nen** be good/bad at sth. • **ich kann nicht ...** I can't ... [kɑːnt] **Kann ich Ihnen helfen? / Was kann ich für Sie tun?** *(im Laden)* Can I help you?
▶ S.170 „können" und „dürfen"
könnte(n): ich/er könnte ... I/he could ... [kəd, kʊd] • **du könntest (vielleicht) Hilfe brauchen** you might need help [maɪt]
konnte(n): ich/er konnte ... I/he could ... [kəd, kʊd]
Kontakt halten keep in touch [ˌkiːp ɪn 'tʌtʃ]
kontrollieren *(überprüfen)* check [tʃek]
Konzert concert ['kɒnsət] • **ein Kon-zert geben** *(einen Auftritt haben)* do a gig *(infml)*
Kopf head [hed]
Kopfhörer headphones *(pl)* ['hedfəʊnz]
Kopfschmerzen headache ['hedeɪk]
Kopie copy ['kɒpi]
kopieren copy ['kɒpi]
Korb basket ['bɑːskɪt] • **ein Korb Äpfel** a basket of apples
Körper body ['bɒdi]
korrigieren correct [kəˈrekt]
kosten *(Essen probieren)* try [traɪ]

kosten: Er/Sie/Es kostet 1 Pfund. It's £1. • **Sie kosten 35 Pence.** They are 35 p. • **Wie viel kostet/kosten ...?** How much is/are ...?
kostenlos free [fri:]
köstlich delicious [dɪ'lɪʃəs]
Kram stuff [stʌf]
krank ill [ɪl]
kränken: jd. kränken *(aus der Fassung bringen)* upset sb. [ʌp'set]
Krankenhaus hospital ['hɒspɪtl]
Krankenwagen ambulance ['æmbjələns]
kriegen get [get]
Krokodil crocodile ['krɒkədaɪl]
Krug jug [dʒʌg] • **ein Krug Orangensaft** a jug of orange juice
Küche kitchen ['kɪtʃɪn]
Kuchen cake [keɪk]
Kugelschreiber pen [pen]
Kuh cow [kaʊ]
kühl cool [ku:l]
Kühlschrank fridge [frɪdʒ]
Kummer worry ['wʌri]
kümmern 1. sich um etwas/jn. kümmern look after sth./sb. [ˌlʊk_'ɑ:ftə]
2. Kümmere dich um deine eigenen Angelegenheiten! Mind your own business. [ˌmaɪnd jər_ˌaʊn 'bɪznəs]
Kumpel mate [meɪt]
Kunde, Kundin customer ['kʌstəmə]
Kunst art [ɑ:t]
Künstler/in artist ['ɑ:tɪst]
künstlich artificial [ˌɑ:tɪ'fɪʃl]
Kurs *(Lehrgang)* course [kɔ:s]
kurz short [ʃɔ:t] • **kurze Hose** shorts *(pl)* [ʃɔ:ts]
Küste coast [kəʊst]

L

lächeln smile [smaɪl]
Lächeln smile [smaɪl]
lachen laugh [lɑ:f]
Lachs salmon ['sæmən]
Laden *(Geschäft)* shop [ʃɒp]
Lage: in der Lage sein, etwas zu tun be able to do sth. ['eɪbl]
Lamm(fleisch) lamb [læm]
Lampe lamp [læmp]
Land *(auch als Gegensatz zur Stadt)* country ['kʌntri]; *(Grund und Boden)* land [lænd] • **auf dem Land** *(im Gegensatz zur Stadt)* in the country; *(nicht auf dem Wasser)* on land
landen land [lænd]
Landkarte map [mæp]
Landwirt/in farmer ['fɑ:mə]
lang long [lɒŋ] • **drei Tage lang** for three days
langsam slow [sləʊ]

langweilig boring ['bɔ:rɪŋ]
Lärm noise [nɔɪz]
lärmend noisy ['nɔɪzi]
Lasagne lasagne [lə'zænjə]
lassen let [let] • **Lass uns ... / Lasst uns ...** Let's ... • **Lass das!** Stop that!
lässig easy-going [ˌi:zi'gəʊɪŋ]
Lastkraftwagen lorry ['lɒri]
Lauf run [rʌn]
Laufbahn *(Sport)* running track [træk]
laufen run [rʌn]
Läufer/in runner ['rʌnə]
Laufschuhe running shoes
laut loud [laʊd]; *(lärmend)* noisy ['nɔɪzi]
Laut sound [saʊnd]
läuten ring [rɪŋ]
leben live [lɪv]
Leben life [laɪf], *pl* lives [laɪvz]
Lebensmittel food [fu:d]
lecker delicious [dɪ'lɪʃəs]
Leder leather ['leðə]
ledig single ['sɪŋgl]
leer empty ['empti]
legen *(hin-, ablegen)* put [pʊt]
lehren teach [ti:tʃ]
Lehrer/in teacher ['ti:tʃə]
Lehrgang *(Kurs, Seminar)* workshop ['wɜːkʃɒp]; course [kɔ:s]
leicht *(nicht schwierig)* easy ['i:zi]
Leichtathletik athletics [æθ'letɪks]
leider I'm afraid [ə'freɪd]
leidtun: Tut mir leid. I'm sorry. ['sɒri]
leise quiet ['kwaɪət]
Leiter/in *(Anführer/in)* leader ['li:də]
Lektion *(im Schulbuch)* unit ['ju:nɪt]
lernen learn [lɜ:n]
Lern- und Arbeitstechniken study skills ['stʌdi skɪlz]
lesen read [ri:d]
Leser/in reader ['ri:də]
letzte(r, s) last [lɑ:st]; final ['faɪnl]
leuchtend bright [braɪt]
Leute people ['pi:pl]; guys [gaɪz] *(AE, infml)*
Licht light [laɪt]
Lichtblitz flash [flæʃ]
Liebe love [lʌv]
Liebe Grüße, ... *(Briefschluss)* Love ... [lʌv]
lieben love [lʌv]
Lieber Jay, ... Dear Jay ... [dɪə]
lieber: etwas lieber mögen like sth. better
Liebling dear [dɪə]; sweetheart ['swi:thɑ:t]
Lieblings-: **meine Lieblingsfarbe** my favourite colour ['feɪvərɪt]

Lied song [sɒŋ]
Liedtext lyrics *(pl)* ['lɪrɪks]
liegen: Das liegt bei dir. *(Das kannst/musst du (selbst) entscheiden.)* That's up to you.
lila purple ['pɜ:pl]
Limonade lemonade [ˌlemə'neɪd]
Lineal ruler ['ru:lə]
Linie: (U-Bahn-)Linie line [laɪn]
linke(r, s) left [left] • **links, auf der linken Seite** on the left • **(nach) links abbiegen** turn left • **nach links schauen** look left
Liste list [lɪst]
Livemusik live music [laɪv]
Löffel spoon [spu:n]
Logo logo ['ləʊgəʊ], *pl* logos
Lokal *(Kneipe)* pub [pʌb]
Löwe lion ['laɪən]
Luft air [eə]

M

machen do [du:]; make [meɪk] • **die Hausaufgabe(n) machen** do homework • **einen Ausflug machen** go on a trip • **einen Spaziergang machen** go for a walk • **eine Spritztour/Fahrt machen** take a ride • **eine Übung machen** do an exercise • **ein Picknick machen** have a picnic • **Fotos machen** take photos • **jm. Vorwürfe machen (wegen)** blame sb. (for) • **Judo machen** do judo • **sich Notizen machen** take notes • **sich Sorgen machen (um, wegen)** worry (about) ['wʌri] • **(Zauber-)Kunststücke machen** do tricks • **Reiten macht Spaß.** Riding is fun.
Mädchen girl [gɜ:l]
Magazin *(Zeitschrift)* magazine [ˌmægə'zi:n]
Magen stomach ['stʌmək]
Magenschmerzen stomach ache ['stʌmək_eɪk]
Magst du ...? Do you like ...? [laɪk] *(siehe auch unter „mögen")*
Mahlzeit meal [mi:l]
Mai May [meɪ]
mailen: jm. etwas mailen mail sb. sth. [meɪl]
Make-up make-up ['meɪkʌp]
Mal(e); -mal time(s) [taɪm(z)]
malen paint [peɪnt]
Maler/in painter ['peɪntə]
Mama mum [mʌm] *(BE)*; mom [mɒm, *AE:* mɑ:m] *(AE)*
man you [ju:]
Manager/in manager ['mænədʒə]

manchmal sometimes [ˈsʌmtaɪmz]
Mann man [mæn], *pl* men [men]
männlich male [meɪl]
Mannschaft team [tiːm]
Mappe *(des Sprachenportfolios)* dossier [ˈdɒsieɪ]
markieren mark up [ˌmɑːkˈʌp]
Markt market [ˈmɑːkɪt]
Marmelade *(Orangenmarmelade)* marmalade [ˈmɑːməleɪd]
März March [mɑːtʃ]
Maschine machine [məˈʃiːn]
Mathematik maths [mæθs]
Matrose sailor [ˈseɪlə]
Mauer wall [wɔːl]
Maulwurf mole [məʊl]
Maus mouse [maʊs], *pl* mice [maɪs]
Medaille medal [ˈmedl]
Mediation *(Sprachmittlung)* mediation [ˌmiːdiˈeɪʃn]
Medien media *(pl)* [ˈmiːdiə]
Meer sea [siː]
Meerschweinchen guinea pig [ˈgɪni pɪg]
mehr more [mɔː] • **mehr als** more than • **mehr als ich** more than me • **nicht mehr** not ... any more **viel mehr** lots more • **keine Musik mehr** no more music
Meile *(= ca. 1,6 km)* mile [maɪl]
meilenweit for miles [maɪlz]
mein(e) ... my ... [maɪ] • **meine neuen** my new ones [wʌnz]
meinen think [θɪŋk]; *(sagen wollen)* mean [miːn] • **Meinst du wirklich?** Do you really think so?
meiner, meine, meins mine [maɪn]
Meinung opinion [əˈpɪnjən] • **anderer Meinung sein (als)** disagree (with) [ˌdɪsəˈgriː] • **meiner Meinung nach** in my opinion
meist: (der/die/das) meiste ...; am meisten most [məʊst] • **die meisten Leute** most people
meistens usually [ˈjuːʒuəli]
Meister/in *(Champion)* champion [ˈtʃæmpiən]
Meisterschaft championship [ˈtʃæmpiənʃɪp]
Melodie tune [tjuːn]
Menschen people [ˈpiːpl]
merken: sich etwas merken remember sth. [rɪˈmembə]
Messer knife [naɪf], *pl* knives [naɪvz]
Meter metre [ˈmiːtə]
Metzger butcher [ˈbʊtʃə] • **beim Metzger** at the butcher's
▶ S.163 at the butcher's / to the doctor's
mich me [miː] • **mich (selbst)** myself [maɪˈself]
▶ S.176 Reflexive pronouns
Mikrofon microphone [ˈmaɪkrəfəʊn]

Milch milk [mɪlk]
mild mild [maɪld]
Million million [ˈmɪljən]
Mindmap mind map [ˈmaɪnd mæp]
Minute minute [ˈmɪnɪt]
mir me [miː]
mischen mix [mɪks]
Mischung mix [mɪks]; mixture [ˈmɪkstʃə]
mit with [wɪð] • **mit dem Auto/ Zug/Rad/... fahren** go by car/ train/bike/...
mitbringen bring [brɪŋ]
mitmachen: bei etwas/jm. mitmachen join sth./sb. [dʒɔɪn]
Mitschüler/in classmate [ˈklɑːsmeɪt]
Mittagessen lunch [lʌntʃ] • **zum Mittagessen** for lunch
Mittagspause lunch break [ˈlʌntʃ breɪk]
Mitte centre [ˈsentə]; middle (of) [ˈmɪdl]
Mitteilung *(Notiz)* note [nəʊt]
Mittel- *(Zentral-)* central [ˈsentrəl]
mittel(groß) medium [ˈmiːdiəm]
Mittelteil middle [ˈmɪdl]
Mitternacht midnight [ˈmɪdnaɪt]
Mittwoch Wednesday [ˈwenzdeɪ, ˈwenzdi] *(siehe auch unter „Freitag")*
Mix mix [mɪks]
mixen mix [mɪks]
Mobiltelefon mobile phone [ˌməʊbaɪl ˈfəʊn]; mobile [ˈməʊbaɪl]
möchte: Ich möchte gern ... (haben) I'd like ... (= I would like ...) • **Ich möchte über ... reden** I'd like to talk about ... • **Möchtest du etwas (Saft) / ein paar (Kekse)?** Would you like some (juice/biscuits)?
Mode fashion [ˈfæʃn]
Modell *(-auto, -schiff; Fotomodell)* model [ˈmɒdl]
Moderator/in presenter [prɪˈzentə]
modern modern [ˈmɒdən]
modisch *(schick, im Trend)* trendy [ˈtrendi]
mögen like [laɪk]; *(sehr mögen)* love [lʌv] • **etwas lieber mögen** like sth. better
möglich possible [ˈpɒsəbl]
Möhre carrot [ˈkærət]
Moment moment [ˈməʊmənt] **genau in dem Moment** just then • **Moment mal!** Wait a minute. [ˈmɪnɪt]
Monat month [mʌnθ]
Mond moon [muːn]
Monitor monitor [ˈmɒnɪtə]
Monster monster [ˈmɒnstə]
Montag Monday [ˈmʌndeɪ, ˈmʌndi] *(siehe auch unter „Freitag")*

morgen tomorrow [təˈmɒrəʊ] • **das Wetter von morgen** tomorrow's weather
Morgen morning [ˈmɔːnɪŋ] • **am Morgen, morgens** in the morning **Guten Morgen.** Good morning. **Montagmorgen** Monday morning
Moschee mosque [mɒsk]
MP3-Spieler MP3 player [ˌempiˈθriː ˌpleɪə]
müde tired [ˈtaɪəd]
Müll rubbish [ˈrʌbɪʃ]
Mülltonne bin [bɪn]; dustbin [ˈdʌstbɪn]
Multiple-Choice multiple choice [ˌmʌltɪpl ˈtʃɔɪs]
Mund mouth [maʊθ] • **Halt den Mund!** Shut up. [ˌʃʌt ˈʌp]
murren grumble [ˈgrʌmbl]
Museum museum [mjuːˈziːəm]
Musical musical [ˈmjuːzɪkl]
Musik music [ˈmjuːzɪk]
Musiker/in musician [mjuːˈzɪʃn]
müssen have to; must [mʌst] **nicht müssen** needn't [ˈniːdnt]
mutig brave [breɪv]
Mutter mother [ˈmʌðə]
Mutti mum [mʌm] *(BE)*; mom [mɒm, *AE:* mɑːm] *(AE)*
Mütze cap [kæp]

N

Na ja ... / Na gut ... Oh well ... [əʊ ˈwel]; anyway [ˈeniweɪ]
Na und? So? [səʊ]
nach 1. *(örtlich)* to [tə, tu] • **nach draußen** outside • **nach drinnen** inside • **nach Hause gehen** go home • **nach Hause kommen** come home; get home • **nach oben** up; *(im Haus)* upstairs [ʌpˈsteəz] • **nach unten** down; *(im Haus)* downstairs [ˌdaʊnˈsteəz] **2.** *(zeitlich)* after [ˈɑːftə] • **Viertel nach 11** quarter past 11 [pɑːst] **3. nach etwas fragen** ask about sth. [əˈbaʊt]
Nachbar/in neighbour [ˈneɪbə]
nachdem after [ˈɑːftə]
nachdenken über think about
Nachmittag afternoon [ˌɑːftəˈnuːn] **am Nachmittag, nachmittags** in the afternoon
Nachricht message [ˈmesɪdʒ] **Nachrichten** *(im Fernsehen, Radio; Neuigkeiten)* news *(no pl)* [njuːz] **Das sind gute Nachrichten.** That's good news.
nachrufen: jm. Schimpfwörter nachrufen call sb. names

Dictionary (German – English) 217

nachschlagen: etwas nachschlagen look sth. up [ˌlʊk_'ʌp]

nächste(r, s): am nächsten Tag the next day [nekst] • **der Nächste sein** be next • **Was haben wir als Nächstes?** What have we got next?

Nacht night [naɪt] • **heute Nacht** tonight [tə'naɪt] • **in der Nacht, nachts** at night

Nachtklub nightclub ['naɪtklʌb]

nahe (bei) near [nɪə]; close (to) [kləʊs]

Nähe: in der Nähe von near [nɪə]

Name name [neɪm]

Nase nose [nəʊz] • **die Nase voll haben (von etwas)** be fed up (with sth.) [ˌfed_'ʌp]

Nashorn rhino ['raɪnəʊ]

nass wet [wet]

national national ['næʃnəl]

natürlich of course [əv 'kɔːs]

Naturwissenschaft science ['saɪəns]

Nebel fog [fɒg]

neben next to ['nekst tə]

neblig foggy ['fɒgi]

nehmen take [teɪk] • **Wir nehmen es.** *(beim Einkaufen)* We'll take it.

neidisch (auf) jealous (of) ['dʒeləs]

nein no [nəʊ]

nennen *(rufen, bezeichnen)* call [kɔːl]; *(benennen)* name [neɪm]

nerven: jn. nerven annoy sb. [ə'nɔɪ]

Nerven: Mein Vater geht mir auf die Nerven. My dad is annoying. [ə'nɔɪɪŋ]

nervös nervous ['nɜːvəs]

nett nice [naɪs]

neu new [njuː]

neueste(r, s) latest ['leɪtɪst]

Neuigkeiten news [njuːz]

nicht not [nɒt] • **nicht mehr** not (...) any more • **Du brauchst eine Schultasche, nicht wahr?** You need a school bag, right? [raɪt] • **Ich weiß es nicht.** I don't know. [ˌdəʊnt 'nəʊ] • **noch nicht** not (...) yet [jet] • **(noch) nicht einmal** not even ['iːvn]

nichts nothing ['nʌθɪŋ]; not (...) anything ['eniθɪŋ] • **Nichts zu danken.** You're welcome. ['welkəm]

nicken (mit) nod [nɒd]

nie, niemals never ['nevə]

niemand nobody ['nəʊbədi]; not (...) anybody ['enibɒdi]

nirgendwo(hin) not (...) anywhere ['eniweə]

noch: noch ein(e) ... another ... [ə'nʌðə] • **noch 45 Pence** another 45 p • **noch einmal** again [ə'gen] • **noch nicht** not (...) yet [jet] • **noch nicht einmal** not even [iːvn] • **(immer) noch** still [stɪl]

Norden north [nɔːθ] • **nach Norden** north • **Richtung Norden** *(Fahrtrichtung)* northbound ['nɔːθbaʊnd]

nördlich north [nɔːθ]

Nordosten north-east [ˌnɔːθ'iːst] • **nach Nordosten** north-east

nordöstlich north-east [ˌnɔːθ'iːst]

Nordwesten north-west [ˌnɔːθ'west] • **nach Nordwesten** north-west

nordwestlich north-west [ˌnɔːθ'west]

nörgeln grumble ['grʌmbl]

normalerweise usually ['juːʒuəli]

Notiz note [nəʊt] • **sich Notizen machen** take notes

November November [nəʊ'vembə]

null o [əʊ]; zero ['zɪərəʊ]; *(beim Sport)* nil [nɪl]
▶ S.171 A football match

Nummer number ['nʌmbə]

nun now [naʊ] • **Nun, ...** Well, ... [wel]

nur only ['əʊnli]; just [dʒʌst] • **nur zum Spaß** just for fun

nützlich useful ['juːsfl]

O

ob if [ɪf]

oben *(an der Spitze)* at the top (of) [tɒp]; *(im Haus)* upstairs [ˌʌp'steəz] • **nach oben** up; *(im Haus)* upstairs

Oberbegriff group word ['gruːp wɜːd]

oberhalb von over ['əʊvə]

Oberteil top [tɒp]

Obst fruit [fruːt]

Obstkuchen pie [paɪ]

Obstsalat fruit salad ['fruːt ˌsæləd]

obwohl although [ɔːl'ðəʊ]

oder or [ɔː] • **Das ist nicht dein Ernst, oder?** You're joking, aren't you?

offen open ['əʊpən]

öffnen open ['əʊpən]

oft often ['ɒfn]

ohne without [wɪ'ðaʊt]

Ohr ear [ɪə]

Ohrenschmerzen earache ['ɪəreɪk]

Ohrring earring ['ɪərɪŋ]

Oje! Oh dear! [əʊ 'dɪə]

okay OK [əʊ'keɪ]

Oktober October [ɒk'təʊbə]

Öl oil [ɔɪl]

Oma grandma ['grænmɑː]; granny ['græni]

Onkel uncle ['ʌŋkl]

online, Online- online [ˌɒn'laɪn]

Opa grandpa ['grænpɑː]; grandad ['grændæd]

Oper opera ['ɒprə]

Operation (an) operation (on) [ˌɒpə'reɪʃn]

Opfer victim ['vɪktɪm]

Orange orange ['ɒrɪndʒ]

orange(farben) orange ['ɒrɪndʒ]

Orangenmarmelade marmalade ['mɑːməleɪd]

Orangensaft orange juice ['ɒrɪndʒ dʒuːs]

ordentlich tidy ['taɪdi]

Ordnung: in Ordnung all right [ɔːl 'raɪt]; fine [faɪn]

organisieren organize ['ɔːgənaɪz]

Ort place [pleɪs]; *(Veranstaltungs-, Wohnort)* location [ləʊ'keɪʃn]

Orts-, örtlich local ['ləʊkl]

Osten east [iːst] • **nach Osten** east [iːst] • **Richtung Osten** eastbound ['iːstbaʊnd]

östlich east [iːst]

Outfit *(Kleidung; Ausrüstung)* outfit ['aʊtfɪt]

P

paar: ein paar some [səm, sʌm]; *(einige wenige)* a few [fjuː]

Paar: ein Paar a pair (of) [peə]

Päckchen packet ['pækɪt] • **ein Päckchen Pfefferminzbonbons** a packet of mints

packen pack [pæk]

Packung packet ['pækɪt] • **eine Packung Pfefferminzbonbons** a packet of mints

Paddel paddle ['pædl]

paddeln paddle ['pædl]; canoe [kə'nuː]

Paket parcel ['pɑːsl]

Palast palace ['pæləs]

pantomimisch darstellen mime [maɪm]

Papa dad [dæd]

Papagei parrot ['pærət]

Papier paper ['peɪpə]

Paralympische Spiele *(Olympische Spiele für Sportler/innen mit körperlicher Behinderung)* Paralympics [ˌpærə'lɪmpɪks]

Park park [pɑːk]

Parkplatz *(für viele Autos)* car park ['kɑː pɑːk]

Parlament parliament ['pɑːləmənt]

Partner/in partner ['pɑːtnə]

Party party ['pɑːti]

passen fit [fɪt] • **passen zu** go with

passieren (mit) happen (to) ['hæpən]

Pause break [breɪk] • **in der Pause** *(zwischen Schulstunden)* at break

Pence pence (p) [pens]

Person person ['pɜːsn]

persönliche(r, s) personal ['pɜːsənl]

Pfad path [pɑːθ]

Pfeffer pepper ['pepə]

Pfefferminzbonbons mints [mɪnts]
Pfeife 1. *(zum Rauchen; Orgelpfeife)* pipe [paɪp]
2. *(Trillerpfeife)* whistle ['wɪsl]
pfeifen whistle ['wɪsl]
Pferd horse [hɔːs]
Pferdeschwanz *(Frisur)* ponytail ['pəʊniteɪl]
Pfund *(britische Währung)* pound (£) [paʊnd] • **Es kostet 1 Pfund.** It's £1.
Piano piano [pi'ænəʊ]
Picknick picnic ['pɪknɪk] • **ein Picknick machen** have a picnic
piepsen bleep [bliːp]
Piepton bleep [bliːp]
Pilz mushroom ['mʌʃrʊm, -ruːm]
pink(farben) pink [pɪŋk]
Pirat/in pirate ['paɪrət]
Pizza pizza ['piːtsə]
Plan plan [plæn]
planen plan [plæn]
Planet planet ['plænɪt]
Platz *(Ort, Stelle)* place [pleɪs]; *(in der Stadt)* square [skweə]; *(runder Platz in der Stadt)* circus ['sɜːkəs]; *(für Squash, Badminton)* court [kɔːt]; *(Einsatzort)* location [ləʊ'keɪʃn]
Plätzchen biscuit ['bɪskɪt]
plaudern chat [tʃæt]
plötzlich suddenly ['sʌdnli]
Pokal cup [kʌp]
Polizei police *(pl)* [pə'liːs]
Polizeiwache, Polizeirevier police station [pə'liːs steɪʃn]
Polizist/in policeman [pə'liːsmən]/ policewoman [pə'liːswʊmən]
Poltergeist poltergeist ['pəʊltəgaɪst]
Pommes frites *(pl)* chips [tʃɪps]
Popcorn popcorn ['pɒpkɔːn]
Pop(musik) pop (music) [pɒp]
populär (bei) popular (with) ['pɒpjələ]
Porträt *(Steckbrief)* profile ['prəʊfaɪl]
Post *(Briefe, Päckchen, …)* post [pəʊst]; *(Postamt)* post office ['pəʊst ˌɒfɪs]
Postamt post office ['pəʊst ˌɒfɪs]
Poster poster ['pəʊstə]
Postkarte postcard ['pəʊstkɑːd]
Präsentation presentation [ˌprezn'teɪʃn]
Preis *(Kaufpreis)* price [praɪs]; *(Gewinn)* prize [praɪz]
pressen squeeze [skwiːz]
pro per [pɜː, pə] • **einmal pro Woche** once a week / once per week
Probe *(am Theater)* rehearsal [rɪ'hɜːsl]
proben *(am Theater)* rehearse [rɪ'hɜːs]
probieren try [traɪ]
Problem problem ['prɒbləm]

produzieren produce [prə'djuːs]
Programm programme ['prəʊgræm]
Projekt (über, zu) project (on, about) ['prɒdʒekt] • **ein Projekt machen, durchführen** do a project
Prospekt brochure ['brəʊʃə]
Provinz province ['prɒvɪns]
Prozent per cent (%) [pə'sent]
prüfen *(überprüfen)* check [tʃek]
Prüfung test [test]
PS *(Nachschrift unter Briefen)* PS [ˌpiː'es] (postscript ['pəʊstskrɪpt])
Publikum audience ['ɔːdɪəns]
Pullover pullover ['pʊləʊvə]
Punkt *(bei Test, Quiz)* point [pɔɪnt]
Punktestand *(Spielstand)* score [skɔː]
▶ S.171 A football match
Pute/Puter turkey ['tɜːki]
putzen clean [kliːn] • **Ich putze mir die Zähne.** I clean my teeth.
Putzfrau, -mann cleaner ['kliːnə]

Q

Querflöte flute [fluːt]
Quiz quiz [kwɪz], *pl* quizzes ['kwɪzɪz]

R

Rad 1. wheel ['wiːl]
2. *(Fahrrad)* bike [baɪk]
Rad fahren cycle ['saɪkl]; ride a bike [ˌraɪd_ə 'baɪk]
Radfahrt bike ride ['baɪk raɪd]
Radiergummi rubber ['rʌbə]
Radio radio ['reɪdiəʊ] • **im Radio** on the radio
Radweg cycle path ['saɪkl pɑːθ]
Rap rap [ræp]
raten *(erraten, schätzen)* guess [ges]
Ratespiel quiz [kwɪz], *pl* quizzes ['kwɪzɪz]
Rätsel riddle ['rɪdl]
Rauch smoke [sməʊk]
rauchen smoke [sməʊk] • **Rauchen verboten.** No smoking.
Raum room [ruːm, rʊm]
realistisch realistic [ˌriːə'lɪstɪk]
Rechnung bill [bɪl]
Recht haben be right [raɪt]
rechte(r, s) right [raɪt] • **rechts, auf der rechten Seite** on the right **(nach) rechts abbiegen** turn right **nach rechts schauen** look right
Rechtschreibung spelling ['spelɪŋ]
rechtzeitig in time [ɪn 'taɪm]
recycelt recycled [ˌriː'saɪkld]
Recycling recycling [ˌriː'saɪklɪŋ]

Redakteur/in editor ['edɪtə]
reden (mit, über) talk (to, about) [tɔːk]; speak (to, about) [spiːk] • **Wovon redest du?** What are you talking about?
Refrain chorus ['kɔːrəs]
Regal(brett) shelf [ʃelf], *pl* shelves [ʃelvz]
Regen rain [reɪn]
Reggae reggae [re'geɪ]
regnen rain [reɪn]
regnerisch rainy ['reɪni]
Reh deer, *pl* deer [dɪə]
reich rich [rɪtʃ]
reichen *(weitergeben)* pass [pɑːs]
Reihe 1. Du bist an der Reihe. It's your turn. [tɜːn]
2. *(Sendereihe, Serie)* series, *pl* series ['sɪəriːz]
Reis rice [raɪs]
Reise trip [trɪp]; *(Fahrt)* journey ['dʒɜːni] • **eine Reise unterbrechen** break a journey
reisen travel ['trævl]
reiten ride [raɪd] • **reiten gehen** go riding
Reitweg bridle path ['braɪdl pɑːθ]
Religion *(Religionsunterricht)* RE [ˌɑːr'iː], Religious Education [rɪˌlɪdʒəs_edʒu'keɪʃn]
rennen run [rʌn]
Reportage (über) report (on) [rɪ'pɔːt]
repräsentieren represent [ˌreprɪ'zent]
Rest rest [rest]
Restaurant restaurant ['restrɒnt]; *(Imbissstube, Café)* café ['kæfeɪ]
Resultat result [rɪ'zʌlt]
retten save [seɪv]
Rettungshubschrauber rescue helicopter ['reskjuː ˌhelɪkɒptə]
richtig right [raɪt]; *(korrekt)* correct [kə'rekt]
Richtung way [weɪ] • **in diese Richtung** this way • **in die falsche Richtung** the wrong way • **in welche Richtung?** which way?
Richtung Norden northbound ['nɔːθbaʊnd] • **Richtung Osten** eastbound ['iːstbaʊnd] • **Richtung Süden** southbound ['saʊθbaʊnd] **Richtung Westen** westbound ['westbaʊnd]
riechen smell [smel]
Riesenrad big wheel [ˌbɪg 'wiːl]
riesig huge [hjuːdʒ]
▶ S.165 big – large – huge
Rindfleisch beef [biːf]
Ring ring [rɪŋ]
Rock skirt [skɜːt]
Rolle role [rəʊl]
Rollenspiel role play ['rəʊl pleɪ]
Rollstuhl wheelchair ['wiːltʃeə]

Dictionary (German – English)

römisch; Römer, Römerin Roman ['rəʊmən]

rosa pink [pɪŋk]

rot red [red]

Rückfahrkarte return ticket [rɪ'tɜ:n ‚tɪkɪt]

Rucksack rucksack ['rʌksæk]

rufen call [kɔ:l]; shout [ʃaʊt] • **die Polizei rufen** call the police

ruhig quiet ['kwaɪət]

rumhängen (mit Freunden/Freundinnen) *(abhängen)* hang out (with friends) [‚hæŋ_'aʊt]

rund round [raʊnd]

Rundgang (durch das Haus) tour (of the house) [tʊə]

runterladen *(downloaden)* download [‚daʊn'ləʊd]

S

Sache thing [θɪŋ]

Saft juice [dʒu:s]

sagen say [seɪ] • **Sagt mir eure Namen.** Tell me your names. [tel]

Salat 1. *(Kopfsalat)* lettuce ['letɪs] **2.** *(Gericht, Beilage)* salad ['sæləd]

Salz salt [sɔ:lt]

sammeln collect [kə'lekt] • **Ideen sammeln** brainstorm ['breɪnstɔ:m]

Sammler/in collector [kə'lektə]

Samstag Saturday ['sætədeɪ, 'sætədi] *(siehe auch unter „Freitag")*

Sandwich sandwich ['sænwɪtʃ, '-wɪdʒ]

Sänger/in singer ['sɪŋə]

Sanitäter/in paramedic [‚pærə'medɪk]

Sattel saddle ['sædl]

Satz sentence ['sentəns]

sauber clean [kli:n] • **sauber machen** clean

sauer sein (auf) be cross (with) [krɒs]

Säule column ['kɒləm]

Sauna sauna ['sɔ:nə] • **in die Sauna gehen** have a sauna

Saxophon saxophone ['sæksəfəʊn]

Schachtel packet ['pækɪt]; box [bɒks]

Schaf sheep, *pl* sheep [ʃi:p]

Schal scarf [ska:f], *pl* scarves [ska:vz]

Schale bowl [bəʊl] • **eine Schale Cornflakes** a bowl of cornflakes

Schallplatte record ['rekɔ:d]

scharf *(würzig)* spicy ['spaɪsi]

Schatz dear [dɪə]; sweetheart ['swi:tha:t]

schätzen *(raten, erraten)* guess [ges]

schauen look [lʊk] • **nach links/rechts schauen** look left/right

Schaufenster shop window [‚ʃɒp 'wɪndəʊ]

Schauspiel drama ['dra:mə]

Schauspieler/in actor ['æktə]

scheinen *(Sonne)* shine [ʃaɪn]

scherzen joke [dʒəʊk]

scheu shy [ʃaɪ]

scheußlich horrible ['hɒrəbl]

schick *(modisch, im Trend)* trendy ['trendi]

schicken (an) *(Post, E-Mail)* send (to) [send]; mail (to) [meɪl] • **jm. eine SMS schicken** text sb. [tekst]

schieben push [pʊʃ]

schießen shoot [ʃu:t]; *(ein Tor schießen)* score (a goal) [skɔ:], [gəʊl]

Schiff boat [bəʊt]; ship [ʃɪp]

Schild sign [saɪn]

Schildkröte tortoise ['tɔ:təs]

Schimpfwort: jn. mit Schimpfwörtern hänseln, jm. Schimpfwörter nachrufen call sb. names

Schinkenspeck bacon ['beɪkən]

Schlaf sleep [sli:p]

Schlafanzug pyjamas *(pl)* [pə'dʒa:məz]

schlafen sleep [sli:p]; *(nicht wach sein)* be asleep [ə'sli:p]

Schlafparty sleepover ['sli:pəʊvə]

Schlafzimmer bedroom ['bedru:m]

schlagen hit [hɪt]; *(besiegen)* beat [bi:t] • **gegen/auf die Windschutzscheibe schlagen** hit the windscreen ['wɪndskri:n]

Schlagzeug drums *(pl)* [drʌmz] **Schlagzeug spielen** play the drums

Schlange snake [sneɪk]

schlau clever ['klevə]; smart [sma:t]

schlecht bad [bæd] • **schlechter** worse [wɜ:s] • **am schlechtesten; der/die/das schlechteste** (the) worst [wɜ:st] • **schlecht abschneiden (in)** do badly (in) • **schlecht in etwas sein; etwas schlecht können** be bad at sth. • **schlechtes Timing** bad timing

Schleuse lock [lɒk]

schließen *(zumachen)* close [kləʊz]

schließlich at last [ət 'la:st]; *(zum Schluss)* in the end

schlimm bad [bæd] • **schlimmer** worse [wɜ:s] • **am schlimmsten; der/die/das schlimmste** (the) worst [wɜ:st]

Schlitten sledge [sledʒ]

Schlittschuhbahn ice rink ['aɪs rɪŋk]

Schloss castle ['ka:sl]; *(Palast)* palace ['pæləs]

Schluss 1. end [end] • **zum Schluss** in the end **2.** *(einer Geschichte, eines Films usw.)* ending ['endɪŋ]

Schlüssel key [ki:]

Schlüsselring key ring ['ki: rɪŋ]

Schlüsselwort key word ['ki: wɜ:d]

schmutzig dirty ['dɜ:ti]

Schnee snow [snəʊ]

Schneeschuh snowshoe ['snəʊʃu:]

Schneeschuhwandern snowshoeing ['snəʊʃu:ɪŋ]

schneiden cut [kʌt]

schnell quick [kwɪk]; fast [fa:st]

Schokolade chocolate ['tʃɒklət]

schon already [ɔ:l'redi] • **schon?** yet? [jet] • **schon mal?** ever? ['evə]

schön beautiful ['bju:tɪfl]; *(nett)* nice [naɪs]; *(gut, in Ordnung)* fine [faɪn] • **schön ordentlich** neat and tidy

Schönheit beauty ['bju:ti]

Schrank cupboard ['kʌbəd]; *(Kleiderschrank)* wardrobe ['wɔ:drəʊb]

schrecklich terrible ['terəbl]; awful ['ɔ:fl]

schreiben (an) write (to) [raɪt]

Schreiber/in writer ['raɪtə]

Schreibtisch desk [desk]

Schreibung *(Rechtschreibung, Schreibweise)* spelling ['spelɪŋ]

schreien shout [ʃaʊt]; scream [skri:m]

Schriftsteller/in writer ['raɪtə]

Schritt step [step]

schüchtern shy [ʃaɪ]

Schuh shoe [ʃu:]

Schuld: Das ist nicht meine Schuld. It's not my fault. [fɔ:lt] • **jm. die Schuld geben (an)** blame sb. (for) [bleɪm]

Schule school [sku:l] • **in der Schule** at school

Schüler/in student ['stju:dənt]

Schulfach (school) subject ['sʌbdʒɪkt]

Schulheft exercise book ['eksəsaɪz bʊk]

Schulleiter/in head teacher [‚hed 'ti:tʃə]

Schulmensa canteen [kæn'ti:n]

Schultasche school bag ['sku:l bæg]

Schulter shoulder ['ʃəʊldə]

Schulterpolster *(beim American Football)* pad [pæd]

Schüssel bowl [bəʊl]

schützen: jn. (vor etwas) schützen protect sb. (from sth.) [prə'tekt]

Schützer *(Knieschützer usw. für Inlineskater)* pad [pæd]

schwach weak [wi:k]

schwarz black [blæk] • **schwarzes Brett** notice board ['nəʊtɪs bɔ:d]

Schweigen silence ['saɪləns]

Schwein pig [pɪg]

Schweinefleisch pork [pɔ:k]

schwer 1. *(Gewicht)* heavy ['hevi] **ein 150 Kilogramm schwerer Bär** a 150-kilogram bear

220 Dictionary (German – English)

2. *(schwierig)* **difficult** ['dɪfɪkəlt];
hard [hɑːd]
3. *(anstrengend)* **hard** [hɑːd]
Schwester sister ['sɪstə]
schwierig difficult ['dɪfɪkəlt]; hard
[hɑːd]
Schwierigkeiten trouble ['trʌbl] • **in
Schwierigkeiten sein** be in trouble
Schwimmbad, -becken swimming
pool ['swɪmɪŋ puːl]
schwimmen swim [swɪm]
  schwimmen gehen go swimming
Schwimmer/in swimmer ['swɪmə]
See 1. *(Binnensee)* lake [leɪk]
  2. *(die See, das Meer)* sea [siː]
Seemann sailor ['seɪlə]
sehen see [siː] • **Siehst du?** See?
Sehenswürdigkeiten sights *(pl)*
  [saɪts]
sehr very ['veri] • **Danke sehr!**
  Thanks very much! • **Er mag sie
  sehr.** He likes her a lot. [ə 'lɒt]
  etwas sehr mögen / sehr lieben
  like/love sth. very much
Seife soap [səʊp]
sein *(Verb)* be [biː]
sein(e) *(besitzanzeigend) (zu „he")*
  his; *(zu „it")* its
seiner, seine, seins his [hɪz]
Seite 1. side [saɪd] • **auf der linken
  Seite** on the left • **auf der rechten
  Seite** on the right
  2. *(Buch-, Heftseite)* page [peɪdʒ]
  Auf welcher Seite sind wir? What
  page are we on?
selbst: über dich selbst about
  yourself [jəˈself, jɔːˈself]
selbstverständlich of course [əv ˈkɔːs]
seltsam *(sonderbar; fremd)* strange
  [streɪndʒ]
senden (an) *(Post, E-Mail)* send (to)
  [send]; mail to [meɪl]
Sendereihe series, *pl* series ['sɪəriːz]
September September [sepˈtembə]
Serie *(Sendereihe)* series, *pl* series
  ['sɪəriːz]
Sessel armchair ['ɑːmtʃeə]
Setup setup ['setʌp]
setzen: sich setzen sit [sɪt] • **Setz
  dich / Setzt euch zu mir.** Sit with
  me.
Shampoo shampoo [ʃæmˈpuː]
Shorts shorts *(pl)* [ʃɔːts]
Show show [ʃəʊ]
sich (selbst) 1. *(zu „she")* herself
  [həˈself, hɜːˈself]
  2. *(zu „he")* himself [hɪmˈself]
  3. *(zu „it")* itself [ɪtˈself]
  4. *(zu „they")* themselves [ðəmˈselvz]
  5. sich (gegenseitig) *(einander)*
  each other [iːtʃ ˈ_ʌðə]; one another
  [wʌn ə'nʌðə]

▶ S.176 Reflexive pronouns
▶ S.177 Reflexiv im Deutschen –
    nicht reflexiv im Englischen

sicher 1. *(in Sicherheit)* safe (from)
  [seɪf] • **nicht sicher** unsafe [ʌnˈseɪf]
  2. sicher sein *(nicht zweifeln)* be
  sure [ʃʊə, ʃɔː]
Sicherheit: in Sicherheit (vor) safe
  (from) [seɪf]
sie 1. *(weibliche Person)* she [ʃiː]
  Frag sie. Ask her. [hə, hɜː]
  2. *(Ding, Tier)* it [ɪt]
  3. *(Plural)* they [ðeɪ] • **Frag sie.** Ask
  them. [ðəm, ðem]
Sie *(höfliche Anrede)* you [juː]
Sieg win [wɪn]
Sieger/in winner ['wɪnə]
Silbe syllable ['sɪləbl]
singen sing [sɪŋ]
Single single ['sɪŋgl]
sitzen sit [sɪt]
Skateboard skateboard ['skeɪtbɔːd]
  Skateboard fahren skate [skeɪt]
skaten skate [skeɪt]
Skater skater ['skeɪtə]
Sketch sketch [sketʃ]
Ski ski [skiː] • **Ski fahren/laufen** ski
  [skiː]
Skipiste ski slope ['skiː sləʊp]
Sklave, Sklavin slave [sleɪv]
SMS text message ['tekst ˌmesɪdʒ]
  jm . eine SMS schicken text sb.
  [tekst]
Snack snack [snæk]
so: 1. so weit/gut/schlecht/... that
  far/good/bad/... • **so süß** so
  sweet [səʊ]
  2. so alt/groß wie as old/big as
Socke sock [sɒk]
sodass so that
soeben just [dʒʌst]
Sofa sofa ['səʊfə]
Software software ['sɒftweə]
sogar even ['iːvn]
Sohn son [sʌn]
sollte(n): Warum sollte ich ...? Why
  should I ...? [ʃəd, ʃʊd]
Sommer summer ['sʌmə]
sonderbar *(fremd; seltsam)* strange
  [streɪndʒ]
Song song [sɒŋ]
Sonnabend Saturday ['sætədeɪ, 'sætədi]
  (siehe auch unter „Freitag")
Sonne sun [sʌn]
Sonnenbrille: (eine) Sonnenbrille
  sunglasses *(pl)* ['sʌnglɑːsɪz]
sonnig sunny ['sʌni]
Sonntag Sunday ['sʌndeɪ, 'sʌndi]
  (siehe auch unter „Freitag")
Sorge worry ['wʌri] • **sich Sorgen
  machen (wegen, um)** worry (about)
  Mach dir keine Sorgen. Don't worry.

sorgfältig careful ['keəfl]
Sorte sort [sɔːt]
Soundfile sound file ['saund faɪl]
sowieso anyway ['eniweɪ]
Spaghetti spaghetti [spəˈgeti]
spannend exciting [ɪkˈsaɪtɪŋ]
sparen save [seɪv]
Spaß fun [fʌn] • **Spaß haben** have
  fun • **nur zum Spaß** just for fun
  Reiten macht Spaß. Riding is fun.
  Viel Spaß! Have fun! / Enjoy your-
  self.
spät late [leɪt] • **Wie spät ist es?**
  What's the time? • **zu spät sein/
  kommen** be late
später later ['leɪtə]
spätestens: bis spätestens 10 (Uhr)
  by ten (o'clock)
  ▶ S.175 German „bis"
spazieren gehen go for a walk [wɔːk]
Spaziergang walk [wɔːk] • **einen
  Spaziergang machen** go for a walk
Specht woodpecker ['wʊdpekə]
Speise dish [dɪʃ]
Speisekarte menu ['menjuː]
sperren lock [lɒk]
Spiegel mirror ['mɪrə]
Spiel game [geɪm]; *(Wettkampf)*
  match [mætʃ]
spielen play [pleɪ]; *(Szene, Dialog)*
  act [ækt] • **Fußball spielen** play
  football • **Gitarre/Klavier spielen**
  play the guitar/the piano
Spieler/in player ['pleɪə]
Spielstand *(Punktestand)* score [skɔː]
  ▶ S.171 A football match
Spion/in spy [spaɪ]
Spitze *(oberes Ende)* top [tɒp] • **an
  der Spitze (von)** at the top (of)
Sport; Sportart sport [spɔːt] • **Sport
  treiben** do sport
Sporthalle sports hall ['spɔːts hɔːl]
sportlich sporty ['spɔːti]
Sportunterricht PE [ˌpiːˈiː], Physical
  Education [ˌfɪzɪkəl_edʒuˈkeɪʃn]
Sportzentrum sports centre ['spɔːts
  ˌsentə]
Sprache language ['læŋgwɪdʒ]
Sprachmittlung *(Mediation)*
  mediation [ˌmiːdiˈeɪʃn]
sprechen (mit) speak (to) [spiːk]
  Hier spricht Isabel. *(am Telefon)*
  This is Isabel.
springen jump [dʒʌmp]
Spülbecken, Spüle sink [sɪŋk]
Staat state [steɪt] • **die Vereinigten
  Staaten (von Amerika)** the United
  States (US) [juˌnaɪtɪd 'steɪts], [ˌjuːˈ_es]
Stadion stadium ['steɪdiəm]

Dictionary (German – English) 221

Stadt *(Großstadt)* city ['sɪti]; *(Klein-stadt)* town [taʊn]
Stadtplan map [mæp]
Stadtzentrum city centre [ˌsɪti 'sentə]
Stahl steel [stiːl]
Stall *(für Kaninchen)* hutch [hʌtʃ]
Stammbaum family tree ['fæməli triː]
Standort location [ləʊ'keɪʃn]
Star *(Film-, Popstar)* star [staː]
stark strong [strɒŋ]
starten start [staːt]
Statue statue ['stætʃuː]
Steak steak [steɪk]
Steckbrief *(Beschreibung)* profile ['prəʊfaɪl]
Stecker plug [plʌg]
Steeldrum steel drum [ˌstiːl 'drʌm]
stehen stand [stænd] • **Hier steht: ...** *(im Text)* It says here: ... • **Wie steht es?** *(beim Sport)* What's the score?
▶ S.171 A football match
stehlen steal [stiːl]
Steigerung comparison [kəm'pærɪsn]
Stein stone [stəʊn]
stellen *(hin-, abstellen)* put [pʊt]
Fragen stellen ask questions
sich (hin)stellen stand [stænd]
etwas auf die Beine stellen get sth. off the ground
sterben (an) die (of) [daɪ]
Stereoanlage stereo ['steriəʊ]
Stern star [staː]
Stichwort *(Schlüsselwort)* key word ['kiː wɜːd]
Stiefel boot [buːt]
still quiet ['kwaɪət]
Stille silence ['saɪləns]
stimmen: Das stimmt. That's right. [raɪt] • **Du brauchst ein Lineal, stimmt's?** You need a ruler, right?
stolz (auf jn./etwas) proud (of sb./sth.) [praʊd]
stoßen push [pʊʃ]
Strand beach [biːtʃ] • **am Strand** on the beach
Straße road [rəʊd]; street [striːt]
Straßenbahn tram [træm]
Streich trick [trɪk]
Streik strike [straɪk] • **in den Streik treten** go on strike • **sich im Streik befinden** be on strike
streiken 1. *(sich im Streik befinden)* be on strike [straɪk]
2. *(in den Streik treten)* go on strike
Streit argument ['aːgjumənt]
streiten; sich streiten argue ['aːgjuː]
streng strict [strɪkt]
Strom electricity [ɪˌlek'trɪsəti]
Stromschnellen rapids *(pl)* ['ræpɪdz]
strukturieren structure ['strʌktʃə]
Strumpf sock [sɒk]

Stück 1. piece [piːs] • **ein Stück Papier** a piece of paper
2. *(Titel auf einer CD)* track [træk]
Student/in student ['stjuːdənt]
Studio studio ['stjuːdiəʊ]
Stuhl chair [tʃeə]
stumm: „stummer" Buchstabe *(nicht gesprochener Buchstabe)* silent letter [ˌsaɪlənt 'letə]
Stunde hour ['aʊə]; *(Schulstunde)* lesson ['lesn] • **eine halbe Stunde** half an hour [ˌhaːf_ən_'aʊə] • **ein 14-Stunden-Flug** a 14-hour flight **ein Supermarkt, der 24 Stunden geöffnet ist** a 24-hour supermarket
Stundenplan timetable ['taɪmteɪbl]
...stündig: ein 14-stündiger Flug a 14-hour flight
Sturm storm [stɔːm]
stürmisch stormy ['stɔːmi]
stürzen *(hinfallen)* fall [fɔːl]
suchen look for ['lʊk fɔː]
Süden south [saʊθ] • **nach Süden** south • **Richtung Süden** *(Fahrtrichtung)* southbound ['saʊθbaund]
südlich south [saʊθ]
Südosten south-east [ˌsaʊθ'iːst] **nach Südosten** south-east
südöstlich south-east [ˌsaʊθ'iːst]
Südwesten south-west [ˌsaʊθ'west] **nach Südwesten** south-west
südwestlich south-west [ˌsaʊθ'west]
Supermarkt supermarket ['suːpəmaːkɪt]
Suppe soup [suːp]
Surfbrett surfboard ['sɜːfbɔːd]
surfen surf [sɜːf] • **im Internet surfen** surf the internet [sɜːf]
süß sweet [swiːt]
Süßigkeiten sweets *(pl)* [swiːts]
Sweatshirt sweatshirt ['swetʃɜːt]
Szene scene [siːn]

T

Tabak tobacco [tə'bækəʊ]
Tafel *(Wandtafel)* board [bɔːd] • **an der/die Tafel** on the board
Tag day [deɪ] • **drei Tage (lang)** for three days • **eines Tages** one day **Guten Tag.** Hello.; *(nachmittags)* Good afternoon. [gʊd_ˌaːftə'nuːn]
Tagebuch diary ['daɪəri]
Tagesausflug a day out
Tagesfahrkarte all-day ticket; *(der Londoner Verkehrsbetriebe)* Travelcard ['trævlkaːd]
Tal valley ['væli]
Talent talent ['tælənt]
Tante aunt [aːnt]; auntie ['aːnti]

Tanz dance [daːns]
tanzen dance [daːns]
Tanzen dancing ['daːnsɪŋ]
Tänzer/in dancer ['daːnsə]
Tanzstunden, Tanzunterricht dancing lessons ['daːnsɪŋ ˌlesnz]
Tasche *(Tragetasche, Beutel)* bag [bæg]; *(Hosentasche, Jackentasche)* pocket ['pɒkɪt]
Taschengeld pocket money ['pɒkɪt mʌni]
Tasse cup [kʌp] • **eine Tasse Tee** a cup of tea
Tätigkeit activity [æk'tɪvəti]
Tatsache fact [fækt]
tausend thousand ['θaʊznd]
Taxi taxi ['tæksi]
Team team [tiːm]
Teddy teddy ['tedi]
Tee tea [tiː]
Teelöffel teaspoon ['tiːspuːn]
Teenager teenager ['tiːneɪdʒə]
Teenager- *(Jugend-)* teen [tiːn]
Teil part [paːt]; *(Abschnitt)* section ['sekʃn]
teilen: sich etwas teilen (mit jm.) share sth. (with sb.) [ʃeə]
teilnehmen (an) take part (in) [teɪk 'paːt]
Telefon *(tele)*phone ['telɪfəʊn] • **am Telefon** on the phone
telefonieren phone [fəʊn]
Telefonnummer *(tele)*phone number ['telɪfəʊn ˌnʌmbə]
Teller plate [pleɪt] • **ein Teller Pommes frites** a plate of chips
Temperatur temperature ['temprətʃə]
Tempus *(grammatische Zeit)* tense [tens]
Tennis tennis ['tenɪs]
Termin appointment [ə'pɔɪntmənt]
Terminkalender diary ['daɪəri]
Test test [test]
teuer expensive [ɪk'spensɪv]
Text text [tekst]; *(Liedtext)* lyrics *(pl)* ['lɪrɪks]
Theater theatre ['θɪətə]
Theaterstück play [pleɪ]
Thema, Themenbereich topic ['tɒpɪk]
Thermometer thermometer [θə'mɒmɪtə]
Tier animal ['ænɪml]; *(Haustier)* pet [pet]
Tierhandlung pet shop ['pet ʃɒp]
Tiger tiger ['taɪgə]
Timing: schlechtes Timing bad timing ['taɪmɪŋ]
Tipp tip [tɪp]
Tisch table ['teɪbl]
Tischtennis table tennis ['teɪbl tenɪs]
Tischtennisschläger table tennis bat [bæt]

Titel title ['taɪtl]; *(Musikstück auf einer CD)* track [træk]
Toast(brot) toast [təʊst]
Tochter daughter ['dɔ:tə]
Toilette toilet ['tɔɪlət]
toll fantastic [fæn'tæstɪk]; great [greɪt]; brilliant ['brɪliənt]
Tomate tomato [tə'mɑːtəʊ], *pl* tomatoes
Tondatei sound file ['saʊnd faɪl]
Top *(Oberteil)* top [tɒp]
Tor gate [geɪt]; *(im Sport)* goal [gəʊl]
ein Tor schießen score (a goal) [skɔ:]
Torfrau, Torwart goalkeeper ['gəʊlki:pə]
Tornado tornado [tɔ:'neɪdəʊ]
Torte cake [keɪk]
tot dead [ded]
töten kill [kɪl]
Tour (durch das Haus) tour (of the house) [tʊə]
Tourist/in tourist ['tʊərɪst]
Track *(auf einer CD)* track [træk]
traditionell traditional [trə'dɪʃənl]
tragen *(Kleidung)* wear [weə]
Trainer/in coach [kəʊtʃ]
trainieren practise ['præktɪs]; train [treɪn]
Trainingsstunde, -einheit training session ['seʃn]
Transport *(Beförderung)* transport ['trænspɔ:t]
Traum dream [dri:m]
träumen (von) dream (of, about), [dri:m] • **Träum weiter!** Dream on!
▶ S.167 on („weiter")
Traumhaus dream house
traurig sad [sæd]
treffen; sich treffen meet [mi:t]
ein Abkommen / eine Abmachung treffen make a deal [di:l]
Treffer: einen Treffer erzielen score (a goal) [skɔ:], [gəʊl]
Treppe(nstufen) stairs *(pl)* [steəz]
Trick *(Zauberkunststück)* trick [trɪk]
Trillerpfeife whistle ['wɪsl]
Trimester term [tɜ:m]
trinken drink [drɪŋk] • **Milch zum Frühstück trinken** have milk for breakfast
Trommel drum [drʌm]
Trompete trumpet ['trʌmpɪt]
trotzdem anyway ['eniweɪ]
Truthahn turkey ['tɜ:ki]
Tschüs. Bye. [baɪ]; See you. ['si: ju:]
T-Shirt T-shirt ['ti:ʃɜ:t]
tüchtig hard-working [,hɑ:d'wɜ:kɪŋ]
tun do [du:] • **Tue, was ich tue.** Do what I do. • **tun müssen** have to do • **tun wollen** want to do [wɒnt]
Tut mir leid. I'm sorry. ['sɒri]

Tunnel tunnel ['tʌnl]
Tür door [dɔ:]
Türklingel doorbell ['dɔ:bel]
Turm tower ['taʊə]
Turnen *(Sportunterricht)* PE [,pi:_'i:], Physical Education [,fɪzɪkəl_edʒu'keɪʃn]
Turnschuhe trainers *(pl)* ['treɪnəz]
Tut mir leid. I'm sorry. ['sɒri]
Tüte bag [bæg]
Typ type [taɪp] *(infml)*
Tyrann *(Schultyrann)* bully ['bʊli]
tyrannisieren bully ['bʊli]

U

U-Bahn: die U-Bahn the underground ['ʌndəgraʊnd] *(BE)*; the subway ['sʌbweɪ] *(AE)*; *(in London)* the Tube *(no pl)* [tju:b]
U-Bahnlinie line [laɪn]
üben practise ['præktɪs]
über 1. about [ə'baʊt] • **über dich selbst** about yourself
2. *(räumlich)* over ['əʊvə]; *(quer über)* across [ə'krɒs]; *(oberhalb von)* above [ə'bʌv]
überall everywhere ['evriweə]
überarbeiten revise [rɪ'vaɪz]
übereinstimmen: mit jm./etwas übereinstimmen agree with sb./sth. [ə'gri:]
überfliegen: einen Text überfliegen *(um den Inhalt grob zu erfassen)* skim a text [skɪm]
überleben survive [sə'vaɪv]
übernachten *(über Nacht bleiben)* stay [steɪ]
überprüfen check [tʃek]
überqueren cross [krɒs]
überraschen: jn. überraschen surprise sb. [sə'praɪz]
überrascht (über etwas) surprised (at sth.) [sə'praɪzd]
Überraschung surprise [sə'praɪz]
Überschrift title ['taɪtl]
übersetzen (aus ... ins) translate (from ... into) [træns'leɪt]
Übersetzung translation [træns'leɪʃn]
übrigens by the way [,baɪ ðə 'weɪ]
Übung *(im Schulbuch)* exercise ['eksəsaɪz] • **eine Übung machen** do an exercise
Übungsheft exercise book ['eksəsaɪz bʊk]
Uhr 1. *(Armbanduhr)* watch [wɒtʃ]; *(Wand-, Stand-, Turmuhr)* clock [klɒk]
2. elf Uhr eleven o'clock • **7 Uhr morgens/vormittags** 7 am [,eɪ_'em] **7 Uhr nachmittags/abends** 7 pm [,pi:_'em] • **um 8 Uhr 45** at 8.45

Uhrzeit time [taɪm]
um 1. *(örtlich)* um ... (herum) round [raʊnd]; around [ə'raʊnd] • **um den See (herum)** around the lake **ganz um die Burg herum** all around the castle
▶ S.164 around
2. *(zeitlich)* **um 8.45** at 8.45 • **um sechs herum** *(gegen sechs)* around six
▶ S.164 around
3. Es geht um Mr Green. This is about Mr Green.
4. um zu to
umdrehen: sich umdrehen turn [tɜ:n]
Umfrage (über) survey (on) ['sɜ:veɪ]
umher: in ... umher round [raʊnd]; around [ə'raʊnd] • **in der Stadt umher** around the town
▶ S.164 around
umher-: umhergehen; umherspazieren walk around • **umherrennen** run around • **umherspringen** jump around
▶ S.164 around
umschreiben *(anders ausdrücken)* paraphrase ['pærəfreɪz]
umsehen: sich umsehen look round [,lʊk 'raʊnd]
umsteigen change [tʃeɪndʒ]
umziehen (nach, in) *(die Wohnung wechseln)* move (to) [mu:v]
uncool uncool [,ʌn'ku:l] *(infml)*
und and [ənd, ænd] • **Und? / Na und?** So? [səʊ]
unentschieden: 2:2 unentschieden 2 all
▶ S.171 A football match
Unentschieden draw [drɔ:]
▶ S.171 A football match
unfair unfair [,ʌn'feə]
Unfall accident ['æksɪdənt]
unfreundlich unfriendly [ʌn'frendli]
ungefähr about [ə'baʊt]
Ungeheuer monster ['mɒnstə]
ungerecht unfair [,ʌn'feə]
ungesund unhealthy [ʌn'helθi]
unglaublich amazing [ə'meɪzɪŋ]
unglücklich unhappy [ʌn'hæpi]
unheimlich scary ['skeəri]
unhöflich rude [ru:d]
Uniform uniform ['ju:nɪfɔ:m]
unklar unclear [,ʌn'klɪə]
unmöglich impossible [ɪm'pɒsɪbl]
unordentlich untidy [ʌn'taɪdi] • **sehr unordentlich sein** *(Zimmer)* be a mess [mes]
Unordnung: alles in Unordnung bringen make a mess [,meɪk_ə 'mes]
Unrecht haben be wrong [rɒŋ]

Dictionary (German – English)

uns us [əs, ʌs] • **uns (selbst)** ourselves [aʊə'selvz]
► S.176 Reflexive pronouns
unser(e) ... our ... ['aʊə] • **unser eigenes Schwimmbad** our own pool [əʊn]
unserer, unsere, unseres ours ['aʊəz]
unten (im Haus) downstairs [,daʊn'steəz] • **am unteren Ende (von)** at the bottom (of) ['bɒtəm] **dort unten** down there • **nach unten** down [daʊn]; (im Haus) downstairs
unter under ['ʌndə]
unterbrechen: eine Reise unterbrechen break a journey [,breɪk_ə 'dʒɜːni]
unterhalten: sich unterhalten (mit, über) talk (to, about) [tɔːk]
Unterricht lessons (pl) ['lesnz]
unterrichten teach [tiːtʃ]
unterschiedlich different ['dɪfrənt]
unterstützen: eine Mannschaft unterstützen support a team [sə'pɔːt]
Untersuchung (über) (Umfrage) survey (on) ['sɜːveɪ]
unverschämt rude [ruːd]
Urgroßmutter great-grandmother [,greɪt'grænmʌðə]
Urgroßvater great-grandfather [,greɪt'grænfɑːðə]
Urlaub holiday ['hɒlədeɪ] (BE); vacation [və'keɪʃn, AE: veɪ'keɪʃn] (AE) • **in Urlaub fahren** go on holiday • **in Urlaub sein** be on holiday • **ein zweiwöchiger Urlaub** a two-week holiday

V

Vater father ['fɑːðə]
Vati dad [dæd]
Verabredung appointment [ə'pɔɪntmənt]
verabschieden: sich verabschieden say goodbye [,seɪ gʊd'baɪ]
verängstigt scared [skeəd]
Veranstaltungsort location [ləʊ'keɪʃn]
verbinden (einander zuordnen) link [lɪŋk]
Verbindung (Verknüpfung) link [lɪŋk] • **in Verbindung bleiben** keep in touch [,kiːp_ɪn 'tʌtʃ]
verboten: Rauchen verboten. No smoking.
verbringen: Zeit verbringen (mit) spend time (on) [spend]
Verein club [klʌb]
vereinigt: das Vereinigte Königreich (Großbritannien und Nordirland)

the United Kingdom (UK) [juː,naɪtɪd 'kɪŋdəm], [,juː'keɪ] • **die Vereinigten Staaten (von Amerika)** the United States (US) [juː,naɪtɪd 'steɪts], [,juː_'es]
verfolgen follow ['fɒləʊ]
vergessen forget [fə'get]
Vergleich comparison [kəm'pærɪsn]
vergriffen sein (ausverkauft sein) be sold out [,səʊld_'aʊt]
verheiratet (mit) married (to) ['mærɪd]
verkaufen sell [sel]
Verkäufer/in (im Geschäft) shop assistant ['ʃɒp_ə,sɪstənt]
Verkehr traffic ['træfɪk]
Verkehrsmittel transport (no pl) ['trænspɔːt]
verkehrsreich (Straße) busy ['bɪzi]
verkehrt (falsch) wrong [rɒŋ]
verknallt: in jn. verknallt sein have a crush on sb. [krʌʃ]
verknüpfen (einander zuordnen) link [lɪŋk]
Verknüpfung link [lɪŋk]
verlassen leave [liːv]
verletzen hurt [hɜːt]
verletzt hurt [hɜːt]
verlieren lose [luːz]
vermissen miss [mɪs]
Vermittlung (Sprachmittlung, Mediation) mediation [,miːdi'eɪʃn]
veröffentlichen publish ['pʌblɪʃ]
verrückt mad [mæd]; crazy ['kreɪzi] **verrückt nach/auf etwas sein** be mad about sth.
Versammlung (morgendliche Schulversammlung, oft mit Andacht) Assembly [ə'sembli]
verschieden (anders) different ['dɪfrənt]
verschwinden disappear [,dɪsə'pɪə]
versprechen promise ['prɒmɪs]
verstecken; sich verstecken hide [haɪd]
verstehen understand [,ʌndə'stænd]
versuchen try [traɪ] • **versuchen zu tun** try and do / try to do
vertreten (repräsentieren) represent [,reprɪ'zent]
verwenden use [juːz]
verwirrt puzzled ['pʌzld]
Video video ['vɪdiəʊ]
viel a lot (of) [lɒt]; lots (of) [lɒts]; much [mʌtʃ] • **viele** a lot (of) [lɒt]; lots (of) [lɒts]; many ['meni] • **Viel Glück (bei/mit ...)!** Good luck (with ...)! • **viel mehr** lots more **Viel Spaß!** Have fun! / Enjoy yourself. • **wie viel?** how much? **wie viele?** how many? • **Vielen Dank!** Thanks a lot!

vielleicht maybe ['meɪbi] • **du könntest vielleicht Hilfe brauchen** you might need help [maɪt]
Viertel: Viertel nach 11 quarter past 11 ['kwɔːtə] • **Viertel vor 12** quarter to 12
violett purple ['pɜːpl]
Violine violin [,vaɪə'lɪn]
Vogel bird [bɜːd]
Vokabelverzeichnis vocabulary [və'kæbjələri]
voll full [fʊl] • **die Nase voll haben (von etwas)** be fed up (with sth.) [,fed_'ʌp]
Volleyball volleyball ['vɒlibɔːl]
von [əv, ɒv]; from [frəm, frɒm] **ein Aufsatz von ...** an essay by ... [baɪ] • **von Montag bis Freitag** from Mondays to Fridays
► S.175 German „bis"
vor 1. (räumlich) in front of [ɪn 'frʌnt_əv] **2.** (zeitlich) **vor dem Abendessen** before dinner [bɪ'fɔː] • **vor einer Minute** a minute ago [ə'gəʊ] **Viertel vor 12** quarter to 12
vorankommen: Wie komme ich voran? (Wie sind meine Fortschritte?) How am I doing?
vorbei (an) (vorüber) past [pɑːst]
vorbei sein be over ['əʊvə]
vorbereiten prepare [prɪ'peə] • **sich vorbereiten (auf)** prepare (for); get ready (for) ['redi] • **Dinge vorbereiten** get things ready
vorbringen: ein Argument vorbringen make a point
Vordergrund foreground ['fɔːgraʊnd]
Vormittag morning ['mɔːnɪŋ]
vorsichtig careful ['keəfl]
vorspielen (pantomimisch darstellen) mime [maɪm]
vorstellen: sich etwas vorstellen imagine sth. [ɪ'mædʒɪn]
Vorstellung (Präsentation) presentation [,prezn'teɪʃn]; (Show) show [ʃəʊ]
vorüber (an) (vorbei) past [pɑːst]
Vorwürfe: jm. Vorwürfe machen (wegen) blame sb. (for) [bleɪm]

W

wählen (auswählen, aussuchen) choose [tʃuːz]
wahr true [truː]
während as [əz, æz]; while [waɪl]
wahrscheinlich probably ['prɒbəbli]
Wald forest ['fɒrɪst]; woods (pl) [wʊdz]
walisisch; Walisisch Welsh [welʃ]

Wand wall [wɔːl]
wann when [wen]
warm warm [wɔːm]
warnen: jn. (vor etwas) warnen warn sb. (about sth.) [wɔːn]
warten (auf) wait (for) [weɪt]
   Warte mal! Wait a minute. ['mɪnɪt]
   Wart's ab! Wait and see!
warum why [waɪ] • **Warum ich?** Why me?
was what [wɒt] • **Was für ein Auto ...?** What kind of car ...? • **Was haben wir als Hausaufgabe auf?** What's for homework? • **Was haben wir als Nächstes?** What have we got next? • **Was ist los? / Was ist denn?** What's the matter? ['mætə] • **Was ist mit ...?** What about ...? • **Was kostet/kosten ...?** How much is/are ...? • **Was war das Beste an ...?** What was the best thing about ...?
waschen wash [wɒʃ] • **Ich wasche mir das Gesicht.** I wash my face.
Waschmaschine washing machine ['wɒʃɪŋ məʃiːn]
Wasser water ['wɔːtə]
Webcam webcam ['webkæm]
Website website ['websaɪt]
Wechselgeld change [tʃeɪndʒ]
weg away [ə'weɪ]
Weg way [weɪ]; *(Pfad)* path [pɑːθ]; *(Gasse)* lane [leɪn] • **auf dem Weg (zu/nach)** on the way (to) • **jm. den Weg beschreiben** tell sb. the way • **jn. nach dem Weg fragen** ask sb. the way • **etwas auf den Weg bringen** get sth. off the ground
wegbleiben *(draußen bleiben)* stay out [steɪ_'aʊt]
weggehen leave [liːv]
wehen blow [bləʊ]
wehtun hurt [hɜːt]
weiblich female ['fiːmeɪl]
Weide field [fiːld]
Weihnachten Christmas ['krɪsməs]
weil because [bɪ'kɒz]
Weise *(Art und Weise)* way [weɪ]
weiß white [waɪt]
weit (entfernt) far [fɑː]
weiter: geradeaus weiter straight on [streɪt_'ɒn]
weitere(r, s): weitere 45 Pence another 45 p [ə'nʌðə]
weiter-: weitergeben pass [pɑːs]
   weitergehen walk on • **weiterlesen** read on • **weitermachen** go on • **weiterreden** go on
   weiterträumen dream on
   ▶ S.167 on („weiter")

welche(r, s) which [wɪtʃ] • **Auf welcher Seite sind wir?** What page are we on? [wɒt] • **Welche Farbe hat ...?** What colour is ...?
wellenreiten gehen go surfing ['sɜːfɪŋ]
Wellensittich budgie ['bʌdʒi]
Welt world [wɜːld] • **auf der ganzen Welt** all over the world • **aus der ganzen Welt** from all over the world
wem? who? [huː] • **Wem gehören diese?** Whose are these? [huːz]
wen? who? [huː]
wenden: sich an jn. wenden turn to sb. [tɜːn]
wenig: am wenigsten least [liːst]
wenigstens at least [ət 'liːst]
wenn 1. *(zeitlich)* when [wen] 2. *(falls)* if [ɪf]
wer? who? [huː] • **Wer ist dran / an der Reihe?** Whose turn is it? [huːz]
werden become [bɪ'kʌm] • **wütend/heiß/... werden** get angry/hot/... **du wirst frieren; ihr werdet frieren** you'll be cold (= you will be cold) [wɪl] • **du wirst nicht frieren; ihr werdet nicht frieren** you won't be cold (= you will not be cold) [wəʊnt]
werfen throw [θrəʊ]
wessen? whose? [huːz]
West- western ['westən]
Westen west [west] • **nach Westen** west • **Richtung Westen** *(Fahrtrichtung)* westbound ['westbaʊnd]
westlich *(westlich von)* west [west]; *(Gebiet)* western ['westən]
Wetter weather ['weðə]
Wettkampf match [mætʃ]
Whisky whisky ['wɪski]
wichtig important [ɪm'pɔːtnt]
wie 1. *(Fragewort)* how [haʊ] • **Wie bitte?** Sorry? ['sɒri] • **Wie geht es dir/Ihnen/euch?** How are you? [ˌhaʊ_'ɑː jə] • **Wie heißt du?** What's your name? • **Wie komme ich voran?** *(Wie sind meine Fortschritte?)* How am I doing? • **Wie spät ist es?** What's the time? • **Wie steht es jetzt?** *(beim Sport)* What's the score? • **wie viel?** how much? • **wie viele?** how many? • **Wie war ...?** How was ...? • **Wie war das Wetter?** What was the weather like? • **Wie wär's mit ...?** What about ...? 2. **so alt/groß wie** as old/big as 3. **wie ein Filmstar** like a film star [laɪk] 4. **wie auch immer, ... / wie dem auch sei, ...** anyway, ... ['eniweɪ]
wieder again [ə'gen]

wiederholen *(Lernstoff)* revise [rɪ'vaɪz]
Wiederholung *(des Lernstoffs)* revision [rɪ'vɪʒn]
Wiedersehen: Auf Wiedersehen. Goodbye. [ˌgʊd'baɪ]
wiederverwendet/-verwertet recycled [ˌriː'saɪkld]
Wiederverwertung recycling [ˌriː'saɪklɪŋ]
wild wild [waɪld]
willkommen: Willkommen (in Bristol). Welcome (to Bristol). ['welkəm] • **Sie heißen dich in ... willkommen** They welcome you to ...
Wind wind [wɪnd]
windig windy ['wɪndi]
Windjacke anorak ['ænəræk]
winken wave [weɪv]
Winter winter ['wɪntə]
wir we [wiː]
Wirbelsturm tornado [tɔː'neɪdəʊ]
wirklich 1. *(tatsächlich)* really ['rɪəli] • **Meinst du wirklich? / Glaubst du das wirklich?** Do you really think so? 2. *(echt)* real [rɪəl]
Wirklichkeit: in Wirklichkeit *(eigentlich)* actually ['æktʃuəli]
wirklichkeitsnah realistic [ˌrɪə'lɪstɪk]
wissen know [nəʊ] • **wissen wollen** wonder ['wʌndə] • **Ich weiß es nicht.** I don't know. • **von etwas wissen; über etwas Bescheid wissen** know about sth. • **..., wissen Sie. / ..., weißt du.** ..., you know. **Weißt du was, Sophie?** You know what, Sophie? • **Woher weißt du ...?** How do you know ...?
Witz joke [dʒəʊk] • **Witze machen** joke
witzig funny ['fʌni]
wo where [weə] • **Wo kommst du her?** Where are you from?
Woche week [wiːk]
Wochenende weekend [ˌwiːk'end] **am Wochenende** at the weekend
Wochentage days of the week
...wöchig: ein zweiwöchiger Urlaub a two-week holiday
Wofür? What for? [ˌwɒt 'fɔː]
Woher weißt du ...? How do you know ...? [nəʊ]
wohin where [weə]; *(in welche Richtung)* which way
wohlauf *(gesund)* well [wel]
Wohltätigkeitsbasar jumble sale ['dʒʌmbl seɪl]
wohnen live [lɪv] • **bei jm. wohnen** stay with sb.
Wohnheim hostel ['hɒstl]

Dictionary (German – English) 225

Wohnort location [ləʊˈkeɪʃn]
Wohnung flat [flæt]
Wohnungstür front door [ˌfrʌnt ˈdɔː]
Wohnwagen caravan [ˈkærəvæn]
Wohnzimmer living room [ˈlɪvɪŋ ruːm]
Wolf wolf, *pl* wolves [wʊlf, wʊlvz]
Wolke cloud [klaʊd]
wollen *(haben wollen)* want [wɒnt]
  tun wollen want to do
Workshop workshop [ˈwɜːkʃɒp]
Wort word [wɜːd]
Wortbildung word building [ˈwɜːd ˌbɪldɪŋ]
Wörterbuch dictionary [ˈdɪkʃənri]
Wörterverzeichnis vocabulary [vəˈkæbjələri]; *(alphabetisches)* dictionary [ˈdɪkʃənri]
Wovon redest du? What are you talking about?
würden: ich würde ... / du würdest ... I would ... / you would ... [wəd, wʊd]
Würfel dice, *pl* dice [daɪs]
Wurst, Würstchen sausage [ˈsɒsɪdʒ]
würzig *(scharf gewürzt)* spicy [ˈspaɪsi]
wütend (über etwas/auf jn.) angry (about sth./with sb.) [ˈæŋgri]

Y

Yoga yoga [ˈjəʊgə]

Z

Zahl number [ˈnʌmbə]
zählen count [kaʊnt]
Zahn tooth [tuːθ], *pl* teeth [tiːθ] • **Ich putze mir die Zähne.** I clean my teeth.
Zahnschmerzen toothache [ˈtuːθeɪk]

zanken; sich zanken argue [ˈɑːgjuː]
Zauberkunststück trick [trɪk] • **Zauberkunststücke machen** do tricks
Zebra zebra [ˈzebrə]
Zeh toe [təʊ]
Zeichen *(Schild)* sign [saɪn]
zeichnen draw [drɔː]
Zeichnung drawing [ˈdrɔːɪŋ]
zeigen show [ʃəʊ] • **auf etwas zeigen** point at/to sth. [pɔɪnt]
Zeile line [laɪn]
Zeit time [taɪm]; *(grammatische Zeit, Tempus)* **tense** [tens] • **Zeit verbringen (mit)** spend time (on) [spend]
Zeitschrift magazine [ˌmægəˈziːn]
Zeitung newspaper [ˈnjuːspeɪpə]; paper [ˈpeɪpə]
Zeitungsartikel article [ˈɑːtɪkl]
zelten camp [kæmp]
Zentimeter centimetre (cm) [ˈsentɪmiːtə]
Zentral- *(Mittel-)* central [ˈsentrəl]
Zentrum centre [ˈsentə]
zerbrochen broken [ˈbrəʊkən]
zerstören destroy [dɪˈstrɔɪ]
Zeug *(Kram)* stuff [stʌf]
ziehen pull [pʊl]
ziemlich gut pretty good [ˈprɪti]; quite good [kwaɪt]
Ziffer number [ˈnʌmbə]
Zimmer room [ruːm, rʊm]
Zitrone lemon [ˈlemən]
zu 1. *(örtlich)* to [tə, tu] • **zu Jenny** to Jenny's • **zu Hause** at home **zum Arzt** to the doctor's • **Setz dich zu mir.** Sit with me. • **auf jn./etwas zu** towards sb./sth. [təˈwɔːdz]
2. zum Beispiel for example [fərˌɪgˈzɑːmpl] • **zum Frühstück/Mittagessen/Abendbrot** for breakfast/lunch/dinner [fə, fɔː]
zum Schluss in the end

3. zu viel too much [tuː] • **zu spät sein/kommen** be late
4. versuchen zu tun try and do / try to do
5. *(geschlossen)* closed [kləʊzd]
zubereiten *(kochen)* cook [kʊk]
Zucker sugar [ˈʃʊgə]
zuerst first [fɜːst]
Zug train [treɪn] • **im Zug** on the train
Zuhause home [həʊm]
zuhören listen (to) [ˈlɪsn]
Zuhörer/in listener [ˈlɪsnə] • **Zuhörer/innen** *(Publikum)* audience [ˈɔːdɪəns]
zulassen, dass jd. etwas tut *(erlauben)* let sb. do sth. [let]
zum *siehe „zu"*
zumachen close [kləʊz]
zumindest at least [ət ˈliːst]
zurück (nach) back (to) [bæk]
zurücklassen leave [liːv]
zusammen together [təˈgeðə]
zusammenpassen, -gehören go together
zusätzlich extra [ˈekstrə]
Zuschauer/innen *(Publikum)* audience [ˈɔːdɪəns]
zusehen watch [wɒtʃ]
zustimmen: jm./etwas zustimmen agree with sb./sth. [əˈgriː] • **nicht zustimmen** disagree with [ˌdɪsəˈgriː]
zuwenden: sich jm. zuwenden turn to sb. [tɜːn]
zwanglos *(entspannt)* relaxed [rɪˈlækst]
zweimal twice [twaɪs]
zweite(r, s) second [ˈsekənd]
Zwiebel onion [ˈʌnjən]
Zwillinge twins *(pl)* [twɪnz]
Zwillingsbruder twin brother [ˈtwɪn ˌbrʌðə]
zwischen between [bɪˈtwiːn]

First names
(Vornamen)

Alexander [ˌælɪgˈzɑːndə]
Alice [ˈælɪs]
Alisha [əˈlɪʃə]
Alison [ˈælɪsn]
Alistair [ˈælɪstə]
Andy [ˈændi]
Annabel [ˈænəbel]
Arthur [ˈɑːθə]
Ashley [ˈæʃli]
Asif [æˈsiːf]
Avril [ˈævrɪl]
Ben [ben]
Bonnie [ˈbɒni]
Charlene [ʃɑːˈliːn]
Charlie [ˈtʃɑːli]
Conan [ˈkəʊnən]
Daniel [ˈdænjəl]
Dermot [ˈdɜːmət]
Diana [daɪˈænə]
Dylan [ˈdɪlən]
Elizabeth [ɪˈlɪzəbəθ]
Elvis [ˈelvɪs]
Emily [ˈeməli]
Emma [ˈemə]
Ewan [ˈjuːən]
Faith [feɪθ]
Fiona [fiˈəʊnə]
Fred [fred]
George [dʒɔːdʒ]
Giles [dʒaɪlz]
Grace [greɪs]
Graham [ˈgreɪəm]
Guy [gaɪ]
Hassan [həˈsɑːn]
Helen [ˈhelən]
Holly [ˈhɒli]
Jake [dʒeɪk]
James [dʒeɪmz]
Jamie [ˈdʒeɪmi]
Jaz [dʒæz]

Jenny [ˈdʒeni]
Jessica [ˈdʒesɪkə]
Jill [dʒɪl]
Joe [dʒəʊ]
John [dʒɒn]
Jonathan [ˈdʒɒnəθən]
Jordan [ˈdʒɔːdn]
Julie [ˈdʒuːli]
Kahasi [kəˈhɑːʃi]
Karen [ˈkærən]
Katie [ˈkeɪti]
Katrina [kəˈtriːnə]
Kaz [kæz]
Keira [ˈkɪərə]
Kelly [ˈkeli]
Ketevan [ˌketəˈvɑːn]
Latisha [ləˈtɪʃə]
Linda [ˈlɪndə]
Liz [lɪz]
Lucy [ˈluːsi]
Madonna [məˈdɒnə]
Marc [mɑːk]
Michael [ˈmaɪkəl]
Mika [ˈmiːkə]
Mitsu [ˈmɪtsuː]
Natalie [ˈnætəli]
Nathan [ˈneɪθən]
Pamela [ˈpæmələ]
Pat [pæt]
Paul [pɔːl]
Peter [ˈpiːtə]
Petunia [pəˈtjuːniə]
Phil [fɪl]
Robbie [ˈrɒbi]
Robert [ˈrɒbət]
Sam [sæm]
Samantha [səˈmænθə]
Sandra [ˈsɑːndrə]
Sarah [ˈseərə]
Sean [ʃɔːn]
Shakira [ʃəˈkɪərə]
Shania [ʃəˈnaɪə]

Shaz [ʃæz]
Sheena [ˈʃiːnə]
Sue [suː]
Tommy [ˈtɒmi]
Walter [ˈwɔːltə]
Wayne [weɪn]
Will [wɪl]
Winston [ˈwɪnstən]

Family names
(Familiennamen)

Bale [beɪl]
Bell [bel]
Brown [braʊn]
Burns [bɜːnz]
Byrd [bɜːd]
Cabot [ˈkæbət]
Cartwright [ˈkɑːtraɪt]
Collins [ˈkɒlɪnz]
Connery [ˈkɒnəri]
Cookson [ˈkʊksn]
Cooper [ˈkuːpə]
Costelloe [kɒˈsteləʊ]
Craig [kreɪg]
Devlin [ˈdevlɪn]
Doyle [dɔɪl]
Fagan [ˈfeɪgən]
Fawkes [fɔːks]
Fleming [ˈflemɪŋ]
Franks [fræŋks]
Gabriel [ˈgeɪbriəl]
Gordon [ˈgɔːdn]
Holmes [həʊmz]
Hooley [ˈhuːli]
Jones [ˈdʒəʊnz]
Kelly [ˈkeli]
Knightley [ˈnaɪtli]
Kowalski [kəˈwɒlski]
Lavigne [læˈviːn]
Lowry [ˈlaʊri]
MacKay [məˈkaɪ]
McDonald [məkˈdɒnld]

List of names   **227**

McFadden [mək'fædn]
McGregor [mə'gregə]
McNamara [ˌmæknə'mɑːrə]
Melua ['meluə]
Nagora ['nægərɑː]
O'Keefe [əʊ'kiːf]
Parsons ['pɑːsnz]
Parker ['pɑːkə]
Penniman ['penɪmən]
Perry ['peri]
Peterson ['piːtəsən]
Potter ['pɒtə]
Presley ['prezli]
Raleigh ['rɔːli]
Rowling ['rəʊlɪŋ]
Shakespeare ['ʃeɪkspɪə]
Stephens ['stiːvnz]
Tilley ['tɪli]
Tonkins ['tɒŋkɪnz]
Twain [tweɪn]
Waites [weɪts]
Watson ['wɒtsn]
Watt [wɒt]
Wilkes [wɪlks]
Williams ['wɪljəmz]

Place names
(Ortsnamen)

Aberdeen [ˌæbə'diːn]
Albert Street ['ælbət striːt]
Aldgate East [ˌɔːldgeɪt_'iːst]
The Atlantic [ət'læntɪk]
Batumi [bɑː'tuːmi]
Beirut [beɪ'ruːt]
Belfast [ˌbel'fɑːst]
Berlin [bɜː'lɪn]
Birmingham ['bɜːmɪŋəm]
Bond Street [bɒnd striːt]
Burslem ['bɜːsləm]
Camden Lock [ˌkæmdən 'lɒk]
Chapleau ['ʃæpləʊ]
Chelsea ['tʃelsi]

Cornwall ['kɔːnwɔːl]
Covent Garden [ˌkɒvənt 'gɑːdn]
Edinburgh ['edɪnbərə]
Flotta ['flɒtə]
Glasgow ['glæzgəʊ, 'glɑːzgəʊ]
Gretna Green [ˌgretnə 'griːn]
Houton ['huːtn]
Hoy [hɔɪ]
Hyde Park [ˌhaɪd 'pɑːk]
Kirkwall ['kɜːkwɔːl]
Kutaisi [ˌkʊtə'iːsi]
Loch Ness [lɒx 'nes]
London ['lʌndən]
The Lowry ['laʊri]
Lyness ['laɪnes]
Majorca [mə'jɔːkə]
Manchester ['mæntʃestə]
Manchester Aquatics Centre
  [ˌmæntʃestər_ə'kwætɪks ˌsentə]
Melbourne ['melbən]
Missinaibi Lake [ˌmɪsɪ'neɪbi 'leɪk]
Moaness ['məʊnes]
Montreal [ˌmɒntri'ɔːl]
Nelson's Column [ˌnelsnz 'kɒləm]
Newcastle-under-Lyme
  [ˌnjuːkɑːsəl_ˌʌndə 'laɪm]
Newfoundland ['njuːfəndlənd]
Nunavut ['nuːnəvuːt]
Old Trafford [ˌəʊld 'træfəd]
Ontario [ɒn'teəriəʊ]
The Orkney Islands ['ɔːkni_ˌaɪləndz]
Ottawa ['ɒtəwə]
Paris ['pærɪs]
Port of Spain [ˌpɔːt_əv 'speɪn]
Portobello Road [ˌpɔːtəʊbeləʊ 'rəʊd]
Princes Street ['prɪnsəz striːt]
Pudding Lane [ˌpʊdɪŋ 'leɪn]
Quebec [kwɪ'bek]
Queensway ['kwiːnzweɪ]
Redhill [ˌred'hɪl]
Richmond ['rɪtʃmənd]
The River Thames [ˌrɪvə 'temz]

Rochdale ['rɒtʃdeɪl]
San Francisco [ˌsæn frən'sɪskəʊ]
Staffordshire ['stæfədʃə]
Stoke-on-Trent [ˌstəʊk_ɒn 'trent]
Stromness ['strɒmnes]
Tbilisi [tə'bliːsi]
Toronto [tə'rɒntəʊ]
Tower Hamlets [ˌtaʊə 'hæmləts]
Tower Hill [ˌtaʊə 'hɪl]
The Tower of London
  [ˌtaʊər_əv 'lʌndən]
Trocadero [ˌtrɒkə'dɪərəʊ]
Turin [ˌtjʊə'rɪn]
Velodrome ['velədrəʊm]
Victoria Station [vɪkˌtɔːriə 'steɪʃn]
Waterloo [ˌwɔːtə'luː]
Westminster ['westmɪnstə]

Other names
(Andere Namen)

The Beatles ['biːtlz]
The Big Issue [ˌbɪg_'ɪʃuː]
Celtic F. C. ['seltɪk]
The Central Line ['sentrəl ˌlaɪn]
The Docklands Light Railway
  (DLR) [ˌdɒkləndz ˌlaɪt 'reɪlweɪ]
Global Deejays [ˌgləʊbl 'diːdʒeɪz]
The Highland Games [ˌhaɪlənd 'geɪmz]
The Jubilee Line ['dʒuːbɪli: ˌlaɪn]
The Lovin' Spoonful [ˌlʌvɪn 'spuːnfʊl]
The Maple Leafs [ˌmeɪpl 'liːfs]
Maroon 5 [məˌruːn 'faɪv]
Nessie ['nesi]
Rangers ['reɪndʒəz]
Traitor's Gate [ˌtreɪtəz 'geɪt]

Countries and continents

Country/Continent	Adjective	Person	People
Africa ['æfrɪkə] *Afrika*	African ['æfrɪkən]	an African	the Africans
America [ə'merɪkə] *Amerika*	American [ə'merɪkən]	an American	the Americans
Asia ['eɪʃə, 'eɪʒə] *Asien*	Asian ['eɪʃn, 'eɪʒn]	an Asian	the Asians
Australia [ɒ'streɪliə] *Australien*	Australian [ɒ'streɪliən]	an Australian	the Australians
Austria ['ɒstriə] *Österreich*	Austrian ['ɒstriən]	an Austrian	the Austrians
Bangladesh [ˌbæŋglə'deʃ] *Bangladesch*	Bangladeshi [ˌbæŋglə'deʃi]	a Bangladeshi	the Bangladeshis
Belgium ['beldʒəm] *Belgien*	Belgian ['beldʒən]	a Belgian	the Belgians
Canada ['kænədə] *Kanada*	Canadian [kə'neɪdiən]	a Canadian	the Canadians
the Caribbean [ˌkærə'bi:ən] *die Karibik*	Caribbean [ˌkærə'bi:ən]	a Caribbean	the Caribbeans
China ['tʃaɪnə] *China*	Chinese [ˌtʃaɪ'ni:z]	a Chinese	the Chinese
Colombia [kə'lɒmbiə] *Kolumbien*	Colombian [kə'lɒmbiən]	a Colombian	the Colombians
Croatia [krəʊ'eɪʃə] *Kroatien*	Croatian [krəʊ'eɪʃn]	a Croatian	the Croatians
the Czech Republic [ˌtʃek rɪ'pʌblɪk] *Tschechien, die Tschechische Republik*	Czech [tʃek]	a Czech	the Czechs
Denmark ['denmɑ:k] *Dänemark*	Danish ['deɪnɪʃ]	a Dane [deɪn]	the Danes
England ['ɪŋglənd] *England*	English ['ɪŋglɪʃ]	an Englishman/-woman	the English
Europe ['jʊərəp] *Europa*	European [ˌjʊərə'pi:ən]	a European	the Europeans
Finland ['fɪnlənd] *Finnland*	Finnish ['fɪnɪʃ]	a Finn [fɪn]	the Finns
France [frɑ:ns] *Frankreich*	French [frentʃ]	a Frenchman/-woman	the French
Georgia ['dʒɔ:dʒə] *Georgien*	Georgian ['dʒɔ:dʒən]	a Georgian	the Georgians
Germany ['dʒɜ:məni] *Deutschland*	German ['dʒɜ:mən]	a German	the Germans
(Great) Britain ['brɪtn] *Großbritannien*	British ['brɪtɪʃ]	a Briton ['brɪtn]	the British
Greece [gri:s] *Griechenland*	Greek [gri:k]	a Greek	the Greeks
Holland ['hɒlənd] *Holland, die Niederlande*	Dutch [dʌtʃ]	a Dutchman/-woman	the Dutch
Hungary ['hʌŋgəri] *Ungarn*	Hungarian [hʌŋ'geəriən]	a Hungarian	the Hungarians
India ['ɪndiə] *Indien*	Indian ['ɪndiən]	an Indian	the Indians
Iran [ɪ'rɑ:n, ɪ'ræn] *Iran*	Iranian [ɪ'reɪniən]	a Iranian	the Iranians
Ireland ['aɪələnd] *Irland*	Irish ['aɪrɪʃ]	an Irishman/-woman	the Irish
Italy ['ɪtəli] *Italien*	Italian [ɪ'tæliən]	an Italian	the Italians
Japan [dʒə'pæn] *Japan*	Japanese [ˌdʒæpə'ni:z]	a Japanese	the Japanese
Lebanon ['lebənən] *Libanon*	Lebanese [ˌlebə'ni:z]	a Lebanese	the Lebanese
the Netherlands ['neðələndz] *die Niederlande, Holland*	Dutch [dʌtʃ]	a Dutchman/-woman	the Dutch
New Zealand [ˌnju: 'zi:lənd] *Neuseeland*	New Zealand [ˌnju: 'zi:lənd]	a New Zealander	the New Zealanders
Norway ['nɔ:weɪ] *Norwegen*	Norwegian [nɔ:'wi:dʒən]	a Norwegian	the Norwegians
Pakistan [ˌpækɪ'stæn, ˌpɑ:kɪ'stɑ:n] *Pakistan*	Pakistani [ˌpækɪ'stæni, ˌpɑ:kɪ'stɑ:ni]	a Pakistani	the Pakistanis
Poland ['pəʊlənd] *Polen*	Polish ['pəʊlɪʃ]	a Pole [pəʊl]	the Poles
Portugal ['pɔ:tʃʊgl] *Portugal*	Portuguese [ˌpɔ:tʃʊ'gi:z]	a Portuguese	the Portuguese
Russia ['rʌʃə] *Russland*	Russian ['rʌʃn]	a Russian	the Russians
Scotland ['skɒtlənd] *Schottland*	Scottish ['skɒtɪʃ]	a Scotsman/-woman, a Scot [skɒt]	the Scots, the Scottish
Slovakia [sləʊ'vɑ:kiə, sləʊ'vækiə] *die Slowakei*	Slovak ['sləʊvæk]	a Slovak	the Slovaks
Slovenia [sləʊ'vi:niə] *Slowenien*	Slovenian [sləʊ'vi:niən], Slovene ['sləʊvi:n]	a Slovene, a Slovenian	the Slovenes, the Slovenians
South Africa [ˌsaʊθ 'æfrɪkə] *Südafrika*	South African [ˌsaʊθ 'æfrɪkn]	South African	the South Africans
Spain [speɪn] *Spanien*	Spanish ['spænɪʃ]	a Spaniard ['spænɪəd]	the Spaniards
Sweden ['swi:dn] *Schweden*	Swedish ['swi:dɪʃ]	a Swede [swi:d]	the Swedes
Switzerland ['swɪtsələnd] *die Schweiz*	Swiss [swɪs]	a Swiss	the Swiss
Turkey ['tɜ:ki] *die Türkei*	Turkish ['tɜ:kɪʃ]	a Turk [tɜ:k]	the Turks
the United Kingdom (the UK) [juˌnaɪtɪd 'kɪŋdəm, ju:'keɪ] *das Vereinigte Königreich (Großbritannien und Nordirland)*	British ['brɪtɪʃ]	a Briton ['brɪtn]	the British
the United States of America (the USA) [juˌnaɪtɪd ˌsteɪts_əv_ə'merɪkə, ju:_es_'eɪ] *die Vereinigten Staaten von Amerika*	American [ə'merɪkən]	an American	the Americans
Wales [weɪlz] *Wales*	Welsh [welʃ]	a Welshman/-woman	the Welsh

English sounds (Englische Laute)

Die Lautschrift in den eckigen Klammern zeigt dir, wie ein Wort ausgesprochen wird.
In der folgenden Übersicht findest du alle Lautzeichen.

Vokale (Selbstlaute)				Konsonanten (Mitlaute)			
[iː]	green	[eɪ]	skate	[b]	box	[f]	full
[i]	happy	[aɪ]	time	[p]	play	[v]	very
[ɪ]	in	[ɔɪ]	boy	[d]	dad	[s]	sister
[e]	yes	[əʊ]	old	[t]	ten	[z]	please
[æ]	black	[aʊ]	now	[g]	good	[ʃ]	shop
[ɑː]	park	[ɪə]	here	[k]	cat	[ʒ]	television
[ɒ]	song	[eə]	where	[m]	mum	[tʃ]	teacher
[ɔː]	morning	[ʊə]	tour	[n]	no	[dʒ]	Germany
[uː]	blue			[ŋ]	sing	[θ]	thanks
[ʊ]	book			[l]	hello	[ð]	this
[ʌ]	mum			[r]	red	[h]	he
[ɜː]	T-shirt			[w]	we		
[ə]	a partner			[j]	you		

The English alphabet (Das englische Alphabet)

a	[eɪ]	h	[eɪtʃ]	o	[əʊ]	v	[viː]
b	[biː]	i	[aɪ]	p	[piː]	w	['dʌbljuː]
c	[siː]	j	[dʒeɪ]	q	[kjuː]	x	[eks]
d	[diː]	k	[keɪ]	r	[ɑː]	y	[waɪ]
e	[iː]	l	[el]	s	[es]	z	[zed]
f	[ef]	m	[em]	t	[tiː]		
g	[dʒiː]	n	[en]	u	[juː]		

Irregular verbs

Infinitive	Simple past form	Past participle	
(to) **be**	**was/were**	**been**	sein
(to) **beat**	**beat**	**beaten**	schlagen; besiegen
(to) **become**	**became**	**become**	werden
(to) **begin**	**began**	**begun**	beginnen, anfangen (mit)
(to) **blow**	**blew**	**blown**	wehen, blasen
(to) **break** a journey	**broke**	**broken**	eine Reise unterbrechen
(to) **bring**	**brought**	**brought**	(mit-, her)bringen
(to) **build**	**built**	**built**	bauen
(to) **buy**	**bought**	**bought**	kaufen
(to) **catch**	**caught**	**caught**	fangen; erwischen
(to) **choose** [u:]	**chose** [əʊ]	**chosen** [əʊ]	(aus)wählen; (sich) aussuchen
(to) **come**	**came**	**come**	kommen
(to) **cut**	**cut**	**cut**	schneiden
(to) **do**	**did**	**done** [ʌ]	tun, machen
(to) **draw**	**drew**	**drawn**	zeichnen
(to) **drink**	**drank**	**drunk**	trinken
(to) **drive** [aɪ]	**drove**	**driven** [ɪ]	(ein Auto) fahren
(to) **eat**	**ate** [et, eɪt]	**eaten**	essen
(to) **fall**	**fell**	**fallen**	(hin)fallen, stürzen
(to) **feed**	**fed**	**fed**	füttern
(to) **feel**	**felt**	**felt**	(sich) fühlen; sich anfühlen
(to) **fight**	**fought**	**fought**	kämpfen
(to) **find**	**found**	**found**	finden
(to) **fly**	**flew**	**flown**	fliegen
(to) **forget**	**forgot**	**forgotten**	vergessen
(to) **get**	**got**	**got**	bekommen; holen; werden; (hin)kommen
(to) **give**	**gave**	**given**	geben
(to) **go**	**went**	**gone** [ɒ]	gehen, fahren
(to) **grow**	**grew**	**grown**	wachsen; anbauen, anpflanzen
(to) **hang out** *(infml)*	**hung out**	**hung out**	rumhängen, abhängen
(to) **have (have got)**	**had**	**had**	haben, besitzen
(to) **hear** [ɪə]	**heard** [ɜː]	**heard** [ɜː]	hören
(to) **hide** [aɪ]	**hid** [ɪ]	**hidden** [ɪ]	(sich) verstecken
(to) **hit**	**hit**	**hit**	schlagen
(to) **hold**	**held**	**held**	halten
(to) **hurt**	**hurt**	**hurt**	wehtun; verletzen
(to) **keep**	**kept**	**kept**	(be)halten
(to) **know** [nəʊ]	**knew** [njuː]	**known** [nəʊn]	wissen; kennen
(to) **lay** the table	**laid**	**laid**	den Tisch decken
(to) **leave**	**left**	**left**	(weg)gehen; abfahren; verlassen; zurücklassen

Irregular verbs 231

Infinitive	Simple past form	Past participle	
(to) let	let	let	lassen
(to) lose [uː]	lost [ɒ]	lost [ɒ]	verlieren
(to) make	made	made	machen; bauen; bilden
(to) mean [iː]	meant [e]	meant [e]	bedeuten; meinen
(to) meet	met	met	(sich) treffen
(to) pay	paid	paid	bezahlen
(to) put	put	put	legen, stellen, *(wohin)* tun
(to) read [iː]	read [e]	read [e]	lesen
(to) ride [aɪ]	rode	ridden [ɪ]	reiten; *(Rad)* fahren
(to) ring	rang	rung	klingeln, läuten
(to) run	ran	run	rennen, laufen
(to) say [eɪ]	said [e]	said [e]	sagen
(to) see	saw	seen	sehen; besuchen, aufsuchen
(to) sell	sold	sold	verkaufen
(to) send	sent	sent	schicken, senden
(to) shine	shone [ɒ]	shone [ɒ]	scheinen *(Sonne)*
(to) shoot [uː]	shot	shot	schießen, erschießen
(to) show	showed	shown	zeigen
(to) shut up	shut	shut	den Mund halten
(to) sing	sang	sung	singen
(to) sit	sat	sat	sitzen; sich setzen
(to) sleep	slept	slept	schlafen
(to) speak	spoke	spoken	sprechen
(to) spend	spent	spent	*(Zeit)* verbringen; *(Geld)* ausgeben
(to) stand	stood	stood	stehen; sich (hin)stellen
(to) steal	stole	stolen	stehlen
(to) stick	stuck	stuck	herausragen, herausstehen
(to) swim	swam	swum	schwimmen
(to) take	took	taken	nehmen; (weg-, hin)bringen; dauern, *(Zeit)* brauchen
(to) teach	taught	taught	unterrichten, lehren
(to) tell	told	told	erzählen, berichten
(to) think	thought	thought	denken, glauben, meinen
(to) throw	threw	thrown	werfen
(to) understand	understood	understood	verstehen
(to) upset	upset	upset	ärgern, kränken, aus der Fassung bringen
(to) wake up	woke	woken	aufwachen; wecken
(to) wear [eə]	wore [ɔː]	worn [ɔː]	tragen *(Kleidung)*
(to) win	won [ʌ]	won [ʌ]	gewinnen
(to) write	wrote	written	schreiben

232 ❓ How am I doing?

Key to the self-assessment tests

Unit 1 ▶ *How am I doing? (p. 29)*

1 Thames
2 Tube
3 Tower Bridge
4 Piccadilly Circus
5 Buckingham Palace
6 **A** ticket
7 **C** get
8 **A** change
9 **B** vegetable

10 **C** onion
11 **B** so
12 **A** After I spoke to the teacher, I tried to work harder.
13 **A** I don't usually like food from different countries, but I liked the food at the Bangladeshi café.
14 **C** Dear Dora

15 **B** went, was
16 **C** took
17 **A** has been
18 **C** Yes, I have.
19 **B** haven't done
20 **D** How long does the journey take?
21 **B** What platform do I need for the train to Bath?

Unit 2 ▶ *How am I doing? (p. 47)*

1 Orkney Islands
2 capital
3 salmon
4 dance/play the fiddle
5 rock
6 **C** car park
7 **B** mountain
8 **B** text message

9 **C** cook dinner
10 **C** Text me when you're back.
11 **B** funktionieren
12 **C** If my brother goes to the party, I will stay at home.
13 **A** If kids in my class were horrible to me, I would tell my teacher.

14 **B** If I was in my best friend's class, I would be happy.
15 **B** speaking
16 **A** message

Unit 3 ▶ *How am I doing? (p. 67)*

1 the steel drum
2 the Lowry
3 Old Trafford
4 Nathan Stephens
5 **C** dinner
6 **D**
7 **B** Berlin.
8 **D**
9 **C** supporter

10 **D** sports hall
11 **1** tennis – **D** court
 2 ice hockey – **C** ice rink
 3 football – **A** pitch
 4 skiing – **B** slope
12 **A** draw
13 **1** living room – **B** armchair
 2 bathroom – **C** shower
 3 bedroom – **A** wardrobe

14 **D** lift
15 **C** who
16 that I want to visit.
17 **B** Most students like Frau Marx.

Unit 4 ▶ *How am I doing? (p. 83)*

1 Ottawa / Toronto
2 snowshoeing, canoeing, hunting, ice hockey
3 singer
4 province
5 **C** per cent
6 **B** easy-going
7 **B** relaxed

8 **C** point
9 **D** blame
10 **A** from
11 **B** lyrics
12 brainstorm ideas, write the text and finally check and revise it.
13 in a list or a mind map
14 adjectives and adverbs/linking words

15 **D** am not allowed to
16 **C** be able to
17 **B** have to
18 **C** is doing
19 John was talking to himself but ...
20 Sam and Robert took photos of each other.

How am I doing?

Key to the self-assessment tests

Unit 1–5 ▸ How am I doing? (p. 100)

1 Scotland, Wales   2 points
2 London, Thames   2 points
3 underground/Tube   1 point
4 Scotland   1 point
5 Manchester   1 point
6 airport, bridge, bus, bus stop, car, driver, harbour, helicopter, lorry, northbound, plane, platform, road, river, sea, ship, station, taxi, tram, Travelcard, Tube, map, tunnel, underground, … ;
   word field: transport
   1 point for three or more words,
   1 point for the name of the word field
7 phone calls, text messages, instant messages, video, DVD, logo, ringtone, computer, games, mix music, chat, internet, …;
   word field: electronic media
   1 point for three or more words,
   1 point for the name of the word field
8 castle, cathedral, church, department store, hotel, lake, market, palace, park, post office, pub, river, station, street, supermarket, tower, town/city centre, …;
   word field: town/city
   1 point for three or more words,
   1 point for the name of the word field
9 football, handball, rugby, tennis, hockey, basketball, court, pitch, half-pipe, pool, bridle path, ski slope, sports hall, running track, badminton racket, table tennis bat, skis, skates and pads, saddle, swimsuit, swimming trunks, running shoes, … ;
   word field: sport
   1 point for three or more words,
   1 point for the name of the word field
10 guitar, steel drum, violin, piano, recorder, flute, trumpet, classical music, folk music, rap, jazz, open-air concert, dance, workshop, album, single, CD player, choir, chorus, lyrics, MP3 player, …;
   word field: music
   1 point for three or more words,
   1 point for the name of the word field

11 bay, canal, castle, cliff, rock, cow, coast, farmhouse, farmer, field, forest, hill, wood, lake, mountain, river, valley, sheep, …;
   word field: country
   1 point for three or more words,
   1 point for the name of the word field
12 scan   1 point
13 skim   1 point
14 paraphrase   1 point
15 brainstorm   1 point
16 topic sentence/first sentence   1 point
17 linking words   1 point
18 who, what, when, where, why;
   you can use them to write a report
   1 point for all 5 Ws,
   1 point for saying what you can use them for
19 Text genau lesen / Wörterbuch nutzen / Rechtschreibregeln beachten / Persönliche Checkliste für häufige Fehler führen
   1 point for one of these answers
20 If you were in London now, what would you want to do?   1 point
21 If we go in May, I won't be able to go with them.   1 point
22 I knew the girl who was hurt in the accident.   1 point
23 I haven't read the book (that) the teacher gave us.   1 point
24 a) The film was very exciting. It was about two spies who were trying to catch each other.   1 point
    b) My sister and I aren't allowed to ride our bikes in the street because my mum is afraid we'll hurt ourselves.   1 point
    c) I felt ill and stayed at home.   1 point
    d) In three years I will be able to speak English better.   1 point

Illustrationen

Roland Beier, Berlin (S. 17 oben und Mitte; S. 18; S. 20; S. 23 oben; S. 24 (u. 107); S. 25; S. 29; S. 38; S. 43 li.; S. 47; S. 50; S. 60 unten; S. 63–64; S. 67; S. 77 (u. 112); S. 79 oben (u. 113); S. 83; S. 91 unten; S. 93; S. 95 (u. 113); S. 100; S. 128–129 (u. 114); S. 134–180); **Carlos Borrell**, Berlin (vordere u. hintere Umschlaginnenseite; S. 6 (u. 52); S. 17 unten re.; S. 30; S. 43 re. (u. 102); S. 74); **Graham-Cameron Illustrations**, UK: **Fliss Cary** (S. 23 unten; S. 26–28; S. 34; S. 39; S. 42 (u. 108); S. 44–46; S. 54; S. 61–62; S. 71; S. 78; S. 79 unten; S. 82; S. 99; S. 101); **John Rabou** (S. 48; S. 51); **Stella Ludin/Aksinia Raphael**, Berlin (S. 60 oben; S. 103); **Linda Rogers Associates**, London: **Gary Rees** (S. 117 (u. 114); **Michael Teßmer**, Berlin (S. 121 (u. 114)); **Korinna Wilkes**, Berlin (S.91 oben; S. 120)

Bildquellen

action press, Hamburg (S. 53 trainers: ALTERPHOTOS; S. 62 Bild 3: Everett Collection, Inc.; S. 92 Bild 1: Action / Zuma Press Inc.; S. 96 oben: All Action, unten: Rex Features Ltd.; S. 97: Wolfgang List; S. 98 oben: 2Vista); S. 141: ALL ACTION DIGITAL; **akg images**, Berlin (S. 75 oben re.: Johann Brandste; Alamy, Abingdon (Inhaltsverz. bear (u. 127): ImageState/Rosemary Calvert; S. 6 (u. 52) unten re.: Paul Doyle, oben Mitte: The Photolibrary Wales, unten Mitte: Photofusion Picture Library/Vehbi Koca; S. 12 Bild 1: Peter Barritt, Bild 2: Ernst Wrba, Bild 3: TNT MAGAZINE; S. 13 Bild 4: Keith Erskine, Bild 5: Caroline Cortizo; S. 15 Bild B: Kevin Allen, Bild C: Richard Cooke; S. 16 road sign: Alice de Maria, oben: Christopher Pillitz; S. 18 Mitte: PCL/picturescolourlibrary; S. 19 oben li. (u. 142): The Print Collector; Mitte: Alex Beaton; S. 20: Brand X Pictures/Burke/Triolo Productions; S. 21 unten (u. 106): Jeremy Hoare; S. 22 oben: Robert Harding Picture; S. 25 Bild A: imagestopshop, Bild B: Stan Kujawa, Bild C: Trevor Smith; S. 30 Bild 1 u. 3: orkneypics; S. 31 Bild 6: Doug Houghton, lamb and sheep: Suzy Bennett, sheep: orkneypics; S. 36 unten li.: Ingram Publishing (Superstock Limited); S. 37 Mitte: Malcolm Fife; S. 40 oben: Worldwide Picture Library/Hugh Webster; Mitte: Robert Harding Picture Library Ltd/Michael Jenner; S. 57 unten (u. 122): artpartner-images.com; S. 61 (u. 110): Eric Nathan; S. 62 Bild 2: UKraft; S. 68 Bild A: DigitalVues, Bild B (M): Chris Cheadle, Bild C background (M): Robert Estall photo agency, girl (M): JUPITERIMAGES/Comstock Images, Bild D: image100, Bild F: Steve Skjold; S. 70 Mitte li.: Geoff du Feu, unten li.: david sanger photography/davidsanger.com, unten re.: RubberBall; S. 72 li.: Alaska Stock LLC: C&C Bear Imagery; S. 74 unten li.: Alaska Stock LLC, unten re.: Elvele Images/Fritz Poelking; S. 75 oben li.: Robert McGouey; S. 76 unten: ACE STOCK LTD; S. 78: RubberBall; S. 80 oben li. u. Mitte li.: Content Mine International, unten: Gary Cook; S. 81 re.: Helene Rogers, li.: Arco Images; S. 88 hat: Bill Brooks; S. 91 oben u. unten li.: Lebrecht Music and Arts Photo Library/Chris Stock/Lebrecht; S. 92 Bild 4: JUPITERIMAGES/Creatas; S. 99 Daniel Radcliffe portrait: All Star Picture Library; S. 104 unten li. u. re.: George S de Blonsky; S. 127 oben (u. 114): Wolfgang Kaehler, unten re.: david tipling; S. 130 unten: Hugh Threlfall; S. 132 video game character (M): JUPITERIMAGES/Brand X/Colin Anderson, unten: Andrew Woodley; **ATW Photography**, Hitchin (S. 120 unten (u. 114)); **Avenue Images**, Hamburg (S. 15 Bild A: Index Stock/David Ball); **A1PIX**, Taufkirchen (S. 65 unten li. (u. 111)); **Bildmaschine.de**, Berlin (S. 92 Bild 5: Peter Engelke); **John Birdsall Social Issues Photolibrary**, Nottingham (Inhaltsverz. kids; S. 7–11; S. 15 (u. 138) Bild D foreground (M); S. 16 Mitte; S. 33 oben; S. 35; S. 52 portrait (u. 53); S. 54–55; S. 56 unten; S. 70 oben li.; S. 73 oben; S. 88–89 kids; S. 90 Latisha); **Blickwinkel**, Witten (S. 31 bird: H.J. Igelmund); **Britain on View**, London (S. 15 (u. 138) Bild D background (M): Nigel Hicks; S. 18 unten re.: www.britainonview.

com; S. 31 Bild 5: Joe Cornish; S. 40 unten: www.britainonview. com); **Cinetext Bildarchiv**, Frankfurt/Main (S. 133(M)); **Corbis**, Düsseldorf (Inhaltsverz. u. 15) Tower Bridge: Angelo Hornak; S. 6 (u. 52) oben li.: Jeremy Horner; S. 18 oben: Toby Melville/Reuters; S. 19 oben re.: Bill Varie; S. 37 oben: Roger Ressmeyer; S. 69 Bild G: Graham Bell, Bild H: Dale C. Spartas, Bild I: Layne Kennedy; S. 70 oben re.: Ajax/zefa; S. 71: Annie Griffiths Belt; S. 72 re.: Dale C. Spartas; S. 75 Mitte re.: Aristide Economopoulos/Star Ledger; S. 85: David Muench; S. 86: James Marshall; S. 95: Comstock; S. 99 Rupert Grint: Phil McCarten/Reuters); **Corel Library** (Inhaltsverz. Hoy); **defd Deutscher Fotodienst**, Hamburg (S. 94 Shrek); **Barbara Derkow Disselbeck**, Köln (S. 32); Digitalstock, Wangen/Markgröningen (S. 65 (u. 111) unten re.); **DK Images**, London (S. 120 oben: Dave King); **Ecopix**, Berlin (S. 22 unten: Beate Weingartner); **Edinburgh Festival Fringe Society**, Edinburgh (S. 37 unten re.); **Erzgebirgische Volkskunst Richard Glässer GmbH**, Kurort Seiffen (S. 65 (u. 111) Mitte angel); **Gareth Evans**, Berlin (S. 41); **fabfoodpix. com**, London (S. 36 Mitte re.); **Fotosearch**, Waukesha (S. 66 boots: Brand X Pictures); Getty Images, München (S. 36 Mitte: Rubberball Productions, unten re.: Tim Graham; S. 57 oben: AFP/Johannes Eisele; S. 58 oben li.: Man Utd via Getty Images/Matthew Peters, Mitte: Gary M. Prior; S. 59 oben li.: Michael Steele, oben re. u. unten re.: Bryn Lennon; S. 62 Bild 6: Evan Agostini; S. 69 Bild J: Alan Bekker; S. 91 unten re.: WireImage/John Stanton; S. 92 Bild 2: AFP/Tim Sloan; S. 94 Franz Ferdinand: Dave Hogan; S. 120 Mitte unten: Dorling Kindersley; S. 122 oben (u. 114): Phil Cole, unten re.: Man Utd via Getty Images: John Peters; S. 123 oben u. unten); **Bonnie Glänzer**, Berlin (S. 21 oben); **Randy Glasbergen**, Sherburne (S. 33 unten); **Harbourfront Centre**, Toronto (S. 88 logo); **Dick Hemingway Photographs**, Toronto (S. 75 Mitte li. u. S. 105: Photographers Direct/Dick Hemingway); **Home Office**, London (S. 118 (u. 114): "ru alone when u meet ur online m8s in real life?" © Crown copyright material is reproduced with the permission of the Controller of HMSO and Queen's Printer for Scotland); **Keystone**, Hamburg (S. 36 oben li.: Topham Picturepoint); **laif**, Köln (S. 38 li.: Hemispheres); **Louise Lazell**, UK (S. 116 oben (u. 114)); **LOOK**, München (S. 87: Thomas Peter Widmann); **The LS Lowry Collection**, Salford (S. 56 oben li.); **The Lowry**, Salford Quays (S. 56 oben re.); **MUML Crest & Imagery © MU Ltd.** (S. 53 poster); **OCS Group Marketing**, Lancashire (S. 66 oben); **PA Photos**, Nottingham (S. 59 Mitte; S. 104 oben); **Jacob Perlmutter**, UK (S. 115; S. 116 unten); **Photofusion**, London (S. 19 unten: Bipinchandra); **Picture Alliance**, Frankfurt/Main (Inhaltsverz. Old Trafford (u. S. 58 oben re.): dpa-Sportreport; S. 58 unten li.: dpa/dpaweb/epa Keystone Patrick B. Kraemer, unten re.: dpa-Report/Abaca Kempinaire-Gouhier; S. 59 unten li.: dpa-Sportreport; S. 61 (u. 110) re.: SCHROEWIG/Graylock; S. 62 Bild 1: dpa-Report/epa Lambert, Bild 4: Schroewig; S. 65 (u. 111) oben: Bildagentur Huber/R. Schmid, Chemnitz u. Mitte re.: ZB-Fotoreport/Wolfgang Thieme; S. 73 unten: dpa-Report/Keystone USA k03; S. 75 unten: dpa/Landov Katie Mcmahon; S. 76 oben: Schroewig/Jens Koch; S. 80 oben re.: dpa; S. 80 oben re.: dpa / Photoshot; S. 94 Kate Moss: dpa/Pa Topshop, Rock am Ring: SCHROEWIG/Jens Koch, Nelly Furtado: dpa/Roland Weihrauch, Alexander Kapranos: dpa/Harald Tittel; S. 98 Michael Ballack: dpa-Report, Heidi Klum: dpa, Jessica Alba: dpa, Tokio Hotel: dpa-Report, Dirk Nowitzki: Picture-Alliance/ASA; S. 99 Daniel Radcliffe film scene: picture-alliance/KPA Archival Collection); **Picture Press**, Hamburg (S. 6 (u. 52) oben re.: Maruan Bahrour; S. 89 oben li.: Frank P. Wartenberg); **www.rountreegraphics.com** (S. 123 Mitte: Stephen Rountree); **Marion Schönenberger**, Berlin (S. 52–53; S. 99; S. 130 oben; S. 131 (u.114)); **Scottish Tartans World Register**, Crieff (S. 36 oben re.); **Nick**

Sharratt (S. 124–126 (u. 114)): illustrations taken from Cliffhanger by Jacqueline Wilson. Reprinted by permission of David Higham Associates Limited, London); **Shutterstock**, New York (S. 18 unten li.: Robyn Mackenzie; S. 38 cow: Norma Cornes; S. 68 Bild B bear country sign (M): Vera Bogaerts, Bild E: Oksana Perkins; S. 70 Mitte re.: Ronen; S. 74 Mitte: Ronnie Howard; S. 76 Mitte: Sascha Burkard; S. 88 basketball: Vincent Giordano, CD (u. 90): Andresr, film: Olga Langerova; S. 92 Bild 3 li.: Rafa Irusta, Bild 3 re.: Danny Smythe; S. 102: Doug Stacey; S. 119: Ronen; S. 127 Mitte: Thomas O'Neil; S. 132 DVD cases (M): 3poD Animation); **Friedrich Stark**, Dortmund (S. 74 oben); Stills-Online, Hamburg (S. 66 helmet); **Stock-Food**, München (S. 120 Mitte oben: Z.Sandmann/Cimbal); **Stuck on Scotland Holidays**, Scotland (S. 38 re.); **Charles Tait Photographic Limited**, Orkney (S. 30 Bild 4: www.charles-tait.co.uk); **Transport for London**, London (S. 14); **The Travel Library Ltd**, Fleet (S. 37 unten li.); **ullstein bild**, Berlin (S. 6 (u. 52) unten li.: Wöstmann; S. 30 Bild 2: Still Pictures; S. 62 Bild 5: Imagno); **webbaviation.co.uk**, Bramhall (S. 59 velodrome exterior); **WILDLIFE**, Hamburg (S. 30 salmon: J. Mallwitz)

Titelbild
Alamy, Abingdon (London Eye (M): Ian MacPherson); Corbis, Düsseldorf (bus (M): Royalty-Free); **IFA-Bilderteam**, Ottobrunn (Union Jack: Jon Arnold Images)

Textquellen
S. 34: *Billy doesn't like school really* by Paul Cookson taken from "The Works – Poems chosen by Paul Cookson". Macmillan Children's Books, London 2000.©Paul Cookson; S. 81: *Dog helps to kill bear* adapted from "Canoeist kills bear", http://www.cbc.ca/canada/story/2006/07/22/bear.html (Stand: 17.01.2008); S. 115–116: *Pull in Emergency* adapted from "Night Haunts for Twilight Teens" by Sophie Heawood, taken from The Times, 12.08.2006. © NI Syndication Ltd. London; S. 121: *The lost girl* adapted from "The Mermaid Bride and other Orkney Folk Tales" told by Tom Muir. The Orcadian Limited (Kirkwall Press), Orkney. © 1998 Tom Muir and Bryce Wilson; S. 124–126: *Tim, a rock and a rope* adapted from "Cliffhanger" by Jacqueline Wilson, published by Corgi Yearling. Reprinted by permission of the Random House Group Ltd.; S. 127: *Safety in bear country* adapted from "The Mountain Guide - Safety in Bear Country" by Parks Canada, http://www.pc.gc.ca/docs/v-g/pm-mp/guidem-mguide/sec4/gm-mg4_e.asp (Stand: 17.01.2008); S. 129: *Snow storm* by Clare Bevan taken from "Read me and Laugh - A Funny Poem for Every Day of the Year" chosen by Gaby Morgan. © Macmillan Children's Books, London 2005; S. 130–133: *Fans* from "Forty Short Plays" by Ann Cartwright. Reprinted by permission of Harcourt Education; S. 136–137: Auszüge von S. 311 and S. 725 aus "English G 2000 Wörterbuch – Das Wörterbuch zum Lehrwerk". Herausgegeben von der Langenscheidt-Redaktion Wörterbücher und der Cornelsen-Redaktion Englisch. © 2002 Cornelsen Verlag GmbH & Co. OHG, Berlin und Langenscheidt KG, Berlin und München

Liedquellen
S. 73: *Sk8er boi* by David Scott Alspach/Lauren Christy/Graham Edwards/Avril Ramona Lavigne. © Almo-Music Corp./Ferry Hills Songs/Mr. Spock Music/Rainbow Fish Publ./Warner-Tamerlane Publ. Co. Neue Welt Musikverlag GmbH, Hamburg. Rondor Musikverlag GmbH, Berlin; S. 116: *Backfoot*. © Pull in Emergency, UK; S. 122: *You'll never walk alone* by Oscar Hammerstein. © Williamson Music Inc. D/A/CH/osteuropäische Länder: EMI Music Publishing (Germany GmbH), Hamburg; *We are the champions* by Freddie Mercury. © by Queen Music Ltd. D/A/CH/Osteuropäische Länder: EMI Music Publishing Germany GmbH, Hamburg

Classroom English

Was *du* im Klassenzimmer sagen kannst

Du brauchst Hilfe
Können Sie mir bitte helfen?
Auf welcher Seite sind wir, bitte?
Was heißt … auf Englisch/Deutsch?
Wie spricht man das erste Wort in Zeile 2 aus?
Können Sie bitte … buchstabieren?
Können Sie es bitte an die Tafel schreiben?
Kann ich es auf Deutsch sagen?
Können Sie/Kannst du bitte lauter sprechen?
Können Sie/Kannst du das bitte noch mal sagen?

Über Texte und Themen sprechen
Ich finde die Geschichte …
schön/interessant/langweilig/schrecklich/….
Es war lustig/gruselig/langweilig/…, als …
Ich fand es gut/nicht gut, als …
Ich finde, Tom hat recht/nicht recht, weil …
Ich bin mir nicht sicher. Vielleicht …
Was meinst du?
Ich stimme … zu/nicht zu, weil …

Hausaufgaben und Übungen
Tut mir leid, ich habe mein Schulheft nicht dabei, Herr …
Ich habe meine Hausaufgaben vergessen, Frau …
Ich kann Nummer 3 nicht lösen.
Entschuldigung, ich bin noch nicht fertig.
Ich habe … Ist das auch richtig?
Tut mir leid, das weiß ich nicht.
Was haben wir (als Hausaufgabe) auf?

Bei der Partnerarbeit
Kann ich mit Julian arbeiten?
Wer ist dran? – Du bist dran.
Ich finde, wir sollten/könnten …
Was machen wir zuerst?

What your teacher says
Open your books at page 24, please.
Look at the picture/line 8/… on page 24.
Copy/Complete the chart/network/…
Correct the mistakes.
Take notes.
Do exercise 3 for homework, please.
Have you finished?
Switch off your mobile phones.
Walk around the class and ask other students.
Discuss … with …
Give a presentation about …
Report to the class.

What *you* can say in the classroom

You need help
Can you help me, please?
What page are we on, please?
What's … in English/German?
How do you say the first word in line 2?
Can you spell …, please?
Can you write it on the board, please?
Can I say it in German?
Can you speak louder, please?
Can you say that again, please?

Talking about texts and topics
I think the story is …
nice/interesting/boring/terrible/…
It was funny/scary/boring/… when …
I liked it/didn't like it when …
I think Tom is right/wrong because …
I'm not sure. Maybe …
What do you think?
I agree/disagree (with …) because …

Homework and exercises
Sorry, I haven't got my exercise book, Mr …
I've forgotten my homework, Mrs/Ms/Miss …
I can't do number 3.
Sorry, I haven't finished yet.
I've got … Is that right too?
Sorry, I don't know.
What's for homework?

Work with a partner
Can I work with Julian?
Whose turn is it? – It's your turn.
I think we should/could …
What are we going to do first?

Was dein/e Lehrer/in sagt
Schlagt bitte Seite 24 auf.
Seht euch das Bild/Zeile 8/… auf Seite 24 an.
Übertragt/Vervollständigt die Tabelle/das Wörternetz/…
Verbessert die Fehler.
Macht euch Notizen.
Macht bitte Übung 3 als Hausaufgabe.
Seid ihr fertig? / Bist du fertig?
Schaltet eure Handys aus.
Geht durch die Klasse und fragt andere Schüler/innen.
Diskutiere/Diskutiert … mit …
Halte/Haltet einen Vortrag über …
Berichte/Berichtet der Klasse.